AUTHOR Daniel L. Akin

SERIES EDITORS David Platt, Daniel L. Akin, and Tony Merida

CHRIST-CENTERED

Exposition

EXALTING JESUS IN

MARK

HOLMAN
REFERENCE

NASHVILLE, TENNESSEE

Christ-Centered Exposition Commentary: Exalting Jesus in Mark

© Copyright 2014 by Daniel L. Akin

B&H Publishing Group

All rights reserved.

ISBN 978-0-8054-9685-7

Dewey Decimal Classification: 220.7
Subject Heading: BIBLE. N.T. MARK—COMMENTARIES \
JESUS CHRIST

Printed in the United States of America
3 4 5 6 7 8 9 10 • 22 21 20 19 18
SB

SERIES DEDICATION

Dedicated to Adrian Rogers and John Piper. They have taught us to love the gospel of Jesus Christ, to preach the Bible as the inerrant Word of God, to pastor the church for which our Savior died, and to have a passion to see all nations gladly worship the Lamb.

—David Platt, Tony Merida, and Danny Akin
March 2013

ACKNOWLEDGMENTS

I would like to thank Michael Guyer, Shane Shaddix, Mary Jo Haselton, Kim Humphrey, Debbie Shugart, and Amy Whitfield, each of whom made significant contributions to this volume. You all have blessed and enriched my life.

—Danny Akin

TABLE OF CONTENTS

SERIES INTRODUCTION

Augustine said, "Where Scripture speaks, God speaks." The editors of the Christ-Centered Exposition Commentary series believe that where God speaks, the pastor must speak. God speaks through His written Word. We must speak from that Word. We believe the Bible is God breathed, authoritative, inerrant, sufficient, understandable, necessary, and timeless. We also affirm that the Bible is a Christ-centered book; that is, it contains a unified story of redemptive history of which Jesus is the hero. Because of this Christ-centered trajectory that runs from Genesis 1 through Revelation 22, we believe the Bible has a corresponding global-missions thrust. From beginning to end, we see God's mission as one of making worshipers of Christ from every tribe and tongue worked out through this redemptive drama in Scripture. To that end we must preach the Word.

In addition to these distinct convictions, the Christ-Centered Exposition Commentary series has some distinguishing characteristics. First, this series seeks to display exegetical accuracy. What the Bible says is what we want to say. While not every volume in the series will be a verse-by-verse commentary—although most will—we nevertheless desire to handle the text carefully and explain it rightly. Those who teach and preach bear the heavy responsibility of saying what God has said in His Word and declaring what God has done in Christ. We desire to faithfully handle God's Word, knowing that we must give an account for how we have fulfilled this holy calling (Jas 3:1).

Second, the Christ-Centered Exposition Commentary series has pastors in view. While we hope others will read this series, such as parents, teachers, small-group leaders, and student ministers, we desire to provide a commentary busy pastors will use for weekly preparation of biblically faithful and gospel-saturated sermons. This series is not academic in nature. Our aim is to present a readable and pastoral style of commentaries. We believe this aim will serve the church of the Lord Jesus Christ.

Third, we want the Christ-Centered Exposition Commentary series to be known for the inclusion of helpful illustrations and theologically driven applications. Many commentaries offer no help in illustrations, and few offer any kind of help in application. Often those that do offer illustrative material and application unfortunately give little serious attention to the text. While giving ourselves primarily to explanation, we also hope to serve readers by providing inspiring and illuminating illustrations coupled with timely and timeless application.

Finally, as the name suggests, the editors seek to exalt Jesus from every book of the Bible. In saying this, we are not commending wild allegory or fanciful typology. We certainly believe we must be constrained to the meaning intended by the divine Author Himself, the Holy Spirit of God. However, we also believe the Bible has a messianic focus, and our hope is that the individual authors will exalt Christ from particular texts. Luke 24:25-27,44-47; and John 5:39,46 inform both our hermeneutics and our homiletics. Not every author will do this the same way or have the same degree of Christ-centered emphasis. That is fine with us. We believe faithful exposition that is Christ-centered is not monolithic. We do believe, however, that we must read the whole Bible as Christian Scripture. Therefore, our aims are both to honor the historical particularity of each biblical passage and to highlight its intrinsic connection to the Redeemer.

The editors are indebted to the contributors of each volume. The reader will detect a unique style from each writer, and we celebrate these unique gifts and traits. While distinctive in approach, the authors share a common characteristic in that they are pastoral theologians. They love the church, and they regularly preach and teach God's Word to God's people. Further, many of these contributors are younger voices. We think these new, fresh voices can serve the church well, especially among a rising generation that has the task of proclaiming the Word of Christ and the Christ of the Word to the lost world.

We hope and pray this series will serve the body of Christ well in these ways until our Savior returns in glory. If it does, we will have succeeded in our assignment.

David Platt
Daniel L. Akin
Tony Merida
Series Editors
February 2013

Mark

The Good News of Jesus Christ the Son of God

MARK 1:1-8

Main Idea: The gospel is the good news that God has kept His promise to send a Messiah, who is Jesus Christ, the Son of God.

I. **We Can Trust God to Keep His Promise (1:1-4).**
    A. God kept His word to send the Messiah (1:1).
    B. God kept His word to send His forerunner (1:2-4).
II. **We Can Trust God to Send His Preachers (1:4-8).**
    A. Like John we should be faithful (1:4-5).
    B. Like John we need to be humble (1:6-8).

The Gospel of Matthew is written to Jews telling them that Jesus is the Messiah King who fulfills Old Testament prophecy. Mark is written to Romans telling them that Jesus is the Suffering Servant who actively ministers on our behalf and gives His life as a ransom for many. Luke is written to Greeks telling them that Jesus is the perfect Son of Man who came to save and minister to all people through the power of the Holy Spirit. John is written to the world, telling that Jesus is the fully human, fully divine Son of God in whom we must believe to receive eternal life.

The Gospel of Mark is fast moving and hard-hitting! By the far the shortest of the four Gospels, it is noted as much for what it omits as what it includes. In Mark there is no genealogy of Jesus, no miraculous birth narrative with Bethlehem and shepherds, no childhood at Nazareth or visit to the temple, no Sermon on the Mount, and few parables.

To summarize, Mark recorded, in rapid-fire succession, specific events from the life and ministry of Jesus to prove to a Roman audience that He is the Christ, the Son of God, who served, suffered, died, and rose again as the Suffering Servant of the Lord depicted by the prophet Isaiah.

As we prepare to walk through this powerful Gospel narrative concerning Jesus Christ, two questions need to be raised and answered. First, who wrote this Gospel? Second, how should we approach any of the Gospels?

3

Authorship

The early church agreed unanimously that a man named John Mark wrote this Gospel. His mother was Mary, whose home in Jerusalem was a meeting place for believers of the early church (Acts 12:12).

The Hebrew name *John* means "God's gift." The Roman name *Mark* means "polite" or "shining." John Mark, though never mentioned by name in the Gospel, may be the naked boy of Mark 14:51-52. John Mark and his cousin Barnabas accompanied Paul on his first missionary journey (Acts 12:25), but Mark turned back before the journey ended (Acts 13:13). This irritated Paul and led to a parting with Barnabas (Acts 15:36-41). Later Paul and Mark were reconciled, and Mark was "useful" to Paul (2 Tim 4:11).

Finally, the early church affirmed Mark was the apostle Peter's interpreter. He recorded Peter's experiences with the Lord Jesus. Mark's account being especially vivid when it involves incidents with Peter supports this view.

Some Basic Presuppositions Concerning Our Gospels

How do we approach the four Gospels and, in particular, the Gospel of Mark? What presuppositions should we bring to our study?

(1) Gospels are historical and not mythological accounts. What they record really did happen. (2) They will vary because they are written by four different men. However, because they were inspired by God, all they wrote will be true. (3) Gospels are more than thematic biographical studies. They are not biographies in the modern sense. They are historical theologies of the person and work of Jesus Christ. (4) Portions may be summarized and not given as exhaustive accounts. (5) Gospels are more concerned about Christ's death than His life (more than one-fourth of each deals with the final week of His life). One scholar said Mark "is a Passion Narrative with an extended introduction" (Stein, *Mark*, 33).

As we begin an exciting journey through this Gospel, what does Mark want us to understand concerning the good news of Jesus Christ, the Son of God?

We Can Trust God to Keep His Promise
MARK 1:1-4

Jesus said in John 5:39, "You pore over the Scriptures because you think you have eternal life in them, yet they testify about Me." God had promised to send a Savior, a Deliverer, a Messiah. Mark says the time has arrived, and He has appeared, as well as the one God called to prepare the way for His arrival—Jesus Christ and John the baptizer.

God Kept His Word to Send the Messiah (Mark 1:1)

Without wasting any words, Mark gives the introduction to Mark 1:1-15 as well as the theme of the entire book: it is about good news of Jesus who is the Christ, the Son of God.

The word *beginning* recalls Genesis 1:1 and John 1:1. Something new and exciting has occurred. The word *gospel* means a message of good news or of joyful tidings. It speaks of the coming Savior who would provide salvation promised by the prophetic word. The time of God's salvation has arrived! God has kept His promise to send a Messiah.

This Messiah is "Jesus Christ, the Son of God." "Jesus" is the Greek name for the Hebrew *Joshua*: "Yahweh is salvation." "Christ" is the Greek equivalent of the Hebrew *Messiah*: "the anointed one." Initially a title, "Christ" would become a common part of the name of our Lord. "Son of God" is a crucial title for the promised deliverer. It takes Christology to a higher level. Bob Stein says, "Son of God reveals Jesus' unique and unparalleled relationship with God. It is the favorite title of Mark for identifying Jesus (1:11,24; 3:11 [cf. 1:34]; 5:7; 9:7; 12:6; 13:32; 14:61-62; 15:39), and when Mark was written, it conveyed to the Christian community the idea of both preexistence and deity (cf. Phil 2:6-8; Col 1:15-20)" (Stein, *Mark*, 41). One cannot avoid the inescapable conclusion that Jesus is indeed God!

And of all Jesus' titles, the title "Son of God" in particular appears at significant points in the Gospel and sometimes in the mouths of some interesting personalities! Perhaps most striking is that the disciples never recognize Jesus as the Son of God in the Gospel of Mark. The demons get it right (3:11; 5:7). Even a Roman centurion understands it (15:39). Yet not until after the resurrection did the disciples get it. If Jesus' disciples failed to see it, there is hope for those who seem the furthest away from seeing it today.

There are four strategic confessions in the second Gospel: (1) Mark's assertion in 1:1: "The beginning of the gospel of Jesus Christ, the Son of God." (2) Peter's confession in 8:29: "He said to them, 'But who do you say that I am?' And Peter answered and said to Him, 'You are the Christ.'" (3) The Messiah's affirmation by the nation through the words of the high priest in 14:61-62: "Again the high priest asked Him, saying to Him, 'Are You the Christ, the Son of the Blessed?' Jesus said, 'I am. And you will see the Son of Man sitting at the right hand of the Power, and coming with the clouds of heaven.'" (4) A Roman (Gentile) soldier's recognition of Jesus as the Son of God in 15:39: "Truly this Man was the Son of God!" This is how

TITLES OF JESUS IN THE GOSPEL OF MARK
1. Jesus Christ, Son of God (1:1)
2. Jesus, Son of the Most High God (5:7)
3. Jesus, Son of David (10:47-48)
4. Christ (1:1; 8:29; 9:41; 12:35)
5. Christ, the Son of the Blessed (14:61)
6. Christ, King of Israel (15:32)
7. Son of Man (2:10,28; 8:31,38; 9:9,12,31; 10:33,45; 13:26; 14:21,41,62)
8. Holy One of God (1:24)
9. Lord of the Sabbath (2:28)
10. Lord (5:19; 7:28; 10:51 [Gk]; 11:3; 13:20 [16:19-20])
11. King of the Jews (15:2,9,12,18,26)

the Gospel of Mark unfolds. It begins here with the declaration that this is the "gospel of Jesus Christ, the Son of God."

God Kept His Word to Send His Forerunner (Mark 1:2-4)

Before the Messiah, God promises to send a forerunner. Mark 1:2-3 combines three texts, a common practice in that day, evoking the themes of the wilderness, a new exodus, and the forerunner Elijah.

The first reference is Exodus 23:20: "I am going to send an angel [messenger] before you to protect you on the way and bring you to the place I have prepared." Next he pulls from Malachi 3:1: "'See, I am going to send My messenger, and he will clear the way before Me. Then the Lord you seek will suddenly come to His temple, the Messenger of the covenant you desire—see, He is coming,' says the Lord of Hosts." The last reference is Isaiah 40:3: "A voice of one crying out: Prepare the way of the Lord in the wilderness; make a straight highway for our God in the desert."

Mark simply references the most significant and well known of the three texts, the prophet Isaiah. God has promised to send His messenger, who will prepare the way; make the road ready ahead of "You," the Messiah. He will loudly proclaim his message where God has continually met His people calling them to repentance: the wilderness. His message is *simple* and *clear.* Level the roads, make them presentable and safe, for the Lord is coming! God kept His word to send His forerunner to prepare the way for the Messiah.

We Can Trust God to Send His Preachers
MARK 1:4-8

The sending of John the baptizer was a fulfillment of biblical prophecy signaling a new day in "redemptive history"—which is the series of events by which God redeems His people from sin and death. The culmination of redemptive history is the cross of Christ. Three observations about John the Baptist elsewhere in Scripture are worth noting. Matthew 11:7-12,14 says,

> *Jesus began to speak to the crowds about John: "What did you go out into the wilderness to see? A reed swaying in the wind? What then did you go out to see? A man dressed in soft garments? Look, those who wear soft clothing are in kings' palaces. But what did you go out to see? A prophet? Yes, I tell you, and far more than a prophet. This is the one it is written about: 'Look, I am sending My messenger ahead of You, he will prepare Your way before You.' I assure you: Among those born of women no one greater than John the Baptist has appeared; but the least in the kingdom of heaven is greater than he. . . . For all the prophets and the Law prophesied until John; if you are willing to accept it, he is the Elijah who is to come."*

John was greatly esteemed in the eyes of our Savior. John was the Elijah to come, the one who would announce the coming of the Messiah. He was truly at a turning point in redemptive history.

While John prepared the way for the Messiah, he rightly understood his role in God's plan of redemption: "He must increase, but *I must decrease*" (John 3:30, emphasis added). His ministry was not about himself; it was rightly centered on Jesus Christ.

The message John declared about the Messiah was true, and many came to believe in Jesus. "Many came to Him and said, '*John never did a sign, but everything John said about this Man was true.*' And many believed in Him there" (John 10:41-42, emphasis added). He was not the Savior, but he pointed many to Him.

Chuck Swindoll says these verses concerning John the Baptist give us the "profile of a strange evangelist!" Indeed! In John the Baptist we see a character and life worth emulating. The great thing is that when we do start living like John the Baptist, we end up looking a lot more like Jesus Christ in our own lives.

Like John We Should Be Faithful (Mark 1:4-5)

Mark records with his usual brevity, "John came baptizing in the wilderness." He suddenly appeared. He was "baptizing," but he was not concerned about mere ritual or ceremonial rite. The message he preached was "a baptism of repentance for the forgiveness of sins." This baptism was preparation for the forgiveness Christ would accomplish by His death and resurrection.

In short, John's message was, "The time is now to get right with God!" Popular with some and unpopular with others, John was faithful to God! He truly lived by the dictum, "All that matters in life is that I please God."

How did the people respond? They came from everywhere to hear him, even Jerusalem! Rich and poor. Rural and urban. They responded to John's preaching by repenting (turning from sin), confessing (acknowledging their sin), and being baptized (an outward sign of humility giving evidence of the inward change of their hearts). He called people to prepare their hearts for the coming of the Messiah.

Like John We Need to Be Humble (Mark 1:6-8)

Our tendency is to want to make John's character like that of a modern man. That will not work. He was not the kind of man to be a presidential cabinet member; rather, he was a wandering preacher who lived in the wilderness. God chose a forerunner entirely different from the type we would have picked. Mark helps us take a straight and honest look at this man. Not only does he appear unusual by today's standards; he was unusual by the standards of his own day. He had no credentials, had not studied in a formal school with Pharisees or rabbis, and wore funny clothes and ate weird food!

Humble in *appearance?* He wore a camel-haired garment with a leather belt. Sounds like Elijah in 2 Kings 1:8.

Humble in *home?* He lived in the desert.

Humble in *diet?* He ate locusts (a clean animal; Lev 11:22) and honey. At least it was high in protein and minerals.

Humble in *message?* John effectively said, "One greater than me is coming [v. 7]. He is so great, I am not worthy to do what only a Gentile slave would do [v. 7]. My baptism is outward with water: a symbol. His baptism is inward with the Spirit: the real thing [v. 8]. The One who is coming is *mightier* than I am! He is *more worthy* than I am! He is *more powerful* than I am! I have touched your body with water. He will touch your soul with the Holy Spirit! I know who I am in God's plan. I know who He is in God's plan too!"

John would not live to 35. He would be imprisoned and beheaded. The world, no doubt, scoffed at this crazy man. Heaven, however, would smile. J. C. Ryle rightly demonstrates the implications of John's life:

> The principal work of every faithful minister of the gospel, is to set the Lord Jesus fully before His people, and to show them His fullness and His power to save. The next great work He has to do, is to set before them the work of the Holy Spirit, and the need of being born again, and inwardly baptized by His grace. These two mighty truths appear to have been frequently on the lips of John the Baptist. It would be well for the church and the world, if there were more ministers like him. (Ryle, *Mark*, 4)

Conclusion

Early Christians used one symbol to mark the tombs of believers or to designate secret meeting places because of Roman persecution. It was sometimes signed in sand to distinguish a friend from an enemy. Further, it captured beautifully the evangelistic intent of Jesus' ministry and the essence of who Jesus was. It also summarizes well the theme of Mark's Gospel. I do not speak of the *cross*, but of the *fish*! The Greek word is ICHTHUS (ΙΧΘΥΣ). It is a perfect acrostic for *Iesous Christos Theou Huios Soter*, or in English, "Jesus Christ, God's Son, Savior!" Here is the essence of Mark's Gospel. Here is the essence of the good news about Jesus.

Reflect and Discuss

1. What is the advantage of having four Gospels, all telling essentially the same story?
2. How might Mark's consciousness of having a Roman audience affect his selection and presentation of the facts?
3. How did Mark's missionary work with Paul and Barnabas and his association with Peter prepare him to write this Gospel?
4. What are the implications of Jesus' title "Christ" in the lives of His followers? What are the implications of His being "the Son of God"?
5. Why did the demons and the Roman centurion recognize that Jesus was the Son of God before the resurrection, but His disciples did not? How does the disciples' slowness give hope for us and our loved ones?
6. How does John the Baptist function as a transitional figure from the Old Testament to the new covenant?
7. How do John and his preaching style compare with current notions of how to gain a following and grow a church?
8. Why do you think John gained a large following? What was his message? How did that message contribute to his popularity and to his death?

9. How is John's humble message about Christ similar to what we should tell others about Christ? How is our message different?
10. God fulfilled His promise to send a messenger and send a Savior. What are some of the other promises of God that have not yet been fulfilled? How does Mark 1:1-8 encourage you concerning these promises?

The Baptism and Temptation of the Servant-King
MARK 1:9-13

Main Idea: Jesus Christ is the eternal Son of God, the Servant-King who fights God's enemies on behalf of God's people.

I. **The Baptism of Jesus Was a Declaration of Sonship (1:9-11).**
    A. It inaugurated His public ministry (1:9).
    B. It identified Him with sinful humanity (1:9).
    C. It associated Him with John's ministry (1:9).
    D. It demonstrated His approval by His Father (1:10).
    E. It revealed the triune God (1:9-11).
    F. It showed His total dependence on the Holy Spirit (1:10).
    G. It declared the type of Messiah He would be (1:11).
II. **The Temptation of Jesus Was a Declaration of War (1:12-13).**
    A. Jesus was submissive to the Spirit (1:12).
    B. Jesus was engaged by Satan (1:13).

God's thoughts are not our thoughts, and God's ways are not our ways. His ways are higher. His thoughts are higher (Isa 55:8-9). His ways surprise us. His plans often are mysterious. Sometimes they seem downright strange.

The beginning of Jesus' public ministry is a perfect example. It starts not in a thriving metropolis but in the rugged wasteland of the Judean wilderness near the Dead Sea; not with a press conference but a baptism; not with a parade and feast but with 40 days of solitude and fasting even further in the desolate and dangerous wilderness, being tempted by the archenemy of God.

To be sure, the baptism and temptation of Jesus show us that God's ways are not our ways, but His ways are, as Romans 12:2 affirms, always good, acceptable, and perfect. What then do we learn from these two critical events in the life of Jesus?

The Baptism of Jesus Was a Declaration of Sonship
MARK 1:9-11

Jesus comes to John probably in the middle or latter days of John's ministry. He comes to be baptized, an event so significant that it is recorded in all four Gospels (cf. Matt 3:13-17; Luke 3:21-22; John 1:28-34). Mark uses the word *baptize/baptism* six times in the first nine verses of the book. Still, this act is surprising: Why was He baptized? Matthew tells us that John the Baptist was opposed to baptizing Christ, and he had a pretty good argument (Matt 3:14; cf. Mark 1:7). Jesus, however, says it must take place "for us to fulfill all righteousness" (Matt 3:15). But then, what does that mean?

I believe we can tease out the answer as we look at seven truths His baptism teaches us. The baptism is the beginning of His humiliation as He faithfully submits to the Father's will and willingly identifies Himself with sinful humanity. It is no more odd for Jesus to be baptized in the Jordan River than for Him to hang on the cross at Calvary as the sinless and spotless Son of God (Dever, "Jesus' Debut").

Jesus' Baptism Inaugurated His Public Ministry (Mark 1:9)

Jesus came from Nazareth, a small town in the middle of nowhere. The region of Galilee was despised because of its distance from Jerusalem and for its infestation of Gentiles. The town of Nazareth was even worse— unknown and unmentioned. Jesus was a nobody from nowhere! But He comes to John and thereby begins His public ministry. He was probably in His early thirties. His public ministry would last only three years or so. The time has come for the Servant King to ascend to the public stage.

Why in the wilderness? God has often met with His people there. Recall the exodus, when God brought His children out of Egypt into the wilderness where He would give them His law, feed them, and lead them by cloud and fire. Again in Hosea 2:14-15 He promised His presence: "Therefore, I am going to persuade her, lead her to the wilderness, and speak tenderly to her. . . . There she will respond as she did in the days of her youth, as in the day she came out of the land of Egypt."

Jesus' Baptism Identified Him with Sinful Humanity (Mark 1:9)

In His baptism Jesus joins those who seek a baptism of repentance and who are confessing their sins. Jesus neither repents of sin nor confesses His sin because He had no sin (2 Cor 5:21; Heb 4:15). Still, He aligns Himself with those He came to save. Like Moses in the first exodus (Exod 32:23), He does not set Himself apart from their sins (Lane, *Mark*, 55).

Jesus' Baptism Associated Him with John's Ministry (Mark 1:9)

Jesus does not hesitate to connect Himself to John the Baptist regarding the fulfillment of prophecy and his message of repentance (cf. 1:15!). No one had higher praise for John than Jesus. As the Christ, the Servant King, He makes His public appearance, He endorses the ministry of His cousin John (Luke 1:36).

Jesus' Baptism Demonstrated His Approval by His Father (Mark 1:10)

Immediately—an important word in Mark's Gospel (here translated "as soon as")—the Holy Spirit descends on Jesus through an opening in the sky. Jesus sees the heavens being "torn open." The word occurs only one other time in Mark's Gospel, when God the Father tears the temple curtain in two from top to bottom! At His baptism and at His crucifixion the Father intervenes supernaturally, eschatologically, declaring that Jesus is the Son of God.

Isaiah 64:1 had predicted this: "If only You would tear the heavens open and come down, so that mountains would quake at Your presence." The tearing apart of the heavens signals a significant moment in history and in the life of the Servant King. In this way the Father first gives His approval through action.

Jesus' Baptism Revealed the Triune God (Mark 1:9-11)

Adrian Rogers said, "The doctrine of the Trinity is not beyond logic and reason—just above it!" And as difficult as it can be to wrap our minds around the concept of a triune God, we clearly see all three persons of the Godhead at Jesus' baptism. The Son is baptized, the Father speaks, and the Spirit descends into (*eis*) Jesus "like a dove." Like the ending of Matthew's Gospel (28:19-20), the beginning of the Gospel of Mark gives us a brief glimpse into the nature of our God, the great Three in One. It also serves as a confirming witness concerning the identity of Jesus the Son.

Jesus' Baptism Showed His Total Dependence on the Holy Spirit (Mark 1:10)

The presence of the Spirit on the Messiah was promised in Isaiah 42:1: "This is My Servant; I strengthen Him, this is My Chosen One; I delight in Him. I have put My Spirit on Him; He will bring justice to the nations." The prophet elaborates on this promise in Isaiah 11:2: "The Spirit of the LORD will rest on Him—a Spirit of wisdom and understanding, a Spirit of counsel and strength, a Spirit of knowledge and of the fear of the LORD."

Jesus is the fulfillment of these promises. *Like* a dove (it was not literally a dove), in gentleness and purity, the Spirit came into Jesus, and He was equipped for His ministry. Even though the Spirit came *into* Jesus (Gk *eis*), this is no "adoptionistic" Christology. He did not become the Son of God at the moment of His baptism. No, He was declared to be and empowered as the Son of God for the Suffering Servant ministry. John Piper says,

> When Jesus was baptized along with all the repenting people who wanted to be on God's side, it was as though the commander-in-chief had come to the front lines, fastened his bayonet, strapped on his helmet, and jumped into the trench along with the rest of us. And when he did that, his Father in heaven, who had sent him for this very combat, signified with the appearance of a dove that the Holy Spirit would be with him in the battles to come. (Piper, "Christ in Combat")

Jesus' Baptism Declared the Type of Messiah He Would Be (Mark 1:11)

Mark 1:11 is surely one of the most important verses in the Bible! It is echoed again at the transfiguration in 9:7, along with the admonition for the disciples to "listen to Him." It is a combination of three massively significant Old Testament texts. The phrase, "You are My Son" comes from Psalm 2:7, and in quoting this Davidic psalm, the Father announces, "You are the Messiah-King, the greater Son of David who will rule the nations." In calling Christ "beloved," we are reminded of the way Abraham saw Isaac, the son he was called to sacrifice (Gen 22:2). It bears the weight of Christ being the "One and Only" Son of the Most High God. The third phrase, "I take delight in You," comes from Isaiah 42:1, which is the first of Isaiah's Suffering Servant songs. These passages climax in the great Isaiah 53 text where the Servant is crushed by God as He bears the sins of the world!

This declaration of the Father's love for His Son cannot be overstated and must not be overlooked. No prophet ever heard words like these! Abraham was a friend (Isa 41:8). Moses was a servant (Deut 34:5). Aaron was a chosen one (Ps 105:26). David was a man after God's own heart (1 Sam 13:4). But only Israel (Exod 4:23) and the king of Israel (as their representative; Ps 2:7) were called God's sons. Now they are united in the person of the Servant King, Jesus of Nazareth! James Edwards says, "Jesus is Israel reduced to one" (*Mark*, 37). As the Messiah and Son of God, Jesus is a second Adam, a new Israel, and a perfect King who will succeed where they each failed!

That we must accept "Son of God" as a declaration of deity is easily demonstrated by the actions of this Son: He forgives sins (2:5), heals the sick (1:40), casts out demons (1:24; 5:1-20), is Lord of the Sabbath (2:28), raises the dead (6:35-43), and ultimately rises from the dead Himself (16:1-8). This declaration coupled with Jesus' life, ministry, miracles, and resurrection make His deity undeniable.

So the Father has attested, "You are the promised Messiah-King—My Son and My delight. But You will realize Your kingdom by being a faithful Servant to Your Father even to the point of a crushing, painful, and humiliating death." Would Jesus accept such an assignment? In light of this lingering question, it is no coincidence that "immediately" Satan came to tempt Him, trying to divert the Savior from His mission.

The Temptation of Jesus Was a Declaration of War
MARK 1:12-13

A commissioning by God is often followed by a time of testing. In this time of testing, will Jesus continue to "trust and obey" the will of the Father now that the course of His life is made clear? The Gospel of Mark gives us a brief summation of the "war in the wilderness" (cf. Matt 4:1-11; Luke 4:1-13). The battle begins here, but it will rage all the way to a Roman cross and an empty tomb. Here is Christ in deadly combat for the eternal souls of men. If He loses, we are lost!

Jesus Was Submissive to the Spirit (Mark 1:12)

Jesus acted "immediately," this time going further into the wilderness to be tempted. But He didn't just decide to go—"the Spirit drove Him" out. He was "impelled" or "cast out." Mark will use the same word to describe Jesus casting out demons! Jesus' temptation was no accidental encounter, no chance meeting. It was a divine appointment scheduled by the Father and implemented by the Spirit. It is not what we would expect to happen after the baptism and the voice from heaven. We would expect a reception or some kind of celebration, but instead we see an expulsion further into the wilderness. The same Spirit that descended is now casting Him into the wilderness.

Thankfully, Jesus yields to the Spirit and embraces this test. The Servant King has a job to do, and the Spirit immediately compels Him. Rather than shrinking back, as Israel was so prone to do, our King, our Commander in Chief, the true Israel goes out to fight in the trenches with us and for us. In so doing He turns back the enemy and provides hope and a pattern for us to do the same.

Jesus Was Engaged by Satan (Mark 1:13)

Now we see a snapshot of what this battle looked like. "He was in the wilderness 40 days, being tempted by Satan." This was the *deep* wilderness. This was no vacation spot. The conditions were grueling, and Jesus was undoubtedly tired and weak. To grumble, complain, or give in would have been easy.

This reminds us of Israel's 40 years of wandering in the wilderness, where they grumbled, complained, and failed to trust their God. This also reminds us of Moses' 40 days on Mount Sinai (Exod 34:28) and Elijah's 40 days at Mount Horeb (1 Kgs 19:8). Jesus is not only a new Adam and a second Israel, but He is also a better Moses and a superior prophet!

Jesus said in John 8:44, "[The Devil] was a murderer from the beginning and has not stood in the truth, because there is no truth in him. When he tells a lie, he speaks from his own nature, because he is a liar and the father of liars." Satan (meaning "adversary"), the Devil (meaning "accuser"), meets our King in the desert.

A few things about this meeting in the desert would have made it especially difficult. (1) Satan meets Jesus in the wilderness, not a garden. (2) Jesus has been fasting 40 days (Matt 4:2). (3) Jesus is alone. (4) The wilderness is filled with wild animals. The wild beasts are mentioned immediately following the mention of Satan, suggesting they are in partnership with him. Further, remember Mark's Roman audience, especially during the Neronian persecution of AD 64–68. The Roman historian Tacitus wrote in his *Annals*, "[Christians] were covered with the hides of wild beasts and torn to pieces by dogs" (*Annals*, 15:44). People associated wild animals with adversity and persecution, so including that detail would undoubtedly heighten the horror and danger of our Lord's 40 days in the desolate and untamed Judean wilderness. It appears from all of these conditions that Jesus does battle with Satan on Satan's home field. It is a divine invasion of enemy territory.

Christian, be encouraged. Christ knows what you are going through. Even more, His angels came to His aid. They may be sent by God to serve us as well (Ps 34:7; Heb 1:14)! First John 3:8 reminds us, "The Son of God was revealed for this purpose: to destroy the Devil's works." In this text we see a wonderful picture of that happening. It is a preview of coming attractions.

What was Satan's goal? He wanted to defeat the Son! But how? Ultimately it seems that Satan's goal was to get Jesus *not to suffer*! Satan was at the baptism I am sure! He saw and he heard it all! The suffering and death of Jesus meant Satan's doom and destruction, and it meant salvation for you and me. This is what was at stake in the war in the wilderness!

Mark does not record our Lord's victory with the same detail as do Matthew and Luke. This is just round one of a 15-round bout. The Servant King won this round. The war in the wilderness was not the end. It was just the beginning, or more precisely it was the resumption of a war begun long ago in Genesis 3:15.

Conclusion

God's ways are not our ways, are they? His ways are often full of unexpected twists and turns we do not see coming. But aren't you glad His ways are good, acceptable, and perfect? If you doubt this, just look at the baptism and the temptation of the Servant King! God's will is not always safe, but it is always best!

Reflect and Discuss

1. What is most surprising or mysterious to you about the way God accomplished the salvation of mankind?
2. What do you consider to be the meaning of the rite of baptism in your church?
3. Why do you think God chooses the wilderness as the place to communicate with His children?
4. What does Mark 1:9-11 teach us about the Trinity?
5. What can we learn from the ideal connection between God the Father and God the Son?
6. In what way does the Holy Spirit represent power in Jesus' life and in ours?
7. What did Jesus do during His life to show He was a second Adam, a new Israel, and a perfect King?
8. How have you been tested since you gave your life to Christ? Are there things you can do now to amend your score on past tests?
9. Satan is a liar and a murderer. How has he shown that in your life?
10. How has popular culture portrayed angels? What does the Bible teach about them?

Building the Kingdom of God

MARK 1:14-20

Main Idea: Jesus came to inaugurate His kingdom by proclaiming the message of the gospel to faithful followers who would carry this message to all people.

I.   **We Must Proclaim the Right Message (1:14-15).**
   A.   The time is fulfilled.
   B.   The kingdom of God has come near.
   C.   Repent!
   D.   Believe in the good news.
II. **We Must Find the Right People (1:16-20).**
   A.   Jesus calls.
   B.   Jesus commissions.
III. **We Must Follow the Right Master (1:17-18,20).**
   A.   See who He is.
   B.   See what He does.

What does it take to build a great organization? How does one attract followers, build devotion, and inspire lifelong commitment? I believe three things are absolutely essential: (1) a *compelling vision*, (2) a *few good people* who can provide the necessary foundation, and (3) a *great leader*.

God brings all three of these essential elements together for the building of His kingdom. A *compelling vision*: "I will make you fish for people! You will play a part in building My kingdom, the kingdom of God" (v. 17). The *few good people*: Simon (Peter) and Andrew (v. 16), James and John (v. 19). A *great leader*: Jesus! The Christ! The Son of God! As we live as citizens of His kingdom, we must hold fast to these same components.

We Must Proclaim the Right Message

MARK 1:14-15

Jesus calls His followers to fish for people. That is accomplished not with bait, hooks, or nets, but with a powerful, confrontational, and compelling message! It is the same message we must proclaim today.

Jesus delayed His preaching ministry in Galilee until John the baptizer was imprisoned. Verses 14-15 summarize well the preaching ministry of Jesus. It is the "good news of God." This is popular in Paul's letters. It refers to the good news *from* God now revealed in His Son Jesus Christ. Jesus will proclaim the gospel, and indeed He *is* the gospel! Further, this gospel is crucial to the coming of something called "the kingdom of God." The message of Jesus breaks down into four components: (1) The time is fulfilled, (2) the kingdom of God is near, (3) repent, and (4) believe in the gospel.

The Time Is Fulfilled

Jesus announces that "the time is fulfilled." He is proclaiming that the One John said would come (1:7) has appeared! The "time" is a decisive and critical moment in history. Now begins "the Great Galilean Ministry," which will last for one and a half years (Robertson, *Harmony*, 30). Jesus returns to Galilee (away from unbelieving Jerusalem) for the inauguration of His public preaching ministry, and it is the occasion for, in effect, a first-century "press release."

The Kingdom of God Has Come Near

Jesus proclaims, "The kingdom of God has come near." This phrase has provided a lot of discussion and disagreement among Bible scholars. I find the comments of Mark Strauss helpful:

> Did Jesus preach that the kingdom was something that would arrive in the future in a dramatic and cataclysmic fashion, or was it a present reality for those who would accept it? . . . Albert Schweitzer claimed that Jesus drew his expectations from the Jewish apocalypticism of his day, which viewed God's kingdom as his dramatic intervention in the future to deliver his people, judge the wicked, and establish his kingdom on earth. (Strauss, *Four Portraits, One Jesus*, 440)

According to Schweitzer's understanding, Jesus was sorely mistaken and was nailed to a cross for His error! Strauss continues:

> British New Testament scholar C. H. Dodd argued that Jesus proclaimed the kingdom as wholly present. Through Jesus' person and work, God's eternal reign had already begun. The hope of the Old Testament prophets has been realized in history. (Strauss, *Four Portraits, One Jesus*, 440)

This understanding of the kingdom is personal, subjective, and inward in focus. A future cosmic kingdom is not in view. Therefore, Strauss concludes,

The problem with both of these views is that they ignore much contrary evidence. Jesus taught *both* present and future dimensions of the
Kingdom. The best interpretation of the data is that the kingdom *has
been inaugurated* through Jesus' life, death, and resurrection but *awaits
consummation* in the future. . . . Jesus proclaimed the kingdom as
both *present* and *future*, as "*already*" but also "*not yet.*" (ibid.; emphasis
added)

With the appearance of the Messiah-King, the "kingdom of God" has
drawn near. In the person of Jesus Christ, men are confronted head-on with
the kingdom—the reign of God. What should be our response? Jesus gives
His hearers two commands.

Repent!

Those who are confronted with the kingdom of God must repent, that is,
"change their minds leading to a change in behavior." It is both a rational
decision and a willful act. It involves a turn from sin and a turn to the Savior.
It is a call that we find in the preaching of John the Baptist, Jesus, and Peter
(Acts 2). It is at the heart and soul of our response to the gospel and the
coming of the King.

Believe in the Good News

When one encounters the kingdom of God, repentance is complemented
by belief in the gospel. Repentance notes that we turn from sin; belief highlights what (or whom) we turn toward. Both *repent* and *believe* are present
imperatives. We are commanded to live in a state of repentance and trust.
This call is not to a momentary, one-time decision that has little if any lasting effect. This is a life-altering change, a radical transformation of our life
orientation! A King has arrived who rightly demands that we follow and
radically obey Him. This is the unchanging and uncompromising message
and vision of the eternal kingdom of God.

We Must Find the Right People
MARK 1:16-20

A great movement must have the right people to get its message out. These
people must embody that message if it is to have lasting impact. Based on
John 1:35-49, Jesus seems to have already met the two sets of brothers we see
in this passage: Simon (Peter) and Andrew, and James and John. All four
were successful fishermen. Jesus capitalizes on this occasion to call them to
a new vocation and a new intimacy with Himself.

Jesus Calls

Verse 17 is crisp and clear: "Follow Me . . . and I will make you fish for people!" This is a call to discipleship and a unique one at that. In the rabbinic schools of the day, the aspiring student sought out the respected rabbi. Further, the student's allegiance was to the Law, not to the teacher. Jesus' form of discipleship is fundamentally different! Jesus seeks them out, and their allegiance will be to Him.

Jesus looks for men and women who will commit to Him, who will learn from Him, who will deny themselves, take up their cross, and follow Him (8:34). As the Messiah King, the Son of God, He has this authority, this right.

There is no prerequisite to following Him. This is a grace call. He does not tell them to improve their moral character or their social acceptability. Jesus finds them where they are, and He simply calls, in effect, "Come! Come as you are, but come, you must and come right now." They are to follow, immediately and in faith. This was a radical call for those fishermen, to be sure, and it is no less radical today!

Jesus Commissions

The Old Testament roots of "fish for people" are often overlooked. It is more than a play on words in light of their vocation. In the Old Testament God fishes for people, and the texts are often foreboding in the context of divine judgment.

> "I am about to send for many fishermen"—this is the LORD's declaration—"and they will fish for them. . . . I will first repay them double for their guilt and sin because they have polluted My land. They have filled My inheritance with the lifelessness of their detestable and abhorrent idols." (Jer 16:16,18)

> This is what the Lord GOD says: "Look, I am against you, Pharaoh king of Egypt, the great monster lying in the middle of his Nile, who says, 'My Nile is my own; I made it for myself.' I will put hooks in your jaws and make the fish of your streams cling to your scales. I will haul you up from the middle of your Nile, and all the fish of your streams will cling to your scales. I will leave you in the desert, you and all the fish of your streams. You will fall on the open ground and will not be taken away or gathered for burial. I have given you to the beasts of the earth and the birds of the sky as food." (Ezek 29:3-5)

> The Lord GOD has sworn by His holiness: Look, the days are coming when you will be taken away with hooks, every last one of you with fishhooks. (Amos 4:2)

"The summons to be fishers of men is a call to the eschatological task of gathering men in view of the forthcoming judgment of God. It extends the demand for repentance in Jesus' preaching. Precisely because Jesus has come fishing became necessary" (Lane, *Mark*, 68).

Like Simon and Andrew, James and John did not hesitate: they left their father and the hired servants in the boat! This is striking and captures what it truly means to follow Jesus. To follow Jesus, we are called to forsake *everyone* and *everything* else. We must not rationalize or explain away Jesus' call as mere hyperbole!

> *Don't assume that I came to bring peace on the earth. I did not come to bring peace, but a sword. For I came to turn a man against his father, a daughter against her mother, a daughter-in-law against her mother-in-law; and a man's enemies will be the members of his household. The person who loves father or mother more than Me is not worthy of Me; the person who loves son or daughter more than Me is not worthy of Me.* (Matt 10:34-37)

> *He replied to them, "Who are My mother and My brothers?" And looking about at those who were sitting in a circle around Him, He said, "Here are My mother and My brothers! Whoever does the will of God is My brother and sister and mother."* (Mark 3:33-35)

> *If anyone comes to Me and does not hate his own father and mother, wife and children, brothers and sisters—yes, and even his own life—he cannot be My disciple.* (Luke 14:26)

The call to follow Jesus is clear and it is unconditional! In essence He puts before us a blank contract and says, "Sign at the bottom, and I will fill in the details!" This is what it means to be the right men and women with the right message. But there is a third essential.

We Must Follow the Right Master
MARK 1:17-18,20

There is only one right Master to follow in life and into eternity. His name is Jesus. Jesus called and they left everything to follow Him. The authority of the call and the immediacy of their responses raise the question as to who this Man is that demands such obedience. Actually, Mark has given us a pretty clear picture of who this Teacher is, even in the opening verses of the book.

See Who He Is

This One we are called to follow is the Christ (1:1), the Son of God (1:1), the Lord (1:3), the mighty One (1:7), the worthy One (1:7), the One who baptizes with the Holy Spirit (1:8), the Spirit-anointed One (1:10), the beloved Son (1:11), the One who pleases God (1:11), and the One who brings the kingdom of God (1:15).

See What He Does

We will learn we are called to follow in radical discipleship the One who is the astonishing Teacher (1:22), the One with authority (1:22), the Holy One of God (1:24), who is able to cast out demons (1:26,32-34,39), heal the sick (1:31-34), and even cleanse lepers (1:42). And this is just chapter 1! The kingdom of God has come near because the King is here. Everything has changed. Nothing will ever be the same again. The hour of decision is now. What will be your response?

Conclusion: Preaching the Gospel to Yourself

Jesus calls us to believe the gospel. One way we do this is to preach the gospel continually, not only to others, but also to ourselves. The result will be that you will see yourself as a much bigger sinner than you thought, but you will also then see Jesus as a much greater Savior than you ever imagined.

How do you preach the gospel to yourself?

See and own your sin. Examine yourself in the mirror of God's Word. Pray that God would bring to light your negative emotions and attitudes as well as blatant rebellion against God's holiness. As you do this, guard yourself against sin's deceitfulness. You will likely feel the tendency to water down God's standard, compare yourself to others, shift blame, or commit to trying harder. These are reflective of man-centered moralism.

See the sin beneath the sin. Push the "Why?" question until you find whatever you are looking to, other than Jesus, for meaning and value in life— your "functional messiah."

Expose the idols of your heart. Idols always disappoint. They are *weak.* They can't deliver when you succeed; they can only raise the bar. They can't forgive you when you fail; they can only lower the boom. They are *harmful.* They hurt you spiritually, emotionally, and physically. They hurt others by undermining your ability to love. They are *grievous.* By going after these idols, you are saying to God, "Jesus is not enough. I also need _____ in order to be happy."

As you expose these idols, confess, "I am a much bigger sinner than I thought. I am a worthy recipient of God's judgment. Trying harder won't cut it. I am helpless and hopeless in myself. *But* there is One who can deliver and rescue, so I flee to Him and Him alone!"

View repentance as a gift. Pray for the gift of repentance. Do not *try* to stop sinning; ask God to change your heart. You may change for a season by your own willpower, but eventually you will become resentful or fall back into worshiping your idols, false saviors that distract you from the true Messiah.

See Jesus as the only true Savior. Jesus *lived* for you; think about and give thanks for specific ways He has lived obediently where you have failed. Jesus also *died* for you; think about Jesus' death on the cross for your specific sins and idolatry. Thank God that your sin has been punished once and for all. God sees you in Jesus; think about how God sees you clothed with Jesus' perfect righteousness. Thank Him specifically for how He provides for you in Christ—ways your idols promised but could never deliver. Jesus lives in you; thank God that He does not leave you to live the Christian life on your own, since the Spirit of Christ now dwells in you. Ask Him to live His righteous life through you, specifically in the areas where you have repented and confessed sin.

Embrace the gospel as your motivation for living. Embrace it and know that the gospel changes you, the gospel empowers you to serve, and through the gospel you meet God. (For this section I have drawn from the insights of Thomas and Wood, *Gospel Coach*, 81–91.)

The King has come, and He calls all of us to repent and believe the gospel, to walk away from the idols of our life, our former allegiances, and to come follow Him. Leave your nets, leave your occupation, leave your friends, leave even your family, and come follow Him. The demands are great, but then Jesus is a great King, and the blessings of knowing Him are far greater!

Reflect and Discuss

1. Think of a great secular organization. How did a compelling vision, a strong core team, and a good leader bring success?
2. If a non-Christian asked you, how would you summarize the good news in two sentences?
3. In what way is the kingdom of God already here? In what way is it yet to come in the future?
4. How is repentance related to confession and obedience?
5. Compare and contrast the words *belief, faith,* and *trust.* In what way is "No, Lord" an oxymoron?
6. Does the assignment to "fish for people" involve grace or judgment? Explain.
7. What have you given up since you responded to Jesus' call, "Follow Me"?
8. Who is Jesus that we should follow Him?

9. What did Jesus do that gave evidence He is the King and Lord, worthy of worship?
10. In your culture, what are the idols many Christians are tempted to rely on for happiness? Which is the most tempting for you?

Why Jesus Should Have Absolute Authority in My Life?

MARK 1:21-28

Main Idea: Jesus' teaching and power over demons give a picture of His kingdom and show that He has absolute authority over all creation.

Jesus Should Have Absolute Authority in My Life

I. **Because of His Teachings (1:21-22,27)**
   A. His teachings are astonishing (1:21-22).
   B. His teachings are with authority (1:22,27).
II. **Because of His Power over Demons (1:23-28)**
   A. Demons recognize Him (1:23-24).
   B. Demons obey Him (1:25-28).

All of us have a source of authority in our lives that will determine how we think and live. For some it is **reason**—I live the way I live because I *think*. For others it is **experience**—I live the way I live because I *feel*. Still others rely on **tradition**—I live the way I live because *we have always done it this way*. Finally, someone might look to **revelation** for their authority—I live the way I live because *God says so*.

For those of us whose authority is revelation, we understand it to take the form of a *proposition* and a *person*—a written Word and a living Word. The written Word we call the Bible. The living Word we know as Jesus. One we love. The other we love and worship. The written Word points us to the living Word, and that One has the right to demand complete and absolute lordship in our lives.

Why should Jesus have absolute lordship in your life? Mark 1:21-28 provides two of many reasons.

Because of His Teachings
MARK 1:21-22,27

Taking along His new followers, Jesus goes to Capernaum. It was located on the north shore of the Sea of Galilee, a freshwater lake, seven miles wide and 13 miles long, teeming with fish. Capernaum was a significant port in Jesus' day with a mixed population of Jews, Gentiles, and Roman soldiers and officials. It was well situated for Jesus to employ as a base while He traveled throughout the region of Galilee evangelizing. Immediately upon His arrival, things kick into action. He begins to teach the crowds, and they learn several things about this new teacher.

His Teachings Are Astonishing (Mark 1:21-22)

Jesus began to teach on the Sabbath, the Jewish day of worship that ran from sundown on Friday to the same on Saturday. His setting was the Jewish synagogue. Analogous to a local church building in our day, the synagogue was an assembly hall where the Scriptures were read and taught. There was only one temple—in Jerusalem—but synagogues were established wherever 10 or more Jewish males, 13 years of age or older, lived. The Jews used them for worship, education, and community gatherings. Their origin can probably be traced to the Babylonian exile in 586 BC.

Mark tells us nothing about the content of Jesus' teaching in this passage. Mark's focus is the One who is teaching, His authority, and the astonishing response of the hearers. The listeners were amazed and alarmed. His teachings were disturbing in their very nature. Today we might say, "They were blown away!"

His Teachings Are with Authority (Mark 1:22,27)

The people immediately saw a contrast between the teachings of Jesus and those of "the scribes." The scribes, also called "teachers of the law," were skilled in the exposition of the Torah, the law of Moses. This much-respected and celebrated group of scholars traced their origin back to Ezra (Ezra 7:6,11). Later called "rabbis," they could render binding judgment on the interpretation of the law. They "combined the offices of Torah professor, teacher and moralist, and civil lawyer, in that order. Their erudition and prestige reached legendary proportion by the first century, surpassing on occasions that of the high priest" (Edwards, *Mark*, 54). Many were Pharisees, though there were also Sadducees and priests among them. The Sanhedrin, the Jewish Supreme Court, was made up mostly of scribes.

Thus, these men were greatly respected—the religious elite—and it was an honor to sit under their instruction. However, they stood in opposition to Jesus and His ministry. Jesus will not challenge the legitimacy of their office, but He will call out their legalism, hypocrisy, and pride.

If some persons fear that they are too bad to be saved, this group ran the risk of believing that they were so good they did not need to be saved! This is a danger those raised in a highly religious context always face.

Mark is careful to contrast the authority of Jesus with the scribes' lack thereof (vv. 22,27). The scribes derived their authority from the "tradition of men" (see 7:8-13). By quoting the fathers of Judaism, they rested on the famous and respected teachers who had preceded them.

Not so with Jesus. Like the prophets His authority came directly from God, His Father (1:11). Lane says, "Jesus' word, presented with a sovereign authority, which permitted neither debate nor theoretical reflection, confronted the congregation with the absolute claim of God upon their whole person" (Lane, *Mark*, 72). The One who brings the teaching that astonishes and has authority is Himself the Christ, the Son of God. He has the right not only to decide what is true but also to demand a decision. Note Mark's second compelling argument for the complete lordship of Christ.

Because of His Power over Demons
MARK 1:23-28

There is "a man with an unclean spirit." The more usual term for "unclean spirit" is "demon" (used 63 times in the New Testament). Who or what is a demon? They could be (1) the spirits of a pre-Adamic evil race, (2) the spirits of evil men, (3) the product of angels cohabitating with women in Genesis 6:1-4, or (4) fallen angels. This fourth option is the most likely. Mark calls them "unclean spirits" 11 times and "demons" 13 times.

What else can we know about demons? (1) From Revelation 12:4, it seems that one-third of the angels fell with Satan in his rebellion against God. (2) Some are now free to roam (Mark 1:21-34). (3) Some will still be free during the tribulation (Rev 9:13-19). (4) Others are confined now, never to roam freely (2 Pet 2:4; Jude 6). (5) They are powerful personalities, though not omnipotent (Mark 1:24). (6) Their activity may have increased during the time of Christ, and it will do so again in the coming end time (see Rev 6–19). (7) They are set up under Satan's control (Eph 6:11-12), probably in rank and possibly in geography (Dan 10:10-12). (8) They have authority and can promote disunity, propagate false doctrine, inflict disease, cause mental difficulties, and hinder Christian growth. (9) Demons can *oppress* but not *possess* believers.

So here is a demon-possessed man in, of all places, a house of worship! If this demon made his way into the first-century synagogue, we should not assume that our own churches are beyond their reach.

Demons Recognize Him (Mark 1:23-24)

Upon seeing Jesus, the demon cries out, "What do You have to do with us, Jesus—Nazarene? Have You come to destroy us? I know who You are—the Holy One of God!" The demon recognizes Jesus in terms of His humanity and His deity: the "Nazarene" and "the Holy One of God." Even the demons stand in awe of the God Man!

The demon is chiefly concerned with Jesus' intentions. "Us" may refer to multiple demons in the man or to the demonic realm as a whole. In either case he recognizes the threat that Jesus is to their authority and power. "Come to destroy" may be a declaration instead of a question. They understand more clearly than humans that the Son of God's coming is a decisive moment in history. It spells their doom!

Confessing Jesus as the "Holy One of God" is perhaps an attempt to gain some power over Jesus by claiming to know His name. It is more likely, however, a recognition of His deity, His sonship, and the great antithesis that exists between an unholy, unclean spirit and the Holy One of God.

Referring to Jesus, demoniacs use language such as "Holy One of God" (1:24), "Son of God" (3:11), and "Son of the Most High God" (5:7). In contrast many of the ordinary sick whom Jesus healed referred to Him more in terms of His humanity: "Lord" (7:8), "Teacher" (9:17), "Son of David" (10:47-48), and "Master" (10:51). It's not that these latter titles were incorrect, but the demons had remarkable theology and a view of Jesus' identity that is frequently loftier than our own.

The kingdom of God goes head-to-head with the forces of evil at the first public ministry of the Son of God. It is a "no contest" event with an immediate and devastating knockout! The "binding of the strong man" has begun (3:27). The demons are forced to acknowledge, grudgingly, what the Father declared in verse 11!

Demons Obey Him (Mark 1:25-28)

Knowing that the demon recognizes Him, Jesus issues a direct command. "Be quiet." It is an imperative, an unqualified rebuke, as though Jesus were saying, "Shut up; muzzle it!" Again He commands, "Come out!" It only takes a few direct words from an absolute authority! No spell or incantation is necessary. He says the word and they obey.

The demon immediately convulsed, cried out, and came out just as the Lord said. The people were "all amazed" ("all" is emphatic in the Greek) and asked, "What is this? A new teaching with authority! He commands even the unclean spirits, and they obey Him." As a result, His fame spread everywhere—not just around Galilee but to surrounding regions! People were hearing the good news of the kingdom everywhere.

Conclusion

The disturbance of men and demons by the Servant King of God has begun. Life will never be the same! Demons are expelled, and broken people are made whole. This is God's kingdom. This is what the great King can do. This is why He should have absolute authority in your life, my life, and every life.

Reflect and Discuss

1. Other than revelation, which source of authority—reason, experience, or tradition—exerts the most influence in your life?
2. How is the respect we show for the Bible, the written Word of God, different from the worship we owe to Jesus, the living Word of God?
3. Which teachings of Jesus do you find astonishing?
4. How can a person show respect for a teacher or preacher of the Bible while still examining the Scriptures to verify their message (Acts 17:11)?
5. What are the advantages to being raised in a "good, Christian home"? What are the disadvantages?
6. What are the limits on the authority of a pastor? How are these limits enforced?
7. What examples of evil are "natural" and what are demonic? What evidence have you heard of or seen that demons are active in the country where you live?
8. Why would demons have better theology than some people?
9. What does Jesus' absolute authority over demons mean for us today? How can it affect your life?
10. In what ways can demonstrations of the authority of Jesus be used to spread the gospel today?

A Day in the Life of Jesus

MARK 1:29-34

Main Idea: Jesus is the Messiah King of the world who came to live as a servant for the sake of His people.

I.   Jesus Came to Heal the Diseased (1:29-34).
II. Jesus Came to Deliver the Demonized (1:32-34).
III. Excursus: Why Did Jesus Conceal His Messiahship During His Ministry?

In a day when pragmatism rules, most people ask two questions: "What can you do for me?" and "What have you done for me lately?" This focus is on utility, performance, and means to an end. Oftentimes those questions enter into the spiritual realm. We arrogantly thrust them before God as if He were our servant, obligated to meet our needs and respond to our call. "OK, God, what have You done for me lately? What have You done for me ever?"

Amazingly, in the incarnation and the sending of His Son, God answers our questions. God does serve us; He does minister to us; He even sacrifices Himself for us. Perhaps the key verse that summarizes the Gospel of Mark and the ministry of Jesus is found in 10:45: "For even the Son of Man did not come to be served, but to serve, and to give His life—a ransom for many." The ransom, the payment for sin, will occur on the cross. His service to wounded and helpless sinners would be characteristic of His ministry from beginning to end, as exemplified on this day in the life of Jesus.

Mark presents these events with five uses of his favorite word: "immediately" (or "right away" or "at once"; 1:21,23,28,29,30). With a sense of mission and urgency, Jesus is here and there, ministering to this one and then another. He truly is the Servant of the Lord, healing the physically sick and setting free spiritual prisoners held captive by the prince of darkness and his demonic hoards! So we ask, "What can Jesus do for me?" The answer is, much more than we ever hoped or imagined!

Jesus Came to Heal the Diseased

MARK 1:29-34

Jesus has just left the synagogue where He taught with authority and delivered a demon-possessed man. Next, He enters Simon Peter's house with His four closest disciples. This will be a "base of operations" for Jesus in and around Capernaum (see 2:1; 3:20; 9:33; 10:10). Peter's mother-in-law[1] is sick with a fever. The nature of the illness is not what is important—the power of the Healer is! "At once" they inform Jesus of her illness, and just as quickly He goes to her, touches her, and heals her!

Again, there are no spells, incantations, or rituals. With compassion and a personal touch, Jesus restores Peter's ailing mother-in-law to full health. Verse 34 adds that on this particular day "He healed many who were sick with various diseases." They kept bringing the sick to Him, and He kept healing them with love and compassion.

This scene raises a theological question: Is there healing in the atonement? Isaiah 53:5 says, "We are healed by His wounds." Matthew 8:17, in the parallel account of these events, even adds a quote from Isaiah 53:4: "Yet He Himself bore our sicknesses, and He carried our pains; but we in turn regarded Him stricken, struck down by God, and afflicted." The answer, then, is a resounding "Yes!" There is healing in the atonement! For some it is *immediate* but *temporary*, since all still die. But for all who trust Jesus as Savior and Lord, it is *eternal* and *permanent*. This is plain in Revelation 21:4-5:

> *He will wipe away every tear from their eyes. Death will no longer exist; grief, crying, and pain will exist no longer, because the previous things have passed away. Then the One seated on the throne said, "Look! I am making everything new." He also said, "Write, because these words are faithful and true."*

Jesus Came to Deliver the Demonized
MARK 1:32-34

Jesus' fame is spreading like wildfire (v. 28). People are probably aware that He is in Peter's house and that He has healed his mother-in-law. Now that the Sabbath has ended (at sundown), people show up from everywhere, bringing the sick, until "the whole town was assembled at the door." With so many around Him, what would Jesus do? "He healed many."

The sick were not the only ones who came: they also brought those who were oppressed by demons, and He "drove out many demons." Satan and his minions had once again met the Savior in spiritual combat (cf. vv. 23-27) and it was no contest. Bring many demons face-to-face with God's Son, and they experience an immediate and decisive thrashing.

---

[1] Obviously, therefore, Peter was married! We have no other details than this.

The last phrase of verse 34 is instructive. Men may be confused as to the identity of Jesus, but never so with the demons: "They knew Him" and they feared Him. What a contrast with foolish, fallen, and unbelieving humans!

A distinction is made between those "who were sick and those who were demon-possessed" (v. 32) and those "who were sick with various diseases" (v. 34). All disease and sickness is the result of sin, but not all disease and sickness is the result of demonic oppression or activity. Satan and his demons *may* inflict physical illness, but not *all* physical afflictions are demonic in origin. The ancients were not as naïve and ignorant as they are sometimes accused of being.

Still, Mark's point in giving this scene is, "Watch the servant serve!" He healed many who were sick. He cast out many demons. The kingdom has come in the person of the great and awesome King, and it is moving forward with great speed and success. And not one thing can stop Him!

Excursus: Why Did Jesus Conceal His Messiahship During His Ministry?

Why does Jesus not permit the demons to speak (v. 34)? Why does Jesus tell the leper to say nothing to anyone (v. 44)? This oddity, called the "Messianic Secret," is an important and interesting issue discussed by both believing and unbelieving scholars. James Edwards helps us see why the question was raised in the first place:

> On three occasions *demons* are enjoined to silence (1:25; 1:34; 3:11). Jesus commands silence after four *miracles* (cleansing of a leper, 1:44; raising of a dead girl, 5:43; healing of a deaf-mute, 7:36; healing of a blind man, 8:26). Twice the *disciples* are commanded to silence (8:30; 9:9). Twice Jesus withdraws from *crowds* to escape detection (7:24; 9:30). Beyond these explicit admonitions to secrecy, Mark implies secrecy in other aspects of Jesus' public ministry. But ironically, the command to silence often results in the opposite: "the more he [commanded to silence], the more they kept talking about it" (7:36; 1:45; 5:20; 7:24). (Edwards, *Mark*, 63)

At least seven observations can be made about this phenomenon.

1. Jesus wanted to avoid the impression of being a mere miracle worker or a magician. Those who conjure up tricks seek attention for themselves. Jesus is different. He came to defeat the power and effects of sin in the whole world.

2. Jesus wanted to avoid unhelpful publicity to have more moments of private teaching with His disciples. Obviously, Jesus' reputation gathered a crowd. This crowd demanded attention, and every moment Jesus spent in public was a moment He could not spend intimately discipling His closest followers.

3. Jesus wanted to avoid the people's misconceptions about the Messiah. His Messiahship was characterized by service and suffering, not sensational displays of miraculous activity that would excite political-Messiah fever. Even with Jesus' attempts to reign in misconceptions, the people still thought He came to overthrow Roman rule.

4. Jesus wanted to express His humility as the Suffering Servant of the Lord.

5. Jesus wanted to inform us that only through the medium of faith, ultimately in a crucified and humiliated Savior, is His messiahship personally apprehended (cf. 1 Cor 1–2). One cannot grasp the fullness of His worth without realizing that He must die. We don't simply like Jesus because He can do miraculous works. We trust Him because His death was on our behalf, and His resurrection is for our victory.

6. Jesus wanted to avoid recognition from an undesirable source such as the demons and the hypocritical religious leaders.

7. He wanted His identity concealed to point to the hostility of the religious and political leaders of the day. There was a stark contrast between Jesus' humble love and the Pharisees' look-at-me religiosity. This disparity is seen most clearly in Jesus' own choice to walk resolutely into the destined hour of His passion.

Some have suggested that Mark invented this portrait of Christ in order to explain why Jesus was not recognized as the Son of God prior to the Easter event, but this suggestion is untenable and should be rejected as liberal conjecture grounded in an antisupernatural bias. The reason nobody recognized Him as the Messiah is that they were looking for a political, military Messiah who would liberate them from Rome. And the Gospel writers were Hebrews rooted in Jewish monotheism. The idea that they would have fabricated Jesus as Messiah in terms of His divine sonship is simply not believable. Instead, we can confidently affirm that the Messianic Secret arose from Jesus Himself. He self-consciously identified with the Suffering Servant of the Lord in Isaiah's prophecy, and He knew the need to guard His messianic identity from premature and false understandings.

He was not the kind of Messiah the first-century world hoped for, but He was the kind of Messiah the first-century world—indeed the whole world—truly needed. Our greatest ailment is not sickness but sin, not demons but death. We did not need a Messiah who would only bring liberation from political oppression and healing from disease. No, we needed a Messiah who would give His life as a ransom for sinners like you and me. Praise God, He sent us the kind of Messiah we needed!

Conclusion

God cares about our problems in this fallen, sin-infested world. God knows that we hurt and that sin is a constant reminder of our finite, mortal humanity. God has remedied our hopeless condition by sending Jesus. As did the diseased and the demonized, we should run to Him and Him alone. And like Peter's mother-in-law, we should be quick to serve Him and serve others out of grateful appreciation for such a wonderful Savior and such a marvelous salvation. It was a normal day in the life of Jesus. It was anything but normal for those who encountered and experienced His saving power!

Reflect and Discuss

1. When Jesus healed Peter's mother-in-law, He did not use any spells, incantations, or rituals. What does this say about His power and authority?
2. What examples of miraculous healing have you seen or experienced?
3. In what way is physical healing temporary? In what way is it eternal and permanent?
4. Why is it important that the Bible distinguishes between those who were sick and those who were demon possessed?
5. How was Jesus different from sensational "miracle workers" and magicians? How should that affect the way we promote Christianity?
6. What is "therapeutic" Christianity? Can emphasis on physical deliverance distract Christians from the message of the gospel these days?
7. How can a pastor's fame distract from the message of the gospel? How can a well-known pastor use his fame effectively for the kingdom?
8. Compare the attitude of the crowds when they were being healed or fed with the response to the crucifixion and to the command that we "take up [our] cross" (8:34).
9. What kind of Messiah were the Jews looking for in Jesus' day? What might have happened if they had become convinced that Jesus was such a Messiah?
10. Do you know of any churches or denominations today that proclaim Jesus to be a political deliverer or a physical healer? How does that fail to tell the whole story?

The Kingdom of God Marches On

MARK 1:35-45

Main Idea: Jesus' life illustrates the advancement of God's kingdom through prayer, proclamation, and healing.

I. The Kingdom Advances Through Prayer (1:35-37).
II. The Kingdom Advances Through Preaching (1:38-39).
III. The Kingdom Advances Through Cleansing (1:40-45).

Shackled by a heavy burden,
'Neath a load of guilt and shame;
Then the hand of Jesus touched me,
And now I am no longer the same.

Since I met this blessed Savior,
Since He cleansed and made me whole;
I will never cease to praise Him—
I'll shout it while eternity rolls.

He touched me, oh, He touched me,
And oh, the joy that floods my soul!
Something happened, and now I know,
He touched me and made me whole. (Gaither, "He Touched Me")

Those words, penned by Bill Gaither in 1963, could have been inspired by the text before us, the healing of a leper, a sure sign that God's kingdom had come and was indeed marching on.

Jesus has just had an extraordinary day of teaching the Scriptures, casting out demons, and healing the sick—all on the Sabbath. He has served the hurting late into the evening, well past sundown (1:32). And even though the day is drawing to a close, there is more to be done to enable the kingdom to advance against the powers of darkness and evil. In this text Jesus exhibits the strategy by which God continues to advance His purposes. Three clear aspects emerge in our text. Bracketed by the miracles of healing and exorcism, we find the essential elements of prayer and preaching. Without both, the advance of the kingdom would have stopped dead in its tracks. The same is true today!

The Kingdom Advances Through Prayer
MARK 1:35-37

Though He had been up late, Jesus still rises "very early" the next morning, "while it was still dark." He leaves Peter's home alone, going "to a deserted place" for solitude and privacy. A place for restoration and fellowship with His Father.

There are three prayers of Jesus in Mark: The first is found here at the beginning, when His ministry is being defined. The second comes in the middle of the Gospel, when the people wanted to "take Him by force to make Him King" (John 6:15). The final prayer is near the conclusion, in Gethsemane, asking the Father to "take this cup away" (Mark 14:32-42). These are critical moments. The setting in each instance is darkness and solitude, recalling the wilderness and the cosmic conflict between our Lord and Satan. Here, Jesus finds strength in the solitude of prayer and intimate fellowship with His Father. What a valuable lesson that too many of us ignore!

Peter and those with him sent out a search party. Apparently the crowds had returned for more miracles. Peter's words are almost a rebuke: "Everyone's looking for You!" In other words, "What are You doing here? This is not where You should be! You need to be with the crowds! We are building a following. Things are beginning to happen. You do not have time to be alone and pray!" Oh, how we are so much like Peter, not understanding the ways of God and how His kingdom will come! Yes, there will be healings and exorcisms. But there must also be prayer.

The Kingdom Advances Through Preaching
MARK 1:38-39

Jesus, as He so often does, responds to Peter in a surprising manner. He will not return to those who are looking for Him. Rather, He says, "Let's move on. Let's go to the next town. I will preach there also. This is why I came."

The crowds at Peter's house came for the miracles. Now, apparently, they want more. The call to repent and believe the gospel (1:15) was not on their spiritual radar. Like so many today, they wanted a Jesus of their liking, a Jesus who would perform miracles and fit into their agenda.

Neither the crowds nor the disciples understood why He had come into the world. But He knew! Jesus came to preach, to herald, to proclaim the gospel of salvation, a message that is both *by* Him and *about* Him. Indeed, He is the gospel! But sadly, the crowds missed Him.

God had only one Son, and He made Him a preacher. No pastor is worthy of the office who does not preach the Word. No church will prosper spiritually without the preaching of the Word. John Stott said, "Christianity is, in its very essence, a religion of the Word of God" (*Between Two Worlds*, 15). Luther would add, "Let us consider it certain and conclusively established that the soul can do without all things except the Word of God, and that where this is not there is no help for the soul in anything else whatever" (*Three Treatises*, 23).

Jesus went throughout all Galilee, preaching the gospel and casting out demons. He did this out of a life of prayer. Prayer and preaching is a one-two punch that cannot be defeated. This is how the kingdom marches on anywhere and anytime.

The Kingdom Advances Through Cleansing
MARK 1:40-45

As He was traveling and ministering, Jesus is met by a leper. This encounter is startling, provocative, and even offensive. A leper was a man whom the culture considered an outcast, the law judged unclean, and the people deemed cursed by God. Even one with AIDS today fares far better than the leper of the first century. A leper was to stay at least 50 paces from others. That he came near to Jesus, so close that Jesus could touch him, was unthinkable.

The word for leprosy covered a number of skin diseases (including what we today call "Hansen's Disease"), each of which was difficult to diagnose and heal. The person with the disease was mocked and shunned. The leper had to wear torn clothes, leave his hair unkempt, cover his face, and cry out "Unclean!" He was forced to live in isolation. Josephus said a leper was "in no way differing from a corpse" (*Antiquities*, 3.264).

Leviticus 13–14 discusses the disease. It was usually regarded as an evidence of divine punishment. As such, the cure could only come from the Lord. Other illnesses could be healed, but leprosy had to be both healed and cleansed. Needless to say, no one in the Bible healed a leper by touch other than Jesus.

Warren Wiersbe notes, "When you read the 'tests' for leprosy in Leviticus 13, you can see how the disease is a picture of sin. Like sin, leprosy is deeper than the skin (v. 3); it spreads (vv. 5-8); it defiles and isolates (vv. 44-46); and it renders things fit only for the fire (vv. 47-59). Anyone who has never trusted the Savior is spiritually in worse shape than this man was physically" (*Be Diligent*, 19).

All of this makes it remarkable that the leper came to Jesus. He violated every convention and custom of society in that day. He was desperate, and he believed only Jesus could heal him and make him clean. He came, knelt, and begged, "If You are willing, You can make me clean." Wow! His faith is astounding! The issue is not whether Jesus *could* heal him, but *would* He? This man comes to Jesus with great courage, great humility, and great faith—the same way we, as sin-sick sinners, must come to Him. He came believing in the only One who could change his life and make him whole.

Surprisingly and scandalously, Jesus makes the unclean clean! Rather than turning away from the man, He turns to him with compassion and touches him, thereby removing his curse, taking away his shame, and removing his defilement. As the Suffering Servant of Isaiah 53:4, He takes on Himself the infirmities of this man, cleanses him, and makes him whole!

Jesus' touch speaks louder than words ever could, yet His words must have thrilled this man's soul: "I am willing." Unlike any ordinary man, the Lord Jesus is not polluted by the leper's disease when He touches him. Instead, the leper is cleansed by the gracious touch and contagious holiness of the Son of God.

It is not surprising that Jesus sends the man to a local priest, according to the ritual for cleansing in Leviticus 14. What is surprising is the stern charge and quick exit Jesus demands. He sends him packing with a command to keep his mouth shut. Jesus does not want persons who merely seek miracles. He wants followers who seek Him! People are always tempted by the sensational. Jesus desires followers who long for truth and want to know Him. He does not want people to come to Him to get what they want. He wants people to come to Him to get Him!

The leper went and talked freely about what Jesus had done. We can understand his enthusiasm. We cannot, however, justify his disregard of our Lord's clear command. He talked of it everywhere. This caused a restriction on Jesus' preaching ministry, as He "could no longer enter a town openly." He again frequented "deserted places" (cf. 1:35). Still, the people "would come to Him from everywhere." What Mark will say in 7:24 is already true now: "He could not escape notice."

Ironically, Jesus and the leper have traded places. The leper is now on the inside with family and friends. Jesus is on the outside in a lonely and desolate place. This picture of substitution is the heart of the gospel. It is why Jesus came. He will take on Himself our sin, our sorrow, and our shame. In return He gives us His forgiveness, His holiness, and His righteousness—praise the Lord! What an exchange!

Conclusion

The rabbis said that it was as difficult to heal the leper as it was to raise the dead. Both are impossible for man; neither is a problem for God's Son. He cleanses the defiled and raises the dead by a simple touch or a simple word. He truly touches lives and makes them whole. He did that for me. Has He done that for you?

Reflect and Discuss

1. How is individual prayer different from corporate prayer? How is individual prayer intensified by isolation?
2. What is the best time for you to spend time in intense prayer: early in the morning, during the day, or in the evening?
3. If you are under pressure, and there is not sufficient time to (1) get enough sleep, (2) spend enough time in prayer, and (3) take enough time to do a job well, which of these are you likely to compromise?
4. Do people still come to church wanting blessings without repentance? What blessings are they hoping to receive?
5. What constitutes "preaching" besides what a pastor does on Sunday mornings? Is there a kind of "preaching" that any Christian man or woman can and should do?
6. What kinds of people are shunned today in a way that approaches how lepers were avoided in Jesus' day? How might we reach out and touch such people?
7. How is asking Jesus, "If You are willing . . ." (1:40) different from asking Him, "If You can do anything . . ." (9:22)?
8. Why was it surprising that Jesus touched the leper? Why was it theologically significant?
9. The leper's publicity of his healing changed what the people expected from Jesus' ministry. What should we publicize about what goes on in our churches in order to give people a true picture of what they should expect?
10. Besides physical health, what did the leper gain from his encounter with Jesus? How does that compare with what we gain?

Jesus of Nazareth: The God Who Forgives Sin

MARK 2:1-12

Main Idea: Jesus is the Son of Man, God incarnate, who is able to forgive the sins of rebellious humanity.

I. **We Should Bring the Hurting to Jesus (2:1-5).**
    A. They need to hear His teaching (2:1-2).
    B. They need to experience His forgiveness (2:3-5).
II. **We Should See Jesus for Who He Truly Is (2:5-11).**
    A. Jesus is God (2:5-9).
    B. Jesus is the Son of Man (2:10-11).
III. **We Should Glorify Jesus for What He Does (2:5,10-12).**
    A. Jesus forgives our sins (2:5).
    B. Jesus heals our diseases (2:10-12).
Excursus: Five Questions We Always Ask of Every Text

All of us at some point in our lives will be forced to consider two critical questions: Can I be forgiven of my sins? Who can forgive me of my sins? That we must face such questions should not surprise us. Sin is our greatest problem. It is our greatest enemy and separates us from God. It renders us spiritually dead, and if left unforgiven, results in eternal death in a place called hell. Sin shatters relationships, causes us to think foolishly, leads us to make bad choices, and moves us to act in evil and destructive ways.

Can I be forgiven? The Bible has a wonderful answer: Yes! Who can forgive me? God can—the God who is revealed in the person of Jesus. This Jesus is the Son of God (1:1), the Son of Man (2:10), and the Holy One of God (1:24) who has come to take away the sins of the world. He is the only One who can deliver me from the penalty of sin, providing for my *justification*. He is the only One who can deliver me from the power of sin, ensuring my *sanctification*. And He is the only One who can deliver me from the presence of sin, promising my future *glorification*. In light of who Jesus is and what He can do, our text provides the appropriate responses.

We Should Bring the Hurting to Jesus
MARK 2:1-5

Mark 2:1–3:6 is a single unit comprising five controversies between Jesus and the Jewish religious leaders in Galilee in northern Israel. There is another series of five controversies with the same antagonists in Jerusalem in Judea (11:27–12:37). In the present section, though, Jesus is back home from His preaching and ministry tour throughout Galilee (1:38-45), likely staying at Peter's house once again (cf. 1:29).

They Need to Hear His Teaching (Mark 2:1-2)

Having heard that Jesus had returned, many gathered to hear Him speak. So many gathered that there is no room—even the doorway is jammed (cf. 1:32-33,37)! They are certainly interested in Jesus, but their interest is for the wrong reason. They want another miracle, but instead Jesus gives them preaching. He preached "the message"—the word (Gk *logos*)—to them (2:2). This involved proclaiming the Scriptures (our Old Testament) and continuing His call to repent and believe the gospel in light of the coming kingdom of God (cf. 1:14-15,22,38-39). "More than any other expression in early Christianity, 'the word' defines the essence of Jesus' ministry" (Edwards, *Mark*, 75). As benefactors of His gracious ministry, we need to hear His preaching.

They Need to Experience His Forgiveness (Mark 2:3-5)

During Jesus' teaching, four men showed up with a man who could not walk (2:3). Obviously, they believed Jesus could heal their friend. However, because of the crowd, they could not get in to see Jesus (2:4). Undeterred, they took the outside staircase up to the flat rooftop. The roof was made of wood beams, cross-laid with branches and packed with a thick layer of grass, mud, and clay. One could easily walk on it. Conveniently, one could also dig through it. The men "unroofed" the roof, showering those below with dirt and sticks. They lowered the man on his bed until he lay there before Jesus.

Jesus saw "their" faith, probably referring to all five men, but at the very least encompassing the four friends. In either case our Lord clearly was impressed, and He honored their faith by pouring out mercy on the paralyzed man.

Jesus addressed him as "son" (Gk *teknon*, "child"), revealing His great affection and compassion for the young man's plight. And with this compassion Jesus told the man, "Your sins are forgiven." This is interesting since the men probably came to Jesus not for forgiveness but for healing. However, Jesus gave them both! In this instance it appears personal sin and physical sickness are related, though this is not always the case (cf. the blind man in John 9).

Seeing the man's whole situation, Jesus lovingly looked past his surface need and met his deeper need; He looked past the man's immediate need and met his real need! Based on who He is and what He would accomplish on the cross, Jesus extended to a paralyzed sinner God's full and complete pardon of sin. He may have needed healing, but even more he—like all of us—needed to experience the forgiveness of sins made possible by Jesus.

We Should See Jesus for Who He Truly Is
MARK 2:5-11

We are hardly stunned by the reaction of the scribes, the religious leaders of Israel. Upon hearing Jesus forgive the man's sin, they immediately accuse Him of blasphemy, the very charge they will use to get Him crucified (14:64-65). To their credit they at least understood the significance of Jesus' actions here. They recognized that the proclamation of forgiveness was not a passing comment but a declaration of deity: "Who can forgive sins but God alone?"

This was a serious charge with serious consequences. They understood Jesus' words to be dishonoring and disrespectful to God. Blasphemy was a grave offense, punishable by death from stoning (Lev 24:15-16). Jesus' words are indeed blasphemous—unless He is in fact God! The whole scenario leaves everyone questioning, "Who is this One claiming to forgive sins?"

Jesus Is God (Mark 2:5-9)

The scribes were correct: only God can forgive sins! That is exactly and precisely what Jesus was asserting, and He will prove it momentarily by healing this man. Later He will prove it for all time in His resurrection from the dead.

In Jewish thinking even the Messiah could not forgive sins! God and God alone has that authority and right. Those first-century Jews knew exactly what was going on: if He can forgive sins, then Jesus is God. Jesus immediately knew what they were thinking (another evidence of deity: omniscience). He immediately confronts them with two direct questions (vv. 8-9). "Why are you thinking these things in your hearts? Which is easier: to say to the paralytic, 'Your sins are forgiven,' or to say, 'Get up, pick up your mat, and walk'?" Jesus knew, as did they, it is one thing to say it; it is something else to prove it.

Jesus Is the Son of Man (Mark 2:10-11)

Jesus introduces us to a specific title that will become His favorite self-designation. He refers to Himself as "the Son of Man." The title is found 81 times in the Gospels. Why did Jesus use this term so often, and what did He mean by it? Why did He not more often use the term "Christ" or "Messiah" or even "Son of God," since that is truly who He is?

A look at the way the term is used can help answer those questions. Sometimes Jesus shows Himself to be the Son of Man who is *serving* (2:10; 2:28). At other times Jesus is the Son of Man who is *suffering* (8:31; 9:9,12; 10:33,45; 14:21,41). Finally, Jesus is the Son of Man who is *coming in glory* (8:38; 13:26; 14:62). The title occurs more often after Peter confesses Jesus as the Christ and Jesus begins to teach clearly about His own death (8:29).

In the Old Testament the term is used in several different ways. In Psalm 144:3 it simply means "human being." However, in Daniel 7:13-14 it refers to One who will come to establish God's kingdom:

> *I continued watching in the night visions, and I saw One like a son of man coming with the clouds of heaven. He approached the Ancient of Days and was escorted before Him. He was given authority to rule, and glory, and a kingdom; so that those of every people, nation, and language should serve Him. His dominion is an everlasting dominion that will not pass away, and His kingdom is one that will not be destroyed.*

Jesus uses the title to refer to Himself with both connotations. As God incarnate, He is a human being who identifies with sinful humanity as He serves and suffers on our behalf. As God, He is the coming Lord of glory.

Jesus avoided the term "Christ" (Messiah) because He was a much different kind of Messiah from what the Jewish nation anticipated in the first century. He first came to suffer, and then He would come in glory. Claiming the title "Son of Man" allowed Him to refer to the total scope of His Messianic mission without all the political overtones.

Only in this present text is the forgiveness of sins linked to the divine title "Son of Man." By implication Jesus does this again in 10:45 when He weds the Son of Man of Daniel 7 to the Suffering Servant of Isaiah 53, thereby redefining who the Messiah is and what He came to do. He is God, a divine heavenly figure who will receive an everlasting kingdom. That kingdom, however, will be realized through suffering service that will climax in death on a Roman cross.

We Should Glorify Jesus for What He Does
MARK 2:5,10-12

In spite of opposition from the religious aristocracy, this story has a happy ending. Those who bring the hurting in faith to Jesus will not be disappointed. William Lane says,

> The announcement [of forgiveness] and presentation of radical healing to a man in his entire person was a sign of the kingdom of God drawn near. The paralytic experienced the fulfillment of God's promise that the lame would share in the joy of the coming salvation. (Lane, *Mark*, 99)

The promise of Isaiah 35:6 is realized here: "Then the lame will leap like a deer."

Jesus Forgives Our Sins (Mark 2:5)

Coming in faith to Jesus, this hurting man received more that he expected and exactly what he needed. He received the full forgiveness of his sins. He and his friends believed Jesus could meet their deepest needs. They were simply wrong on what was really needed.

Often we think we know what our greatest need is, but really we are only focusing on our circumstances. In reality the problem you are facing today is not your spouse, children, or parents. It is not your job, boss, or coworkers. It is not your lack of resources, shortage of time, or insufficient income. Just like this young man, your greatest need is for the Messiah Himself.

Jesus saw everything clearly—far more clearly than we do. He used this teachable moment to make the point concerning our greatest need in this life or the life to come! Jesus forgives the sins of all who come to Him in faith.

Jesus Heals Our Diseases (Mark 2:10-12)

As a proof of His power to forgive sins, something we cannot see, Jesus healed the paralytic, something everyone could see. He is simple and direct in His statement: "'But so you may know that the Son of Man has authority on earth to forgive sins,' He told the paralytic, 'I tell you: get up, pick up your mat, and go home.'" The man responds with the obedience of faith and does just that "in front of everyone"!

The response of the man and the crowd is appropriate. Even the Pharisees and teachers of the law, who "had come from every village of

Galilee and Judea, and also from Jerusalem" (Luke 5:17), could not deny this man had been healed and his sins forgiven. Nor could they deny that it had all been done by this man named Jesus. They may not like it, but they could not deny it! Thus we see forgiveness of sins declared (2:5), questioned (2:6-9), validated (2:11), and recognized (2:12).

Excursus: Five Questions We Always Ask of Every Text

What does this text teach me about God? If the Bible is, in fact, God's revelation of Himself in written form, then we should first be concerned not with what it teaches about us but primarily with what it teaches us about Him. In this text we can surely say that only God can forgive our sins. Jesus, the religious leaders, and even the crowds clearly understood that. We can also say that God is compassionate to those wounded by sin. Jesus did not leave the man paralyzed or in sin. He healed him both physically and spiritually. Finally, we see that God honors all who come to Him in faith.

What does this text teach me about sinful humanity? When studying Scripture, we must take into account that we are created in the glorious image of God, but that image is marred by sin. This text shows that our greatest need is not physical healing but spiritual forgiveness. It also teaches that those who are the most religious are often the most judgmental. The scribes and Pharisees exhibit this truth throughout the Gospels. We also see that sometimes, though not always, physical maladies and personal sin are related.

What does this text teach me about Jesus Christ? He is the crux of the entire Bible, so we must ask how this text relates to His person, work, and teaching. Mark reveals Jesus as God—who knows our hearts, who forgives our sins, and who heals our diseases. Ultimately He is the Son of Man who fulfills the glorious vision of Daniel 7:13-14, who has all authority in heaven and earth.

What does God want me to know? In other words, what truths are there in this passage that I need to learn? Here we learn that we need the ministry of the Word. God's Word spoken into our heart is what He uses to transform our lives. Also, we need to flee to Jesus and Jesus only for the forgiveness of sins. Finally, God wants us to know that Jesus can forgive sins because He is God.

What does God want me to do? How does this text change the way I live? Mark reveals here that God wants us to act on our faith, just as these men did. He also wants us to glorify Him for all He does for us in Jesus. Indeed, worship is the only appropriate response to the work of God in the life, death, and resurrection of His Son, Jesus.

Conclusion

In his classic work *Mere Christianity*, C. S. Lewis gets at the heart of the identity of Jesus with his famous "trilemma." He pinpoints the astonishing claims of Jesus and carefully leads us to the logical and unavoidable conclusions we must face:

> Among these Jews there suddenly turns up a man who goes about talking as if He was God. . . . [W]hat this man said was, quite simply, the most shocking thing that has ever been uttered by human lips.
> . . . I am trying here to prevent anyone saying the really foolish thing that people often say about Him. "I'm ready to accept Jesus as a great moral teacher, but I don't accept His claim to be God." That is the one thing we must not say. A man who was merely a man and said the sort of things Jesus said would not be a great moral teacher. He would either be a lunatic—on a level with the man who says he is a poached egg—or else he would be the Devil of Hell. You must make your choice. Either this man was, and is, the Son of God; or else a madman or something worse. You can shut Him up for a fool, you can spit at Him and kill Him as a demon, or you can fall at His feet and call Him Lord and God. But let us not come with any patronizing nonsense about His being a great human teacher. He has not left that open to us. He did not intend to. (Lewis, *Mere Christianity*, 54–55)

Jesus is the God who forgives sin. The questions you must answer are clear: Is He your God? Has He forgiven your sins?

Reflect and Discuss

1. What are the most important questions a thoughtful person should ask about life?
2. How was Jesus' teaching more profitable than His healing ministry? Is the gospel still more valuable than health and wealth?
3. How is faith in God's ability to do something through us related to our tenacious persistence in getting it done?
4. When you see someone who is crippled, starving, deformed, or poor, do you also think the person really needs salvation?
5. Can a Christian pronounce that another person's sins are forgiven? (See Matt 16:19.) How would that be different from what Jesus did here?
6. Why is it easy to point at someone and make statements about their spiritual state? What else do charlatans say to and about people that is impossible to prove?
7. What does Jesus' title "Son of Man" say about His purpose in His first and second coming?

8. What is the difference between circumstances and needs? How can the church avoid getting caught up in addressing circumstances and focus on the true needs of people?
9. Why did the people of Jesus' day accept the healing of the paralytic as evidence that Jesus had forgiven his sins? Today, what serves as evidence of forgiveness?
10. Of the five questions we must ask of every Bible text, which one do you tend to overlook? Which one is most profitable?

Jesus: The Friend of Sinners
MARK 2:13-17

Main Idea: Jesus is the true Servant King, as He befriends the most wretched of sinners, including you and me!

I. **Jesus Calls the Seemingly Unlikely to Follow Him (2:13-14).**
II. **Jesus Calls the Socially Undesirable to Fellowship with Him (2:15).**
III. **Jesus Calls the Spiritually Unhealthy to Follow Him (2:16-17).**
    A. Who are the Pharisees?
    B. Jesus' Mission

Jesus! What a Friend for sinners! Jesus! Lover of my soul!
Friends may fail me, foes assail me, He, my Savior, makes me whole.

Jesus! What a Strength in weakness! Let me hide myself in Him;
Tempted, tried, and sometimes failing, He, my Strength, my vict'ry wins.

Jesus! What a Help in sorrow! While the billows o'er me roll,
Even when my heart is breaking, He, my Comfort, helps my soul.

Jesus! What a Guide and Keeper! While the tempest still is high,
Storms about me, night o'ertakes me, He, my Pilot, hears my cry.

Jesus! I do now receive Him, More than all in Him I find,
He hath granted me forgiveness, I am His, and He is mine.

Refrain
Hallelujah! What a Savior! Hallelujah! What a Friend!
Saving, helping, keeping, loving, He is with me to the end. (J. Wilbur Chapman, "Jesus! What a Friend for Sinners," 1910)

Are you a friend of sinners? Do you spend time with persons who do not know Christ, whose lives may be offensive to you, and whose reputation among "good people like us" is an embarrassment and even a scandal? Do you love sinners, care for sinners, reach out to sinners, and serve sinners? Are you—am I—a friend of sinners? Are you—am I—like Jesus?!

This section of Mark, what some have called "the scandal of grace" (MacArthur, "Scandal"), has the potential to bring great conviction to the hearts of many of us. Why? First, many if not most of us do not spend much time with sinners. Second, many of us think like modern-day Pharisees. We are like the Pharisee of Luke 18:11 who said, "God, I thank You that I'm not like other people—greedy, unrighteous, adulterers, or even like this tax collector." Instead, we imagine ourselves to be supersaints, and God is fortunate to have us on His team. "I fast twice a week; I give a tenth of everything I get" (Luke 18:12).

How much better would it be for us to pray like the tax collector in Luke 18:13: "God, turn Your wrath from me—a sinner!" We are sinners in desperate need of the mercy of God instead of entitlement. Thankfully we are forgiven sinners through "the scandal of amazing grace," and that grace should lead us, like Jesus, to be a friend of sinners.

In this text we see Jesus, the friend of sinners, as He reaches out to the seemingly unlikely, the socially undesirable, and the spiritually unhealthy. Look carefully at all the characters in the story and ask, "With whom do I most identify? Am I loving and serving sinners as Jesus did?"

Jesus Calls the Seemingly Unlikely to Follow Him
MARK 2:13-14

Jesus is again doing what He loved doing: teaching the Word and calling disciples to follow Him (cf. 1:16). He left the small house for a large open area where the crowds could get close to Him and hear Him. The crowd kept coming to Him, and He kept on teaching.[2] Thus, Jesus is out among the people, with those who need His touch and His teaching. There is a simple principle here: to reach the lost, you have to be with the lost, and you must share the gospel.

Jesus purposefully crosses paths with a tax collector named Levi. This is almost certainly the man we know as Matthew (cf. Matt 9:9). His name means "gift of God." The one who had been a thief will now receive a gift

---

[2] Both verbs occur in the imperfect tense, indicating a recurring action.

from God and become a gift of God to the people whom he had previously swindled. What a transformation!

Now, why would I call him a thief? Tax collectors were notorious in that day and were hated by the Jewish people as traitors and abusers of their own people. They were a mafia-like organization in the first century. They served Rome, the Gentile occupying power of Israel. They were like dishonest IRS agents who overcharged the people for their own profit. The Jewish writings known as the Mishnah and Talmud set them beside thieves and murderers. They were expelled and banned from the synagogue. The touch of a tax collector rendered a house unclean. Jews could lie to a tax collector with impunity. With money as his god, Levi was a social pariah who was spiritually bankrupt, having sold his soul to sin and self. His was a soul in need of a touch from Jesus.

With amazing brevity a shocking scene unfolds. Jesus sees this man named Levi and says, "Follow Me." In response to Jesus' direct imperative, Levi gets up and follows Him. By calling Levi to follow Him, Jesus once more commits a scandalous act. It would rival His touching a leper. But He refuses to yield to social pressure. He came to call sinners to Himself, and that is what He was going to do!

Levi counted the cost, took the risk, and followed Jesus (Luke 5:28). This was a radical decision! He gave up his lucrative business and all of his stuff, and there was no going back. He turned his back on his former way of life for a completely new one.

Why would Levi leave everything and follow Jesus? Even more, why would Jesus invite such an outcast to do so? Levi saw something in Jesus that he wanted to join, and Jesus saw in Levi what he could become. Jesus saw a sinner in need of salvation, not a lowlife deserving condemnation. Jesus saw not the wicked life of a tax collector and extortionist but the changed life of a disciple, an evangelist, an apostle, and a Gospel writer. That's the scandal of grace! Jesus sees in us what no one else can see and turns us into what we were intended to be—mature image bearers who reflect His glory. All this is made possible by scandalous grace and His choice to be the friend of sinners!

Jesus Calls the Socially Undesirable to Follow Him
MARK 2:15

Now we find Jesus in Levi's house, sharing a meal and having a good time. This is appropriate because the day of salvation should be a day of celebration (Luke 15:7,10,32). Levi must have owned a large home because he invited a large number of friends and acquaintances over to the house to eat and meet with Jesus. It was surely an impressive banquet (Luke 5:29). Perhaps it was a farewell party. Perhaps it was to celebrate his new life and calling. In any case there is no doubt that it was to honor Jesus and to share Jesus with his friends.

The term "sinners" may be a technical term for the common people who did not live by the rigid rules of the Pharisees. They were alienated and rejected. These are people who needed God's grace and knew it. They were no doubt stunned that the famous young Rabbi would share table fellowship with them. And they weren't the only ones: the religious leaders shared their amazement. But while the "tax collectors and sinners" were humble and thankful, the religious hypocrites were offended and angered.

Though not the main point of this passage, these religious leaders show us an important truth: bigotry is always ugly and pathetic. It betrays the fear and depravity of our hearts and is clear evidence that we are sinful people that desperately need the scandal of grace in our own lives, even as we proclaim that grace to others. Jesus will certainly welcome the targets of such prejudice as honored guests and beloved members of God's family, provided they come through faith in Him.

Jesus, in this event, tells us the Messiah calls and eats with sinners, extending forgiveness to all who would follow Him. The meal itself was something of a foreshadowing and anticipation of the great Messianic banquet at the end of the age (Rev 19:9), when persons from every tribe, tongue, people, and nation who have experienced this scandalous grace, including the unlikely and the undesirable, will recline with King Jesus at a great banquet that will never end.

Jesus Calls the Spiritually Unhealthy to Fellowship with Him
MARK 2:16-17

In verse 16 we are introduced to a group that is not happy with what Jesus is doing and who will consistently oppose Him throughout His ministry, all the way to the cross: "the scribes and the Pharisees." Though not all Pharisees were scribes, most of them were. These scribes were most likely outside the home, looking through the windows or the open door. They did not like what they saw.

In response to Jesus' apparent comfort, the scribes interrogate His disciples as to why He would lower Himself to eat with tax collectors and sinners—those who do not follow their traditions and rules. Before we see the answer Jesus gives, it might be helpful for us to further explore the identity, origins, and practices of the Pharisees

Who Are the Pharisees?

The Pharisees were the pious Jews who rigorously followed the law of Moses and opposed Greek and Roman influence. Josephus claims they numbered about six thousand in Jesus' day. While the Sadducees were mostly upper-class aristocrats and priests, the Pharisees appear to have been primarily middle-class laypeople, perhaps craftsmen and merchants. The Sadducees had greater political power, but the Pharisees had broader support among the people.

The most distinctive characteristic of the Pharisees was their strict adherence to the law of Moses, the Torah. They carefully obeyed not only the written law but also the oral law, a body of extrabiblical traditions that expanded and elaborated on the Old Testament law (e.g., "the tradition of the elders" in Mark 7:3). The Pharisees' goals were to apply the Torah's mandates to everyday life, and to "build a fence" around the Torah to guard against any possible violation. Hands and utensils had to be properly washed. Food had to be properly grown, tithed, and prepared. Since ritual purity was so important, the Pharisees refused to share table fellowship with those who ignored these matters. The common "people of the land" were often shunned, and the Gentiles even more so!

In contrast to the Sadducees, the Pharisees believed in the resurrection of the dead (Acts 23:8), and they steered a middle road between the Sadducees' belief in free will and the determinism of the Essenes. They hoped for the coming of the Messiah, the Son of David, who would deliver them from foreign oppression. This made them anti-Roman but with less inclination to active resistance than the Zealots and other revolutionaries.

Jesus condemned the Pharisees for raising their traditions to the level of Scripture and for focusing on the outward requirements of the law while ignoring matters of the heart. For their part the Pharisees denounced Jesus' association with tax collectors and sinners, and they deplored the way He placed Himself above Sabbath regulations.

Despite these differences Jesus was much closer theologically to the Pharisees than to the Sadducees, sharing similar beliefs in the authority of Scripture, the resurrection, and the coming of the Messiah. Conflicts arose because He challenged them on their own turf, and He was a threat to their leadership and influence over the people.

Today the term *Pharisee* is often equated with hypocrisy and legalism but not so in first-century Israel. The Pharisees were held in high esteem for their piety and devotion to the law. Indeed, the Pharisees' fundamental goal was noble: to maintain a life of purity and obedience to God's law.

The Old Testament law forbids work on the Sabbath, but it gives few details (Exod 20:8-11; Deut 5:12-15). The rabbis, therefore, specify 39 categories of forbidden activities. So, while knot-tying is unlawful, certain knots, like those which can be untied with one hand, are allowed. A bucket may be tied over a well on the Sabbath but only with a belt, not a rope. While such minutiae may seem odd and arbitrary to us, the Pharisee's goal was not to be legalistic but to please God through obedience to His law.

Jesus criticized the Pharisees not for their goals of purity and obedience but for saying one thing but doing another, for raising their interpretations (mere "tradition of men") to the level of God's commands (cf. 7:8), and for becoming obsessed with externals while neglecting justice, mercy, and faith. They "strain out a gnat, yet gulp down a camel" (Matt 23:23-24). Of course such hypocrisy is not unique to the Pharisees but is common in all religious traditions, including ours! It is easy to follow the form of religion and miss its substance. (This discussion of the Pharisees draws heavily on Strauss, *Four Portraits*, 132–33.)

Jesus' Mission

Jesus hears the Pharisees' criticism. He responds with a proverb that explains His mission and justifies His actions: "Those who are well don't need a doctor, but the sick do need one. I didn't come to call the righteous, but sinners" (2:17). Jesus uses irony to expose the hypocrisy of His detractors. The Pharisees, the religiously moral and upright, were just as needy of a spiritual doctor, healing, and medicine as the tax collectors and wicked. Sadly they did not recognize that they, too, had a spiritually terminal disease that only the Great Physician named Jesus could heal.

In essence Jesus says, "To those who think they are righteous I have nothing to say. To those who know they are sinners in need of salvation I have come, to heal them and call them to Myself." You must see yourself as lost before you can be saved. You must know you are spiritually sick before you can be spiritually healed. You must know you are spiritually dead in sin before you can be made spiritually alive by a Savior!

Conclusion

Jesus was a friend of sinners. He called the seemingly unlikely, reached out to the socially undesirable, and healed the spiritually unhealthy. He cared for them, He spent time with them, and He loved them. If this is true of our Master, then it should also be true of us.

Reflect and Discuss

1. What kinds of "sinners" are you reluctant to befriend? What kind of weakness or fear keeps you from showing the love of Jesus to them?
2. In what ways do you identify with Levi, the outcast tax collector? What do you appreciate about God's grace?
3. Do you know someone like Levi, who most people would think is not worthy of a call to follow Christ? Why might they in fact quickly and eagerly respond to an invitation?
4. Have you ever been offended when you saw a fellow Christian reaching out to a certain class of people?
5. Which people do you think Jesus would hang out with today?
6. What is commendable about the Pharisees' teaching and practice?
7. What aspects of the Pharisees' teaching and practice did Jesus condemn?
8. In what ways do some Christians act like Pharisees, whether the good aspects or the bad? Have you ever found yourself doing these things?
9. Do you know someone who does not realize he or she is spiritually terminally sick? What might you say that could convince them of their condition?
10. Negatively, the unsaved are spiritually terminally sick. Positively, the gospel offers salvation from sin and death. Which motivates you more for evangelism and missions?

Everything Changes with Jesus

MARK 2:18-22

Main Idea: Old forms of religion and ritual cannot adequately communicate the good news of Jesus' new kingdom.

I. **Jesus Came to Bring Joy, Not Sorrow (2:18-20).**
    A. Do not fast and mourn when it is time to celebrate (2:18-19).
    B. Fast and mourn when you consider what your sins cost (2:20).
II. **Jesus Came to Make Things New, Not to Perpetuate the Old (2:21-22).**
    A. False religion is like an old garment that needs to be discarded (2:21).
    B. False religion is like old wineskins that cannot contain new life (2:22).

One of my favorite verses in the Bible is 2 Corinthians 5:17: "Therefore, if anyone is in Christ, he is a new creation; old things have passed away, and look, new things have come." Jesus did not come to reform us but to regenerate us, not to improve us but to make us new. This is true on a personal level and on the corporate level as well—whole religious systems. The gospel of Jesus Christ didn't add to Judaism or reform it. The gospel fulfilled Judaism and superseded it. The new covenant replaced the old.

It is popular today to say all religions are basically the same—that all roads lead to God. This "religious pluralism" claims, for example, that if you follow the teachings of Buddha, you will eventually find yourself in a right relationship with God. Additionally, pluralists claim, there are multiple Hindu ways to multiple Hindu gods. And, of course, they claim there is a Muslim way to God, a Jewish way to God, and for us, a Christian way to God. Whichever path you take, you'll get to the same destination eventually. All roads lead to the divine.

Similar, yet narrower, is the idea that there are at least two ways to God: a Jewish way and a Christian way. This "dual covenant theology" has grown in popularity in recent years. One author has explained, "[Two-covenant theology] holds that God's covenant with Israel through Abraham establishes all Jews in God's favor for all times, and so makes faith in Jesus Christ for salvation needless so far as they are concerned" (Myers, "Do Jews Really Need Jesus?"). Consider also this report in *The Houston Chronicle* about popular television preacher John Hagee:

> Trying to convert Jews is a "waste of time." Everyone else, whether Buddhist or Baha'i, needs to believe in Jesus, he says. But not Jews. Jews already have a covenant with God that has never been replaced with Christianity. "The Jewish people have a relationship to God through the law of God as given through Moses. I believe that every Gentile person can only come to God through the cross of Christ. I believe that every Jewish person who lives in the light of the Torah, which is the word of God, has a relationship with God and will come to redemption." (Duin, "San Antonio Fundamentalist," 1)

The text before us addresses directly such a misunderstanding of the relationship between Judaism and Christianity. Our Lord makes clear that there is a discontinuity between Judaism and Christianity. The new wine of Christianity cannot be contained by the old wineskins of Judaism. With the coming of Jesus, it is a new day. With the coming of Jesus, everything changes!

Jesus Came to Bring Joy, Not Sorrow
MARK 2:18-20

This is the third of five controversies Jesus has with the religious leaders as recorded in 2:1–3:6. In 2:1-12 the question was, "Who can forgive sins but

God alone?" In 2:13-17 the question was, "Why does He eat with tax collectors and sinners?" Jesus answered these questions with authority! However, the scribes and Pharisees missed the joy of Jesus' kingdom. They could not rejoice over a paralytic being healed and sinners being saved. All they saw was Jesus saying and doing the wrong things. Soon they are "plotting with the Herodians against Him, how they might destroy Him" (3:6).

Here the issue is fasting. Once more, in their opinion Jesus doesn't get it right. Why did He continue to upset them?

Do Not Fast and Mourn When It Is Time to Celebrate (Mark 2:18-19)

The disciples of John and the disciples of the Pharisees are fasting regularly. John's disciples were probably fasting in anticipation of the coming of the Messiah. The Pharisees, on the other hand, strictly observed all the ritual fasts prescribed in the Old Testament. They had also added fasting on Monday and Thursday, probably as an expression of personal piety and consecration.

People are observing the party in Levi's house (2:15-16). They do not like what they see, so they come to Jesus with an accusatory question: "Why do John's disciples and the Pharisees' disciples fast, but Your disciples do not fast?" (v. 18). Basically they are asking, "If You are so spiritual, why do You not make Your followers live up to our high religious standards?"

The Day of Atonement is the only annual fast mentioned in the New Testament (Acts 27:9), and it was the only fast mandated for all of Israel in the Old Testament. There were other fasts for various reasons—expressing humility and repentance or preparing to inquire of God—but none were biblically mandated. After the exile, though, four other annual fasts were observed (Zech 8:19).

Despite the prophets' warnings that fasting without a repentant heart and right conduct was in vain (Isa 58:3-6; Zech 7:5-6), many believed that vigorous fasting was a foolproof method of earning God's favor or action. The Pharisees' own intentions resembled this misconception since they sought to earn God's rescue from Roman oppression through national purity and obedience. It makes sense, then, that they would want to know why Jesus' disciples are not fasting. Does He not care about God's deliverance?

The only time the Gospel writers show Jesus fasting is during His temptation. This 40-day fast at the inauguration of His public ministry is reminiscent of that of both Moses (Exod 34:28) and Elijah (1 Kgs 19:8). Jesus was not opposed to fasting. He actually assumed His followers would fast (Matt 6:16). Their fasts were to be genuinely directed at God, though, and not publicly displayed to earn the praise of men. (For this section on fasting, I have drawn heavily from Belben, "Fasting," 364.)

When we know that Jesus expected His followers to fast, His answer is interesting. He responds with a parable in which He is the bridegroom and His disciples are guests: "The wedding guests cannot fast while the groom is with them, can they? As long as they have the groom with them, they cannot fast. But the time will come when the groom is taken away from them, and then they will fast in that day" (Mark 2:19-20).

Jesus is essentially saying, "I am here now with My followers. Like a Jewish wedding feast, this is a joyous occasion where the bridegroom and his friends celebrate, not mourn." Fasting would be inappropriate, out of the question. His presence with them is a time of joy and celebration, not a time of sorrow and sadness.

We would do well to heed Jesus' words. A relationship with Jesus is not a solemn, boring affair. It is a celebration, a spiritual banquet of joy and blessing! Of course we should be holy, but we must not be somber. We should be moral but not legalistic and righteous but not stern. Why? Because there is joy in Jesus! Christian, do not mourn when it is time to celebrate.

Fast and Mourn When You Consider What Your Sins Cost (Mark 2:20)

There is a time for fasting and all that goes with it "when the groom is taken away." This is the first allusion to Jesus' death in Mark's Gospel. Joy is exchanged for sorrow, and celebration turns to mourning. This is an abrupt and surprising image. Edwards points out, "In a normal wedding the guests eventually leave. Jesus interjects the alien thought of the groom being forcibly removed from the wedding celebration.

"Already there are storm clouds over Jesus' ministry, initiated by the consternation of the scribes and Pharisees over Jesus' presumption to forgive sins in 2:10 and His consorting with sinners in 2:13-17. Jesus is aware of the future consequences of His confrontations with the authorities (see 3:6). Like Isaiah's 'Servant of the Lord,' Jesus, too, will be 'cut off from the land of the living' (Isa 53:8).

"The kingdom of God has made a personal appearance in Jesus, but the final victory is far from realized. In order to overcome sin and death, the bridegroom first must become their victim. The reference to the bridegroom being taken from the disciples, and their subsequent fasting, was surely an exhortation to perseverance for Mark's congregation in Rome, itself the victim of Nero's depraved persecution. Mark is telling the church at Rome,

'There will be days when Jesus will seem far from you, just as the Father was far from Jesus in His passion'" (see 14:36; 15:34; Edwards, *Mark*, 91).

The bridegroom, our Lord Jesus, would be snatched away to suffer alone on a cross to atone for our sins, to die the death we should have died, to pay the price for sin we should have paid. He died in my place. He bore my wrath. He took on my judgment. God killed His Son so He would not have to kill me. There is an appropriate time to fast and mourn. It is when I consider the infinite price paid for my sin by my Savior.

Jesus Came to Make Things New, Not to Perpetuate the Old
MARK 2:21-22

The imagery now shifts to two concise parables. The connection is to Jesus and what His first coming means. Jesus came to save sinners, not the self-righteous (v. 17). Jesus came to bring gladness, not sadness (v. 19). The pertinent question isn't why Jesus' disciples didn't fast, but why the Pharisees didn't feast and celebrate the presence of the Messiah! Here Jesus informs us that He came to make things new and not perpetuate the old. With the coming of the Messiah, Judaism must give way to Christianity—and rightly so, for in Jesus the Hebrew faith finds its fulfillment and completion.

False Religion Is like an Old Garment That Needs to Be Discarded (Mark 2:21)

In the first parable, attempting to unite the gospel of Jesus and the old religion of Judaism—exemplified by the Pharisees' ritualistic fasting—is as foolish as trying to patch an old, worn-out garment with a new, unshrunk piece of cloth. When the new piece becomes wet, it will shrink, tear away, and make an even larger hole. With the coming of Jesus, everything is new. The old was not bad, but it is no longer usable. It has been replaced by something better. To continue to try to prop it up and give it a new face is useless. It is futile.

When the real thing has arrived, we do not continue to worship the shadow (Heb 10:1). To do so is to create a false religion—one that cannot save but can only damn.

False Religion Is like Old Wineskins That Cannot Contain New Life (Mark 2:22)

In the ancient world the skins of goats were stripped off as nearly whole as possible. They were then filled with new wine. Their natural elasticity and flexibility, as well as their strength, would allow the skin to stretch and securely contain the new wine as it fermented and expanded. However, if you put new wine in old wineskins that had become brittle and weak, when fermentation took place, the expansion would burst the skins, and both the wine and the wineskins would be lost.

This parable and the one about the patch both illustrate the radical new era in Jesus' coming. Jesus is the new cloth and the new wine. He is not an attachment, addition, or appendage to the status quo. He cannot be integrated into or contained by preexisting structures—even Judaism, the Torah, and the synagogue (Edwards, *Mark*, 92).

The question is not whether the Pharisees will add Jesus' teachings to their list of traditions and rituals—like sewing a new patch on an old garment—but whether they will forsake the shadow of the old covenant and embrace the reality of the new covenant. Nor is it a question whether disciples will incorporate Jesus in their old way of life—like refilling an old container—but whether they will become entirely new receptacles for the expanding fermentation of Jesus and the gospel in their lives.

Conclusion

With Jesus and His life, ministry, atoning death, and glorious resurrection, everything changes. It changes for the better and it changes for good. There can be no compromise between Judaism and Christianity, between works-based religion and salvation by grace alone through faith alone in Christ alone, or between my old life and my new life.

Warren Wiersbe said,

> Jesus came to usher in the new, not to unite with the old. The Mosaic economy was decaying, getting old, and ready to vanish away (Heb 8:13). Jesus would establish a new covenant in His blood (Luke 22:19-20). The Law would be written on human hearts, not on stones (Heb 10:15-18; 2 Cor 3:1-3); and the indwelling Holy Spirit would enable God's people to fulfill the righteousness of the Law (Rom 8:1-4).

> . . .

> Salvation is not a partial patching up of one's life; it is a whole new robe of righteousness (Isa 61:10; 2 Cor 5:21). The Christian life is not a mixing of the old and the new; rather, it is a fulfillment of the old in the new.

> Jesus fulfilled the prophecies, types, and demands of the Law of Moses. The Law was ended at Calvary when the perfect sacrifice was once [for all] offered for the sins of the world (Heb 8–10). When you

trust Jesus Christ, you become part of a new creation (2 Cor 5:17), and there are always new experiences of grace and glory. How tragic when people hold on to dead religious tradition when they could lay hold of living spiritual truth. Why cherish the shadows when the reality has come? (Heb 10:1ff). In Jesus Christ we have the fulfillment of all that God promised (2 Cor 1:20). (Wiersbe, *Be Diligent*, 28–29)

Jesus lived, died, and rose again on our behalf, and that changes everything!

Reflect and Discuss

1. How would you respond to a friend in church who asked if there weren't several roads that lead to God? How would you respond to the same question from a non-Christian stranger?
2. If you had a close acquaintance or good friend, and you later learned that he or she was Jewish, how would you counsel that person to pursue a relationship with God?
3. Some Pharisees fasted to show they were deeply concerned about spiritual matters. How is this commendable? How were they mistaken?
4. Some people fast to earn God's favor or to get Him to act on their behalf. How is that conception mistaken?
5. How can Christians demonstrate to the world that we are celebrating with the living bridegroom, rather than continuing to mourn His death?
6. How does rejoicing in our life with the living Savior fit in with fasting and praying for Jesus' return?
7. Under what circumstances would you consider fasting?
8. What aspects of Old Testament Judaism are represented by the "old garment" or the "old wineskins" that must be discarded now that they have been fulfilled in Christ?
9. How is our life before salvation like an "old garment" that cannot be merely patched up?
10. How is our relationship with God in Christ like "new wine" that cannot be contained within our old way of life?

When Man-Made Rules Get in the Way of God's Gracious Plans

MARK 2:23-28

Main Idea: As Lord of the Sabbath, Jesus releases us from legalistic pressure and frees us to joyful obedience.

I. Do Not Let Man-Made Religious Rules Make You a Spiritual Slave (2:23-24).
II. Remember that the Lord's Day Is to Be a Blessing, Not a Burden (2:25-27).
III. Let the Lordship of Jesus Christ Be Your Anchor and Guide (2:28).

Few things are more destructive, seductive, and deceptive to a true and vital relationship with God than the deadly poison of legalism. It is *destructive* because it breeds death rather than life. It is *seductive* because it has a natural allure for the flesh that causes us to look to ourselves rather than to Christ for our spiritual status before God. It is *deceptive* because it makes us think we are the spiritual elite when actually we are spiritual slaves.

Legalism is raising to the level of biblical mandate and command what God has neither commanded nor prohibited in His Word. It is taking our traditions and preferences and imposing them on others as an act of spiritual superiority, even though the Bible does not make such practices universally prescriptive.

Legalism is characterized by looking for the shortcomings in others rather than in oneself. It looks for what is wrong in someone's life in order to criticize and condemn them rather than what is right in order to commend and encourage them. It reinforces feelings of spiritual superiority and elitism that are man centered rather than Christ centered. It focuses on external behavior rather than the internal issues of the heart! It says, "I don't dance, cuss, smoke, have immoral sex, or do drugs, so I'm better than you. You don't use the right Bible translation, listen to the right music, wear the right clothes, or contribute the right amount, so you're not as close to God as I am."

The Pharisees had their own lists, including, "You don't properly honor and respect the Lord's Day." This issue caused the Pharisees much vexation. Jesus did not conduct Himself properly on the Sabbath, the Jewish day of worship, as outlined and detailed by the religious establishment through their traditions. Jesus will respond to this accusation in the last two of the five religious controversies (2:1–3:6). He will set the record straight, explaining that the Sabbath was made for man, not man for the Sabbath (2:27), and that it is always right to do good, even on the Sabbath (3:4). We will address the first of these here.

Do Not Let Man-Made Religious Rules Make You a Spiritual Slave
MARK 2:23-24

This is the fourth of five controversies with the religious leaders. First, they complained that Jesus claimed to be God and to forgive sins (2:1-12). Next, they were offended because He consorted with sinners (2:13-17). Then He did not fast according to their religious traditions (2:18-22). Now they take issue because He does not honor the Sabbath the way they believe He should (2:23-28 and 3:1-6).

The Sabbath ran from sunset Friday to sunset Saturday, and the Jews were commanded to set it aside as holy to the Lord. Islam may honor Mecca and the Koran, and Hindus may honor the Ganges River, but neither of them has a comparable day of rest and worship. The Sabbath proclaimed Yahweh as Lord of creation and time. It set the Jews apart as a holy and unique people.

The fourth commandment, the longest of the ten, addressed the Sabbath (Exod 20:8-11; Deut 5:12-15). It was a special sign between Israel and Yahweh (Exod 31:13-17), and Jews were to abstain from every kind of work since God Himself rested on the seventh day of creation. However, it is not precise in details, so the Jews built an elaborate wall of tradition around the observance to assure that it would not be violated. The general rule was, "Do no work that is not absolutely necessary." It was understood that nothing was "absolutely necessary" except those tasks that could result in loss of life if left undone.

In this story, as Jesus and His disciples were walking, the disciples picked a few heads of grain. In the eyes of the Pharisees, they were guilty of a double violation. First, they were *traveling*, which was defined as walking more than 1,999 paces. However, the Pharisees focus on the second violation, which was *reaping*. Deuteronomy 23:25 says, "When you enter your neighbor's standing grain, you may pluck heads of grain with your hand." According to this law the disciples were in the clear. However, Exodus 34:21 says, "You are to labor six days but you must rest on the seventh day; you must even rest during plowing and harvesting times." Plucking was considered "harvesting" in the eyes of the Pharisees.

Jesus was held responsible for the actions of His disciples, so they addressed Jesus with a question in the form of a rebuke. *It would be better for you to go hungry than break our rules*, they thought.

Perhaps with good intentions the Pharisees had constructed a mountain of rules that enslaved those who tried to follow them. In a reversal of Genesis 50:20, what God had meant for good they had turned to evil. In a sense the clash is not over the rules but over who makes the rules. Jesus will gladly honor the law when it conforms to God's intentions. However, when it doesn't, you can expect Him to challenge the status quo!

Remember that the Lord's Day Is to Be a Blessing, Not a Burden
MARK 2:25-27

Jesus' response is fascinating. In an apparent tangent He turns to an event in the life of King David. In 1 Samuel 21:1-6, David and his men were in need and hungry, so they went into the house of God and ate "the bread of the Presence," the consecrated bread of the temple. This offering was 12 loaves of unleavened bread, representing Israel's 12 tribes, set out on a table in the holy place.

Jesus' point is simple. While it was not normal or lawful for David and his men to eat the bread of the Presence, it was even more the case that God did not want them to starve. God was primarily concerned with caring for His servant David, the anointed king of Israel. Scripture nowhere condemns their actions.

In His appeal to David, Jesus is inviting a comparison between David and Himself. God in His Word is noting the parallel between the lesser David and His greater Son. This is the first of such allusions that we will see in Mark's Gospel.

Jesus concludes with the principle that should have guided Jewish observance all along: "The Sabbath was made for man and not man for the Sabbath." The Sabbath was made to bless man, not man to bless the Sabbath. The Sabbath was made for man's enjoyment, not man for the Sabbath's significance. Jesus' liberating vision of the Sabbath frees us from legalistic constraints instead of binding us with unbearable burdens.

Colossians 2:16-17 brings clarity for those of us who live under the new covenant inaugurated through the death and resurrection of King Jesus:

"Therefore, don't let anyone judge you in regard to food and drink or in the matter of a festival or a new moon or a Sabbath day. These are a shadow of what was to come; the substance is the Messiah." The Lord's Day, indeed every day, is a blessing that lifts us up, not a burden that weighs us down. It is to help us grow in grace and maturity, not strangle us with rules and regulations.

Let the Lordship of Jesus Christ Be Your Anchor and Guide
MARK 2:28

Modern readers in the Western context cannot easily grasp the striking declaration of verse 28. Jesus weds the "Son of Man" title to that of "Lord of the Sabbath" and declares that He is both. This, just like 2:10, is nothing less than a declaration of deity and divine rights! The divine man of Daniel 7:13-14, whom demons recognize as both the Holy One of God (Mark 1:24) and the Son of God (3:11), is also the Lord of the Sabbath.

Jesus once more puts Himself in the place of and with the authority of God. As the Lord of the Sabbath, He determines what is lawful and unlawful on the Sabbath day. He makes the call, and there is no higher authority. John MacArthur explains the significance of this statement well:

> Jesus dropped the bomb of all bombs on their self-righteous minds in verse 28. . . . "I am," He says, "the sovereign ruler over the Sabbath. . . . I am the sovereign of this day. I designed this day. I am the Creator." Doesn't John say that at the beginning of his Gospel? Everything made was made by Him, and without Him was [not] anything made, so it was He who ceased to work. It was He who rested. It was He who ordained this day to be blessed and separated from work. "I am the sovereign of this day. I am the interpreter of the will of God for this day. You do not rule the Sabbath. You do not set the standards of behavior for the Sabbath, I do. I interpret God's will and God's Word." Yes, Jesus is the interpreter of God's will. He is the interpreter of God's Word. He is the interpreter of God's Law, not men. (MacArthur, "Jesus Is Lord")

The Pharisees relied on their own traditions for guidance, and in doing so, they missed the Lawgiver entirely. For Christians, He is our anchor of spiritual authority in all things. In sum, "Jesus says . . ." settles all issues. As God, He is Lord of the Sabbath! We do not get to choose whether we will allow Him to be such. It is a fact, regardless of our permission. The question to ask is, Have you surrendered to Him as your God and the Lord of your life? Man-made rules will never get you to God! Only the Lord of the Sabbath, the Son of God, will get you there. Trust in His work and not your own. You will not be disappointed.

Reflect and Discuss

1. Do you have more of a tendency to find faults in other people or to find ways to commend and encourage them? Is there any situation where it is our right and our duty to find fault in others?
2. What rules do you find yourself using to judge the spirituality of yourself and others?
3. In what way did Jesus "fulfill" the Sabbath? Does this mean Christians can ignore the Sabbath?
4. How should a Christian treat the fourth commandment: Honor the Sabbath? Are there principles that still apply in the new covenant?
5. What is the value of "building a wall around the law" to make sure we don't violate it? (Do 1 Cor 6:18 and 1 Thess 5:22 imply we need to carefully define sin so we can avoid it?) How do we avoid turning this into legalism?
6. One question Jesus addressed here is, Who makes the rules? How do we make sure we are teaching what the Bible says rather than adding to it and making our own rules?
7. To what extent is a teacher responsible for the conduct of his students? Were the Pharisees justified in condemning Jesus for His disciples' actions? Did Jesus argue about this aspect of the charges?
8. If God loved His people Israel, why did He give them so many restrictive laws?
9. Was the Sabbath law meant to be punitive or celebrative? Was it meant to be a restriction or a benefit? How should that affect the Christian view of the Sabbath?
10. How can a person honor the Sabbath without becoming legalistic?

It Is Always Right to Do Good

MARK 3:1-6

Main Idea: It is always right to bless others and do good, no matter what the enemies of God's kingdom might say or do.

I. **Doing Good for the Glory of God Will Invite Critical Scrutiny (3:1-2).**
    A. Be sensitive to those who need compassion (3:1).
    B. Be ready for those who always criticize (3:2).

II. **Doing Good for the Glory of God Will Require Personal Conviction (3:3-5).**
   A. Be right in what you do (3:3-5).
   B. Be right in what you say (3:4).
   C. Be right in what you feel (3:5).
III. **Doing Good for the Glory of God Will Encourage Hostile Opposition (3:6).**
   A. The enemy of my enemy is my friend.
   B. The enemy we fear most we will seek to destroy.

In 2:1–3:6 we have seen the buildup to what seems like an inevitable confrontation. The religious leaders of Israel are certainly tiring of Jesus humiliating them and asserting His own authority. The worst part is He continually backs up His claims with acts of undeniable power and teaching with inherent authority.

The hostility now reaches a climax in this fifth controversy, resulting in anger on both sides. For Jesus the anger stemmed from the religious leaders placing limits on when it was right to do good and to save a life. For the Pharisees and the Herodians, it was over the young Rabbi's continuous undermining of their traditions, their religious rules, and the overall status quo. So great is their outrage that they will begin, at this early stage of Jesus' ministry, to plot how they might destroy Him (3:6).

Jesus will not back off, though He understands where this will lead. Consumed with the will of His Father and emboldened by an uncompromising conviction, He will move ahead with His face set toward the cross, unalterably convinced that it is always right to do good!

Doing Good for the Glory of God Will Invite Critical Scrutiny
MARK 3:1-2

For Jesus, doing good for the glory of God would not be restricted by date or location. This encounter occurs in the synagogue, the local meeting house for Jewish worship. Further, it is the Sabbath. Jesus has just violated their religious sensibilities by allowing His disciples to pluck some grain on the Sabbath (2:23). The Pharisees considered this work, a heinous offense on the Sabbath (2:24).

Jesus seems to be deliberately provoking a confrontation with the religious leaders. Don't claim to forgive sins (2:5), they effectively tell Him. Don't consort with sinners (2:16). Don't neglect fasting as we dictate (2:18). Don't work in order to eat on the Sabbath (2:24). Their hardness of heart is almost overwhelming, and Jesus' frustration has reached a boiling point. Undoubtedly He is overtly inviting their critical judgment by what He is about to do!

Be Sensitive to Those Who Need Compassion (Mark 3:1)

In the synagogue Jesus sees a man with a withered hand. This man was disabled and in need of love and compassion. One can imagine the repeated embarrassment he endured every time he lifted up his hands in prayer, as was the custom. Some may have drawn the conclusion that his deformed hand was a curse from God for a sin by him or his parents, as the disciples assumed concerning the man born blind (John 9:2-3). And just like the blind man, this man needed Jesus' attention, and his healing would be the occasion for God's power to be put on display. Jesus, with sensitivity and compassion, took notice of this man.

Be Ready for Those Who Always Criticize (Mark 3:2)

When you have a legalistic spirit, you become critical, always on the lookout for what is wrong and seldom on the lookout for what is right. The Pharisees are now eyeballing Jesus, "watching Him carefully" to see if He messes up. The verb for "watching" is in the imperfect tense, indicating that this had become a continuing practice of theirs.

They had one goal in mind: they sought "to accuse Him," presumably with a legal charge. The Pharisees permitted healing on the Sabbath only for the sake of saving a life. This man's problem was not life threatening, so he and Jesus should wait. If Jesus healed him today, they could accuse Him of breaking the Sabbath, an offense punishable by death according to Exodus 31:14-17.

So concerned were the Pharisees about not violating the Sabbath that one rabbi, Rabbi Shammai, opposed praying for or visiting the sick on the Sabbath, since it was to be a day marked by joy (Arnold, *Mark*, 23). "Heal another day, but not today! Do good another day, but not today!" Such was their thinking. "What manner of madness is this?!" we cry. It is the type that grows out of a life of criticism and faultfinding, one that enslaves itself to man-made rules. Remember what Jesus said about them: "They tie up heavy loads that are hard to carry and put them on people's shoulders, but they themselves aren't willing to lift a finger to move them" (Matt 23:4). Jesus also said, "Woe to you, scribes and Pharisees, hypocrites! You travel over land and sea to make one proselyte, and when he becomes one, you make him twice as fit for hell as you are" (Matt 23:15). The Pharisees were enslaved to their own critical hearts, and they did their best to enslave others as well.

Doing Good for the Glory of God Will Require Personal Conviction
MARK 3:3-5

You could probably cut the tension with a knife. They are glaring at Jesus (3:2), and He is glaring at them (3:5). Will He blink, back down, or give in? Will He walk away just this once to keep the peace?

No, this Servant King "did not come to bring peace, but a sword" (Matt 10:34). There will be no retreat in His message and no backing down in His actions. With the courage of His convictions, He will press forward, obedient to the will of God regardless of the consequences. Note the example He provides for us.

Be Right in What You Do (Mark 3:3-5)

Jesus commands the man, "Stand before us" (3:3). He intends to make a public scene to provoke the Jews. Next Jesus commands the man, "Stretch out your hand" (3:5). Immediately his hand is restored. The ravages of the curse are reversed as a foretaste of life in the kingdom when "He will wipe away every tear from their eyes. Death will no longer exist; grief, crying, and pain will exist no longer, because the previous things have passed away" (Rev 21:4).

Jesus actually fulfills the intent and heart of the Mosaic law. He will make this clear when He answers a scribe who asked, "Which command is the most important of all?"

> "This is the most important," Jesus answered: "Listen, Israel! The Lord our God, the Lord is One. Love the Lord your God with all your heart, with all your soul, with all your mind, and with all your strength. The second is: Love your neighbor as yourself. There is no other command greater than these." (Mark 12:29-31)

In this act of mercy, Jesus loves His Father by expressing God's character and compassion toward this man, who is undoubtedly one of God's precious creatures. Likewise, He loves this man through His kind, healing touch. The Pharisees knew nothing of this love and thus were far from fulfilling the law of Moses.

Be Right in What You Say (Mark 3:4)

Sometimes in life and ministry we must confront and provoke others. It is neither easy nor fun. However, sometimes it is necessary, especially when the right thing is not being said or done. Here Jesus raises the right question given the situation of the man and the foolish regulations of the Pharisees: "Is it lawful on the Sabbath to do what is good or to do what is evil, to save life or to kill?" Notice how Jesus frames the questions in terms of polar opposites. He's clarifying a situation that the Pharisees have made unnecessarily complicated. This should be an easy call. Another time Jesus silenced His critics by asking, "What man among you, if he had a sheep that fell into a pit on the Sabbath, wouldn't take hold of it and lift it out? A man is worth far more than a sheep, so it is lawful to do what is good on the Sabbath" (Matt 12:11-12).

It is both shocking and sad to think that the Pharisees could not correctly respond. Their silence condemns them, and it reveals a tragic flaw in their theology concerning the nature of our God—a God of grace and mercy, love and compassion. Thankfully, Jesus knew just what to say to expose their fault.

Be Right in What You Feel (Mark 3:5)

After questioning the Pharisees, Jesus surveys the room carefully, looking into the eyes of each Pharisee. He is both angered and grieved at their hardness of heart. Jesus never became angry at tax collectors and sinners, only self-righteous religious leaders! The religious outcasts at least acknowledged their depravity, whereas the religious elite imagined themselves pure and holy. Pride is dangerously deceitful, and it, unlike any other sin, provoked our Lord to righteous anger. It was right for Him to feel that way with the Pharisees, and it is right for Him to feel that way today, for pride still deceives us all.

Doing Good for the Glory of God Will Encourage Hostile Opposition
MARK 3:6

Doing a good thing made others mad simply because Jesus did not do it the right way from their perspective. Today one does not need to look far before he finds a similar mind-set in many Christian circles. It is not enough to do the right thing. If you do not arrive at the "correct" destination by the "correct" route, then you get criticized and misrepresented. Indeed, you may even find former enemies aligning themselves against you.

The Enemy of My Enemy Is My Friend

The Pharisees and Herodians hated each other. However, their common disdain for Jesus made them strange bedfellows as they made a pact to get rid of this Galilean troublemaker. They "immediately" conspired together. They wasted no time in forming a pact to bring Jesus to His knees.

The Herodians show up here for the first time. They do not appear to be a distinct group or political party like the Pharisees and Sadducees. Instead they appear to be wealthy and influential supporters of the Herods and their dynastic rule. There are only three passing references to this group in the New Testament (see Mark 12:13; Matt 22:16), and they appear each time in a surprising alliance with the Pharisees. This is unexpected because the Herodians were supportive of Hellenistic (Greco-Roman) influences, and they gladly supported Roman rule, both of which the Pharisees strongly opposed. Despite their hatred for one another, though, their common hatred of Jesus was enough to bring them together to plot against Him.

The Enemy We Fear Most We Will Seek to Destroy

The Pharisees and Herodians did not want to slow down or stop Jesus; they wanted to destroy Him. They wanted to assassinate Him and get Him out of the way. This would be their full-time occupation for at least the next year or so. Their hatred was coupled with fear, and both were held with great fervency. As a combination it would lead them, as it can lead us, to do unspeakable evil.

Conclusion

Perhaps this was also the day of this man's salvation. John 10:10 tells us that Jesus came to heal our diseases and bear away our sins that we might have a more abundant life. Most likely that is what happened to this man. I am so glad Jesus, as Acts 10:38 says, "went about doing good." He did a good thing in healing this man, and He did a good thing in saving our souls. And, through word and deed, He teaches us well: It is always right to do good!

Reflect and Discuss

1. Have you ever seen someone resisting something good only because they are defending their "turf" or because they resent the one proposing it? Explain.
2. What reasons would the Pharisees have given that Jesus had to be destroyed?
3. When is it a good idea to do something that you know will result in public criticism?

4. What public or private situations might tempt us to withhold compassion from someone who needs it?
5. How are a legalistic spirit and a critical attitude related?
6. How can a long-term habit of criticism and faultfinding result in ridiculous restrictions and foolish regulations?
7. How did Jesus' question in 3:4 clarify the situation? How can a well-formed question sometimes function better in a debate than simply stating a proposition?
8. What kinds of people make you angry? Is it people who are caught up in a cycle of self-destructive sin? Is it people who claim to be righteous but who flout the ways of God?
9. What "strange bedfellows" have you seen united in their opposition to Christianity?
10. Why are hatred and fear such powerful motivators of evil actions?

The Pressures That Come with Faithful Ministry
MARK 3:7-21

Main Idea: Jesus models perseverance in faithful ministry in the midst of distraction and opposition.

I.   **Expect to Be Pressured by Those Who Want Something from You (3:7-12).**
   A.   They will impose on you (3:7-10).
   B.   They will seek to hinder you (3:11-12).
II. **Expect to Be Pressured by Those Who Want to Be with You (3:13-19).**
   A.   Call out the ones you want to spend time with (3:13-18).
   B.   Recognize that some will still disappoint you (3:19).
III. **Expect to Be Pressured by Those Who Misunderstand You (3:20-21).**
   A.   They may try to control you (3:20-21).
   B.   They may try to stop you (3:21).

Vince Lombardi (1913–1970), the coach of the Green Bay Packers, led his football team to victories in the first two Super Bowls. Lombardi was undoubtedly a great coach, but he was also a man of great wit and insight. Much of his wisdom applied both on and off the field. For example:

"Confidence is contagious. So is lack of confidence."

"Football is like life. It requires perseverance, self-denial, hard work, sacrifice, dedication and respect for authority."

"If you accept losing, you can't win."

"It's not whether you get knocked down, it's whether you get up."

"Once you learn to quit, it becomes a habit."

"It is essential to understand that battles are primarily won in the hearts of men."

The following quotes fit well with this section of Mark's Gospel:

"Men respond to leadership in a most remarkable way, and once you have won their heart, they will follow you anywhere."

"People who work together will win."

"Fatigue makes cowards of us all." (Lombardi, "Quotes")

Leadership, teamwork, and fatigue run throughout Mark 3:7-21. They are always present when trying to handle the pressure that comes with faithful ministry. Jesus knew this, and we discover in this text how He dealt with the pressures. Whether it is opposition from the Pharisees (2:1–3:6), the press of the crowd (3:7-12), the failure of a former follower (3:19), or the rejection of family (3:20-21), Jesus provides a model for us to follow. He will accept the pressure all the way to the cross, where He will die as a ransom for sin (10:45). There is much here for us to learn.

Expect to Be Pressured by Those Who Want Something from You
MARK 3:7-12

Large crowds keep flocking to Jesus (3:7-9,20; 4:1). The Pharisees and the Herodians may have put out a contract on Him, but the people were crazy about Him. Note the diversity: Some came from Galilee in northern Israel and were mostly Jews, though there were probably some Gentiles too. Others came from Judea in southern Israel and Jerusalem and would have been predominantly Jews. Those who came from Idumea, southeast of Judea, would have been a mix of Jews and Gentiles. Still others came from the East, across the Jordan, from the area of the 10 predominantly Gentile cities known as the Decapolis. Finally, some people came from Tyre and Sidon, northwest of Galilee. These too would have been mostly Gentiles.

This ethnic mix is appropriate since the kingdom of God is to be made up of people from every tribe and nation around the world. Jesus would consistently affirm such diversity and would even command it in His Great Commission (Matt 28:18-20).

Growing popularity also means great pressure. Jesus experienced this pressure in all of its many forms. Anyone who pursues faithful ministry should be prepared for the same.

They Will Impose on You (Mark 3:7-10)

Jesus has withdrawn, hoping for some quiet time with His disciples. We often picture Jesus sitting under a tree in beautiful green grass with white fluffy sheep in the background and children in His lap. However, this idyllic vision is a myth! The reality of His public ministry is more often mayhem and bedlam. Here, the press of the crowd is so great that He asked for a getaway boat!

Jesus had been healing the sick (3:10) and casting out demons (v. 11), and people wanted in on it. They did not care about Him but only what they could get from Him. They were not concerned about His privacy, His need for time alone, or His need for food and rest (cf. 3:20). They only wanted to use Him for His miraculous power.

This will too often be the experience of those who work hard for the Lord. It is truly unavoidable, but to a certain degree you can control it. Still, understand this reality: people you serve will impose on you and not give it a second thought. It is simply the nature of the work.

They Will Seek to Hinder You (Mark 3:11-12)

Jesus continues to confront and conquer the demonic as a proof that the kingdom of God has arrived in Him (see also 1:23-28,32,39). Demons fall down before Him, acknowledging that He is the Son of God (3:11). Jesus again demands their silence (v. 12). A demonic declaration of His deity will not help His mission. It is both the wrong source and the wrong time. Jesus will be fully revealed not by demonic confession but by the cross of Calvary. After a futile attempt to control Jesus, the demons are silenced by His sovereign authority. Jesus will carry forward and complete His mission on God's terms—on His terms—not theirs.

The same must be true for us! We must do the will of God in God's way and in God's time. We must not allow ourselves to be manipulated by ungodly agendas regardless of the praise we may be paid, the positions we may be proffered, or the prosperity we may be promised.

Expect to Be Pressured by Those Who Want to Be with You
MARK 3:13-19

Jesus goes up a mountain, away from the crowds. Mountains are important. The mountaintop is where Jesus experienced the climax of His temptation by Satan (Matt 4:8-11). Likewise, a mountain is where He preached the great Sermon on the Mount (Matt 5–7). Mountains were also the setting for Jesus' transfiguration (Mark 9:2), the Olivet Discourse (Matt 24–25), and the giving of the Great Commission (Matt 28:16-20).

Here, Jesus calls the 12 disciples to Himself (Mark 3:13). These would be tasked with leading the early church and proclaiming the gospel among the nations. He prayed all night before calling them (Luke 6:12). Clearly Jesus saw this as a crucial decision in His ministry and in the building of His kingdom.

Call Out the Ones You Want to Spend Time With (Mark 3:13-18)

Jesus called out 12 specific individuals and they came. As His disciples (3:7), they would follow Him, be with Him, and learn from Him. They were like apprentices. As His "apostles" (3:14), they would be sent by Him with His authority to proclaim Him in the gospel.

On the mountain Jesus "appointed" them to carry out His mission. They will have the authority to preach and to cast out demons. In word and action they are to carry on His work of building the kingdom of God. The work is so serious, though, that He wants them with Him for three years, watching and learning from the Master Himself. And, in choosing 12, He shows that He is establishing a new, holy nation—a new community called the church (1 Pet 2:9).

Each of the four Gospel writers gives a list of Jesus' 12 closest followers. The lists are not all the same. Matthew and Mark list Thaddaeus while Luke names Judas (son of James). Judas may have been his original name, and it was changed later to Thaddaeus in order to avoid the stigma attached to the name Judas Iscariot. "Simon the Canaanite" is the transliteration into English of a Greek word that probably represents an Aramaic word meaning "zealous." The Zealots in Judaism were a group that advocated revolutionary tactics to overthrow the power of Rome. Bringing him and Matthew the tax collector together is something only the gospel could do!

This group of men came from a variety of different backgrounds. They had different passions, interests, and agendas. But the thing they have in common was that Jesus called them out, committed Himself to invest in them, and used them to change the world. Likewise, we must call out those we wish to invest in as we continue to make disciples of Jesus today.

Recognize That Some Will Disappoint You (Mark 3:19)

The Bible is brutally honest. It notes successes and failures. It has integrity in its reporting. One example of the ugliness of fallen humanity is Judas Iscariot, the one who betrayed Jesus. In every list of the apostles he is listed last. In every list his betrayal is noted.

Judas was chosen by our Lord to be with Him (3:14). He did not worm his way in, and he would serve well for a while. He gave evidence of loyalty. He even served as treasurer (John 12:4-6), though he was dishonest in his assignment.

All of this is to remind us that if you live long enough and serve long enough you will be disappointed by people whom you love and who you thought loved you. You would let them guard your back, believing they would take a bullet for you, only to discover the knife in your back has their prints on it.

Expect to Be Pressured by Those Who Misunderstand You
MARK 3:20-21

It is one thing to be misunderstood, let down, and betrayed by a friend. It is hard to put into words what it feels like when it is your family. In this text Jesus has returned home, probably to Capernaum, the home of Peter and Andrew.

They May Try to Control You (Mark 3:20-21)

Once more the crowds descend on Jesus with a selfish vengeance. It seems to never end. The house is so full of people He cannot find time or space to eat. The people are completely socially unaware; they care for no one but themselves. They will monopolize Jesus if they can, using Him only for His power to heal. They completely misunderstand that His true mission and agenda are to get to the cross and deal with their real need: their sin!

Still today socially unaware people and people who lack a kingdom mind-set reflect the ancient crowd's mistake. They often flock to big-name preachers and cling to them because they are popular. However, they completely miss the message these leaders preach, and they will smother them if given the chance.

They May Try to Stop You (Mark 3:21)

This is the first mention of Jesus' family. It does not reflect well on them. They hear that Jesus is swamped, apparently to the extent that He is unwilling even to care for His own physical needs. Thus, they decide to "restrain Him," convinced "He's out of His mind." The word *restrain* means "to lay hold" and is used elsewhere of an "arrest." The charge "He's out of His mind" is shocking and disturbing. They understand neither who He is nor what He came to do. Perhaps they are genuinely concerned for Him. However, "in a culture in which honor and shame were critically important, there may also have been an attempt to prevent shame on the family caused by Jesus' . . . behavior" (*EBC*, 745).

From His family's perspective, Jesus is a religious fanatic who is hurting the family name, and He is also a danger to Himself. He has to be stopped. He needs a straitjacket and padded cell. Today they might have said, "Give the man some drugs that will calm Him down!" Oh, if they only knew what He was doing on their behalf!

Conclusion

What words of wisdom can we glean from this text so that we might have a faithful ministry where we start well, run well, and finish well? Jesus perfectly exemplified a master teacher and a faithful minister of the gospel of the kingdom, and we can list several points of application from His pattern:

1. Know who you are and why you are here (3:10-12).
2. Make time to get away. Take control of your schedule and calendar. If you don't, others will (3:13).
3. Surround yourself with others you can train, delegate to, and send out to do the work of ministry (3:13-19).
4. Recognize that no matter how hard you try and how much you invest, some are going to disappoint you (3:19).
5. Remember that ministry is a 24–7 calling that requires your constant attention and management (3:20).
6. Understand that those closest to you may misunderstand you and even oppose you (3:21).
7. Never forget: all that matters in life and ministry is that you please God and do His will (3:35).

Don't lose sight of the goal. Jesus certainly did not. The cross was never out of view. It was His divine destiny. Praise God He did not let the pressures of ministry distract Him or deter Him! He stayed focused. He was faithful in His mission and ministry all the way to Calvary!

Reflect and Discuss

1. What makes Vince Lombardi's quotes great? How do they compare with Solomon's proverbs or Jesus' parables?
2. What happens in ministry if a leader fails to make time to be alone?
3. What is the value in a leader's taking the time to work with a few apprentices?
4. What effect can the constant pressure of public appearances have on a spiritual leader? What is the appeal to the leader? What is the danger?
5. What do various types of churchgoers want from church leaders?
6. Why is it amazing that Matthew (Levi) and Simon the Zealot served together under Christ? Does the gospel still have the power to bring contrary people together? Think of an example of people you know personally.
7. Keeping in mind the deity of Christ and His omniscience and foreknowledge, why do you think He chose Judas Iscariot as one of His apostles?
8. Do you know of friends or family members who have not supported someone's conversion to Christianity? Is a family member more or less likely than a friend to support a zealous devotion to ministry?
9. If you were to meet a famous Christian leader, what could you do to encourage and edify him or her rather than draining energy?
10. Which is more demanding, trying to please people or trying to please God? Which is more tiring? More rewarding?

The Unpardonable Sin

MARK 3:22-30

Main Idea: Some are so hardened in their rejection of Jesus as God's true Messiah that they attribute to Satan the works of the Holy Spirit done through Jesus, and they will never be forgiven.

I. **It Reveals a Hardened Heart That Calls Good Evil (3:22).**
II. **It Reveals Spiritual Blindness That Is Willful and Intentional (3:23-27).**
III. **It Involves a Verbal Declaration That Is Continual and Unforgivable (3:28-30).**

The phrase "the unpardonable sin," to any spiritually sensitive person, strikes terror and fear. It is like hearing the words "Antichrist," "false prophet," "great tribulation," or "lake of fire." They all serve as striking reminders that sin is real and judgment is sure. Actually the phrase "the unpardonable sin" does not occur in the Bible. However, the concept is identified in our text as "an eternal sin" (3:29). This does not soften the impact of the words.

This denotes a sin that, once committed, will never be forgiven and will condemn us eternally to hell—the lake of fire (Rev 20:11-15). Is there really an unforgivable/unpardonable sin? If there is, what exactly is it? Also, can a Christian commit this sin?

Whatever this sin is, we must approach it with the greatest possible gravity and seriousness. When God effectively says, "Commit this sin and I will never forgive you," there is then no longer any hope for heaven and eternal life. When God says "never," He really means never! A billion years from now, His judicial verdict will stand like stone. John Piper is correct: "If forgiveness is withheld for eternity, guilt is sealed for eternity. God is never neutral to sin. He either forgives it or punishes it. . . . Not to be forgiven by God forever is to suffer His wrath forever" (Piper, "Beyond Forgiveness").

This concept is discussed directly following the accusation by Jesus' family that "He's out of His mind" (Mark 3:21). An official religious delegation from Jerusalem has just arrived to investigate this young Jewish rabbi. In the midst of their harsh judgment and criticism, we see the general characteristics of the sin that can never be forgiven. If ever there was a warning that would compel us to run from sin with fear and trembling and to flee to Jesus in faith and repentance, surely this is it! So, what do we learn about the unpardonable sin?

It Reveals a Hardened Heart That Calls Good Evil
MARK 3:22

Jesus is preaching, healing, and casting out demons around the clock. The crowds are growing daily. His family wants to stop Him and take Him home because they fear He is losing it (3:21)! Meanwhile, some scribes have come down from Jerusalem to check Jesus out. Apparently they reached an instantaneous verdict: Jesus was a demon-powered apostate who should be silenced quickly.

The scribes claim, "He has Beelzebul in Him!" Beelzebul was the prince of demons, whose name could possibly mean "lord of the flies/carrion." He was lord of that which is rotten and repulsive, lord of the dung heap. More likely, however, the name means "lord of the house/temple." This would be like calling Him "Baal the prince." Thus, He is the ruler of a house or dynasty of demons. They are claiming that Jesus is possessed, that He is controlled by Satan, who is the prince or ruler of the demon world. In His teaching, healing, and casting out demons, He acts, they say, by the power of Satan.

The verb in verses 22 and 30, "they were saying," is the imperfect tense, which means "they were continually saying." They consistently hurled this slur at Jesus, trying to destroy His reputation. With a hardened heart, which Bavinck calls "a sin against the gospel in its clearest manifestation" (Bavinck, *Sin*, 156), they look at the supremely good One and call Him the supremely evil one. It is a persistent rejection of and declaration against what the Spirit of God is doing in and through Jesus.

Those who move in the direction of the unpardonable sin are aware of the miraculous works of Jesus that cannot be denied. The scribes at no point deny He has cast out demons! In addition, this unpardonable sin is characterized by consistently rejecting the obvious and logical conclusion that these spiritual works are done by the Spirit of God. Instead, those guilty will declare verbally and consistently that these spiritual works are actually from Satan. Such actions reveal a hardened heart that calls evil good and that will not celebrate the works of God in Christ. Anyone who continues down this road will never be forgiven by God.

It Reveals Spiritual Blindness That Is Willful and Intentional
MARK 3:23-27

Jesus responds by calling the religious elite to hear a short proverbial saying that quickly refutes their accusations and reveals the absurdity of their logic. He first makes a simple observation in verse 23. Why would Satan act against himself? The logic is inconceivable! If what they say is true, Satan is destroying himself. And Jesus states the obvious: "If a kingdom is divided against itself, that kingdom cannot stand" (3:24). If Satan were fighting against himself, he would be utterly powerless to do anything to advance his kingdom, and obviously that is not the case. One only needs to look at all the misery he causes to see that.

Satan *is* attempting to build a kingdom. "Satan extends his kingdom by sowing chaos and enslaving humans, not by setting them free" (Arnold, *Mark*, 26). It is ridiculous to suggest that Jesus was fighting for Satan by releasing his captives. To not see this reveals intentional spiritual blindness: "My mind is made up! Don't confuse me with the facts!"

Jesus then changes the analogy. He says, "If a house is divided against itself, that house cannot stand." Pick your context—marriage, family, business, sports, church—the truth remains: a division in the ranks will cause the institution to fail, destroying itself. Jesus states things so explicitly in verse 26: "If Satan rebels against himself and is divided, he cannot stand but is finished!"

Jesus gives a parable. Satan is the "strong man," and Jesus is the One breaking into his house, his realm, to bind and plunder. Satan is indeed a strong man in this world. His house is a house of horrors, filled with sin, sickness, death, demon possession, and all that is evil and wicked. His possessions are human beings, enslaved by all these evils. Demons are his agents who delight in carrying out his diabolical agenda. No one but Jesus can invade his realm and carry away his possessions. No one but Jesus is more powerful than this strongman.

Jesus' point is that He *has* come, and He can and will bind Satan. This is what Jesus is doing and will do climactically at the cross. It is self-evident and indisputable that the Son of God has come to destroy the works of the Devil (cf. 1 John 3:8). In denying this truth, the scribes reveal their intentional spiritual blindness.

It Involves a Verbal Declaration That Is Continual and Unforgivable
MARK 3:28-30

Jesus now begins to conclude the matter by saying, "I assure you," literally "amen." This word is found only in the Gospels. In every case the word is said by Jesus. It is a serious and solemn affirmation. In using it, Jesus attests His words are completely true and reliable because He is uniquely the true witness of God. Put this in the mouth of any other person, and it is completely out of place. With Jesus there is a perfect fit.

Jesus declares the gracious forgiveness and mercy of God in forgiving sins. "All sins," literally, "whatever blasphemies they may blaspheme," will be forgiven. All sinners can find the forgiveness of God if they will come to Him in repentance and faith. However, verses 29-30 note the one tragic and fearful exception. If someone speaks against the Holy Spirit verbally and continually, with willful and malicious intent that reveals a hardened heart beyond the possibility of repentance, there is no forgiveness, and they are "guilty of an eternal sin."

I cannot improve on the insights at this point of New Testament scholar William Lane:

> Blasphemy against the Holy Spirit forever removes a man beyond
> the sphere where forgiveness is possible. This solemn warning must
> be interpreted in the light of the specific situation in which it was

uttered. Blasphemy is an expression of defiant hostility toward God
. . . "the profanation of the Name." . . . This is the danger to which
the scribes exposed themselves when they attributed to the agency
of Satan the redemption brought by Jesus. The expulsion of demons
was a sign of the intrusion of the Kingdom of God. Yet the scribal
accusations against Jesus amount to a denial of the power and greatness of the Spirit of God. By assigning the action of God to a demonic
origin the scribes betray a perversion of spirit which, in defiance of
the truth, chooses to call light darkness. In this historical context,
blasphemy against the Holy Spirit denotes the conscious and deliberate rejection of the saving power and grace of God released through
Jesus' word and act. . . . The failure of the scribes to recognize him
as the Bearer of the Spirit and the Conqueror of Satan could be
forgiven. The considered judgment that his power was demonic,
however, betrayed a defiant resistance to the Holy Spirit. This severe
warning was not addressed to laymen but to carefully trained legal
specialists whose task was to interpret the biblical law to the people. It
was their responsibility to be aware of God's redemptive action. Their
insensitivity to the Spirit through whom Jesus was qualified for his
mission exposed them to grave peril. Their own tradition condemned
their gross callousness as sharply as Jesus' word. The admonition concerning blasphemy of the Holy Spirit is not to be divorced from this
historical context and applied generally. Mark emphasizes this by ter-
minating the incident with a reference to the specific accusation that
Jesus was possessed by an unclean spirit. . . . [R]epetition and a fixed
attitude of mind . . . brought the scribes to the brink of unforgivable
blasphemy. (Lane, *Mark*, 145–56)

Conclusion

The unpardonable sin is *to knowingly, willingly, and persistently attribute to
Satan the works of God done by and in Jesus through the power of the Holy Spirit,
who testifies to these truths in your heart.* (1) It is a sin of full knowledge. (2) It
is an ongoing disposition of the heart that resists the conviction of the Holy
Spirit. (3) It is a verbal act that attributes the works of the Holy Spirit to
Satan. (4) It is a willful rejection of God's grace in Jesus. (5) It is rooted in
unbelief. (6) It is a sin a Christian cannot commit. (7) It is a sin not committed by one who is concerned that he may have committed it.

Despite this last point this unpardonable offense should still awaken all
of us to the seriousness of all sin committed against a holy and righteous
God, who never winks at sin. It is a sin that should lead all of us to confess
with Jesus in 9:42-43,

But whoever causes the downfall of one of these little ones who believe in Me—
it would be better for him if a heavy millstone were hung around his neck and
he were thrown into the sea. And if your hand causes your downfall, cut it
off. It is better for you to enter life maimed than to have two hands and go to
hell—the unquenchable fire.

There is a boundary of sin where, once passed, there is no possibility or hope of return. Do not even think of going there. Instead, run to Jesus in faith and repentance. You will find open arms there! You will find forgiveness free and eternal. Today, do not delay: run from any and all sin and, instead, run to Jesus!

Reflect and Discuss

1. Have you ever spoken to anyone who worried that they had committed the unpardonable sin? Was there ever a time when you were afraid you had done so? Was this a result of a vague explanation of the unpardonable sin?
2. Why did Mark include this episode in Jesus' ministry right after the report that His family thought He was out of His mind? Is there a logical or topical connection?
3. Why would the scribes sent by the Jerusalem Sanhedrin come to the conclusion quickly that Jesus was collaborating with Satan?
4. What is the significance of the imperfect tense of the verb "said" in 3:22 and "they were saying" in verse 30?
5. Can you think of any examples today of people attacking Christianity using ridiculous logic?
6. What do Jesus' parables in 3:23-27 teach us about Satan's goals and tactics in the world?
7. As a preface to 3:29-30, how is verse 28 encouraging?
8. How would you counsel a Christian who was concerned that he or she had committed the unpardonable sin?
9. How would you caution a non-Christian concerning the nature of the unpardonable sin?
10. Even though a Christian cannot commit the unpardonable sin, how does it still function as a warning and exhortation for Christians?

Who Is Part of the Family of God?

MARK 3:31-35

Main Idea: We are not brought into the family of God by physical relationships, but by faith in Jesus Christ leading to humble obedience.

Being Part of the Family of God Is . . .

I.   Not by Physical Descent or Relationship (3:31-33).
II. Not the Result of Finding Jesus Interesting or Helpful (3:34).
III. Revealed by Doing the Will of God (3:35).

In the spirit of tolerance, nonjudgmentalism, and sentimental inclusivism, some theologians teach, and many people believe, that everyone is a child of God. We call this teaching "universalism." Keith DeRose lays out what it affirms: "Universalism refers to the position that eventually all human beings will be saved and will enjoy everlasting life with Christ. . . . In short, then, it's the position that every human being will, eventually at least, make it to the party" (DeRose, "Universalism"). While some like DeRose seek to marshal sophisticated arguments to support their thesis, such a belief gets crushed on the rock-solid truth of many passages of Scripture, including this one.

Jesus' intent was not to shoot down the false doctrine of universalism; yet He does just that, even at the expense of His own family. They have accused Him of being deranged and in need of forced confinement (3:21). In this context Jesus makes clear who is family and who is not, who is in and who is out. His words could not be more striking or any clearer.

Being Part of the Family of God Is Not by Physical Descent or Relationship

MARK 3:31-33

Mary and the brothers of Jesus come to where He is staying, probably at the home of Peter's mother-in-law in Capernaum. Jesus has at least four brothers:[3] James, Joseph, Simon, and Judas (Matt 13:55). He also had sisters (Matt 13:56). They are "standing outside" while others are on the inside—

---

[3] Technically they are half brothers and sisters, since their father is Joseph, but Jesus' Father is God.

the symbolism is striking! They called Him, and the crowd relayed the message: "Look, Your mother, Your brothers, and Your sisters are outside asking for You."

Jesus' response, "Who are My mother and My brothers?" was shocking to the ethnocentric, family-centered culture of that day. He implies here, and makes clear in verse 35, that (1) no physical family connection is ultimately necessary to be in God's family; (2) no particular racial or cultural background is ultimately essential; (3) when you are a member of the family of God, you are part of the only family that really matters; (4) the family of God is a spiritual reality and not a physical one, joining together Zealots, tax collectors, thieves, murderers, liars, cheats, legalists, self-righteous religionists, and all kinds of others sinners just like you and me.

The nature of Mary and the brothers' request was natural, normal, and expected. The response of Jesus was not!

Being Part of the Family of God Is Not the Result of Finding Jesus Interesting or Helpful
MARK 3:34

If physical relationships are not the key to a spiritual relationship with God, what else might be ruled out as a false perspective on this crucial issue? In verse 34 the room is overflowing with those who were attracted to Jesus. They loved His miracles and exorcisms. They loved the show and what He could do for them. Remember, the crowds are never viewed in a favorable light in Mark. Crowds do not follow and stay for the long haul. Individuals do, of their own volition and decision. Hence Jesus looked around at those who were seated around Him.

Who is in the room? The Twelve, including Judas, are there, along with some scribes from Jerusalem. It is also possible that those encountered earlier in the chapter are still hanging around: the Pharisees (3:6), the Herodians (3:6), as well as those healed of demon possession (3:11) and of disease (3:16). And, of course, some were simply curious.

People follow Jesus for different reasons and with different agendas. Some reasons are good and others are bad. Some want Him; others want what He can give them and do for them. Some follow for who He is; others follow for what they make Him out to be. They want someone they can fit into their world, wants, plans, priorities, and preconceived notions. Oh how insightful John 2:23-25 is at this point!

> *While He was in Jerusalem at the Passover Festival, many trusted in His name when they saw the signs He was doing. Jesus, however, would not*

entrust Himself to them, since He knew them all and because He did not need anyone to testify about man; for He Himself knew what was in man.

He said His true family was "here," but not all of them were included. In His next statement He narrowed it down.

Being Part of the Family of God Is Revealed by Doing the Will of God
MARK 3:35

Jesus provides a clear, simple, blanket statement concerning who is part of the family of God: anyone who "does the will of God." Luke 8:21 says it is "those who hear and do the word of God." Kent Hughes says, "Obedience does not originate a relationship with God (faith does that), but obedience is a sign of it" (Hughes, *Mark*, 98). Hughes also notes this new family relationship is far superior, far stronger, far more satisfying, far more demanding, and far more dear than any human family relationship (ibid.). It is an eternal relationship that is marked by unshakeable grace, and those who receive such grace are marked by humble obedience.

Tim Keller relates our text to the Prodigal Son:

Jesus . . . is the true elder brother. He willingly brings us into the Father's family at his expense. He died for us, he was plundered for us. We sit at the Father's table dressed in Jesus' clothes, with his ring on our finger. All through him. We must celebrate and live out the fact that we are members of a kingdom family, and it is all at the expense of our big brother, Jesus Christ. Do you live every day as if you are a member of God's family, accepted and loved? Remember, a child in a family obeys not in order to be loved and accepted, but because he already is loved and accepted. (Keller, "Mark," 37–38)

The "will of God" is critically important throughout the Bible:

After removing him, He raised up David as their king and testified about him: "I have found David the son of Jesse, a man loyal to Me, who will carry out all My will." (Acts 13:22)

Do not be conformed to this age, but be transformed by the renewing of your mind, so that you may discern what is the good, pleasing, and perfect will of God. (Rom 12:2)

Paul, an apostle of Christ Jesus by God's will. (2 Cor 1:1)

Don't work only while being watched, in order to please men, but as slaves of Christ, do God's will from your heart. (Eph 6:6)

For this is God's will, your sanctification: that you abstain from sexual immorality. (1 Thess 4:3)

Give thanks in everything, for this is God's will for you in Christ Jesus. (1 Thess 5:18)

. . . in order to live the remaining time in the flesh, no longer for human desires, but for God's will. (1 Pet 4:2)

And the world with its lust is passing away, but the one who does God's will remains forever. (1 John 2:17)

Conclusion

After studying passages like this, it is helpful to make some biblical and theological observations. In light of this text, what can be said about the family of God and the will of God?

1. We became children of God by spiritual birth, not by physical birth (John 3:1-8).
2. No one is born a Christian. You become a Christian and a member of God's family only by adoption (Rom 8:12-16; Gal 4:4-7).
3. Becoming part of the family of God begins when we receive and believe in Jesus, which is a sovereign work of His will, not ours (John 1:12-13).
4. Doing the will of God gives evidence that we are part of God's family (Mark 3:35).
5. Those incapable of knowing and understanding the will of God are objects of God's saving grace and mercy in Christ. People spend eternity in hell as a result of their conscious and willful acts of rebellion and disobedience against the revelation of God they have received, and those who are incapable of understanding God's will cannot rebel in this way (see Deut 1:39; 2 Cor 5:10; Rev 20:11-12). (For more on this, see commentary on Mark 10:13-16 and Akin and Mohler, "Why We Believe.")
6. Revelation brings responsibility. The more you know of God's revealed will, the greater is your accountability. Punishment is not all the same in hell, and rewards are not all the same in heaven.
7. In spite of sophisticated and even well-intended arguments, there is no biblical warrant or evidence that people will have an opportunity after death to believe in Jesus or that eventually all persons (and perhaps even demons) will be saved. Just as eternal life is forever, so is eternal death.

8. If it were true that all will eventually be saved, evangelism would be unnecessary, and missions would be a waste of time, lives, and money.

9. Because the Bible promises that people from every tribe, tongue, people, and nation will be in heaven at the throne to worship the Lamb (Rev 5; 7), we rejoice in knowing that the family of God will consist of the 16,600-plus people groups scattered around the world, 7,000-plus of which are still unreached.[4] It is the will of God that they hear and believe and that we go and get them for His glory.

Reflect and Discuss

1. What are some other Bible passages that argue against universalism—the belief that all people will go to heaven regardless of faith in Jesus Christ?

2. What passages might proponents of universalism cite? How would you explain that those passages do not in fact teach universalism?

3. What else can we conclude from the fact that Jesus had brothers and sisters?

4. How is Jesus' response to His family good news for Gentiles? For sinners?

5. How is finding Jesus "interesting" or "fascinating" insufficient for inclusion in the family of God?

6. In what ways do some people find Jesus "helpful" today?

7. How does Jesus' statement about doing the will of God fit together with the fact that one comes into right relationship with God only through faith?

8. How is Jesus like the older brother in the parable of the prodigal son (Luke 15:11-32)? How is He different?

9. What aspect of salvation is emphasized in John 1:12-13? What aspect is emphasized in John 3:14-16?

10. How does Jesus' statement about His spiritual family being those who do the will of God function as motivation for world missions?

---

[4] For a continual updating of unreached people groups, see http://www.joshuaproject.net.

Do You Have Ears That Hear?

MARK 4:1-20

Main Idea: Jesus calls His followers to hear, respond to, and share the gospel, while sin, the cares of this world, and opposition hinder kingdom growth.

I. **We Must Spread the Gospel That People Might Hear the Word (4:1-9).**
II. **If We Do Not Listen to the Word, We Will Not Benefit (4:10-12).**
III. **The Fruitfulness of the Gospel Depends on the Hearer's Receptivity (4:13-20).**
   A. The soil of some hearts is hard (4:14-15).
   B. The soil of some hearts is shallow (4:16-17).
   C. The soil of some hearts is distracted (4:18-19).
   D. The soil of some hearts is fruitful (4:20).

Biblical writers often refer to body parts, sometimes to make an important spiritual observation, other times to illustrate a biblical truth. For example:

> *How beautiful on the mountains are the feet of the herald, who proclaims peace, who brings news of good things, who proclaims salvation, who says to Zion, "Your God reigns!"* (Isa 52:7)

> *And the tongue is a fire. The tongue, a world of unrighteousness, is placed among the parts of our bodies. It pollutes the whole body, sets the course of life on fire, and is set on fire by hell.* (Jas 3:6)

> *The eye is the lamp of the body. If your eye is good, your whole body will be full of light.* (Matt 6:22)

> *But even the hairs of your head have all been counted.* (Matt 10:30)

> *Then He said, "Anyone who has ears to hear should listen!"* (Mark 4:9)

Our text is about our ears and how well they hear spiritual truth. It is about those who come to a church gathering, attend a Bible study, or have the gospel shared with them. Just as James 3:1-12 teaches us there is a spiritual connection between the heart and the tongue, Mark 4 teaches us there also is a spiritual connection between the heart and the ear. In verse 3 Jesus says, "Listen!" In verse 9 He says, "Anyone who has ears to hear should listen!" In verse 12 He speaks of those who "may listen and listen, yet not understand."

And in verse 20 He speaks of those who "hear the word, welcome it, and produce a crop." What is Jesus' point?

We Must Spread the Gospel That People Might Hear the Word

MARK 4:1-9

Jesus is "again" by the sea teaching, drawing a great crowd. "He taught them many things in parables." Parables are the most striking feature of the teaching ministry of Jesus. The popular idea that a parable is "an earthly story with a heavenly meaning" is helpful, but it needs to be expanded.

(1) Parables provide insight into the nature, coming, growth, and consummation of the kingdom of God. They give us pictures of this kingdom that "has come near" (1:15). (2) Parables are by design provocative and surprising. (3) Parables are used to stimulate thinking and cause the hearer to contemplate what they are hearing. (4) Parables use everyday objects, events, and circumstances to illustrate spiritual truth, usually with a new twist. (5) Parables reveal more truth to those with receptive ears, and they hide truth from others. This is critical to understanding 4:10-12. (6) Parables make up 35 percent of Jesus' teaching in the Gospels. (7) Parables usually, but not always, focus on a single truth. We should not allegorize them seeking a meaning for every detail. (8) Parables in the Gospels ultimately draw attention to Jesus as God's Messiah and call us to make a personal decision concerning Him.

Verses 3-8 constitute what is often called the "parable of the sower." I think the "parable of the soils" is a better designation. In "broadcast sowing" a farmer would spread the seed everywhere. The difference in growth resulted from the type of soil it landed on. In Jesus' illustration there are four types: the path (v. 4), the rocky ground (vv. 5-6), the soil with thorns (v. 7), and the good and productive soil (v. 8).

The kingdom of God, through the preaching of the gospel, will break into this world like seed being sown by a farmer. It will fall in various places, receive various responses, but eventually experience a tremendous harvest.

The parable begins with a challenge for Jesus' hearers to pay careful attention. A spiritually alert heart and hungry mind are needed to understand what He is teaching. The message of the parable for Christians is clear: we must sow the seed of the gospel that others might hear and respond. Responses will vary, but that is not our concern. Our assignment is to sow and sow generously, even promiscuously! God is responsible for the harvest (1 Cor 3:5-9).

Jesus also closes the parable with an admonition to pay attention: "Anyone who has ears to hear should listen!" (Mark 4:9). It seems He is challenging them to consider His message. C. F. D. Moule paraphrased it as, "Now think that one out for yourself, if you can!" (Wessel, "Mark," 648).

If We Do Not Listen to the Word, We Will Not Benefit
MARK 4:10-12

Verses 10-12 are something of an interlude between telling the parable (vv. 3-9) and explaining it (vv. 14-20). The Twelve and "those who were around Him" wanted to know more about why He spoke in parables (v. 10). His answer constitutes what some would classify as one of the "hard sayings" of Jesus. It requires consideration and reflection. Addressing the Twelve and those who want more of Him and His teachings, He says they will be granted access and insight to the secrets of the kingdom of God. In contrast, those on the "outside" will get no explanation but only more parables.

Then He quotes Isaiah 6:9-10 to drive home His point and to demonstrate that the Scriptures are being fulfilled in Him: "So that they may look and look, yet not perceive; they may listen and listen, yet not understand; otherwise, they might turn back—and be forgiven." His point is that, just as the sun that hardens the clay also melts the wax, so the Word of the gospel offends the resistant and rebellious while it is enthusiastically received by the receptive. Those outside are not denied the possibility of belief, but if they persist in their unbelief, they will not receive more evidence or revelation. That clarifies verse 25: "For to the one who has, it will be given, and from the one who does not have, even what he has will be taken away." Love the Word and you will get more satisfaction and understanding in who God has revealed Himself to be. Refuse the Word and even the understanding you do have will be taken away.

The secret of the kingdom is that God's present plan for growing it is seed sowing. Later the kingdom will flourish like seeds that mature into fruit. His rule has come in an unexpected manner, but it has come. Do you have ears that hear? Will you see it grow?

The Fruitfulness of the Gospel Depends on the Hearer's Receptivity
MARK 4:13-20

Jesus explains the parable. He starts with a mild chiding. His words note the essential and foundational nature of this parable. If they do not understand this one, they will struggle to understand the others. If children cannot add and subtract, they will scarcely be able to multiply and divide; and geometry, trigonometry, and calculus will be hopeless.

Jesus then proceeds to explain the four soils.

The Soil of Some Hearts Is Hard (Mark 4:14-15; cf. 4:4)

The sower in this story is Jesus, or anyone who shares the gospel, and the seed is the Word of God. The path represents hard-hearted or tough-minded individuals. The Word comes to them, and "immediately," as soon as they hear it, Satan snatches it away. They are resistant and thus unresponsive. They suffer from what might be called "gospel deafness." Like skeptics, they dismiss the Word without giving it careful consideration. For whatever reason they are hardened to the gospel. The book closes when the service ends, and so do their ears and hearts.

The Soil of Some Hearts Is Shallow (Mark 4:16-17; cf. 4:5-6)

The next soil is welcoming but not substantive enough to maintain the growth of the seed. The people represented by this soil hear the Word and receive it with joy. They endure for a while and even show signs of maturity, just as the plant sprouts quickly, grows well at first, and looks promising.

However, these people are shallow and have no roots. Soon tribulation and persecution—seen in the "sun" of Jesus' parable—come because of the presence of the Word. When (not if!) oppression comes, these people "immediately" fall away (4:6,17). They are "quickly green and quickly gone" (Dever, "Ignoring or Hearing?").

The Soil of Some Hearts Is Distracted (Mark 4:18-19; cf. 4:7)

This group of people receives the Word better than the first two. However, they eventually get distracted by worry, wealth, and craving for other things. Theirs is a partial commitment, which is, in reality, no commitment at all. This present life is more important to them than the life to come, and stuff is more important than the Savior.

In John 8:31, Jesus says those who "continue" are "really" disciples. Therefore those in this group show themselves to be false disciples. There is no real surrender to Christ as Lord. They find more pleasure in cash than in Christ, more pleasure in their cravings than in their Creator.

The Soil of Some Hearts Is Fruitful (Mark 4:20; cf. 4:8)

The final soil is noticeably different from the first three. It represents those who hear the Word, accept it, and bear fruit. Tribulation and persecution do not deter them. Worries, wealth, personal desires, and sinful cravings do not distract them. Their hearing is active, not passive. They aggressively pursue the Word, allow it to take root, and then rejoice in its abundant growth.

Note the promise that comes with receptivity to God's Word: It will grow and produce fruit. Failure to do so proves that it is really sown on another soil class. A fruitless Christian is an oxymoron. John 15:5 says, "The one who remains in Me and I in him produces much fruit." If we are not producing anything, that shows we are not really connected to the power of God through faith in His Word.

Conclusion

Christianity is a religion of the Word and therefore of the ear. Do you have ears that hear? Do you tune in to the words of Scripture and the gospel, or do you tune them out? Think carefully before dismissing Jesus' words. Hearing God's Word is dangerous. What you do with it is critical to your soul.

My challenge is this: Be greedy for the Word. Go after it, grab hold of it, and do not let it go. Like a starving beggar who has found bread, seize it with all your might and cherish it for the life-sustaining food that it is! He who has ears to hear, let him hear.

Reflect and Discuss

1. Why do you think the Holy Spirit inspired the biblical writers to refer frequently to body parts?
2. When have you found telling stories (parables) to be an effective way to communicate? What made them effective?
3. Why do some people call this the parable of the sower and some call it the parable of the soils? Which do you prefer, and why?
4. How did Jesus' parables give His disciples more understanding without giving any benefit to those who rejected Him?
5. Give current examples of cases where those who already understand the gospel gain more understanding while those who have rejected Jesus remain in the dark.
6. Was it unfair of Jesus to obscure His teaching from those who rejected Him by using parables? Whose fault was it ultimately that they did not understand?
7. Why is this parable foundational to comprehending other parables?

8. Is one kind of soil prevalent in our culture? Is there a particular way we should present the Word of God that might make people more receptive? How can we change the presentation without changing the message?
9. As with the "path," is Satan also responsible for the failure of the other kinds of unfruitful soil?
10. What part do we play in being good soil for God's Word? What can we do to grow in holiness and to produce fruit by making disciples?

What Do We Learn About Jesus and His Kingdom from a Lamp, a Bunch of Seeds, and One Small Seed?

MARK 4:21-34

Main Idea: The kingdom of God is guaranteed to grow by the power of God until it encompasses people from every nation.

I. **The Light of Jesus Will Not Be Hidden (4:21-25).**
   A. If you hide it, you misuse it (4:21-23).
   B. If you hide it, you will lose it (4:24-25).
II. **God Will See to It That His Kingdom Grows (4:26-29).**
   A. There is a mystery to the growth of the kingdom (4:26-27).
   B. There is a certainty to the growth of the kingdom (4:28-29).
III. **God's Kingdom May Begin Small, but It Will Grow Large (4:30-34).**
   A. God's kingdom program will experience amazing results (4:30-32).
   B. God's kingdom program requires careful explanation (4:33-34).

Sometimes the work of the Lord can become frustrating and disappointing. We work hard but see little fruit. We shine the light of the gospel and sow the seed of the Word, but not much happens. It seems almost futile, and we wonder, *Why even continue?*

William Carey (1761–1834), the father of the modern missionary movement, labored in India seven years before seeing his first convert. He shared the gospel for more than 40 years, but the fruit of his labor was minimal. Still he could say, "The future is as bright as the promise of God" and "Expect great things [from God], attempt great things [for God]."

Likewise, Adoniram Judson (1788–1850) labored in Burma for seven years before seeing his first convert. He would die disappointed that his labors for the gospel yielded so little fruit. Yet like Carey, he was faithful to the end and could voice these words: "In spite of sorrow, loss, and pain, our course be onward still; we sow on Burma's barren plain, we reap on Zion's hill."

These men, as well as many others, may have been inspired to press on by a little lamp, a bunch of seeds, and one small mustard seed.

The Light of Jesus Will Not Be Hidden
MARK 4:21-25

Mark 4:1-34 consists of four parables. Verses 21-34 comprise the final three of these. The theme of all of them is how God's kingdom emerges and grows with the appearance of Jesus of Nazareth, the Messiah, who came to give His life as a ransom for many (10:45). Mark brings these parables together to reinforce the main parable of the soils (4:1-20). These stories drive home the need for the response of faith to God's revealed Word.

Jesus begins this set of parables with a commonsense illustration about a lamp. However, a literal translation of the key phrase in verse 21 is, "Comes the lamp. . . ." This is a reference to Jesus Himself, who has "come as a light into the world" (John 12:46). He is "the light of men" (John 1:4), "the true light" (John 1:9), and the "light of the world" (John 8:12). How then do we respond to this extraordinary Lamp?

If You Hide It, You Misuse It (Mark 4:21-23)

The Lamp, and for that matter any lamp, is not brought to be put under a basket or a bed. The very idea is ridiculous. No, you put a lamp up high in the open. Likewise, God has sent this Lamp to bring light to a dark world. He has come to reveal truth, enlighten minds, and conquer the darkness!

The light may be, for the most part, hidden at the moment. However, eventually the whole world will see the glory of this light. That which is hidden will be manifest. The resurrection of the crucified King assures this revelation. The second coming of the glorified King will establish it. The world may try to hide Jesus, but it will fail miserably in those attempts.

I like *The Message* paraphrase of verse 23: "Are you listening to this? Really listening?" This call to listen is found in verses 3,9,13,23, and 24. Hearing the Word and acting on it is of tremendous importance, so a new set of ears is absolutely essential. Why?

If You Hide It, You Will Lose It (Mark 4:24-25)

Verse 24 repeats the call to have listening ears. What follows is a critically important theological principle in the form of a proverb: "By the measure you use, it will be measured and added to you. For to the one who has, it will be given, and from the one who does not have, even what he has will be taken away." A similar proverb said, "In the pot in which you cook for others, you'll be cooked" (Edwards, *Mark*, 140).

Here the means of measuring is "hearing." If your hearing is good, rich, and receptive to the Word, you will receive it back and even more. Indeed, "to the one who has, it will be given." Proverbs 9:9 says, "Instruct a wise man, and he will be wiser still; teach a righteous man, and he will learn more." Respond to God's truth and more truth will follow. Embrace the kingdom now when it is small, and you will share in it when it is worldwide!

In radical contrast, for the one who rejects the Word, "even what he has will be taken away." Refuse Jesus and the Word, and you lose the little you may once have had. This is a critical spiritual principle. Our spiritual health, our spiritual eternity, is at stake. How we respond to Jesus day by day is of the utmost seriousness. Do not take for granted the relationship you have today. It could all be lost tomorrow.

God Will See to It That His Kingdom Grows
MARK 4:26-29

This is Mark's only unique parable. Jesus crafts a second parable about sowing seeds. In the parable of the soils, the focus was on the necessity of sowing and the receptivity of the soils (vv. 3-8). Here the emphasis falls on the innate power of the seed. The Word of God has within it the power of its own success and triumph. Let the Word loose and watch it work.

This parable is instructive concerning the nature of the kingdom in a comprehensive sense. It notes the kingdom's sowing (v. 26), growing (vv. 27-28), and harvesting (v. 29). From beginning to end, the sovereignty of Christ and the power of the Word stand forth in absolute authority.

There Is a Mystery to the Growth of the Kingdom (Mark 4:26-27)

The man is not important; the seed is the focus. The man is passive because the power for the seed to sprout and grow is not in him. The seed has within itself the power of its own generation. James, the half brother of Jesus, wrote in James 1:21, "Humbly receive the implanted word, which is able to save you." Plant the word in a receptive soul and off it goes!

The coming of the kingdom of God is not contingent or dependent on human activity. The seed of the gospel prospers and grows of itself. Once it is sown, a process is set in motion that cannot and will not be stopped, even though its growth is a total mystery to us.

There Is a Certainty to the Growth of the Kingdom (Mark 4:28-29)

The Greek word *automatē* is fronted here for emphasis. It literally reads, "Automatically the earth bears fruit." Once the process has begun, it is destined to be completed: blade, ear, grain, harvest. The process that brings about the fullness of the kingdom of God is not spectacular, but it is certain. Even now it is present and growing, whether or not you see it.

God did not design His kingdom to come like a tidal wave or a bolt of lightning, to come quickly and disappear quickly. No, God planted it in the coming of a Galilean peasant, a homeless man from Nazareth, who gathered about Him a bunch of nobodies. The ways of God are mysterious indeed, but He will be successful.

The "sickle" is often a symbol of the arrival of the kingdom of God and the judgment that will accompany it. Revelation 14:15 says, "Another angel came out of the sanctuary, crying out in a loud voice to the One who was seated on the cloud, 'Use your sickle and reap, for the time to reap has come, since the harvest of the earth is ripe.'"

Who would have imagined that starting with only a group of 12 men, Christianity would grow to where it is today? But it won't stop there. It will continue to grow until every people group on the planet is found in the kingdom. God will ensure this growth. Are you certain you are part of it?

God's Kingdom May Begin Small, but It Will Grow Large
MARK 4:30-34

The final parable in this chapter is about a single seed, a tiny little mustard seed. The phrase "the kingdom of God" (cf. 4:11,26) is the unifying theme of the four parables in Mark 4. Jesus begins this parable with two rhetorical questions. He has exactly the right analogy to help us see where the kingdom of God is headed.

God's Kingdom Program Will Experience Amazing Results (Mark 4:30-32)

The mustard seed was renowned for its size in Palestine because it was the smallest of all the seeds sown. In Matthew 17:20 Jesus uses the mustard-seed image to represent a minimal quantity of faith. Here Jesus wants to draw an analogy between the mustard bush's microscopic beginning and its large mature state. At the beginning a small seed is sown. But soon the small seed explodes in growth. It produces something completely out of proportion to itself.

Likewise, from small and meager beginnings, God's kingdom will expand and grow for all to see. What began as the smallest becomes the greatest! Unlike His first coming, when Christ returns, all the world will see as He surpasses all the earth's kingdoms in power, glory, and majesty. What an encouraging word for those who think they labor in vain, who endure rejection and persecution, and who may even experience martyrdom!

Some have suggested that "the birds of the air" represent Satan, connecting these birds back to the ones in 4:4. Others believe this reference indicates shelter for kingdom citizens. Still others suggest the birds represent the nations coming into the kingdom. Finally, some believe the birds are simply part of the story and have no special significance. I like number three: the nations! Passages such as Psalm 104:12; Ezekiel 17:23 and 31:6; and Daniel 4:9-21 would all support this. That the birds "nest in its shade" settles the issue for me. In effect, Jesus is asserting that all the peoples of the world are going to be there.

Yes, there is surprising growth to God's kingdom, and all the nations will enter and enjoy it! This is a parable of growth and grace, of joy and celebration.

God's Kingdom Program Requires Careful Explanation (Mark 4:33-34)

This section of Mark ends with an explanatory word from Mark about the importance of parables in Jesus' teaching (cf. vv. 10-12). At least 39 parables are found in the Synoptic Gospels of Matthew, Mark, and Luke. He spoke in parables so they would understand the nature of the kingdom and the central role both He and the Word would play in it.

For the tenth time in chapter 4, the importance of hearing is noted. "As they were able to understand" implies that the parables either enlighten or obscure, depending on one's ability to hear and respond. He purposely chose this teaching method, knowing what would happen.

However, to those who drew close to Jesus as His disciples, He explained everything. Only in close communion and connection to Jesus can one understand "the language about God" (Edwards, *Mark*, 146). Draw close to Jesus and you get more of Him and His Father; draw back from Jesus and you lose both Him and the Father (2 John 9).

Conclusion

Yes, the kingdom starts small, but it will grow large. And the biggest and best of this growth is yet to come! If you doubt that, listen to Revelation 7:9-10:

> *After this I looked, and there was a vast multitude from every nation, tribe, people, and language, which no one could number, standing before the throne and before the Lamb. They were robed in white with palm branches in their hands. And they cried out in a loud voice:*
> > *Salvation belongs to our God,*
> > *who is seated on the throne,*
> > *and to the Lamb!*

Reflect and Discuss

1. What inspires you to persevere when progress seems painfully slow?
2. When we are told that Jesus is the light of the world, what is our responsibility?
3. Have you found that in the seasons of your life when you were actively responding to God's Word, these were the times when you grew the most? What made those days so productive?
4. What makes some seasons in your life spiritually unproductive and stale? How can you avoid such times?
5. How does the parable of the seeds emphasize God's sovereignty?
6. Why is it reassuring to know that God intends the kingdom to grow automatically as well as slowly but surely?
7. Does your understanding of biology, botany, ecology, and agriculture diminish or enhance the parables of the seeds and the mustard seed (4:26-32)? Why?
8. How is the parable of the mustard seed encouraging for those who work and pray for the expansion of the kingdom of God?
9. What is the argument in favor of the birds in the branches of the mustard plant representing the nations?
10. Jesus explained the parables to His disciples. In what way do Christians today actually have an advantage over those disciples?

The One Who Can Control the Storm

MARK 4:35-41

Main Idea: Jesus' authority over the wind and the sea demonstrate His identity as God and as the One we can trust.

I. God Is Working in the Circumstances of Our Lives (4:35-37).
II. Jesus Is Human Aside from Sin (4:38).
III. We Panic When We Lose Faith in the One We Should Trust (4:38).
IV. Jesus Has Authority over Nature Because He Is God (4:39).
V. Trials and Difficulties Come for the Benefit of Our Faith (4:40).
VI. The Identity of Jesus Is an Issue We All Must Settle (4:41).

Psalm 107 celebrates the goodness of God and His great works of deliverance. In light of the story of Jesus' calming the storm, verses 23-32 are especially powerful:

Others went to sea in ships, conducting trade on the vast waters.
They saw the LORD's works, His wonderful works in the deep.
He spoke and raised a tempest that stirred up the waves of the sea.
Rising up to the sky, sinking down to the depths,
their courage melting away in anguish,
they reeled and staggered like drunken men,
and all their skill was useless.

Then they cried out to the LORD in their trouble,
and He brought them out of their distress.
He stilled the storm to a murmur,
and the waves of the sea were hushed.
They rejoiced when the waves grew quiet.
Then He guided them to the harbor they longed for.
Let them give thanks to the LORD
for His faithful love
and His wonderful works for all humanity.
Let them exalt Him in the assembly of the people
and praise Him in the council of the elders.

These verses point to the inescapable truth for those who have ears to hear and eyes to see (Mark 4:1-34): Jesus is the God of Psalm 107 who "stilled the storm to a murmur, and the waves of the sea were hushed" (v. 29).

This is the first of a series of historical accounts that bear witness to Jesus' power as a miracle worker. He has authority over nature (4:35-41), over demons (5:1-20), over sickness (5:25-34), and over death (5:21-24,35-43).

Mark 4:35-41 is marked by careful accuracy and detail. No doubt we have the reminiscences of Peter, the eyewitness authority behind Mark's Gospel. He remembered the time of day ("evening," v. 35), the cushion in the boat (v. 38), and the place where Jesus slept ("in the stern," v. 38). Further, the less-than-flattering picture of the apostles—their embarrassing fear and lack of faith (v. 40)—is not the kind of thing one makes up about oneself.

God orchestrates an event in the lives of the apostles to increase their faith in the One they should already trust. Few stories have been more poorly applied than this one. It is *not* about Jesus' getting you through the storms of life. He does that, of course, but this account is about the One who is the sovereign and all-powerful Lord. Demons rightly recognize Him as God (5:7), and we should fully trust Him.

Six biblical truths stand out for our consideration and edification.

God Is Working in the Circumstances of Our Lives
MARK 4:35-37

Jesus has had a full day of teaching ("on that day," v. 35). It is now evening, and He and the Twelve need to get some rest. There is nothing unusual about this.

He tells them, "Let's cross over to the other side of the sea" (v. 35). He heads east toward "the region of the Gerasenes" (5:1) with a flotilla ("other boats were with Him," 4:36; even now He cannot get away). Once in the boat Jesus immediately falls into a deep sleep.

Suddenly everything turns upside down. A "fierce windstorm" arose. The word speaks of hurricane-type winds, and they were taking on water. Many aspects of this story echo the story of Jonah (Jonah 1). Seasoned sailors and fishermen suddenly find themselves in a storm unlike anything they have ever experienced. There is a crucial detail: it was Jesus who led them into the storm! This was not accidental. This did not catch God off guard.

We should not be alarmed by surprises in our lives. They are divinely ordained moments whereby God is working in the everyday circumstances of our lives to reveal who He is, who we are, and who we need! Trials and tribulations, difficulties and desperate moments are when God does His greatest work in our lives. When He brings us to the end of ourselves, we are driven to Him and Him alone as Savior and Rescuer. If He does not act, we will not be saved. Would you really want it any other way? Faith answers a resounding no!

Jesus Is Human Aside from Sin
MARK 4:38

The Bible affirms, and the church has always believed, that Jesus is both fully God and fully man, two natures united in one person. He is 100 percent divine and 100 percent human in the one person, the God man.

The only qualification related to His humanity is that He is without sin. He had no sin nature, and He never committed a single sin—not one. Two texts make this clear:

> *He made the One who did not know sin to be sin for us, so that we might become the righteousness of God in Him.* (2 Cor 5:21)

> *For we do not have a high priest who is unable to sympathize with our weaknesses, but One who has been tested in every way as we are, yet without sin.* (Heb 4:15)

Both His humanity and His deity are put on display in this story, and it is humanity that appears so clearly when He is in stern of the boat, fast asleep on a cushion. The Bible repeatedly teaches our Lord's full and true humanity. He got hungry (Matt 4:2). He got angry (Mark 3:5). He cried (John 11:35). He died (the cross). Now we see He slept. He had an exhausting day, and He kept on sleeping right through the storm. This is the only time in the Gospels that we read of Jesus sleeping.

Yes, He is human. But there is something else. He has complete trust in the providential care of His Father. The veteran seamen may be terrified, but the Carpenter from Nazareth sleeps soundly. Lottie Moon said, "I have a firm conviction that I am immortal till my work is done" (Akin, *10 Who Changed*, 64). We are all essentially immortal until our work on earth is finished. Jesus knew He had a work to complete on the cross. He was confident in His Father's promise to see Him finish.

We Panic When We Lose Faith in the One We Should Trust
MARK 4:38

Here we see the normal human reaction to something we cannot control. We do not see the spiritual response one would expect from those who have been with Jesus.

The apostles, in a panic, wake Jesus up. Just as the captain of Jonah's ship chewed him out for sleeping while they were perishing, so the apostles criticize Jesus as well. Mark says they called Him "Teacher." Matthew 8:25 says "Lord." These are terms of respect and honor.

But then they demand, "Do you not care that we are perishing?" They question His love and concern for them. Frustrated by what appears to be indifference to their plight and facing a desperate situation they have no hope of handling themselves, they lash out in a rude outburst rather than exhibiting faith in the One who has proven Himself trustworthy.

It pains me greatly to see myself in the disciples. Jesus has proven Himself faithful to me over and over, yet when caught by surprise and squeezed in a vice of trouble, I fume rather than show faith.

Spurgeon, the great Baptist preacher, said, "God is too wise to err, too good to be unkind; leave off doubting Him, and begin to trust Him, for in so doing, you will put a crown on His head" (Spurgeon, *Spurgeon's Sermons*, 3:1857). Let's crown Him in faith, not doubt Him in unbelief.

Jesus Has Authority over Nature Because He Is God
MARK 4:39

God and only God is thrice "omni." He is omniscient: He knows all things (actual and potential). He is omnipresent: He always exists everywhere. He is omnipotent: He is all-powerful.

Jesus' gracious humility is on display as He does not chasten the disciples for their less-than-charitable summons. In a simple, nonmagical statement He rebukes the wind and says to the sea, "Silence! Be still!"

The word "rebuke" can mean censure. It is the same word used in 1:25 when Jesus rebukes the demons! Could this storm have been demonically instigated? "Be still" carries the idea of "muzzle." The idea is "be still and stay still." The response of both wind and wave is immediate because their Master has spoken.

Here is our Lord's deity on full and glorious display! Hurricane force winds are stopped with a single word. Only God could do this. Jesus must be God. This is the direction in which Jesus seeks to drive the disciples.

Trials and Difficulties Come for the Benefit of Our Faith
MARK 4:40

Jesus now turns from addressing the storm to addressing the disciples. He expresses a mild rebuke: "Why are you fearful? Do you still have no faith?" By now they should have a greater comprehension and increased faith in

His person. This was a golden teaching moment, but they came up short. In the eye of the storm, rather than trusting Him, the disciples accuse Jesus of forsaking them (v. 38). Unfortunately, this will not be the last time Jesus must point out their lack of faith (7:18; 8:17,21,33; 9:9). Until they see the resurrected Christ and fully understand what He did for them on the cross, they are going to struggle.

We, in contrast, have no excuse. We know Jesus is all-powerful and all-knowing God. We know He has taken care of all our sin. We know He rose from the dead. We know He can be trusted no matter what! Trials and difficulties are divine appointments to strengthen our faith. So why are we still afraid? Do we still have no faith?

The Identity of Jesus Is an Issue We All Must Settle
MARK 4:41

This story ends with the disciples' asking a question every one of us must face.

The text says they were "terrified." The fear of the disciples at what Jesus has done and who He might be exceeds the fear they had over the storm. The presence of God is far more frightening than the most destructive forces of nature. One can take your life. The other can claim your soul. They ask, "Who then is this? Even the wind and the sea obey Him!" Despite their recent experiences with Jesus as He taught and performed miracles, they still aren't sure just who He is.

This is the first of three boat scenes in Mark's Gospel (cf. 6:45-52; 8:14-21). Each is associated with a miracle. Each is a challenge to understand and settle the identity of Jesus. Each is adequate for them to draw the conclusion we must draw as well—"You are the Christ, the Son of God."

The famous atheist Bertrand Russell (1872–1970) was asked what he would say to God if he discovered upon his death that God existed and he was wrong. His response was: "I will say, 'Not enough evidence, God, not enough evidence'" (Dawkins, *Delusion*, 141). That excuse will not fly. The evidence is in and it is overwhelming. The time to settle the issue is now.

Conclusion

The parallels between Jesus stilling the storm and the story of Jonah should not surprise us. Jesus called Himself the true Jonah in Matthew 12:40. He is the true Jonah who was consumed by the stormy sea of God's wrath as He hung on the cross. He endured the storm so that we could find peace and be saved. Jesus calmed the only storm that could truly drown us: God's wrath and judgment. He went down in the storm only to emerge three days later as the One who stilled the just and righteous wrath of God against sinners.

"Who then is this?" Ask the demons (Mark 5:7)—they know Him! And we can know Him and trust Him regardless of our circumstances.

Reflect and Discuss

1. Why is it unlikely that the disciples made up this story? If you were going to make up a story about being there when Jesus calmed a storm, how would you tell it?
2. How is it comforting to know that Jesus, in His sovereignty, led the disciples into this predicament?
3. How should the disciples have reacted to the fact that the Son of God was sleeping soundly in their boat during the storm? How does this help us as we face our own mortality?
4. Is it possible to show genuine respect (by calling Him "Teacher") and disrespect (by accusing Him of indifference) at the same time? Can you think of a time when you questioned God's love or justice?
5. Is it biblically sound to say that we drive a nail into Jesus' hand when we doubt Him, and we put a crown on His head when we trust Him?
6. What are the differences between the way Jesus calmed the storm and the way false religions use magic and incantations in an attempt to control the weather?
7. Are you encouraged to see that the disciples who were with Jesus when He was on the earth were slow to fully understand who He was? On the other hand, do you see why we do not have an excuse to be as unperceptive as they were?
8. In what way would it be comforting to be in the presence of Jesus? In what way would it be terrifying?
9. Does something you have read in the Gospels make you stop and say, "Who then is this?" What about Christ amazes you the most?
10. How is the lesson "Jesus calms the storms of your life" an inadequate interpretation of this episode? What is the greater lesson?

Can the Demonized Be Delivered?

MARK 5:1-20

Main Idea: Jesus is the Servant King who liberates those enslaved in a fallen world by wielding absolute authority, even over demons.

I.   **Jesus Confronts the Demonic (5:1-5).**
    A.   Satan attempts to defile the image of God in man (5:1-2).
    B.   Satan attempts to deface the image of God in man (5:3-4).
    C.   Satan attempts to destroy the image of God in man (5:5).
II. **Jesus Conquers the Destructive (5:6-13).**
    A.   Our Savior is a liberator (5:6-13).
    B.   Satan is a murderer (5:13).
III. **Jesus Commissions the Delivered (5:14-20).**
    A.   Let Jesus change you (5:14-17).
    B.   Let Jesus command you (5:18-19).
    C.   Let Jesus consume you (5:20).

In his classic fable *The Screwtape Letters*, C. S. Lewis provides a glimpse into the strategies of Satan's demons. An older and wiser demon named Screwtape is mentoring the younger Wormwood. In his preface to the imaginary correspondence, Lewis writes,

> There are two equal and opposite errors into which our race can fall about the devils. One is to disbelieve in their existence. The other is to believe, and to feel an excessive and unhealthy interest in them. They themselves are equally pleased by both errors, and hail a materialist or magician with the same delight. (Lewis, *Screwtape*, 3)

Lewis is right, and the human race has fallen into both errors. The materialists of the "Age of Reason" or Enlightenment were fooled into disbelieving in the existence of demons or any spirit beings. New ageism and postmodern mysticism have been enamored with angels, demons, and spirits beyond this world. Beginning in 1969 with *Rosemary's Baby* and in 1973 with *The Exorcist*, Americans have been engaged in a peculiar fascination with the occult and the demonic. Simply surveying Hollywood since then reveals this trend: *Hostage to the Devil* (1976); *The Omen* (1976); *The Possessed* (1977); *Exorcist II: The Heretic* (1977); *The Entity* (1982); *My Demon Lover*

(1987); *The Blair Witch Project* (1999); *Bedazzled* (2000); *The Little Vampire* (2000). Likewise, television series like *Buffy the Vampire Slayer, Charmed,* and *Touched by an Angel* are ever before us. Add to this the hotly debated issues of SRA (Satanic Ritual Abuse) and Halloween, and you have a significant element of our culture awash in spiritism and the occult.

We need a good dose of biblical balance and sanity. Mark 5 provides an excellent starting point. Yes, Jesus believed demons were real, and that should settle for all of us the question of their existence. Yet beyond this fact, we see in our Lord's encounter with the Gerasene demoniac the power, mercy, and authority of the Son of God, who commands the demon with merely a word. In this text we will see the purpose of Satan to destroy and the power of the Savior to deliver. Whether it is a demonic man (5:1-20), a diseased woman (5:24-34), or a dead little girl (5:21-43), Jesus has the power to save.

Jesus Confronts the Demonic
MARK 5:1-5

Jesus has just calmed the sea, rebuking it and commanding it, "Silence! Be still" (4:39). The sea immediately became calm, provoking the disciples to ask, "Who then is this?" They are about to get their answer but from an unlikely source.

Satan Attempts to Defile the Image of God in Man (Mark 5:1-2)

Crossing a now-calmed Sea of Galilee, Jesus and the Twelve arrive in the area of the Gerasenes. Gadara was a major city in the region (cf. Matt 8:28; Luke 8:26,37). South of the town called Gerasa was a steep slope only 40 yards from the shore. Two miles from there were cavernous tombs.

As they got out of the boat, a man with an unclean spirit came out of the tombs to meet Jesus. Because he was possessed, this man was defiled. Additionally, a Jew would view the touching of a dead body as an act of great defilement, and here was a man living among the dead. Satan had taken him down and was close to delivering a knockout blow.

Satan Attempts to Deface the Image of God in Man (Mark 5:3-4)

It is heart wrenching to think the Devil could so deface one who was created in the image of God. This man lived in the tombs. He often had been bound with shackles and chains but had snapped them off. Deranged and utterly depraved in his behavior, this man was not a maniac but a demoniac.

The people of his town had driven him away. Defiled and defaced, he descended into a life of filth, loneliness, and terror. People feared him because of his Herculean strength, but they did not respect him. It is shameful to see what Satan had conquered and captured.

Satan Attempts to Destroy the Image of God in Man (Mark 5:5)

Jesus says in John 10:10, "A thief comes only to steal and to kill and to destroy," and in John 8:44, "[The Devil] was a murderer from the beginning." Peter adds, "Your adversary the Devil is prowling around like a roaring lion, looking for anyone he can devour" (1 Pet 5:8). This was the plan the Devil had in mind for this poor demon-possessed soul. He was howling like a wild animal and cutting himself against the jagged rocks of the land. Some believe this is depraved pagan worship. Others see wild but futile attempts to drive out the demons. I believe it is a failed attempt to end his pain and suffering by suicide. Running about wild, naked, and unkempt, he was by now a mere shell of cuts, bruises, lacerations, scabs, and infected tissues. He tried again and again to end his unbearable existence in death. This was the agenda of the demons inside him. Perhaps the only thing that prevented his death was the last vestiges of the image of God in him and the common grace of God about him. Defiled and defaced, he was daily staring death in the face. A more miserable existence could hardly be imagined.

But something happened that would turn things upside down and reverse the course of his despair: this man met Jesus.

Jesus Conquers the Destructive
MARK 5:6-13

The Jewish Talmud gave four signs of madness: (1) walking about at night, (2) spending the night on a grave, (3) tearing one's clothes, and (4) destroying what one was given. This man met these criteria and more. His situation appears hopeless until he meets "Jesus, Son of the Most High God."

Our Savior Is a Liberator (Mark 5:6-13)

Seeing Jesus from a distance, this madman did something surprising. He knelt down before Him. However, kneeling was not an act of worship but an acknowledgment of authority. He then yelled, "What do You have to do with me, Jesus, Son of the Most High God? I beg You before God, don't torment me!" The demons reacted this way because Jesus had told them to "come out of the man."

This spiritual encounter is completely one-sided! The demon-possessed man must drop to his knees. The demons always confess Christ accurately and truthfully (cf. 1:24). Their knowledge of Jesus' identity is superior to the disciples' knowledge, at least at this point in their journey. The demon's confession in 5:7 answers the disciples' question in 4:41. The demoniac knows who Jesus is, and he knows his existence is at stake. His time has run out.

The title "Son of the Most High God" is nothing less than a recognition of deity. Still, "The full address is not a confession of Jesus' dignity but a desperate attempt to gain control over him or to render him harmless, in accordance with the common assumption of the period that the use of the precise name of an adversary gave one mastery over him" (Lane, *Mark*, 183–84). The demon actually appeals to God for protection, though his request will certainly not receive a positive response. Jesus has commanded him to come out, and come out he will.

The full impact of the control and horrifying grip this demon had on this man now becomes painfully evident (vv. 9-10). The demon gives his name as "Legion . . . because we are many." A *legion* is a contingency of 6,000 Roman soldiers. This man was not possessed by just one demon but by thousands of demons working as one evil force. Captured by this alien army, his natural mind, will, and emotions had all but been destroyed. These soldiers of Satan had trampled his soul. His only hope was in a Liberator whose power and authority were greater than what now possessed him. That Liberator was Jesus Christ, the Son of God.

In a microcosm of the battle between good and evil, Jesus gives a preview of the fate of Satan and his demons. The demons, through the voice of the man, keep begging Jesus not to send them out of the region. The tormentor is now the tormented as he contemplates his destiny. Luke 8:31 is more specific: "They begged Him not to banish them to the abyss," a place of spiritual confinement before final, eternal judgment.

The demons attempt to bargain with Jesus. A large herd of pigs was there, feeding on the hillside. The demons begged Him, "Send us to the pigs." Jesus complied, giving them permission to transfer hosts. The tormented man had met his Savior, his Liberator.

Satan Is a Murderer (Mark 5:13)

I am convinced that when the man was cutting himself with stones, the demons in him were driving him to commit suicide. That judgment is supported by what happens now: "Then the unclean spirits came out and entered the pigs, and the herd of about 2,000 rushed down the steep bank into the sea and drowned there." The volition of a human being made in God's image is stronger than that of an animal. What Legion could not get the man to do was easily accomplished in a large herd of pigs. The pigs could not withstand the will of Legion, and they were driven to their death.

Satan is a murderer of human beings, while Jesus is their Savior. Still, why did Jesus allow the demons to enter into this herd of pigs? William Lane provides a plausible explanation:

> First, Jesus recognized the time of the ultimate vanquishment of the demons had not yet come; his encounter and triumph over the demonic does not yet put an end to Satan's power. It is the pledge and the symbol of that definitive triumph, but the time when that triumph will be fully realized is yet deferred. It must await the appointment of God. Therefore, Jesus allows the demons to continue their destructive work, but not upon a man. The second element is related to this: Jesus allowed the demons to enter the swine to indicate beyond question that their real purpose was the total destruction of their host. (Lane, *Mark*, 186)

We can add two further observations. (1) The demons, not Jesus, destroyed the pigs. (2) The event demonstrates that God cares more for man, whom He created in His image and recreates in salvation, than He does for animals that do not bear His image.

Several important theological truths arise from this story thus far (Arnold, "Exorcism," 58).

1. Demons are real and dangerous. A demon (or many demons!) can inhabit and take possession of a person.
2. Demons can make themselves known by speaking through people and even taking control of their bodies.
3. Demons are fallen angels and powerful spiritual beings. They can exhibit enormous strength through a person under their control.
4. Demons can inflict serious personal injury to the one possessed and to others, with the ultimate goal of that person's death.
5. Demons can move or be transferred from one host to another.
6. Demons can resist leaving their host. They may even beg, out of self-interest, for their own well-being.
7. Demons recognize and are subject to appropriate spiritual authority.
8. If demonic spirits attempted to resist the incarnate Christ, we can be sure they will also attempt to resist us.
9. Jesus spoke directly to the demon, even asking for his name. This may provide a pattern for us to follow.

10. Jesus, unlike the exorcists of His day that used elaborate rituals and incantations, simply gave the command, and the demons were forced to obey.

When it comes to our confronting the demonic, in the name of Jesus and by the power of His bloody work on the cross, we can see the demonized delivered and the spiritually captive set free.

Jesus Commissions the Delivered
MARK 5:14-20

Paul says in 2 Corinthians 5:17, "Therefore, if anyone is in Christ, he is a new creation; old things have passed away, and look, new things have come." Never was this more real than in this man whom the Lord Jesus had delivered from a legion of demons. You would think there would be joy and thanksgiving all around. Sadly some of the people responded with fear. Still the focus is on this "new man" in Christ. What Jesus did in saving him from Satan and his sin He will also do for you if you simply come to Him in faith.

Let Jesus Change You (Mark 5:14-17)

When the demon-possessed pigs plunged into the sea and drowned, the men who tended them ran off and reported it. The people came out to see what had happened. I'm sure they were shocked! "They came to Jesus and saw the man who had been demon-possessed by the legion" (5:15). But was this really him? Their confusion is understandable. He was simply sitting there, not running about wild and in a rage. And he was dressed, not half naked in ragged, dirty clothes. And even more wonderful, he was in his right mind! He knew who he was and who they were. He sat clothed, calm, and a new creature because of what Jesus had done for him.

Perhaps the man was smiling, rejoicing in his salvation and deliverance. Perhaps with gratitude and devotion his eyes were fixed on Jesus. However, the townspeople had something else on their minds, and they began to beg Jesus to leave. What a surprising and disappointing response! Jesus has just rid their village of a menace, and they're concerned about the pigs!

Now to be fair, we should note, "they were afraid." A combination of commercial concern (two thousand pigs) and fear of the One who can cast out demons by a word was more than they could handle. What else can this man named Jesus do? What demands might He make? If He can change and transform a demoniac what might He do with us? With me? Pathetically, they decide it would be best all-around if Jesus left.

> Rabbi, be gone! Thy powers
> Bring loss to us and ours.
> Our ways are not as Thine.
> Thou lovest men, we—swine.
> Oh, get you hence, Omnipotence,
> And take this fool of Thine!
> His soul? What care we for his soul?
> What good to us that Thou hast made him whole,
> Since we have lost our swine? (Hughes, *Mark*, 122)

The townspeople may not have cared for the demoniac's soul, but the Son of God did. Jesus made him a new man. Heaven was glad, but his fellow humans wanted him gone. What a sad commentary on the wickedness and self-centeredness of the human heart void of the grace of God.

Let Jesus Command You (Mark 5:18-19)

Jesus does not stay where He is not wanted. Whether out of ignorance, fear, or greed, the people in the region of Gerasenes had decided they had had enough of this miracle worker. However, one man felt altogether differently. He had met Jesus, and his life had been wonderfully transformed. No one had ever shown him such love and compassion, mercy and kindness. The townspeople may be begging Jesus to leave, but this man begged and pleaded with Jesus to remain.

If, however, Jesus would not stay, "Fine, then let me go with You," he might have said. "I've never met anyone like You. No one has ever done, could ever do, what You did for me. I love You. I want to be with You. *Where* does not matter, as long as I am in Your presence, walking by Your side." Somewhat surprisingly, though, Jesus denied his request. In gratitude this man wanted to follow Jesus. Our Lord, however, had an evangelistic assignment. Go and tell others what I, the Lord, have done for you. Start in your home and work from there. Go to your family and friends and share with them. "Tell them of My mercy," Jesus basically tells the man. "Be My witness; give your testimony. You were lost but now you are saved. You once belonged to Satan, but now you belong to the Son of God."

The Gerasenes might not have wanted Jesus, but Jesus still wanted them. He would not leave them without a witness. He commissioned the former demoniac to tell them how much the Lord had done for him, and what He may also do for them.

Let Jesus Consume You (Mark 5:20)

Unlike so many followers of Jesus, this man did not argue, complain, or refuse his assignment from his Master. He accepted his marching orders without question. "He went out and began to proclaim in the Decapolis how much Jesus had done for him" (5:20). And the response for those who heard was appropriate: "They were all amazed." It is easy to imagine the scene as people who had only known Legion now met this new man who had been transformed by Christ and was consumed by His grace. I imagine he stopped friends and strangers alike to tell them how much Jesus had done for him. All the while, I am convinced, he was on his way to obeying the words of Jesus: "Go back home."

Using a little imagination, one can sense the excitement building within his heart as he got closer to home. Perhaps he had a wife and children. How long had it been since he saw them, kissed his wife, and held his children? Is it possible they had been praying for him all this time?

"Lord, rescue the soul of my husband."

"Dear God, please help my daddy and bring him back home."

Finally, this man sees a home he has not seen for a long time. A little boy turns from playing in the dirt and sees his daddy. Running out the front door is his precious little girl. She stops in her tracks when she sees him, and with the excitement only a daughter can have for her daddy, she begins to scream at the top of her lungs, "Mommy, Mommy! It's Daddy! It's Daddy! He's come home!" No longer walking, the man is now in a sprint, gathering in his arms his little boy and little girl who had run to him. Then, there in the doorway, stood a lady, his wife. With tears streaming down her face and a sweet smile, she is speechless, all caught up in the joy of the moment. Now they are all embracing and crying tears of joy. How could this be? What happened?

Wiping the tears from his eyes, the man looks at his wife and children and begins, "I met a man named Jesus. He is the Son of the Most High God. Let me tell you what He has done for me." I imagine this was a wonderful story told many, many times. After all, those who are forgiven much, always love much (Luke 7:47).

Reflect and Discuss

1. If you were involved in a conversation about movies featuring demons, vampires, and even angels, how might you steer the conversation to a balanced, biblical view of demonic activity?

2. How would you respond to a Christian who questions, in this modern day, whether we still need to believe in angels and demons?
3. What were some of the ways the Devil debased this man? How do people these days end up being disgraced when they listen to the Devil's lies?
4. Why do you think Herculean strength is often a characteristic of demoniacs?
5. Why does demonic activity ultimately lead to suicidal despair? Why is Jesus the only decisive answer to such despair?
6. Why do the demons know precisely who Jesus is?
7. How is Jesus' command to the demons different from the way exorcism is portrayed in the movies?
8. Have you ever seen someone come to Christ, and the people around him or her are more concerned with trivial matters than with the salvation of souls?
9. In what ways can someone who has just been saved be a better evangelist than someone who has been a Christian and studied the Bible for a long time? How can the latter improve his or her message?
10. Describe a scenario where Jesus might change someone you know so that they would once again be in their right mind and come home. Pray for that person.

Jesus Is the Great Physician

MARK 5:21-43

Main Idea: We can come to Jesus with our requests, and He will honor even imperfect faith when the object of that faith is Him.

I. **Jesus Hears the Cries of the Distressed (5:21-24).**
   A. We can come to Jesus with our request (5:21-23).
   B. We must come to Jesus in faith (5:23-24).
II. **Jesus Responds to the Pain of the Diseased (5:24-34).**
   A. We can approach Jesus in our suffering (5:24-27).
   B. We must approach Jesus in faith (5:28-34).
III. **Jesus Has Authority over the Power of Death (5:35-43).**
   A. We can believe in Jesus in spite of the circumstances (5:35-36).
   B. We can believe in Jesus regardless of the skeptics (5:37-40).
   C. We can believe in Jesus because He can be trusted (5:41-43).
Excursus: Five Questions We Always Ask of Every Text

Jesus! What a Friend for sinners! Jesus! Lover of my soul!
Friends may fail me, foes assail me, He, my Savior, makes me whole.

Hallelujah! What a Savior! Hallelujah! What a Friend!
Saving, helping, keeping, loving, He is with me to the end.
(Chapman, "Jesus! What a Friend for Sinners")

Mark 5 provides what could be called "three cases of incurables." However, when Jesus shows up, everything changes. Jesus is Lord over demons, disease, and even death! Our Lord is man's Savior (5:1-20), woman's Savior (5:24-34), and the child's Savior (5:35-43). Yes, He is indeed a friend of sinners and the healer of the hurting.

Jesus Hears the Cries of the Distressed
MARK 5:21-24

This text has what we call a "sandwich structure," beginning with the story of Jairus (5:21-24), interrupted by the story of a suffering woman (5:24-34), and ending with Jairus again (5:35-43). The purpose is to make comparisons.

Themes in these stories are also found in the stories of Jesus calming the sea (4:35-41) and healing the demon possessed (5:1-20). First, Jesus cares for those in trouble. Second, Jesus is the omnipotent God! He has authority over what is impossible for you and me. Nature, demons, diseases, and even death surrender completely and immediately to His sovereign authority.

We Can Come to Jesus with Our Request (Mark 5:21-23)

Great crowds still follow (3:7,8,9,20,32; 4:1 [2x],36). He just can't be hidden.

A man shows up by the name of Jairus, a ruler of the synagogue. He is a man of distinction, respect, and standing; yet he shows great humility. Basically he begs Jesus on his knees with his face to the ground! His little girl is dying, and in spite of the growing opposition of the religious establishment, he bucks the trend and comes to Jesus. She is his only daughter (Luke 8:42).

We Must Come to Jesus in Faith (Mark 5:23-24)

Jairus came to Jesus because he believed Jesus could do for him what no one else could! His humble faith is a model we all should emulate. His request was straight and to the point, delivered in *dependency* and *urgency* (v. 23). Our Lord's response is simple and immediate (v. 24). He went with him. Well, it was almost immediate!

Jesus Responds to the Pain of the Diseased
MARK 5:24-34

What occurs in verses 24-43 cannot be fully appreciated apart from the urgency of the situation and the Hebrew laws concerning ceremonial uncleanness (Lev 15:25-30; 22:1-9; Num 5:1-4). Jesus is not too busy in one task to stop and help someone else who is hurting, especially one who is determined, humble, and hopeful (has faith) in Him.

We Can Approach Jesus in Our Suffering (Mark 5:24-27)

The crowd is still there—bedlam reigns. A woman suddenly appears. She has a discharge of blood, making her ceremonially unclean and forbidding her access to the temple. She has been sick for 12 long years, and she is probably unmarried and childless, two additional cultural curses added to her pitiful state. She has suffered much from many physicians—she spent all she had and did not get better.

She heard about this miracle worker named Jesus. Possibly with pagan superstition, she believes that if she could just touch Him or His clothing she could be healed. Her theology may be weak but her faith is strong!

We Must Approach Jesus in Faith (Mark 5:28-34)

Though hundreds thronged about Him, only one woman connected with Him in faith. Spiritually and physically desperate, she did the unthinkable and unacceptable. She reached out and touched Him, and she did so in faith.

She is "instantly" healed and she knows it! She feels it! What extraordinary joy she must have experienced, well and whole for the first time in 12 years! The amazing grace of God through Christ had healed her body just as it heals our soul when we place our faith in Him.

Jesus "at once" perceives a loss of power. He had taken on her uncleanness and sickness and imparted to her His purity and health! The Suffering Servant of Isaiah 53 strikes again (see especially Isa 53:3-4)! Jesus looks for the one who touched Him *in faith*. The woman falls down and confesses everything (cf. 5:6,22). He welcomes her into the kingdom, commends her faith, and blesses her with "shalom." She has experienced salvation, both physically and spiritually.

Jesus Has Authority over the Power of Death
MARK 5:35-43

Jairus by now must be beside himself in anxiety and frustration. His daughter is at death's door. This woman has been sick for 12 years—she could have waited another 30 minutes! Unlike Nicodemus, who came in the dark of night, he came in daylight, humble and begging. He demanded nothing, and look where it got him!

Note the similarities between Jairus and the nameless woman: (1) they knew only Jesus could help them; (2) they knew they were unworthy; (3) they fell down; and (4) they believed Jesus could heal. She got what she wanted. However, things for Jairus appear to go from bad to worse.

We Can Believe in Jesus in Spite of the Circumstances (Mark 5:35-36)

Jesus is interrupted with bad news: Jairus' daughter is dead. Hope is suddenly gone. Jesus responds to the bad news with a challenge. It is as if He is saying: "Despite all appearances I am neither distracted nor disinterested in your need. I work in My time, not others' time. I will not be hurried or dictated to. Believe and watch what I do."

We Can Believe in Jesus Regardless of the Skeptics (Mark 5:37-40)

He takes the inner circle of Peter, James, and John. This is the first time He separates them from the others. Professional mourners had arrived to accompany the family with their "loud wailing." It would have been quite a scene. Jesus rebukes them with a shocking statement that only invites their ridicule. He kicks them out of the house (!) and goes in with just the three disciples and the little girl's parents.

Hard-core realists who breathe the air of skepticism will always be with us. They will mock our faith in a crucified Jew and ridicule our trust in a God we cannot see. They will laugh at your love for the Savior who has cleansed you of sin's defilement and given you spiritual life by His atoning work on the cross. Nevertheless, believe. Have faith—not faith in faith, which is spiritual nonsense, but faith in the omnipotent, sovereign Lord Jesus whose authority and power are absolute and know no rival.

We Can Believe in Jesus Because He Can Be Trusted (Mark 5:41-43)

Jesus again does the unthinkable in that culture, a taboo of enormous magnitude: He touches the dead body of the little girl! With a gentle touch, as

Mom and Dad look on through tears, He says, "Little girl, I say to you, get up!"

The response, by now, should not surprise us! Immediately she got up, obeying the Master. They were "immediately overcome with amazement," which is one of the great understatements of Scripture.

He gave a command to keep this quiet (for Messianic reasons). He instructed them to give her something to eat (for practical reasons). This little lady had been completely restored to full health. Like her spiritual sister in verses 24-34, her gender, namelessness, uncleanness, and impossible condition did not stop her from experiencing the healing touch of the great physician. Yes, we can believe in Jesus no matter what. Hallelujah, what a Savior!

Excursus: Five Questions We Always Ask of Every Text

What does this text teach me about God? God honors the faith of all who come to Him through Jesus. Social status, gender, or any other distinction does not matter. God cares for the demon possessed, the man of distinction, the outcast woman, and the little girl who is powerless. God truly loves the world of people without distinction (John 3:16).

What does this text teach me about sinful humanity? Disease and death are realities we must face in our fallen and sinful world. Ours is a world that desperately needs the touch and grace of God mediated through Jesus.

What does this text teach me about Jesus Christ? Jesus cares for the hurting. Jesus does His work on His timetable. When Jesus touches the unclean, they become clean as He takes on their uncleanness. Jesus gives healing and life to those who trust Him as He takes on our diseases and dies our death (Isa 53). He willingly gives up power for those who have no power.

What does God want me to know? We can come to Jesus with our request no matter who we are or what we have done. We must come to Jesus in faith, believing and not fearing (cf. Mark 6:5-6). God honors imperfect faith from a sincere heart when the object of that faith is Jesus.

What does God want me to do? God wants you to come to Him with any and every request. God wants you to trust Him regardless of the circumstances or situation. Why? Because He can be trusted to heal our diseases and conquer the great enemy called death. How do we know? We look to the cross and an empty tomb. Hallelujah! What a Savior!

Reflect and Discuss

1. Do you know anyone who came to Jesus in desperation, convinced He was the only One who could help? Have you ever felt that way?

2. Are you willing to be interrupted? If you are busy helping one person, will you still take the time to help someone who is hurting? How do you prioritize?
3. Have you known anyone whose initial interest in Jesus was misguided? What deliberate steps can you and your church take to lead such a person to saving, biblical faith?
4. What does the woman's healing tell us about the role of physicians and the role of faith?
5. Jesus felt it when He took on the woman's uncleanness and bestowed grace on her. How does knowing this affect your attitude toward the many times you have experienced forgiveness and grace? Forgiveness is free; is it cheap?
6. Jesus commended the imperfect faith of the woman. How can we be more encouraging of spiritual babes in our churches without condoning bad theology?
7. Have you ever been frustrated with God's timing? Have you ever felt He waited until it was too late—but then He came through? Explain.
8. When our prayers turn into demands, are we trying to manipulate God, like magicians attempt to do, or are we commanding God, as if He were our butler?
9. How would you respond to someone who urged your family to "have faith in faith"?
10. How do these stories encourage us that no person and no situation are beyond Jesus' ability to restore?

Jesus: A Prophet Without Honor!

MARK 6:1-6

Main Idea: We cannot come to Jesus on our terms. We must see Him for who He truly is.

I. **When You Consider Jesus, Are You Only Amazed (6:1-3)?**
   A. His teachings should astonish you, but that is not enough (6:1-2).
   B. His miracles may captivate you, but that is not enough (6:2).
   C. His background will not impress you, but so what (6:3)?
II. **When You Consider Jesus, Are You Offended (6:3-4)?**
   A. In spite of clear evidence, you may reject Him (6:3).
   B. In spite of close proximity, you may dishonor Him (6:4).
III. **When You Consider Jesus, Are You Guilty of Unbelief (6:5-6)?**
   A. Unbelief is one thing that limits Jesus (6:5).
   B. Unbelief is one thing that amazes Jesus (6:6).

N o prophet is accepted in his hometown." Jesus would say this on more than one occasion (Luke 4:24; John 4:44). Applied to you or me, it may be a moment of sadness and disappointment. Applied to Jesus, it is an event of tragic eternal consequences that even causes our Savior to be "amazed" at such unbelief (Mark 6:6).

This is Jesus' second recorded, and His last, visit to His hometown of Nazareth as far as we know. His previous homecoming did not go well at all (Luke 4:16-30). Initially impressed by His preaching (Luke 4:22), the town He grew up in turned on Him and attempted to murder Him (Luke 4:28-30). In spite of such treatment, Jesus returns, this time with His 12 apostles. It will be a painful training time.

As we consider how Jesus was treated by His own hometown, His own family and friends, it might be good for us to reflect on how we treat this Servant King and how we respond to the One who was rejected by those who were certain they knew Him best. It is critically important that we see Jesus as He truly is and as He is revealed in Scripture, not as we might hope, wish, or want Him to be.

When You Consider Jesus, Are You Only Amazed?
MARK 6:1-3

Few people are neutral when it comes to Jesus. Everyone has an opinion. Unfortunately, those opinions often fail to measure up to the full biblical portrait. Too often we take a "cafeteria approach," selecting those parts of Jesus that we find pleasing to our taste. Other aspects of His person and work we simply pass over.

Jesus leaves the area around the Sea of Galilee and heads to His hometown of Nazareth (cf. 1:9,24). Nazareth was a nowhere town made up of nobodies. The population is estimated to have been between 150 and 200. It is never mentioned in the Old Testament, Apocrypha, or rabbinic literature. It only receives scant attention in the New Testament. Little wonder that Nathanael said in John 1:46, "Can anything good come out of Nazareth?"

His Teachings Should Astonish You, but That Is Not Enough
(Mark 6:1-2)

On this return trip Jesus brings His disciples. This will prove to be most instructive for their upcoming ministry assignment (6:7-13, esp. v. 11). What their Master encounters, they will too.

Once again, on a Sabbath He taught in the synagogue. Again the people were "astonished," overwhelmed, struck by what they were hearing from the son of Joseph (Luke 4:22) and Mary (Mark 6:3). Their amazement again turns to skepticism (vv. 2-3). They began to bat around five questions among themselves:

1. Where did this man get these things?
2. What is the wisdom given to Him?
3. How are these miracles performed by His hands?
4. Isn't this the carpenter, the son of Mary, and the brother of James, Joses, Judas, and Simon?
5. And are not His sisters here with us?

These are meant as disparaging questions. They did not deny He was saying and doing these things. This makes their rejection all the more amazing and makes them culpable. If He did not get these things, this wisdom, and these mighty works from God, then from whom? How? They choose to leave the question open.

Some chalked up what He said and did to Satan (cf. 3:22). In our day some chalk it up to a superior intellect and wit. Thus those who deny the supernatural—His miracles and His resurrection—can applaud His teaching. His teachings should astonish us, but that is not enough.

His Miracles May Captivate You, but That Is Not Enough (Mark 6:2)

The number of miracles is growing!

1. Peter's mother-in-law (1:29-31)
2. Many more in Capernaum (1:32-34)
3. A leper (1:40-45)
4. A paralyzed man (2:1-12)
5. A man with a deformed hand (3:1-6)
6. Many again (3:7-12)
7. The storm and sea (4:35-41)
8. The Gerasene demoniac (5:1-20)
9. The woman who bled for 12 years (5:25-34)
10. Jairus' daughter who had died (5:35-43)

His hometown does not deny all these things, but these things do not bring them to faith. They simply cannot reconcile what He has done with who they think He must be!

It is as if they are saying, "This is the Christ? This One we have known all our lives is the Son of God? Are you kidding? We may not be able to explain

His miracles, but we know who He is. He is nothing and a nobody; of that we are certain."

Apart from the eyes of faith, no one will see Jesus for who He truly is. In and of themselves, miracles are not enough. His miracles point to Him. They are divinely ordained signs, declaring in capital letters that this One is the Christ, the Son of God! Believe Him! Follow Him!

His Background Will Not Impress You, but So What? (Mark 6:3)

The derisive comments peak in verse 3.

"Isn't this the carpenter?" Jesus is nothing more than a commoner who works with His hands. As a *tekton*, He builds things and repairs things. He is a handyman, a construction worker! He is a "man's man" to be sure. Still, His occupation was not impressive, certainly not the stuff of an esteemed rabbi. He was blue-collar through and through.

"Isn't this . . . the son of Mary?" Perhaps this is nothing more than an indication that Joseph had died. On the other hand, this might be a cheap shot at the scandal of His birth. If so, they were taunting Him that He was an illegitimate child born to a whore.

His brothers James (Jacob) and Joseph were named after the patriarchs. Judah and Simon were named for famous Jewish revolutionaries. Here is a family hoping for the rescue and redemption of Israel. The Redeemer was indeed right there with them, but they missed it.

All of this is to say, "If anyone should know who you are, we should! You are nothing special. You are just one of us. You are a nobody, and you were a bastard child to top it off!"

Publius the Syrian (c. 2 BC) said, "Familiarity breeds contempt." Apparently this was the case with Nazareth and "the local boy makes good" named Jesus. He was just too ordinary. Our minds are made up about this homeboy! We will not let the evidence get in our way, and nothing will change our mind.

When You Consider Jesus, Are You Offended?
MARK 6:3-4

Not everyone responds to Jesus in the same way. Paul says His death on the cross as our substitute is a stumbling block to Jews and foolishness to Gentiles (1 Cor 1:23). However, even before the cross, those who knew Jesus best found His ministry a scandal! Jesus' teachings and miracles do not automatically produce faith. They actually offended those who changed

His diapers, who learned the Torah and enjoyed table fellowship with Him, and who at one time gave Him hugs and kisses. Not anymore. All that has changed.

In Spite of Clear Evidence, You May Reject Him (Mark 6:3)

The word "offended" in verse 3 is *skandalizomai*. They are "scandalized" by all this talk and hoopla about Jesus. He offends their personal sensibilities. His works they cannot deny, and His words they cannot handle, but they do not care! In spite of overwhelming evidence they will not believe He is the Christ, the Son of God.

So two thousand years ago they were thinking, "A Jew from nowhere executed unjustly is the Savior and only Savior of the world? Impossible! No way! I am offended." We are not the first to think so.

In Spite of Close Proximity, You May Dishonor Him (Mark 6:4)

Jesus responds with a saying He made famous. Aligning Himself with the prophetic tradition, He acknowledges with a broken heart His rejection by those who knew Him best, those you would have expected would stand with Him no matter what anyone else said or did. They knew Him but could not explain Him, so they rejected Him. His hometown, His relatives, even His own household cast their ballot against Him. This prophet from God meets the same fate as so many others who had gone before Him.

Sometimes we spend so much time with someone that we no longer appreciate them. For those of us raised in a Christian environment, this is certainly an ever-present danger we must guard against. In a sense we should *never* get comfortable with Jesus. His goal is not to make us comfortable. His goal is to bring us to repentance and faith, humbly falling at His feet confessing Him as Lord and God. He is not your homeboy, your buddy, or your soul mate. He is not your genie in a bottle obligated to grant your every wish.

Nor is He some ordinary guy who lived two thousand years ago, stirred things up for a few years, and got nailed to a cross for His troubles. His hometown got it wrong. His relatives, at least for a while, got it wrong. The religious leaders got it wrong. Rome got it wrong. And still today people get Him wrong!

Do you see Him for who He truly is and call Him Lord, Savior, Master, King? Do you let Jesus set the agenda for your life and—as 8:34-38 says—for your death?

When You Consider Jesus, Are You Guilty of Unbelief?

MARK 6:5-6

Jesus left His hometown of Nazareth and moved on to teach in other villages. To our knowledge He never again returned home. The *unbelief* of the *Nazarenes* brought about a twofold reaction.

Unbelief Is One Thing That Limits Jesus (Mark 6:5)

Jesus did no mighty works in His hometown. He healed just a few.

How could the omnipotent Son of God be bound, limited by the unbelief of Nazareth? He *could not* do miracles because He *would not* in the face of blatant unbelief. Morally and spiritually He was constrained not to reveal His power in such an environment of rejection and unbelief. "He laid His hands on a few sick people and healed them." Oh, but imagine what He would have done in the presence of faith!

Come to Him in faith like Jairus and the woman who bled for 12 years, and He will heal your body and bring your only daughter back from death (5:21-43). Reject Him in unbelief, and He does not do for you what He does for others. You also send Him on His way in search of those who will listen to His message and embrace Him as Lord.

Tim Keller is helpful here: "Jesus' miracles were not 'magic tricks' designed to prove how powerful he was, but 'signs of the kingdom' to show how his redemptive power operates. His miracles always healed and restored and delivered people in ways that revealed how we are to find him by faith and have our lives transformed by him. . . . He 'could' not do a deed that would not redeem" (Keller, "Mark," 62).

Hebrews 11:6 reminds us, "Now without faith it is impossible to please God, for the one who draws near to Him *must believe* that He exists and rewards those who seek Him" (emphasis added).

Unbelief Is One Thing That Amazes Jesus (Mark 6:6)

Only twice in the Bible is Jesus said to be amazed. In Luke 7:9 He saw the faith of a Roman centurion who believed He could heal from a distance with just a word. And in Mark 6:6 He was amazed by the unbelief of those of His own hometown. Compare versions.

Jesus and His hometown are dumbfounded, each by the other. They could not get past Jesus' humble origins and familiar feel. Jesus was astounded at their unbelief in light of what He said and did. This sadly foreshadows the unbelief of the nation of Israel as a whole, of many in our world, and even of many in our churches.

It is a shock to our system that the sovereign God would come to us from such a humble town, a humble family, a humble trade, and a humble nation. It is a scandal to be sure. Once again we see, "God's ways are not our ways!"

The preacher Phillips Brooks (1835–1893) said, "Familiarity breeds contempt, but only with contemptible things or among contemptible people" (Wiersbe, *Be Diligent*, 59). The contempt shown by the citizens of Nazareth said nothing about Jesus, but it said a lot about them.

What about you and me? Do we show contempt toward the Jesus revealed in Scripture? Are we "scandalized" by the simplicity of His gospel? Are we offended by the unfairness of its message that says a child molester or even a serial rapist and murderer on death row can be made right with God by childlike faith in Jesus Christ? Or do we allow the biblical evidence to slay our biases and reshape our preconceived notions of who Jesus must be for us to accept Him and trust Him?

Or again, have we become so familiar with Him, having been raised in church all our lives, that His words no longer convict, His miracles no longer astonish, and His death on the cross no longer strikes the chord of "Amazing Grace"? Familiarity can blind us to the greatness and glory of a Savior if we are not careful. Spiritually inoculated at some point in life, we become immune to the real thing. I have seen it far too many times. We must not come to Jesus on our terms but on His. This prophet was without honor in His own hometown. We cannot make the same mistake in our own hearts. The consequences are eternal.

Reflect and Discuss

1. Did any of your classmates surprise you at your class reunion because of the good things they had accomplished? How did you feel about it: Were you happy, proud, or skeptical?
2. Why might the people in Jesus' hometown have resented Him? Is the response of a person's hometown and family a reliable indicator of whether the "prophet" is genuine and legitimate?
3. List some of the things Jesus said and did that are astonishing. Do non-Christians acknowledge that He said and did those things?
4. How is it possible for a person to see what Jesus did and yet deny that He is the Savior, the Son of God?
5. What kinds of credentials do you expect spiritual leaders to have? Are the most important credentials where they went to school, how well-spoken they are, who recommends them, or something else?
6. Should we avoid offending people when we tell them about Jesus?

7. Are you familiar and comfortable with any "famous" person? Do you sometimes forget that other people hold them in awe? Have you become too familiar with Jesus?
8. Can you think of any songs or dramatic presentations that treat Jesus too familiarly?
9. What are some biblical examples of God or Jesus doing miracles in spite of people's unbelief?
10. Have you ever been amazed that people don't believe in Jesus despite the evidence? Do you sometimes display amazing lack of trust in Jesus?

Advance the Kingdom

MARK 6:7-13

Main Idea: Even in the face of rejection or death, our mission is to preach the gospel and advance the kingdom.

I.   **Go with Jesus' Authority and as a Team (6:7).**
II. **Go Mean and Lean with Nothing Nonessential (6:8-9).**
III. **Go Where You Are Welcomed and Move On When Rejected (6:10-11).**
IV. **Go Preaching the Word and Doing the Work of the Kingdom (6:12-13).**

Those who follow Jesus have the honor and joy of advancing and extending His kingdom, actually sharing in what He is doing. There are some specific aspects to our calling. First, He calls us to go and we obey. Period. Second, He sends us out with His authority in on-the-job training. And third, we actually continue and extend the ministry of Jesus as we preach the gospel to the nations and minister to the hurting there (cf. Matt 28:16-20).

Jesus has just left His hometown of Nazareth, where He was rejected for a second time (Luke 4:16-30; Mark 6:1-6). That experience will impact the counsel He gives His 12 apostles as they go on their evangelistic/mission assignment (6:4,11). He moves on to other villages where He continues His teaching ministry. He may be disappointed (as all of us will be from time to time), but He is not deterred from fulfilling the will of His Father.

After discipling and mentoring the Twelve for an extended period, it is now time for them to get their feet wet, to move to the next level. Though all aspects of their training and instruction do not apply to us, we would be wise to consider some significant principles in our particular assignment as we join hands with Jesus to "advance the kingdom."

Go with Jesus' Authority and as a Team
MARK 6:7

Jesus begins to send out (*apostellō;* root of "apostle") the apostles two by two. Jesus sends them out as teams for several reasons. First, it is safer and wiser. Lone Rangers are easy targets of the evil one. As Ecclesiastes 4:9 says, "Two are better than one." Also, the law required two witnesses to verify a matter (Deut 17:6; 19:15; 2 Cor 13:1). This was in keeping with a cultural norm for that day.

He also gives them His authority over demons and unclean spirits. The Twelve were His authorized and appointed representatives. The Twelve were (as are we) extensions of King Jesus. Indeed a man's representatives were viewed as the man Himself. What an honor! What a responsibility! Paul complements this: "We are ambassadors for Christ, certain that God is appealing through us" (2 Cor 5:20). We represent the King! Called as fishers of men (Mark 1:16-20) and those who are set apart to be with Jesus (3:13-19), they are now ready to go out on their own as extensions of their Master.

Go Mean and Lean with Nothing Nonessential
MARK 6:8-9

To be effective in God's work, we must do what we do unencumbered, with no excess baggage that could impede our mission. Further, we must go in radical faith and dependence on our God.

The instructions Jesus provides for the Twelve also provide principles for our work. They are to travel light, taking nothing that is not absolutely essential, only a staff. In the parallel accounts the apostles are told not to take a staff (Luke 9:3) or sandals (Matt 10:9-10). The idea in those two accounts may be to not purchase *additional items.* Further, Mark may have in view the shepherd's staff for walking, while Matthew and Luke may have in view the shepherd's club for protection (Lane, *Mark,* 207n31). The bottom line is that the most basic preparation is to be made.

They do not travel first class! They do not make their ministry a means for accumulating stuff. They are to stay mean and lean. The four items required of the Twelve are identical to what God told the Hebrews to take on their flight from Egypt (Exod 12:11). Is a new exodus under a greater Moses (Deut 18:15-18) in view? Is the emphasis on faith in God to provide what we need the point of the passage? According to James Edwards, "True service of Jesus is characterized by dependence on Jesus, and dependence on Jesus is signified by going where Jesus sends despite material shortfalls and unanswered questions. . . .They must trust him alone who sends them" (Edwards, *Mark*, 181). Little provisions require big faith in God to meet your needs (cf. Phil 4:19)!

Go Where You Are Welcomed and Move On When Rejected
MARK 6:10-11

Jesus now tells them where to stay and when to move on. When you find a receptive home, stay there until your work is done in that area. Do not impose yourself on multiple homes or seek out nicer accommodations. This is not a pleasure tour. Adequacy is your goal. Accept what is offered and be grateful. Do not dishonor the kindness of a lesser home by moving to a nicer one and thereby become an offense to the gospel. Don't be aloof. Live among the people. Be dependent on them. Be accountable. Share life with them. Live in community. Be transparent. Show integrity!

If you do not receive a warm reception in a "short-term" mission (a crucial contextual point), if they will not receive you or listen to you, move on and leave a sign of their personal responsibility and prospective judgment (shake off the dust). We should anticipate rejection by some. When turned away, move on, at least for now. When you leave, in "a merciful prophetic act" (Hughes, *Mark*, 1:136), shake off the dust from your feet to warn them of what they are rejecting. This was something pious Jews did when they had traveled outside Israel to signify their disassociation from their paganism and the divine judgment that awaited them.

There will be times, with a broken heart, that we must warn others of the danger of rejecting Christ and the judgment they will experience (Ezek 33:1-20). It hurts but it is necessary.

Go Preaching the Word and Doing the Work of the Kingdom
MARK 6:12-13

The final two verses of this section summarize the specifics of the apostles' mission. It mirrors what they had seen Jesus do. With His authority and enablement, they cast out *many* demons. They anointed with oil *many* who were sick and healed them (cf. Jas 5:14-16). They went out and preached repentance, the same message preached by both John the Baptist (Mark 1:4) and Jesus (1:15). They were to go as servants. They were not to compromise their message even if it brought rejection and persecution. They had to have the courage to tell the truth about Jesus and the gospel.

If "repentance" was the first word out of the mouth of John, Jesus, and the apostles (Acts 2:38), it must be an important component of the gospel and the Christian life.

Thomas Watson, English Puritan (ca. 1620–1686), wrote a helpful treatise on repentance. He stated, "Repentance is a grace of God's Spirit whereby a sinner is inwardly humbled and visibly reformed" [Watson, *Doctrine*, 18]. . . .

Watson identified six ingredients necessary for true repentance. The first is *sight of sin*, whereby a person comes to themselves (Luke 15:17) and clearly views their lifestyle as sinful. If a disciple fails to see their sin, they are rarely motivated to repent. . . .

The second ingredient for true repentance is *sorrow for sin* (Ps 38:18). We need to feel the nails of the cross in our soul as we sin. Repentance includes godly grief, a holy agony (2 Cor 7:10). . . . The fruits of repentance will be expressed in genuine, anguishing sorrow over the offense itself and not just its consequences. This sorrow for sin is more than just a "worldly grief"; it will be seen in the ongoing actions it produces. . . .

The third ingredient is *confession of sin*. The humble sinner voluntarily passes judgment on themselves as they sincerely admit to the specific sins of their heart. . . . In the Scriptures, we find at least seven benefits to confession:

1. Confession of sin gives glory to God (Josh 7:19).
2. Confession of sin is a means to humble the soul (2 Chr 26:19).
3. Confession of sin gives release to a troubled heart (Ps 51:11-12).
4. Confession of sin purges out sin (Neh 3:13). Augustine called it "the expeller of vice."
5. Confession of sin endears Christ to the soul that needs atoning (Rom 7:25).
6. Confession of sin makes way for forgiveness (2 Sam 12:13; 1 John 1:9).
7. Confession of sin makes way for mercy (Prov 28:13).

Fourth, *shame for sin* is an ingredient for true repentance. . . . Repentance causes a holy bashfulness. Ezra prayed, "O my God, I am ashamed and blush to lift my face to You, my God, for our iniquities have risen higher than our heads, and our guilt has mounted up to the heavens" (Ezra 9:6). The repenting prodigal was so ashamed of his sin that he did not feel he deserved to be a son anymore (Luke 15:21). Sin makes us shamefully naked and deformed in God's eyes and puts Christ to shame, the one who took the scorn of the cross on himself.

The fifth ingredient in repentance is *hatred of sin*. We must hate our sin to the core. We hate sin more deeply when we love Jesus more fully. Repentance begins with the love of God and ends with hatred of sin. . . . Tolerating sin is a willful leap toward committing it. True repentance loathes sin deeply.

Finally, the sixth progressive ingredient of repentance is *turning from sin and returning to the Lord* "with all your heart" (Joel 2:12). This turning from sin implies a notable change, "performing deeds in keeping with their repentance" (Acts 26:20). Ezekiel records these words of God to the house of Israel: "Repent and turn away from your idols, and turn away your faces from all your abominations" (Ezek 14:6). We are called to turn away from *all* our abominations—not just the obvious ones or the ones that create friction in others. The goal of repentance is not to manufacture peace among others with perfunctory repentance, but rather to turn to God wholly.

Most importantly, though, this repentance is not just a turning away from sin; it is also a turning "of repentance toward God and faith in our Lord Jesus" (Acts 20:21). [We should repent of our] doubt by believing in the goodness, greatness and graciousness of God, and [turning] in faith to trust in the freedom Christ offers in the gospel. Repentance is rooted in a hatred of sin *and* a joyful awareness of God's loving-kindness, which leads to joy: "God's kindness is intended to lead you to repentance" (Rom 2:4). We rejoice that Christ has done everything for us—all that we need to secure our salvation and our growth in holiness. Our prayer is, "Lord, I am an adopted child, not a slave to sin. I am accepted because of Christ. I have forgotten how loved, secure, rich and free I am in Christ. Please let me be astonished by your love." (Thomas and Wood, *Gospel Coach*, 87–90)

The mission of the Twelve (Mark 6:7-13,30-32) brackets an interesting and tragic event in biblical history: the murderous beheading of John the Baptist (6:14-29). What are we to learn? Could it be—at least in part—that the kingdom advances mysteriously in the midst of rejection and even the death of God's choice servants? We go as a team, and we may suffer and die as a team. We go with little, and even what we have can be taken away. Some will welcome us, but others will not only reject us; they will try to destroy us. Preaching the Word and helping others may result not in our praise but in our death.

This was the fate of John and of Jesus and of the Twelve (minus perhaps the apostle John). This may be your fate or my fate. But did not Jesus say in

John 15:18, "If the world hates you, understand that it hated Me before it hated you"?

As we advance the kingdom of King Jesus, if indeed we are rejected and persecuted, may our Lord give us the heart of the apostles, "[who were] rejoicing that they were counted worthy to be dishonored on behalf of the Name" (Acts 5:41). Carry His Name and you may suffer shame and even pain, but do not forget the great gain now and forever!

Reflect and Discuss

1. Have you served in any sort of apprenticeship? What do you remember about the first time you did the work on your own?
2. What are the advantages of working as a team in mission work? What are the dangers of going alone?
3. When people know that you are Jesus' ambassador, what do they see?
4. How should Jesus' restrictions on what the apostles should take with them be applied today?
5. What are the advantages to having few possessions? What are the advantages to having abundant possessions? What are the dangers of either situation?
6. What are the advantages to staying in someone's home on the mission field, as compared to staying in paid lodging or on a missionary compound?
7. What might we do or say as an equivalent to the custom of shaking the dust off one's feet when leaving an unreceptive town?
8. How would you define *repentance* to someone who had never been in a church?
9. What are the thematic connections between the story of Jesus' sending the Twelve on their mission and the beheading of John the Baptist?
10. What is the true definition of *success* with regard to missions? What, then, is the nature of failure?

What Do You Get for Faithful Service to God?

MARK 6:14-29

Main Idea: Faithful service to God may cause the kings of this world to oppose you, even kill you, but it will bring great pleasure to the true King, Jesus.

I. **Expect That Some Will Fear You (6:14-16).**
   A. Let your good works honor you (6:14-15).
   B. Let your good works haunt them (6:16).

II. **Expect That Some Will Try to Stop You (6:17-20).**
   A. Guilt will drive some to oppose you (6:17-18,20).
   B. Hatred will drive others to oppose you (6:19).
III. **Expect That Some Will Attempt to Destroy You (6:21-29).**
   A. Accept that the ungodly will use ungodly means to get you (6:21-23).
   B. Accept that the ungodly may get your head on a platter (6:24-29).

What are the rewards for faithfully serving our God? What are the blessings for a life of devotion to King Jesus? Jesus will actually address these questions later when He tells His disciples, "I assure you . . . there is no one who has left house, brothers or sisters, mother or father, children, or fields because of Me and the gospel, who will not receive 100 times more, now at this time—houses, brothers and sisters, mothers and children, and fields, with persecutions—and eternal life in the age to come" (10:29-30). You see, sometimes the rewards and spiritual benefits include persecution.

On March 2, 2011 Shahbaz Bhatti—age 42 and the only Christian serving in Pakistan's cabinet—was brutally murdered when gunmen sprayed his body with bullets. Al-Qaeda claimed responsibility, saying the attack was a "fitting lesson for the world of infidelity, the crusaders, the Jews and their aides. . . . This is the fitting end of the accursed one which [will] serve as an example to others. And now with the blessing and aid of Allah, the mujahedeen will send all of you, one by one, to hell." Shahbaz Bhatti knew the risk he was taking as a devoted follower of King Jesus. A few months before his martyrdom, he said, "I want to share that I believe in Jesus Christ who has given His own life for us. I know what is the meaning of the cross. And I'm ready to die for a cause. I'm living for my community and suffering people and I will die to defend their rights" (Belz, "Ready," 15). And indeed, he did just that.

Yes, you may lose your life for faithfully serving King Jesus. You may actually lose your head, as John the Baptist found out. Mark 6:14-29 is something of a parenthesis and flashback that records the imprisonment and execution of John the Baptist. John is the forerunner of Jesus' message and ministry. He is also the forerunner of His death. Jesus has just warned the 12 apostles that their preaching would not always be welcomed. The brief ministry and abrupt end of John the Baptist would confirm Jesus' point: the cost of discipleship is great indeed.

This tragedy in many ways foreshadowed the miscarriage of justice when our Savior was put to death on the cross. In both cases cowardly men capitulated to pressure and executed God's man. A servant is not greater than his master. If they treated Jesus with cruelty, they will do the same to His followers. The life of John the Baptist perfectly illustrates what we might expect as we faithfully serve our God.

Expect That Some Will Fear You
MARK 6:14-16

When we are doing the work of God, some may rejoice in our good works and praise God for them (Matt 5:16). Others may oppose and reject us (Mark 6:11). Still others may actually fear us, not liking what we say or do but being unable to deny that God is at work. This was the reaction of a man Mark sarcastically refers to as "King Herod," a title Herod demanded from the locals but never received from Rome.

He was Herod Antipas, a mere tetrarch, ruler of one-fourth of his father Herod the Great's kingdom. Antipas ruled over Galilee and Perea until AD 39. He requested the title of "king" from Emperor Augustus and was soundly turned down. His nephew Herod Agrippa received the title of "king" form Caligula in AD 37. Antipas's adulterous wife Herodias became jealous and egged him on to request again the title. This ultimately played into his dismissal and exile.

This wicked, henpecked politician did not know what to do with a man like John. He feared John (v. 16) and was "very disturbed" by him. How do we respond if we find ourselves in such a mess of confusion and intrigue?

Let Your Good Works Honor You (Mark 6:14-15)

Herod heard of the ministry of Jesus and the 12 apostles. Jesus' miraculous works were not denied, but neither did they lead to faith. They did, however, lead to some interesting speculation. Herod entertained three options concerning Jesus: (1) He is John the Baptist raised from the dead; (2) He is Elijah; (3) He is a prophet like those of old.

Preaching and doing the work of the kingdom caused serious jitters in Herod's court and kingdom. Like the people of Nazareth, Herod wondered at the source of His "supernatural powers." Surprisingly, Herod's conclusion comes closer to the truth. Jesus, John, the Twelve, Elijah, and the prophets all allowed their good works to honor them. Even their enemies could not deny their works.

Let Your Good Works Haunt Them (Mark 6:16)

The generally held opinion of the common people was that Jesus was a prophet. Not so with Herod. He was convinced that Jesus was John the

Baptist raised from the dead. We are now informed that John had already been beheaded by Herod. This miracle child—born to a priest named Zacharias and his wife Elizabeth in their old age (Luke 1:5-56), uniquely called from his mother's womb, and who Jesus said was the greatest man who ever lived (Matt 11:11)—Herod had wickedly put to death.

John was a man of great courage and moral fiber. Herod was not. John loved God and boldly proclaimed His Word. Herod did not. John denounced sin and called people to repentance and a radical change in life. Herod murdered an innocent man, a prophet of God. It haunted him, and rightly so. John's blood was on his hands.

We need not defend ourselves if we walk with God. We need never employ methods of violence and coercion as we represent King Jesus and extend His kingdom. Our good works will honor us before men, and our good works will haunt those who oppose us, now or in eternity.

Expect That Some Will Try to Stop You
MARK 6:17-20

We now move into the lurid events that led to the execution of John. It is an all too familiar story of sex, power, pride, lust, and revenge. Herod may have been weak and paranoid, but his wife Herodias was conniving and ruthless. She would stop at nothing, even prostituting her daughter. Divorce, adultery, incest, drunkenness, striptease dancing, and murder characterized the Herods. It was "sin on steroids." And in the midst of all of this is a man consumed with a guilty conscience for not doing the right thing.

Guilt Will Drive Some to Oppose You (Mark 6:17-18,20)

Herod Antipas had met his niece, Herodias, in Rome. At the time she was married to his half brother, Herod Philip, making her also his sister-in-law. He evidently seduced her (or she him!), she left her husband, and they married. This was a clear act of adultery and bigamy.

Leviticus 18:16 says, "You are not to have sexual intercourse with your brother's wife; it will shame your brother," and Leviticus 20:21 says, "If a man marries his brother's wife, it is impurity. He has shamed his brother." This is a sinful situation that requires the man of God to speak.

John spoke up more than once ("had been telling," Mark 6:18). This greatly offended Herodias, the first-century Jezebel. It also caused problems for her weakling husband! So Herod had John arrested and imprisoned, even while he knew in his heart that John was right.

Amazingly, Herod feared John, since he knew John was a righteous and holy man. He therefore kept him safe and kept listening to him. He was greatly perplexed, yet he heard him gladly. He feared John but was fascinated with him. John, on the other hand, had no fear of the powerful and influential. He boldly confronted these royals in their sin. And though Herod could not help but listen, he was too weak and sinful to obey John's message.

The contrast between John the Baptist and Herod Antipas sets the stage for the final act of this tragedy:

JOHN THE BAPTIST	HEROD ANTIPAS
A hair-coated prophet	A gorgeously robed ruler
Austere and simple	Flamboyant and ornate
Righteous	Debaucherous
A prophet without price	A man who could be bought
Moral courage	Spineless coward
A clear conscience	A troubled conscience
Maintained his integrity and lost his head	Forfeited his integrity and lost his soul
A man of the Spirit	A man of the flesh

Jesus and Pilate will provide a similar contrast when our Lord endures His passion and goes to the cross for sinners.

Hatred Will Drive Others to Oppose You (Mark 6:19)

Herod did not know what to do with John, but unfortunately his Jezebel knew exactly what she wanted. Herodias "held a grudge against" John and "wanted to kill him." But her weak husband kept him safe in prison, so any assassination plan would have to be put on hold. Herodias felt that "the only place where her marriage certificate could safely be written was on the back of the death warrant of John the Baptist" (Wessel, "Mark," 670). All she needed was an opportune moment.

Expect That Some Will Attempt to Destroy You
MARK 6:21-29

The adage "Hell hath no fury like a woman scorned" is certainly appropriate here (though often attributed to William Shakespeare, these words were actually penned by a man named William Congreve in a 1697 play titled *The Mourning Bride*). Herodias had been condemned by John as a treacherous and adulterous woman. How far she is willing to go to get revenge is truly amazing.

Accept That the Ungodly Will Use Ungodly Means to Get You (Mark 6:21-23)

Herod threw a birthday party for himself. The Jews viewed birthday parties as pagan celebrations. Herod did not care. He had invited the important people of his little kingdom. Herodias's daughter enters the room filled with drunken men. There is little doubt she was sent by her mother, and there is little doubt Salome (we learn her name from Josephus's writings) danced seductively and greatly appealed to the lustful passions of these unregenerate, pagan men.

Most likely she was only in her teens. The daughter of Herodias and Philip, she was also Herod's stepdaughter and niece! This is how low Herodias stooped. She cared more about the head of John the Baptist than she did the dignity and reputation of her daughter.

Salome's dance pleased Herod and his guests. Parroting the language of Esther 5:2-3, he utters a proverbial saying that binds him to grant a generous gift for her performance. The ungodly has used ungodly means to get what she wants, and in God's mysterious providence, she succeeds.

Accept That the Ungodly May Get Your Head on a Platter (Mark 6:24-29)

Salome goes to Mommy and says, "What should I ask for?" The unhesitating response is, "John the Baptist's head!" "Immediately she hurried" to tell Herod. Not surprisingly, Herod was sad but spineless in his response. He could not afford to lose face in front of his guests, so the executioner is immediately sent and John is beheaded. The executioner brings John's head in to Herod; Herod directs it to Salome; Salome then gives it to Herodias. It's done and John is gone!

Herod feared displeasing his wife and losing face with man more than he feared God. Pride took him down, just like it did Satan and Adam. Herodias feared and hated John because he was right and she knew it. John was a nuisance to her conscience and a cancer to her reputation. He had to go. His head on a platter would solve all her problems, or at least she thought so.

Isn't it amazing that John the Baptist was declared by Jesus to be the last and greatest prophet? Yet John died in his early 30s, never performed a single miracle, and had a public ministry that lasted only about a year. Bad things do happen to good people. Life is often unfair. The righteous do suffer. And yes, sometimes good things happen to bad people. But never forget, God sees. He knows!

"When Jesus heard about it, He withdrew from there by boat to a remote place to be alone" (Matt 14:13). There is no doubt He was grieved, He was hurt, and He wept. And He would not forget! Note Jesus' opinion of Herod: "He said to them, 'Go tell that fox, "Look! I'm driving out demons and performing healings today and tomorrow, and on the third day I will complete My work"'" (Luke 13:32). And when the two met (Luke 23:8-9), the encounter revealed this tension: "Herod was very glad to see Jesus; for a long time he had wanted to see Him because he had heard about Him and was hoping to see some miracle performed by Him. So he kept asking Him questions, but Jesus did not answer him."

Conclusion

Death cannot silence a life. Murdering someone will not put an end to their testimony. Remember the saying, "Even though he is dead, he still speaks through his faith" (Heb 11:4). Today no one names their son Herod. Millions, on the other hand, bear the name of John. One's tombstone may serve as a trumpet, one's grave a megaphone of a life well lived for the glory of a great King whose name is Jesus. Throughout history the message of the martyrs continues to ring loud and clear. These choice servants of Jesus are a wonderful source of strength and encouragement. None fulfills that assignment better than John the Baptist. Herod and Herodias may have received his head on a platter, but our Lord received his soul into heaven for all eternity. John lost his head, but Herod and Herodias lost their souls. In the end there is no question who won and who lost. Bad things do happen to good people. But great things happen to godly people who put it all on the line, even their head on a platter, for the truth of God's Word and the glory of His name!

Reflect and Discuss

1. Which is harder, dying for Jesus once or living radically sold out to Jesus day after day, year after year?
2. What is the most recent example you have heard of a martyr for Christ? What is the most recent example of persecution you heard of in your own country?

3. What reactions have you seen in today's world that could be characterized as fear of Christianity?
4. Why did Herod fear John, and why was he tormented after his death? If you lived radically for Christ, who might fear you, and why?
5. What are the right reasons non-Christians should fear Christians? What are some bad ways some Christians cause fear and loathing in society?
6. What unbiblical practices in your own country are popular, so that if you spoke out against them, you would be persecuted? Should you speak out anyway?
7. What other cases do you know of where someone has used sex and lust to manipulate a leader? How can a leader prepare his or her mind and heart to resist such manipulation?
8. Is there any person or leader you fear more than God? Are you tempted to protect your own reputation rather than honoring God?
9. How would you explain to a non-Christian why bad things happen to good people and good things happen to bad people? How would you explain it in a Sunday school class?
10. Who do you think of that, "even though he is dead, he still speaks through his faith"?

The Feeding of the Five Thousand

MARK 6:30-44

Main Idea: Jesus' mission of love and rescue is demonstrated in His feeding of the five thousand.

I. **Like Jesus We Should Find Rest from Ministry (6:30-32).**
    A. Rejoice in God's blessings on your ministry (6:30).
    B. Get away for some rest and relaxation from your ministry (6:31-32).
II. **Like Jesus We Should Have Compassion for Others (6:33-37).**
    A. People have spiritual needs we should address (6:33-34).
    B. People have physical needs we should address (6:35-37).
III. **Like Jesus We Should Seek to Meet the Needs of Others (6:37-44).**
    A. Do what only you can do (6:37-40).
    B. Trust Jesus to do what only He can do (6:41-42).
    C. Recognize that a little can become a lot with Jesus (6:43-44).

Fyodor Dostoevsky said, "The most pressing question on the problem of faith is whether a man as a civilized being can believe in the divinity of the Son of God, Jesus Christ, for therein rests the whole of our faith" (source unknown).

Perhaps no story in the Bible, other than the resurrection of Jesus from the dead, confronts us with this reality of our Lord's deity more directly than the feeding of the five thousand. Only God could do what occurred on that remarkable day in Israel. This story, so popular and captivating for children—and yes, adults—is so important in the life and ministry of Jesus that it is the only miracle, outside of the resurrection, that is recorded in all four Gospels (Matt 14:13-21; Mark 6:30-44; Luke 9:10-17; John 6:1-13). Mark also will record a second feeding miracle in 8:1-10, with four thousand men in attendance.

John 6:15 informs us that this miracle made such an impact on the crowd that they attempted to take Jesus "by force to make Him king." Our Lord would refuse their advance and stay the course to the cross, as was His divine destiny.

Many lessons are contained in this story. We will structure our study in three parts.

Like Jesus We Should Find Rest from Ministry
MARK 6:30-32

Mark returns to the evangelistic mission of the Twelve (6:7-13), which had been interrupted by his account of the execution of John the Baptist (6:14-29). The "apostles," the word here meaning sent-out "missionaries," returned and rehearsed "all that they had done and taught" (v. 30). Jesus had sent them out, as He sends us out, with a job to do. They had experienced great success. When Jesus authorizes us and empowers us, we can anticipate God's blessings in what we do. We must simply believe and go.

They now return to evaluate their successes as well as their failures. This was how our Lord mentored His men:

- Teach them.
- Send them out.
- Have them return.
- Report and evaluate.

I doubt we can improve on this model of discipleship and training.

Rejoice in God's Blessings on Your Ministry (Mark 6:30)

They shared with the Lord "all that they had done and taught." They had cast out *many* demons, healed *many* who were sick, and preached the gospel of repentance (6:12-13) just like John the Baptist (1:4) and Jesus (1:15). One can imagine their excitement as they shared what they had been able to do in His name and with His delegated authority (6:7). They had worked hard, putting in many long hours. Still the blessings and joys of ministry were evident.

Get Away for Some Rest and Relaxation from Your Ministry (Mark 6:31-32)

Some people "rust out" in ministry because they are lazy. Others "burn out" because they never take a break. Vance Havner says, "If we don't come apart, we will come apart" (*Jesus Only*).

Jesus tells His apostles, "Come away by yourselves to a remote place and rest for a while" (v. 31; cf. vv. 32,35). Why? So many were coming and going they could not even eat (cf. 3:20)! They need some "down time," a "break in the action," much-needed R & R. Jesus gives a command: "Rest for a while." It was not a sin for them to take a brief sabbatical. It would have been a sin for them not to. The same is true for us! In fact, the greater the demands, the greater our need to find time alone with Jesus.

We can glean several practical insights. (1) There is a time to work (cf. John 9:4). Laziness has no place in the Christian life. (2) We should have periods of rest because Jesus tells us to. Being a workaholic is not spiritual and actually can be sinful. Some make ministry an idol. (3) Rest is best when accompanied both by solitude and companionship. (4) Rest is for a specific period of time. It is not permanent. (5) Even while resting, be prepared for ministry if necessary. A devoted follower of Jesus is *never* off duty.

Like Jesus We Should Have Compassion for Others
MARK 6:33-37

Often the Bible pictures our Lord as a Shepherd and us as His sheep. Jesus is the "Lord" who is "my shepherd" of Psalm 23. Jesus is the rejoicing Shepherd of Luke 15:4-6 who goes after the one lost sheep. Jesus is the "good shepherd" of John 10:11 who lays down His life for His sheep. Jesus is the "chief Shepherd" of 1 Peter 5:4 who honors His servants. Jesus is the "great Shepherd" of Hebrews 13:20. Jesus is the Shepherd Lamb of Revelation 7:17 who guides us to springs of living water.

We, on the other hand, are stupid sheep who cannot take care of ourselves and cannot save ourselves. Dietrich Bonhoeffer understands the desperate situation "human sheep" face without a shepherd: "There were questions but no answers, distress but no relief, anguish of conscience but no deliverance, tears but no consolation, sin but no forgiveness" (Garland, *Mark*, 258). We desperately need a shepherd, One who is compassionate and able to provide for us and protect us. We need a Shepherd Savior.

People Have Spiritual Needs We Should Address (Mark 6:33-34)

The people saw Jesus and the disciples leaving and ran ahead of them. When Jesus and the disciples went ashore, already "He saw a huge crowd." Was He angry? Frustrated? Depressed? No. First, He "had compassion on them." He was deeply moved, and His heart went out to them. Second, He saw them "like sheep without a shepherd." The spiritual leaders of Israel had become hirelings (cf. John 10:12-13; Ezek 34:1-24!). The nation of Israel was lost, helpless, without guidance, malnourished, and lacking protection. Third, "He began to teach them many things" (cf. 1 Pet 5:2).

In the wilderness Moses pleaded with the Lord to raise up a leader "that the Lord's community won't be like sheep without a shepherd" (Num 27:17). God raised up Joshua in anticipation of the greater Joshua named Jesus. In Ezekiel 34 the Lord rails against the evil shepherds who have neglected and abused the people. He promises, "I will appoint over them a single shepherd, My servant David, and he will shepherd them. . . . I, Yahweh, will be their God, and My servant David will be a prince among them" (Ezek 34:23-24). That Davidic Shepherd King has now appeared in Jesus. Now when the people are once again lost in the wilderness, "a desolate place," the Good Shepherd Jesus has arrived to spiritually guide them and feed them by His Word. His compassion moves Him to meet their greatest needs, their *spiritual* needs, and their other needs as well.

People Have Physical Needs We Should Address (Mark 6:35-37)

Jesus cares for our souls and our spiritual needs. He said, "For what does it benefit a man to gain the whole world yet lose his life?" (8:36). However, He also cares for our body and our physical needs. In Matthew 25:31-46 He tells us to feed the hungry, give water to the thirsty, give rest to the stranger, clothe the naked, care for the sick, and visit prisoners. There is no social gospel, but there are social ministries that are the natural outgrowth of the gospel. As Jesus had compassion for spiritual and physical needs, so should we.

The hour is now late. The disciples bring this to Jesus' attention and actually command Him to "send [the people] away" so they can "buy themselves something to eat." The tone of their request may be a bit harsh, but we can certainly understand the logic of it. Further, the people are becoming something of a nuisance.

The number of men present was five thousand. Add women and children and the number may have been between 15,000 and 20,000! This makes Jesus' response all the more outlandish: "You give them something to eat." The Twelve say, "Send them off," and Jesus says, "Feed them."

God wants us to have compassion on those in need, and He wants us involved in their lives meeting both spiritual and physical needs. We indeed minister to the whole person. That's what Jesus did.

Like Jesus We Should Seek to Meet the Needs of Others
MARK 6:37-44

It is one thing to recognize a legitimate need. It is another to do something about it (cf. Jas 2:14-17).

At first blush Jesus' command to feed them seems unreasonable, even insane. Still the disciples give it their best shot. Full of unbelief, they at least obey the instructions of their Master, and they will actually participate in one of the Lord's greatest miracles.

Do What Only You Can Do (Mark 6:37-40)

Given a command to feed the people, the apostles do a quick cost assessment. They calculate it would take two hundred denarii—eight months' wages—to feed the crowd. They do not have that kind of money. Strike one!

Jesus then asks them what they have. They quickly survey the crowd: five loaves and two fish. John 6:9 teaches us these sardines and crackers were given by a young boy. So all they have is the lunch a mother would pack for her boy. This is strike two!

The disciples obeyed, and this is all they were able to do. Their problem was now clearly beyond their resources. If Jesus does not intervene, then it's not going to happen. But He does intervene. He commands them to get organized, so in obedience they sit down by groups of fifties and hundreds (cf. Exod 18:21). Now let the party begin!

Trust Jesus to Do What Only He Can Do (Mark 6:41-42)

God loves to demonstrate His power and sufficiency in our lives. Often He allows problems to invade our lives that are far beyond our abilities or resources to handle. Why? He wants us to look to Him. Warren Wiersbe is exactly right: "Jesus looked at the situation, not as a problem, but as an opportunity to trust the Father and glorify His name" (*Be Diligent*, 65).

Jesus now serves as the Host of a messianic banquet. The desolate place becomes a place of plenty. As Moses met Israel's physical needs with manna and quail, a greater Moses, who is not only the "good shepherd" (John 10:11) but also the "bread of life" (John 6:35), will now feed His people with an abundant feast unlike any they have ever known.

He took the five loaves and two fish and blessed it. Perhaps He prayed the common table prayer of the Hebrews: "Praise be to you, O Lord our God, King of the world, who makes bread to come forth from the earth, and who provides for all that you have created" (Edwards, *Mark*, 192). Then He broke it into pieces and distributed it through the disciples to the people.

"And they all ate and were satisfied." None left hungry. His compassion is overflowing. His provision is satisfying.

Recognize That a Little Can Become a Lot with Jesus (Mark 6:43-44)

Following the banquet, the leftovers were gathered. It was 12 small baskets *full*, one for each of the apostles. Where we see a lack, Jesus sees abundance. Where we see human problems, He sees and accomplishes divine possibilities. A little can become a lot with Jesus!

Sally Lloyd-Jones writes, "The Bible is not a book of rules, or a book of heroes. The Bible is most of all a story. . . . You see, the best thing about this story is—it's true. There are lots of stories in the Bible, but all the stories are telling the one big story. The Story of how God loves his children and comes to rescue them" (*Storybook Bible*, 17). Jesus showed His love and came to the rescue in a desolate place to feed the five thousand. He showed His love and came to the rescue in a lonely place on a hill called Calvary. There is a great hero in the Bible. He is our God. He is our Rescuer. He is our Shepherd. He is our Savior. He is Jesus.

Spurgeon said, "Come, then, weary hungry sinner. You have nothing to do but to take Christ. . . . Open your mouth and receive the food! Faith to receive what Christ provides is all that is needed" (*Spurgeon's Sermons*, 21:1218).

Isaiah 40:11 says, "[The Lord] protects His flock like a shepherd; He gathers the lambs in His arms and carries them in the fold of His garment." Let Him gather you. Let Him carry you.

Reflect and Discuss

1. What do you think was Jesus' purpose in having the apostles report about their mission? What benefit is there in sharing failures with a group? What benefit in sharing successes?
2. Do you have a tendency to work too much or too little? When Jesus invited the disciples to come away to a remote place, what does that say about the balance of work and rest?

3. What would be your ideal timing for periods of rest? What kind of activity in what kind of place restores your spiritual energy and equips you to resume ministry with renewed vigor?
4. How is a spiritual sabbatical different from a vacation? Can the two be combined?
5. Have there ever been times that you were so tired you seemed to have no compassion? What is the remedy for this deficiency?
6. Are peoples' "felt needs" sometimes different from what they really need? How can you determine what are the real needs of the people to whom you minister?
7. How can we meet the physical needs of people without turning our ministry into a "social gospel"? How can we advance the gospel of salvation without neglecting the physical needs of people? How is the response of the crowd a warning for us (John 6:15,26-27)?
8. How did Jesus keep the feeding of the five thousand from being a mere social gospel? Was the miracle for the benefit of the crowd or for the disciples (see Mark 8:16-21)?
9. Have you ever known of a situation where the resources and manpower were clearly inadequate to complete the ministry task that God had unquestionably assigned? What happened?
10. What are some events that have brought you the most spiritual encouragement and prompted the most praise to God? Do these often arise out of impossible challenges?

Jesus: The One Who Walks on Water and Heals the Hurting

MARK 6:45-56

Main Idea: Jesus' miraculous acts of walking on water and healing point to His true identity as the great "I AM."

I. **Jesus Is the One in Whom We Should Have Faith (6:45-52).**
   A. We are guided by His plans (6:45).
   B. We are encouraged by His prayers (6:46).
   C. We are blessed by His power (6:47-50).
   D. We are blessed by His person (6:50-51).
   E. We are blessed by His patience (6:52).
II. **Jesus Is the One to Whom We Should Come When We Hurt (6:53-56).**
   A. Jesus can be sought by those in need (6:53-55).
   B. Jesus will bless those who believe in Him (6:56).

In the conflict between supernaturalism and naturalism, between miracles and rationalism, few stories draw the line in the sand more clearly than Jesus walking on the water. For example, the "Christian Biblical Errancy Debate" webpage states,

> If you are tired of having Bible-quoting friends and relatives throw Scripture in your face and would like to have an avalanche of information to throw back at them, you have come to the right place. . . . We provide a level playing field for Biblicists to defend the Bible's absurdities, contradictions, fallacies and inconsistencies. ("Welcome")

Now, how do they handle the absurdity of Jesus walking on water? Unlike the Enlightenment skeptics who postulated "an optical illusion caused by Jesus walking along the shore, or a deception caused by his walking on a sand bar" (Edwards, *Mark*, 196), they take the more postmodern approach and consign it to the fanciful world of mythology. They compare Jesus to the Egyptian sun god Horus who walked on mythical waters in another world. Their conclusion: "When it is conclusively proved that the Christian miracles are nothing more than a pagan mode of symbolic representation literalized, there is no longer any question of contravening, or breaking, or even challenging any well-known laws of nature. The discussion as to the probability or possibility of miracle on the old grounds of belief and doubt is closed for ever" (Massey, *Ancient Egypt*, 688). In other words, "dead men don't rise," and "men don't walk on water."

I hope you will not be surprised when I say I agree! Men don't rise from the dead, and they don't walk on water! However, God can do both. Further, Peter reminds us, "For we did not follow cleverly contrived myths when we made known to you the power and coming of our Lord Jesus Christ; instead, we were eyewitnesses of His majesty" (2 Pet 1:16). The early church knew of the mythical views of the Egyptians, Greeks, and Romans, and they rejected them. Instead, they followed and worshiped "what we have heard, what we have seen with our eyes, what we have observed and have touched with our hands" (1 John 1:1). This story has none of the trappings of mythology. It gives all the evidences of a real event told by an eyewitness (i.e., Peter). Finally, if Jesus was truly raised from the dead, we can also believe that He really walked on the water (Mark 6:45-52) and He really healed the hurting (6:53-56).

What, then, would God have us learn that we might not lack understanding or have a heart that is hardened (v. 52)? How should we respond to the "wonder on the water"?

Jesus Is the One in Whom We Should Have Faith
MARK 6:45-52

Jesus has just fed 15 or 20 thousand people (Mark 6:30-44). Messianic excitement is at a fever pitch. The crowds want to make Him king now (John 6:14-15). However, it is neither the time nor the means whereby He would receive His kingdom. A throne awaits Him, but there is a cross on the way.

This "man for others" has business to which He must attend before He sits on the throne prepared for Him by His Father (2 Sam 7:14-16; Pss 2; 110). He will reveal His deity on the Sea of Galilee. This obedient Son will do God's work in God's way and be glorified in it all, on the water and on the cross.

We Are Guided by His Plans (Mark 6:45)

Jesus takes control in this politically charged situation and makes the disciples "get into the boat and go ahead of Him to the other side, to Bethsaida." Thus the disciples are exactly where Jesus wants them to be. Spurgeon said, "Their sailing was not merely under his sanction, but by his express command. They were in the right place and yet they met with a terrible storm" (*Spurgeon's Sermons*, 55:3,128). Jesus purposefully sent them into trouble!

Jesus may indeed send us into trouble and difficulty but with a redemptive purpose. There our understanding of His providence and power is increased. There our faith and dependence on Him and Him alone grow. His plans are not always easy or what we want, but they are always best. Believe! Don't doubt.

We Are Encouraged by His Prayers (Mark 6:46)

Jesus leaves the crowd, goes up to an unspecified mountain (Mark calls it "*the* mountain") and prays.

Mark only records three times that Jesus prays: (1) at the beginning of the Gospel when His ministry is being defined (1:35); (2) here, in the middle of the Gospel after He feeds the five thousand (6:46); (3) near the end of His ministry in Gethsemane, just before He goes to the cross (14:32-42).

What do we learn? Any time He faced a critical moment, Jesus prayed. He most often got away and prayed in private. In each instance overtones of spiritual conflict and warfare were in the air (cf. Eph 6:18). Prayer for Jesus was intense. It was war. John Piper well says, "Until you believe that life is war, you cannot know what prayer is for" ("Prayer"). Jesus knew this better than any of us. He sought His Father in the heat of the battle raging about Him.

No doubt He prayed for *Himself.* No doubt He prayed for the *crowd* for whom He had compassion. And I suspect He prayed for His *disciples* who were in need of His prayers and His power.

We Are Blessed by His Power (Mark 6:47-50)

It is now late in the evening—the fourth watch of the night was between 3:00 and 6:00 a.m. The boat is at sea, and Jesus is alone on the land enjoying prayer communion with His Father.

He sees them (miraculously!) struggling on the sea. No doubt moved again with compassion (cf. v. 34), He does what no one had done before or since: "He came to them walking on the sea." Walking perhaps several miles[5] in pitch-black darkness, our Lord makes His way to those He has called, loves, and cares for. He knows where they are and what they are going through.

The phrase "He wanted to pass by them" has troubled many. David Garland summarizes the more common interpretations:

- Jesus intends to overtake the disciples and playfully surprise them on other side.
- Jesus wants to pass by but does not do so when He sees the disciple's distress. However, He had already seen their distress.
- Jesus is trying to test their faith.
- The phrase should be translated, "He was about to pass by them." But this is unlikely.
- The phrase refers to the disciples' mistaken impression—they think He intends to pass by them.
- The phrase means He intends simply to go beside them.
- Jesus wants to be seen walking on the sea but wishes to remain unrecognized—something that supposedly fits the author's theology of the messianic secret.
- Another view takes its cue from Amos 7:1–8:3 and interprets the phrase metaphorically: Jesus wanted to help the disciples in their difficulty (Garland, *Mark*, 262).

---

[5] The Sea of Galilee is over eight miles wide. Bethsaida is on the north end, so the "other side" could be as much as 13 miles away. Matthew 14:24 says, "The boat was already over a mile from land."

There is, however, a better understanding of this phrase rooted in the Old Testament understanding of a theophany, an appearance and manifestation of God Himself. In Exodus 33:18,20-23,

> *Then Moses said, "Please, let me see Your glory."*
> *. . . But He answered, "You cannot see My face, for no one can see Me and live." The LORD said, "Here is a place near Me. You are to stand on the rock, and when My glory passes by, I will put you in the crevice of the rock and cover you with My hand until I have passed by. Then I will take My hand away, and you will see My back, but My face will not be seen."*

And in 1 Kings 19:11 we see this encounter with Elijah: "Then He said, 'Go out and stand on the mountain in the LORD's presence.' At that moment, the LORD passed by."

As the Lord "passed by" Moses at Sinai and Elijah at Horeb, so now the God of the Old Testament, who is Christ, "wanted to pass by" His disciples so that they might see His glory and believe! Only God can walk on water, and Jesus is showing them beyond question that is who He is!

Unfortunately, the disciples still do not see (cf. Mark 8:17-18). Oh, they see someone walking on the sea, and they conclude it is an evil "water spirit," a "ghost" (Gk *phantasma*). It is no surprise that they scream in terror. I confess to some sympathy for them. I suspect all of us would have had the same reaction. A man—no, God—walking on the sea is not something you see every day or night.

In Matthew 14:28-31 we are given the record of Peter stepping out of the boat, walking on the water, sinking, and being rescued. But Mark is more interested in the One walking on the water than the ones in the boat. "The bread of life" (John 6:35) has just fed five thousand men plus women and children. The One who gives us "living water" (John 7:38) has just walked on the water. Mark chooses to focus on Him and His power to save and deliver. But He is not finished with his portrait of the deity of this divine Servant King!

We Are Blessed by His Person (Mark 6:50-51)

This miraculous event was not just about Jesus rescuing the disciples from their problem. It was a manifestation of His deity. Now He adds His words.

Seeking to calm the terror of the Twelve, Jesus gently speaks to them saying, "Have courage!" They are in the place of obedience, and Jesus is there.

Next He says, "It is I" (Gk *ego eimi*). We will return to this in a moment.

Third, He says, "Don't be afraid," a command telling them to stop an action in progress: "Stop fearing!"

"Then He got into the boat with them, and the wind ceased" (cf. 4:39). Their response? "They were completely astounded."

But now let us consider the statement, "It is I." In the Greek it is simply "I am." "Have courage!" Jesus says, "I am." These are the words God spoke to Moses at the burning bush (Exod 3:14)! Our Savior declares Himself to be the great "I AM" (John 8:58) who led the Hebrews out of Egypt and safely through the waters of the Red Sea. Jesus not only walks where only God can walk, He also bears God's name! The "I AM" has passed by, showing and declaring His deity. Deity is in the boat! The disciples are overwhelmed, but they still don't get it, and they won't until the resurrection.

We Are Blessed by His Patience (Mark 6:52)

Once again we see the disciples being exposed for their lack of trust in Jesus. The miracle "about the loaves," the feeding of the five thousand, did not make a lasting impression on them. They remain in ignorance, and their hearts are becoming callous. Believe it or not, I find encouragement here. I see myself in them. There is hope!

Jesus could feed 20,000 people. He had previously calmed the sea (4:35-41). Could He not protect them in this situation too? We say, "Yes God, I know You can, and that You have done _____, but my situation is different. I know You can do the impossible, but my situation *is beyond impossible.*" Not so with the God of Luke 1:37.

They receive no rebuke from their Master, the compassionate Shepherd (Mark 6:34). He knows they still have much to learn and endure. He will not give up on them. Praise God, He did not give up on us in our ignorance and hard-heartedness either!

Jesus is the One in whom we should have faith. He has proved Himself over and over.

Jesus Is the One to Whom We Should Come When We Hurt
MARK 6:53-56

Jesus has delivered the disciples from the storm on the sea. He now has more work to do.

No doubt this is a general summary of events that transpired over a period of time, as the word "wherever" would indicate. Once more the compassionate shepherd will care for His sheep without hesitation or discrimination. They hurt, and He heals. What a wonderful Savior He is!

Jesus Can Be Sought by Those in Need (Mark 6:53-55)

The boat lands in the area of Gennesaret (not Bethsaida). The strong winds had sovereignly sent them to a different location. More hurting people are in need of a helping hand, a divine touch. The people recognize Him, and they run throughout "the whole region" to bring the sick to Him.

Gregg Anderson, who works in the "Marketplace" focusing on those who serve in government, describes what was happening:

> Scenes such as those that greeted Jesus should be easily imagined.
> . . . Desperate times require utilizing any available resources and
> space. Two thousand years ago, the resources would have included
> the beds on which the infirm were brought to Jesus. . . . The best
> locations were deemed to be open-air marketplaces in cities large
> enough to have them and any open spaces in the villages and coun-
> tryside where everyone gathered to buy, sell, trade and socialize.
> From the "big city" to the suburbs to the country, the expectation
> was the same—with the needy all assembled in common areas where
> Jesus was likely to go, it was more likely they would experience the
> healing touch they sought. With the eager anticipation of a hospital
> patient and family members awaiting the physician's rounds, those
> gathered in advance of Jesus' arrival strained to see any indication of
> His imminent arrival. Many may very well have been long-time char-
> ity cases, suffering from their handicap for years. These, accustomed
> to begging to survive, were presumably the first to "implore Him."
> (Anderson, "Healing")

Jesus most certainly can be sought anywhere, anytime, and by anyone in need. There is not one whom He will turn away.

Jesus Will Bless Those Who Believe in Him (Mark 6:56)

Wherever He went, they brought the sick to Him, and He healed them. Minimally they believed He could heal, or they would not have come.

Men and women on mission for others brought people to the public square that they might meet and be healed by Jesus. Once there they "begged" continually (imperfect tense) to "touch just the tassel of His robe"—the tassels the law required as a reminder of the Lord's commands (Num 15:37-41; Deut 22:12).

And they were not disappointed: "And everyone who touched it was made well" (cf. Mark 5:27-29). There was nothing magical about the tassels. It was all about having faith in the One inside that garment: deity in a first-century Hebrew robe.

J. I. Packer says, "The true God is great and terrible, just because He is always with me and His eye is always upon me. Living becomes an awesome business when you realize that you spend every moment of your life in the sight and company of an omniscient, omnipotent Creator" (Packer, *Knowing God*, 86).

Jesus *knows* you better than you know yourself. He *loves* you more than you love yourself (which is a great deal). He is *more compassionate* than you could ever hope. He is *more powerful* than you could ever imagine. And He *knows your needs more perfectly* than you or I could ever comprehend. This "Bread of Life" allowed His body to be broken that your soul might receive the spiritual nourishment it needed. He walked the stormy waters through the dark night that led to the cross, so that He might rescue us and that we might never again be terrified or afraid. Through the wonderful touch of His bloody, redemptive hands, we can forever be healed of sin's diseases and made well forever. He walked across the stormy waters of judgment in our place, and He took on our sicknesses in His own body. "Take heart," He says. Understand, "I AM!"

Reflect and Discuss

1. If someone told you that it is impossible for a man to walk on water, how would you respond?
2. If someone suggested that the disciples created myths about Jesus after His death, how would you respond?
3. What was the crowd hoping for when they wanted to crown Jesus king immediately?
4. Have you ever felt that you were doing the will of God obediently, but you still ended up with trouble and difficulty? How did you feel during the trouble? How did it turn out in the end?
5. Mark records three of the instances when Jesus prayed (1:35; 6:46; 14:32-42). How might you change the time, place, and nature of your prayers in light of those accounts?
6. Try to imagine what you would have done if you had seen your favorite teacher walking on water. Why were the disciples terrified?
7. What are some of the other situations where God says, "Be courageous," or "Don't be afraid"? Where Jesus says, "I am . . ."?
8. How are you encouraged by the disciples' slowness to understand who Jesus was?

9. What does Jesus' willingness to heal all who came to Him mean for us today? How do we avoid the heresies of the "health and wealth gospel" or "moralistic therapeutic deism"?
10. How was the experience of being healed by touching the tassel of Christ's robe similar to the snake on a pole (Num 21:4-9)? How could this means be misunderstood (2 Kgs 18:4)?

The Deadly Lures of Legalism

MARK 7:1-23

Main Idea: Jesus calls us to trust not in our own external righteousness (legalism) but in His perfect work on our behalf.

I. **Legalists Honor God with Their Lips, Resulting in False Worship (7:1-8).**
    A. They love to compare themselves to others (7:1-5).
    B. They actually play the hypocrite with a distant heart (7:6-8).
II. **Legalists Make Void the Word of God, Resulting in Spiritual Disobedience (7:9-13).**
    A. They reject the commands of God and establish their own (7:9).
    B. They manipulate God's Word to their own advantage (7:10-13).
III. **Legalist Are Confused Concerning the Source of Defilement, Resulting in a Lack of True Understanding (7:14-23).**
    A. Defilement has its root on the inside (7:14-20).
    B. Defilement reveals its fruit on the outside (7:21-23).

Let me introduce you to a prospective church member. He will attend every service, including special events. He will go on mission trips with a passion to convert the heathen. He will tithe, sing in the choir, read his Bible daily, and memorize Scripture. He will be happy to pray in corporate worship. He is thoroughly orthodox in his theology. He is an inerrantist and believes in heaven and hell. He never gets drunk, is not addicted to porn, never uses profanity, is a family man, loves his country fervently, weeps on July 4, and votes the right way. His reputation in the community is stellar. If any man ever earned the right to go to heaven, it is this man. His religion is certainly something to admire.

Sadly this is a man headed for hell. I have just introduced you to a twenty-first-century Pharisee! A Pharisee in the first century was not scorned as a legalist. No, he was looked up to as a model citizen and a person of piety and religion. Unfortunately Pharisees had, as Paul says, a "zeal for God, but not according to knowledge" (Rom 10:2). Amazingly we can have a passion for God yet not know God. We can be deceived, captured, and enslaved by the deadly lure of legalism. Tragically, those who have been raised in the church are the most susceptible to this deception. Our pride in our religious rituals, church practices, and cultural traditions blind us to both our great sinfulness and the great Savior who alone can rescue us from our sin.

In *Mere Christianity* C. S. Lewis writes,

> There is one vice of which no man in the world is free; which everyone in the world loathes when he sees it in someone else; and of which hardly any people, except Christians, ever imagine that they are guilty themselves. I have heard people admit that they are bad-tempered, or that they cannot keep their heads about girls or drink, or even that they are cowards. I do not think I have ever heard anyone who was not a Christian accuse himself of this vice. And at the same time I have very seldom met anyone, who was not a Christian, who showed the slightest mercy to it in others. There is no fault which makes a man more unpopular, and no fault which we are more unconscious of in ourselves. And the more we have it ourselves, the more we dislike it in others. . . . The vice I am talking of is Pride or Self-Conceit. . . . Pride leads to every other vice: it is the complete anti-God state of mind. (Lewis, *Mere Christianity*, 108–9)

And the Scriptures contain harsh language to convey the Lord's disdain for pride:

> *The Lord protects the loyal, but fully repays the arrogant.* (Ps 31:23)

> *The Lord destroys the house of the proud.* (Prov 15:25)

> *Pride comes before destruction, and an arrogant spirit before a fall.* (Prov 16:18)

> *I will put an end to the pride of the arrogant.* (Isa 13:11)

> *As to the terror you cause, your presumptuous heart has deceived you. You who live in the clefts of the rock, you who occupy the mountain summit, though you elevate your nest like the eagle, even from there I will bring you down. This is the Lord's declaration.* (Jer 49:16)

> *For everyone who exalts himself will be humbled, and the one who humbles himself will be exalted.* (Luke 14:11)

God resists the proud, but gives grace to the humble. (Jas 4:6)

Why is God so opposed to pride? It is because human pride is in opposition to God. It thinks more of itself than it should. It thinks more of itself than God does! And amazingly, such pride may be lurking in unsuspecting locations, such as in religion in the guise of legalistic bondage to the traditions of men. What, then, does the deadly lure of legalism look like?

Legalists Honor God with Their Lips, Resulting in False Worship
MARK 7:1-8

Pharisees and scribes, teachers of the Torah (law), come again (cf. 3:22) from Jerusalem amid the growing popularity of Jesus. By now we know they are up to no good. They are certain they know who Jesus is, and they are determined to take Him down.

Too often we have our minds made up in advance as to the character of a person. With our opinions firmly formed, we look only for evidence that will confirm our judgments. Facts will not get in the way of our opinions. And if we cannot find a fault that will stick to him, then we will go after his friends, associates, and followers: "guilt by association." This is the strategy the Pharisees pursue. Too often we play the game as well.

They Love to Compare Themselves to Others (Mark 7:1-5)

The religious and spiritual elite surround Jesus looking for anything they can use to denounce Him. His disciples provide the perfect opportunity: they eat with "defiled," that is ceremonially unclean, unwashed hands. This had nothing to do with hygiene. It was all about ritual purity and religious traditions that went beyond scriptural command. These traditions were used to establish the spiritual superiority of the Pharisees and scribes over the common people. Writing to a Gentile, Roman audience, Mark provides an explanation:

> *For the Pharisees, in fact all the Jews, will not eat unless they wash their hands ritually, keeping the tradition of the elders. When they come from the marketplace, they do not eat unless they have washed. And there are many other customs they have received and keep, like the washing of cups, jugs, copper utensils, and dining couches.* (vv. 3-4)

So you might have touched something unclean, therefore you must wash. You might have touched a Gentile, so you must wash. If you disregard the "traditions of the elders," you sin.

Religious ritual and legalistic traditions had taken over their lives, enslaving them rather than freeing them. However, they are blind to their own self-imposed bondage, so they challenge Jesus with an air of pride, spiritual superiority, and self-righteousness, asking Him, "Why don't Your disciples live according to the tradition of the elders?" Even they cannot cite a scriptural justification for their practice. No matter. They perceive themselves to be firmly established in the "religious right." Jesus and His disciples were not.

All this religious washing had a good intent, namely to remind Jews that they were unclean before God. But they were completely off base on the true source of their impurity. Their problem was not outside but inside. It wasn't their hands but their hearts.

However, it is pretty difficult to compare hearts, which only God can see. So instead, they decided to draw up a list of external religious activities and see who came out on top. That is much easier.

They Actually Play the Hypocrite with a Distant Heart (Mark 7:6-8)

One thing Jesus consistently did was call out hypocrites and expose them for who they truly were. Jesus makes no reference to the conduct of His disciples. Instead, He exposes the heart of the matter: Is the true source of spiritual authority "traditions of men," or is it the "Word of God"? What will determine how you think and live your life?

Jesus begins with a scathing indictment, calling the Pharisees and scribes "hypocrites"! They were nothing more than religious actors and pretenders. The prophet Isaiah also condemned their hypocritical religion (Isa 29:13). They say the right things about God, but their hearts are still ungodly. Their religion is all words and show. The result was vain, purposeless worship—worship that God neither welcomes nor receives. For evidence, Jesus says they teach as doctrines the commands of men, and they abandon the command of God and hold to the traditions of man. They held that the ultimate authority for spiritual life was both Scripture and tradition, but if there was a conflict between the two, tradition won out every time. Sometimes the Bible wasn't even considered. "We have our traditions. That is all we need."

Some potential examples of this legalism in the contemporary church can be found in church business meetings, deacons meetings, church discipline, and religious practices (e.g., church names, meeting times, dress, worship styles, public invitation or no invitation). If we have all the right boxes checked, we're good! But lists are so easy to check off. Examining our hearts isn't. Can you provide a scriptural basis for what you believe and do? Are you a text-driven or tradition-driven Christian? The difference is crucial.

Legalists Make Void the Word of God, Resulting in Spiritual Disobedience
MARK 7:9-13

Not all traditions are bad. They become bad when we put them on the same level as Scripture or in the place of Scripture. It is a "Bible-plus" kind of religion. In adding to the Bible, you for all practical purposes make void the Bible and nullify its truth and power in your life (v. 13). Jesus makes this crystal clear as He moves into round two with the Pharisees. Again, it is no contest. The "beat down" is ugly! And the exposure of sinful hearts is painful.

They Reject the Commands of God and Establish Their Own (Mark 7:9)

A. T. Robertson noted "the strong contrast here between the command of God and the traditions of men" (*Word Pictures*, 322). They think they are establishing the command of God, protecting it. In actuality they are rejecting God's commands, and in the process they establish their traditions as if they were God's commands. They set aside what is the revealed Word of God and replace it with "made up" traditions of men. How ludicrous! How insane! How human.

Man-made rules and regulations become the object of obedience while God's commands get set aside. "The constitution and bylaws have the final word in this church." I have seen it. I have heard it with my own ears. Warren Wiersbe says, "We must constantly beware lest tradition take the place of truth. It does us good to examine our church traditions in the light of God's Word and to be courageous enough to make changes" (*Be Diligent*, 71).

We foolishly push away the only trustworthy and infallible source of authority. It is an act of pure spiritual suicide. Have you seen the sad progression? First, they teach the commands of men (v. 7). Then they leave the commands of God (v. 8). Next they reject the commands of God (v. 9). And finally they make void the Word of God (v. 13). And if we are not careful, we will fail to see our own hypocrisy in this progression. Oh, we know it is possible to be a hypocrite. We see it so clearly in others. It is when it is in us that we go spiritually deaf, dumb, and blind.

They Manipulate God's Word to Their Own Advantage (Mark 7:10-13)

Jesus now gives His own example that settles the issue. The verdict will not please the religious elite. He goes to the Scriptures, the writings of Moses, pointing out what they clearly teach. Exodus 20:12 and Deuteronomy 5:16 both contain the fifth commandment: "Honor your father and mother." Exodus 21:17 and Leviticus 20:9 show the punishment for breaking this command: "Whoever curses his father or his mother must be put to death." The principle is clear: God calls children to honor and respect their parents.

However, the Pharisees created a theological loophole. They simply declared what they would have given to their parents "Corban," a Hebrew term referring to "a gift dedicated to God." This allowed them to dishonor their parents by neglecting their needs, but they still feel good about it because it was done in service to God. "I serve God by disobeying His expressed command to honor my parents." What kind of logic is that?!

Jesus tells them that kind of reasoning makes void the Word of God, sets up man-made traditions over God's commands, and opens the door for many more such actions (Mark 7:13). That kind of reasoning reveals the hardness of our hearts, the hypocrisy of our worship, and the disobedience of our actions, all in the name of religion! These are not atheists and secularists. These are the religious and spiritual leaders of Israel.

They had positioned their traditions in the place of Scripture and themselves in the place of God. The heart truly is an idol factory, and religious traditions are some of its best tools. This truth should concern us all. I may be as guilty as the Pharisees of Jesus' day and not even see it.

Legalists Are Confused Concerning the Source of Defilement, Resulting in a Lack of True Understanding
MARK 7:14-23

Every human heart has the root of every human sin in it. It is entirely possible to look nice on the outside while being dead on the inside. The most deadly contamination is not what I touch. The most deadly contamination is what is in my heart.

Defilement Has Its Root on the Inside (Mark 7:14-20)

Jesus charges all who are listening in on the theological debate to pay attention and understand. He then delivers a little parable. When His disciples ask the meaning of this parable, Jesus once again (cf. 6:52; 8:17-18) chides them for their lack of understanding. This is one of the most critically important spiritual lessons in the whole Word of God. Jesus explains that corruption is not external but internal. Impurity is not a matter of the stomach but of the heart. Defilement is not what goes in but what comes out.

Jesus' words are spiritually revolutionary! He is saying that the real issues of religious and spiritual faith are internal not external. Sin always proceeds from within. Food ends up in the stomach, but sin begins in the heart. Food is eaten, digested in the stomach, and expelled. Sin, however, remains in the heart and then produces all manner of defilement and death. The basic problem of fallen humanity is not *what we do* but *who we are*! Real filth, impurity, and defilement are inside and unseen, but eventually they will show themselves, as verses 21-23 make clear.

By the way, note Mark's editorial comment in verse 19: "As a result, He made all foods clean." I believe the study note in the *ESV Study Bible* (emphasis in original) captures the meaning succinctly:

> Mark notes that Jesus' teaching, in essence, **declared all foods clean.** The Mosaic ceremonial laws distinguished between "clean" and "unclean" foods (see Lev. 11:1-47). Their purpose was to instill an awareness of God's holiness and of the reality of sin as a barrier to fellowship with God. But once defilement of the heart is thoroughly removed and full fellowship with God becomes a reality (through the atoning death of Jesus; see Mark 10:45; Rom. 14:14; Heb. 8:6-13; 9:10,14), the ceremonial laws have fulfilled their purpose and are no longer required.

The point is quite simple: it was always about the heart.

Defilement Reveals Its Fruit on the Outside (Mark 7:21-23)

Mark Dever calls verses 21-23 "the fingers of sin" ("Jesus and Filth"). They are evidence of a corrupt heart. Inevitably, sin's root will produce sin's fruit. And it is an ugly, destructive crop to behold. Jesus provides a selective list of sin's fruit. He highlights no less than 13 characteristics of the evil actions that flow naturally from a sinful heart—actions that always result in sorrow, harmful behavior, and death. The list has a strong Old Testament grounding.

Evil Thoughts	Evil devising and schemes. They set the stage for what follows.
Sexual Immorality *(porneia)*	General word identifying any and all sexual sins contrary to God's will. It includes premarital, extramarital, and unnatural sexual behavior.
Theft	Stealing. Taking from another what is not yours. The eighth commandment (Exod 20:15; Deut 5:19).
Murder	Taking an innocent life. The sixth commandment (Exod 20:13; Deut 5:17).
Adultery	Violating the marriage covenant by engaging in sexual behavior mentally (Matt 5:28) or physically with someone you are not married to. The seventh commandment (Exod 20:14; Deut 5:18).
Greed	Coveting, a desire for more at the expense or exploitation of another. The tenth commandment (Exod 20:17; Deut 5:21).
Evil Actions	Behavior that is bad, wicked; deliberate malice.
Deceit	Deception, dishonesty, cunning treachery.
Promiscuity	Unbridled, shameless living that is lacking in moral discernment or restraint.
Stinginess (lit. "an evil eye")	Figure of speech for envy, jealousy, rooted in unbelief. It believes God is withholding His best from you. A heart ailment that has the seeds of its own destruction sown within. It is never satisfied! It always wants more.
Blasphemy	Slander; defaming; speaking evil of man or God.
Pride	Arrogance, haughtiness.
Foolishness	Senselessness; spiritual insensitivity.

These evil actions arise from one's heart, which is the source of sin that condemns.

Conclusion

There are basically only two approaches to religion, each of which can be summed up in a single word: *do* or *done*. The world says the problem is out there, and the solution is to answer the question, What can I do? The Bible says the problem is inside of us, and the answer is what Christ has done! You see, in legalism we think better of ourselves than Jesus does. But in salvation we think the same of ourselves as Jesus does: we are hopeless, helpless sinners in desperate need of a Savior.

First Samuel 16:7 says, "Man does not see what the Lord sees, for man sees what is visible, but the Lord sees the heart." When the Lord examines your heart, what does He see? Does He see a self-righteous legalist trusting in what "I do" or a humble sinner trusting only in what Jesus has done? The difference is of eternal significance.

Reflect and Discuss

1. Would the Romans of Jesus' day likely consider pride a vice or a virtue? How do non-Christians generally view pride today?
2. What is different about the Christian worldview that makes us have a different judgment on the value of pride?
3. What is the connection between pride and legalism?
4. Do you have any tendencies toward legalism? How would you recognize such tendencies in yourself? How would you battle against them?
5. What is wrong with the logic behind "guilt by association"? Do you know a person who is godly but who chooses to associate with less reputable types?
6. Which rituals in your church are possible to do as merely external show without necessitating an internal spiritual reality?
7. Which of your practices are long-held traditions that have no basis in Scripture?
8. What are some of your least favorite or most challenging verses in the Bible? Do you sometimes create ways to excuse yourself from obeying those verses, perhaps by employing some work-around or a fanciful interpretation?
9. In what ways do other religions focus on external actions? How is Christianity different from each of those religions?
10. What is the remedy for the list of sinful heart conditions? Why is "trying harder" inadequate and even counterproductive?

Jesus Christ: The God Who Astonishes Beyond Measure

MARK 7:24-37

Main Idea: No one is so unworthy that they cannot receive the blessing of Jesus Christ.

I. **Jesus Is the Savior Who Cannot Be Hidden (7:24-30).**
   A. Jesus cares for the nations, and so should we (7:24).
   B. Jesus cares for the Jews, and so should we (7:25-27).
   C. Jesus cares for the individual, and so should we (7:28-30).
II. **Jesus Is the Savior Who Does All Things Well (7:31-37).**
   A. Jesus hears our cries for help (7:31-35).
   B. Jesus deserves our praise for all He does (7:36-37).

Jesus Christ is the *greatest missionary* who ever lived. He came the *greatest distance*, from heaven to earth, to bring the good news of salvation. He also made the *greatest sacrifice*, giving His life in the place of sinners that we might be reconciled to God. Yet in spite of having no planes or trains or cars, in His brief three years of earthly ministry He made time to travel to foreign soil to give us a glimpse of Great Commission Christianity, demonstrating beyond question that God's kingdom knows no ethnic, racial, national, or gender barriers. Indeed, all who come to Him will find salvation from the One who "could not escape notice" (v. 24), the One who does "everything well" (v. 37).

Mark sets side by side two healing miracles that take place in pagan, Gentile territory. One is the healing of a demon-possessed little girl (vv. 24-30). The other is the healing of a deaf man with a speech impediment (vv. 31-37). Both demonstrate that God's kingdom has come and that Jesus is God's man for all peoples. Contrary to religious and racial bigots, no one is so unclean that they cannot receive the blessing and the touch of Jesus Christ—the God who astonishes (v. 37).

Jesus Is the Savior Who Cannot Be Hidden
MARK 7:24-30

Our Lord knew that His Father had mapped out His life from beginning to end. It would involve days of happiness as well as times of trial and opposition, pressure and disappointment. Jesus has just engaged the Pharisees in a heated discussion over religion versus the gospel (vv. 1-23). Things are building to an inevitable showdown that will result in His crucifixion. However, it is not yet the appointed time. So Jesus leaves Galilee to get away from His enemies, spend some teaching time with His disciples, and get a little R & R. However, He is denied the last and, in the process, teaches us spiritual truths about the heart of God.

Jesus Cares for the Nations, and So Should We (Mark 7:24)

Jesus heads north to the district of Phoenicia—what is today Lebanon—to the seaport city of Tyre. He went there primarily to get away to rest, but "He could not escape notice." This is not surprising, especially since a delegation from Tyre and Sidon had earlier come down to see Him (3:8). Further, the brilliant glory of the Son of God cannot be hidden!

That Jesus chose to get away in the region of Tyre and Sidon is missiologically significant. As best we can tell, this is the only time Jesus ventured beyond the borders of Israel. Further, Tyre and Sidon were inhabited by pagan Gentiles, and the region had a long history of opposition to Israel. This had been the home of Jezebel (1 Kgs 16:31-32). Both Ezekiel (ch. 26) and Zechariah (ch. 9) prophesied against her. James Edwards says, "Tyre probably represented the most extreme expression of paganism, both actually and symbolically, that a Jew could expect to encounter" (Edwards, *Mark*, 217). Yet Jesus goes there and graciously expands the scope and reach of the Messiah beyond what Israel expected. Unfortunately, like Jonah, too many Jews of that day could not imagine that God would extend His salvation beyond the borders of Israel. "From a socioreligious perspective, Jesus' visit to Tyre universalizes the concept of Messiah in terms of geography, ethnicity, gender and religion in a way entirely unprecedented in Judaism" (Edwards, *Mark*, 217). This Savior is not for just one nation. He is for all nations, and we should be as well.

Jesus Cares for the Jews, and So Should We (Mark 7:25-27)

Word gets out quickly that Jesus is in the house. A most unlikely individual shows up asking for His help. She is a woman, she is a Gentile, and she is a Syrophoenician by birth. Matthew 15:22 calls her "a Canaanite woman." A pagan, Gentile woman could not have been further from "the citizenship of Israel" (Eph 2:12). No doubt she knew how socially unacceptable it was for her to approach a Jewish rabbi on any level. Yet she "kept on asking" Jesus "to drive the demon out of her daughter." She came boldly but humbly ("she fell at His feet"), and she was persistent.

Jesus' verbal response is one of the most shocking and controversial statements He ever made. "He said to her, 'Allow the children to be satisfied first, because it isn't right to take the children's bread and throw it to the dogs.'" This sounds like a massive insult unworthy of our Lord. Yes, Jews often referred to Gentiles as dogs—unclean scavengers unworthy of salvation. Is this what Jesus meant? Not at all. (1) The very words of Jesus are something of a parable rather than a direct statement. (2) The word for "dogs" is a word that corresponds to our word *puppies*. It is not a street scavenger but a household pet, which the parable makes clear. (3) There is the crucial word "first." Jesus was, I believe, testing the woman's faith by saying, "I must first minister to Israel before I minister to Gentiles." Paul said the same thing in Romans 1:16: "For I am not ashamed of the gospel, because it is God's power for salvation to everyone who believes, first to the Jew, and also to the Greek."

Our Lord has a deep love for the Jewish nation. He wept bitterly over her rejection of Him as her Messiah (Matt 23:37). In spite of her unbelief, He still loves her. God is not through with the Jews! Paul in Romans 11:25-29 makes this crystal clear:

> So that you will not be conceited, brothers, I do not want you to be unaware
> of this mystery: A partial hardening has come to Israel until the full number
> of the Gentiles has come in. And in this way all Israel will be saved, as it is
> written, "The Liberator will come from Zion; He will turn away ungodliness
> from Jacob. And this will be My covenant with them when I take away
> their sins." Regarding the gospel, they are enemies for your advantage, but
> regarding election, they are loved because of the patriarchs, since God's
> gracious gifts and calling are irrevocable.

God cares for the Jews, and so should we.

Jesus Cares for the Individual, and So Should We (Mark 7:28-30)

It would have been easy for this woman to walk away in bitter disappointment. Yet she fires back with a burst of boldness! Tim Keller says, "There are cowards, there are regular people, there are heroes, and then there are parents. Parents are not really on the spectrum from cowardice to courage because if your child is in jeopardy, you simply do what it takes to save her" (*King's Cross*, 86). With wit, courage, and faith, the woman responds. She does not take offense. She does not question the accuracy of Jesus' words. She simply and humbly carries His analogy one step further. "Lord, even the dogs under the table eat the children's crumbs." What insight! What humility! What faith! Jesus commends her for what He calls "mega faith" (Matt 15:28) and dismisses her with the promise that her daughter is healed.

What a magnificent picture of salvation we have in this story! Yes Lord, we are all dogs under the table with no rights whatsoever as members of the family. I acknowledge I don't deserve a place *at* the table, but I believe there is enough even for me *on* the table! Just a few crumbs will be enough. That I believe. Then in amazing grace and mercy our Savior lifts us up, no longer a dog (sinner) but a child (saved), no longer under the table but now a member of the family at the table.

Are you willing to see yourself as the dog you are that you might be transformed into the child you might become? Perhaps your sin is greater than you realize, but His grace is greater than you could ever imagine.

Jesus Is the Savior Who Does All Things Well
MARK 7:31-37

Perhaps this particular miracle had special significance to Peter, the eyewitness source for much of Mark's Gospel, because he saw it as a physical parallel to his own spiritual experience. I can identify with that!

Jesus went north to Sidon before turning southeast to the region of the Decapolis ("10 cities"). All together this horseshoe-shaped journey would have constituted a 120-mile walk. It is an unusual course. It may have been taken to further avoid the Herodians and Pharisees who were after Him. It may also have been intended as an extension of His ministry to the Gentiles. More dogs are to receive crumbs from His table.

Jesus Hears Our Cries for Help (Mark 7:31-35)

A man is brought to Jesus who was deaf and had a speech impediment. Like the Syrophoenician woman, the man's friends were persistent in begging Jesus to lay His hand on the man. That they did not specifically ask for healing may indicate that all they were asking for was our Lord's blessing. This they would receive, and more!

Jesus takes the man aside. His attention is personal and compassionate. Entering the man's world, our Lord uses "sign language."

> The man could not hear Jesus and he was also incapable of verbal communication. So Jesus "spoke" to him in the language he could understand—sign-language. The fingers placed in his ears and then removed meant, "I am going to remove the blockage in your hearing." The spitting and the touching of the man's tongue meant, "I

am going to remove the blockage in your mouth." The glance up to heaven meant, "It is God alone who is able to do this for you." Jesus wanted the man to understand that it was not magic but God's grace that healed him. (Ferguson, *Mark*, 116)

As Jesus looked up to heaven, first He sighed. I believe this is an expression of our Lord's love and compassion for this man and also His great grief over the fall of man and the terrible consequences of sin. It is the sigh of God over a broken creation. Second, He said, in Aramaic, "Ephphatha," that is, "Be opened." The result is given in simple, straightforward language: "Immediately his ears were opened, his speech difficulty was removed, and he began to speak clearly" (v. 35). The original text says literally, "The shackle of his tongue was released." Like a prisoner bound in chains, Jesus broke the fetters of his captivity and set him free.

Jesus Deserves Our Praise for All He Does (Mark 7:36-37)

One can only imagine the first words of clear speech uttered by this man. No doubt he was praising and glorifying God. Jesus charged him and his friends not to spread the news (v. 36), "But the more He would order them, the more they would proclaim it." We cannot condone their disobedience, but we certainly can understand their response.

Mark's conclusion has deep theological significance. "He has done everything well (good)" echoes creation and God's work in Genesis 1–2. "He even makes deaf people hear, and people unable to speak, talk" recalls Isaiah, who wrote that when the Messiah comes, "the eyes of the blind will be opened, and the ears of the deaf unstopped. Then the lame man will leap like a deer, and the tongue of the mute will sing for joy, for waters will gush in the wilderness, and streams in the desert" (Isa 35:5-6). Again James Edwards captures the great significance of this when he writes:

> The allusion of Isaiah 35 is of supreme significance for Mark's presentation of Jesus, not only because the restoration of speech signals the eschatological arrival of the Day of the Lord but also because the desert wastelands of *Lebanon* (Isa 35:2) will receive the joy of God. The regions of Tyre and Sidon are, of course, precisely the Lebanon of Isaiah 35. Jesus' healing . . . in the Decapolis becomes the firstfruit of the fulfillment of Isa 35:10, that Gentile Lebanon will join "the ransom of the Lord [and] enter Zion with singing"! Salvation thus comes to the Gentile world in Jesus, who is God's eschatological redeemer from Zion. As we have noted before, the only categories adequate for Mark to describe the person and work of Jesus are ultimately the categories of God. Once again, as in the story of the Syrophoenician

woman (7:24-30), "salvation is from the Jews" (John 4:22). (Edwards, *Mark*, 224–25; emphasis in original)

Thus we see the "grand redemptive storyline" in a miracle put on display. Creation (what God does is good) → Fall (a man deaf because of sin) → Redemption (the miracle of healing) → Restoration (God's kingdom has arrived). Oh, there is so much here we need to see! There is so much here we need to "zealously proclaim."

A beautiful hymn written by Charles Wesley wonderfully captures the heart of this text as well as our joyful response. "Hear" the words of stanzas 1, 4, and 5.

> 1. O for a thousand tongues to sing
>   My great Redeemer's praise
> The glories of my God and King
>   The triumphs of His grace!

> 4. Hear Him, ye deaf; His praise, ye dumb,
>   Your loosened tongues employ,
> Ye blind, behold your Saviour come;
>   And leap, ye lame, for joy!

> 5. My gracious Master and my God,
>   Assist me to proclaim,
> To spread through all the earth abroad
>   The honours of Thy Name. (Wesley, "Thousand Tongues," 1739)

Jesus is the God who cannot be hidden. He is the Lord who does all things well!

Reflect and Discuss

1. What constitutes an effective missionary strategy in our day? How did Jesus begin to instruct His followers about successful missions?
2. Is there any nation you would be tempted to skip over in missions? What makes them unworthy in your mind? What would Jesus do?
3. What should be our attitude toward the Jewish people as a political nation? As individual souls?
4. Why would Jesus' ministry in Gentile lands have shocked His disciples? How does it presage Peter and Paul's ministries in the book of Acts?
5. Why was the Syrophoenician woman happy with mere "crumbs"? What can we learn from her attitude?
6. How can boldness and humility both be demonstrated at the same time in our prayers?
7. How would you respond to someone who suggested that Jesus was using some kind of magic in 7:33-34?

8. Why do you think Jesus "sighed deeply" before he healed the deaf man? How does that encourage your faith in Him?
9. How was Jesus' healing ministry associated with the gospel of a restored relationship with God?
10. What part do the old hymns play in your worship experience? How do new songs and choruses help you perceive and worship God?

Sometimes We Just Don't Get It!

MARK 8:1-26

Main Idea: Jesus has the power to overcome our spiritual blindness and open our eyes that we may see.

I. Jesus Always Has a Plan, but We May Only See a Problem (8:1-10).
- A. Jesus cares (8:1-3).
- B. Jesus provides (8:4-7).
- C. Jesus satisfies (8:8-10).

II. Unbelievers Will Demand a Sign but Reject One When They See It (8:11-13).
- A. They test the Lord (8:11).
- B. They grieve the Lord (8:12).
- C. They lose the Lord (8:13).

III. Disciples Will See Great Works but Fail to Fully Understand (8:14-21).
- A. We still may misunderstand our Lord's words (8:14-16).
- B. We still may misunderstand our Lord's work (8:17-21).

IV. The Blind May See, but It May Come Gradually (8:22-26).
- A. We can bring the hurting to Jesus (8:22).
- B. We can trust the hurting to Jesus (8:23-26).

Repetition is a wonderful and effective teacher. Sometimes on the first, second, and even third attempt, we just don't get it. If you are a slow learner like me, it may be on the eleventh try that a valuable lesson finally sinks in. Take heart. We are in good company! The apostles were just like us.

Mark 8:1-30 parallels 6:30–7:37. We have similar events recorded in the same order.

1.	Feeding of a great multitude.	6:30-44 || 8:1-9
2.	A boat trip	6:45-56 || 8:10
3.	Confrontation with the Pharisees	7:1-23 || 8:11-13

4. A conversation about bread	7:24-30 ‖ 8:14-21
5. A miraculous healing	7:31-36 ‖ 8:22-26
6. A significant confession	7:37 ‖ 8:27-29

These events likely happened this way in terms of their *history*. I also believe Mark recorded them in this order for the purpose of *theology*, especially as it relates to discipleship. Remembering what we have seen our Lord do in the past should help us trust Him in the present. Unfortunately, we are sometimes forgetful and even hard-hearted (8:17). In spite of seeing the Lord work in our past, we are not sure He can handle our present. We just don't get it. Four events in Mark 8:1-26 will prepare us for the great confession of Peter in 8:29. They, in a sense, bring us to the end of the first part of this, the shortest of the Gospels.

Jesus Always Has a Plan, but We May Only See a Problem
MARK 8:1-10

"In those days" informs us that the miracle of the feeding of four thousand people probably took place in the region of Decapolis (7:31) as an extension of the Lord's mission to the Gentiles—though some Jews may also have been present.

Some skeptics have denied there were two feedings, arguing that the author of Mark somehow got the tradition confused. However, there is no confusion; there are clear differences:

FEEDING THE 5,000	FEEDING THE 4,000
5,000 men (15,000–20,000 people)	4,000 people total
5 loaves and 2 fish	7 loaves and a few small fish
1 day in the wilderness	3 days in the wilderness
springtime/North of Galilee	no mention of time/SE of Galilee
12 basketfulls of leftovers	7 basketfulls of leftovers
one prayer	two prayers
mostly Jews	mostly Gentiles

Further, and most decisively, Jesus clearly states there were two feedings in 8:19-20.

Jesus has a plan. He wants us to see His love and concern for Gentiles as well as Jews. Yes, He is the long-expected Jewish Messiah. He is also the Savior of the world (John 3:16).

Jesus Cares (Mark 8:1-3)

In 6:34, Mark said Jesus had compassion because He acted compassionately. Now Jesus Himself says He has compassion.

Jesus emphasizes that the crowd has nothing to eat. He also says, "If I send them home hungry, they will collapse on the way, and some of them have come a long distance." What careful attention to their situation! He saw their need just as He sees yours and mine!

Jesus Provides (Mark 8:4-7)

Once again Jesus involves His disciples in the problem. This is another teachable moment. So He calls them to Himself (v. 1), shares His heart (v. 2), and explains the situation (vv. 2-3).

The Twelve respond with a question. It is not one of unbelief as much as it is of their bad location and lack of resources (v. 4). The implication is, "We can do nothing. What then will You do? Jesus, You are the only hope!" Good!

Jesus quickly moves into action. First, He finds out just what is available. Second, He seats the crowd, blesses the bread, and gives it to the disciples to distribute. Third, a few sardines are discovered. He blesses these and the newly created dead fish that are perfectly edible (!), and He has the Twelve pass those out as well. Twice He has taught the people to thank God for their daily provision and to trust Him as their sole and sufficient resource to give them what they need. This miracle also "foreshadows the gathering together of those from every nation under heaven to the heavenly feeding of God's people" (Ferguson, *Mark*, 119).

Jesus Satisfies (Mark 8:8-10)

"They ate and were filled." They gathered the leftovers and filled "seven large baskets," not small baskets like before (cf. 6:43). Jesus could now send them on their way home.

Just another normal day in the life of Messiah Jesus, who satisfies all who follow Him. A little can become a lot in the hands of the Creator God. This is a sign of the inbreaking of God's kingdom. However, some still just don't get it. Time to move to act 2.

Unbelievers Will Demand a Sign but Reject One When They See It
MARK 8:11-13

Mark abruptly introduces another conflict with the religious Gestapo—the Pharisees. We have been here before (2:6-7,16,18,24; 3:1-6,22; 7:1-5). In spite of His numerous miracles and teachings that give evidence that He is the Messiah, they reject what they see and hear, and they raise the stakes in their confrontation with Jesus. "My mind is made up about this fellow Jesus. Let's not let the facts get in the way."

They Test the Lord (Mark 8:11)

Mark says they began to argue with Him. Perhaps this is a resumption of the conflict in 3:22-30 and 7:1-5. They ask for "a sign from heaven," something that would demonstrate *what He is doing*, something they amazingly do not deny is truly of God. Their motive was "to test Him." Their goal is again to discredit Him before the people, not to test Him with a view of authenticating His ministry. It is one thing to put the Lord to a test in faith. It is another thing to test Him in unbelief.

They Grieve the Lord (Mark 8:12)

For the second time in two chapters, our Lord "sighs" with deep emotion. This time His anguish was directed at minds that refused the evidence, hearts that remained hard, eyes that refused to see, and ears that refused to hear (cf. 8:17-18). In effect He said, "You want a sign? Read the Scriptures! Listen to My words. See what I do! Beyond that, *'No sign will be given to this generation!'* If you cannot see God at work in Me, no evidence will convince you otherwise. Your demand is just an expression of unbelief. I will not play your evil and wicked game."

They Lose the Lord (Mark 8:13)

Nothing more can be said. Abruptly, as if a sign of divine judgment, Jesus leaves them. These religious zealots were physically so close to our Lord, but they had never been further away where it really mattered: in their hearts. They have lost Him. Not long from now they will crucify Him. Unbelief is evil and tragic when it says no to the gospel and God's Son.

Disciples Will See Great Works but Fail to Fully Understand
MARK 8:14-21

The Pharisees were not the only ones who did not understand, who had hardened hearts and did not spiritually see or hear. However, unlike the unbelieving Pharisees who were moving in the wrong direction, the disciples were making progress, slow though it was. They still had a ways to go, as verses 14-21 and also 32-34 so plainly testify.

We Still May Misunderstand Our Lord's Words (Mark 8:14-16)

They got in the boat with only "one loaf of bread." It is amazing that with seven large basketfulls, this is all they snagged. They began to discuss their predicament, perhaps even blaming one another. They failed to see the irony of the situation, and they forgot who was in the boat and what He could do!

Jesus used the visual aid at hand to teach them. He cautioned them, "Watch out! Beware of the yeast of the Pharisees and the yeast of Herod." A small amount of leaven will permeate a whole batch of bread dough. The leaven of unbelief has gripped the hearts of the Pharisees and Herod and has taken control of their entire lives. Watch out! Don't let unbelief take you down and away from the divine truth you see and hear in Me.

They don't get it, and they begin again to talk about having only one loaf of bread. Jesus is speaking of spiritual matters, but their minds are stuck on the mundane.

We Still May Misunderstand Our Lord's Work (Mark 8:17-21)

Jesus steps in with a series of questions:

1. "Why are you discussing that you do not have any bread?" Uh . . . (v. 17).
2. "Don't you understand or comprehend?" Sadly, no (v. 17).
3. "Is your heart hardened?" Sadly, yes (v. 17).
4. "Do you have eyes, and not see?" Sadly, yes (v. 18).
5. "Do you have ears, and not hear?" Sadly, yes (v. 18).
6. "Do you not remember?" Apparently not (v. 18).
7. "When I broke the five loaves for the five thousand, how many basketfulls of pieces of bread did you collect?" Uh, twelve (v. 19).
8. "When I broke the seven loaves for the four thousand, how many large basketfulls of pieces of bread did you collect?" Uh, seven (v. 20).
9. "Don't you understand yet?" Again, apparently not (v. 21)!

These questions are not intended to shame but to instruct. For sure, they are slow learners, but then, so are we. How hesitant we are to embrace the truth of Luke 1:37 ("For nothing will be impossible with God."), of Philippians 4:12-13 ("I both know how to have a little, and I know how to have a lot. In any and all circumstances I have learned the secret of being content—whether well fed or hungry, whether in abundance or in need. I am able to do all things through Him who strengthens me."), and of Philippians 4:19 ("And my God will supply all your needs according to His riches in glory in Christ Jesus."). Like the 12 apostles, we often see our Lord's great works in our lives but still fail to fully understand and trust Him.

The Blind May See, but It May Come Gradually
MARK 8:22-26

These verses constitute a visual parable that, though historically true, also symbolizes the spiritual pilgrimage of the disciples. Mark purposely sandwiches it between 8:14-21 and 8:27-38. The two-step healing Jesus uses is intentional. It is meant to portray the gradual, step-by-step understanding of the disciples.

Jesus could have healed this man instantly. That He doesn't is pedagogical. The disciples are slowly coming to see and understand that Jesus is the Messiah. However, even after Peter's great confession in 8:29, they still have only partial sight and understanding. He is not the kind of Messiah they expected. Only after the cross and resurrection do they finally get it. They are just like this blind man who received his sight gradually.

We Can Bring the Hurting to Jesus (Mark 8:22)

They arrive at Bethsaida on the northeast shore of the Sea of Galilee (cf. 6:45). They are immediately met by a delegation who "brought a blind man to Him and begged Him to touch him" (cf. 7:32). No doubt they have heard of His compassion (6:34; 8:2) and what He is capable of. They believed "He has done everything well" (7:37) and are hopeful He will do something good for their friend. We will never be disappointed when we bring our friends to Jesus, and neither were they!

We Can Trust the Hurting to Jesus (Mark 8:23-26)

Jesus is again tender in His treatment of this blind man as He had been with the deaf man in 7:31-37. (1) He took the blind by the hand; (2) He led him away for privacy; (3) He spit on his eyes and asked, "Do you see anything?"

The Son of God did not expect complete healing at this point. He was not surprised.

The man responds, "I see some, more than ever before, but I still don't see clearly." Jesus then proceeded to heal his eyes perfectly.

> What is the significance of this? Was it that this man was a particularly "difficult case" for Jesus? Hardly! Was this miracle then—like others— a sign? Yes! But to whom? To the man? No!—to the disciples. And this is confirmed by the fact that Jesus had already asked them about their vision of Him (v. 18). He was now leading them by the hand to the point at which their sight would become much clearer, and Peter would confess "You are the Christ" (v. 29). Their spiritual understanding did not come instantaneously, but gradually. They, too, needed the second touch from the hands of their Master. (Ferguson, *Mark*, 125)

As before, Jesus sent him home with a command not to enter the village. No need for a show. No desire to make him a spectacle. This miracle was for his physical eyes, and it was for the disciples' spiritual eyes. That it accomplished those two purposes was enough.

> Amazing grace how sweet the sound,
> That saved a wretch like me.
> I once was lost but now I'm found,
> Was blind but now I see. (Newton, "Amazing Grace")

That was true for this blind man. It was true for the Twelve. It was certainly true for me. Now, what about you?

Reflect and Discuss

1. Which subjects did you enjoy in school? Which subjects required a lot of instruction and assistance before you "got it"?
2. How would you respond to someone who claimed the feeding of the five thousand (6:35-44) and the feeding of the four thousand (8:1-9) are really the same event reported twice by Mark (and Matthew)?
3. What is the significance of this feeding taking place in Gentile territory?
4. How is Jesus' compassion and concern for the physical needs of the Gentile crowd indicative of His concern for our spiritual state?
5. When we are faced with an impossible situation and we want to turn it over to God, how do we go about doing that?
6. How do these miraculous feeding episodes serve as a sign of the inbreaking of the kingdom of God?
7. What is the difference between testing God in faith and testing Him in unbelief?

8. Have you ever encountered someone who wouldn't accept your explanation of Christianity even if you used sound logic? What would it take to get through to such a person?

9. As we face new challenges, how can we increase the chances that we will remember God's mighty works from the past and His words of encouragement?

10. How was Jesus' method of healing this blind man an encouragement for His disciples? How is it encouraging for you?

The Normal Christian Life: Following and Serving the King

MARK 8:27-38

Main Idea: The normal Christian life involves dying to self that we may find life in Christ.

I. **You Must Know and Personally Confess Who Jesus Is (8:27-30).**
   A. There is an inescapable question (8:27-28).
   B. There is one acceptable answer (8:29-30).

II. **You Must Learn and Affirm the Ways of God and Not Man (8:31-33).**
   A. God's ways are often hard but clear (8:31-32).
   B. God's will is often a challenge but perfect (8:32-33).

III. **You Must Understand and Accept That Jesus Calls You to Die (8:34-38).**
   A. The self-centered life must be put to death (8:34).
   B. The safe life must be put to death (8:35).
   C. The self-serving life must be put to death (8:36-38).

Today there is a faulty perspective of Jesus that is extremely dangerous and seductive. This is exposed by David Platt in his book *Radical*. In a blog David wrote,

> We American Christians have a way of taking the Jesus of the Bible and twisting him into a version of Jesus that we are more comfortable with. A nice middle-class American Jesus. A Jesus who doesn't mind materialism and would never call us to give away everything we have. A Jesus who is fine with nominal devotion that does not infringe on our comforts. A Jesus who wants us to be balanced, who wants us to avoid dangerous extremes, and who for that matter wants us to avoid

danger altogether. A Jesus who brings comfort and prosperity to us as we live out our Christian spin on the American Dream. (Platt, "My Take")

Any fair and honest reading of Scripture will reveal that this is not who Jesus is and not what Jesus demands. Jesus says, "Die and then follow Me."

This text will provide the answer to three crucial questions: Who is Jesus? What did He come to do? What does He expect of you? It is the beginning of the "Great Discipleship Discourse" (8:31–10:52), in which three times Jesus predicts His passion (8:31-33; 9:30-32; 10:32-34). Immediately following each time, He instructs them concerning true discipleship and what it means to truly follow Him because they just do not get it! In 8:32, Peter tries to correct Him on what kind of Messiah He will be. In 9:34, they are debating greatness in the kingdom. And in 10:37, James and John preempted the others in asking to sit on His right and left in the kingdom.

So our Lord explains what the normal Christian life looks like and what it means to follow a King who came to die and serve, who calls His followers to die and serve as well.

You Must Know and Personally Confess Who Jesus Is
MARK 8:27-30

Jesus takes the Twelve north for a time of private instruction. Caesarea Philippi is an unlikely location for the first human proclamation of Jesus as the Messiah. It represents the outer regions of paganism, idolatry, and hostility to the Hebrew faith. We are at a crucial turning point. As Jesus brought gradual physical sight to the blind man of Bethsaida (8:22-26), He will now bring gradual spiritual sight to the disciples concerning who He is and what kind of Messiah He will be.

There Is an Inescapable Question (Mark 8:27-28)

Jesus asks a straightforward question, a question the Twelve have pondered since He calmed the sea in 4:41: "Who then is this?"

The disciples give the popular opinions making the rounds (cf. 6:14-16). Some agreed with Herod Antipas that He was some kind of reincarnation of John the Baptist. Others judged He was Elijah, the prophetic forerunner before the eschatological "Day of the Lord" (Mal 3:1; 4:5-6). Still others made a simpler claim: "He is one of the prophets," perhaps the One promised by Moses (Deut 18:15,18).

These were favorable assessments to be sure. Each is positive and affirming, much like those who today would applaud Him as a great moral teacher, the example all should emulate. They honor Him but misrepresent Him. They applaud Him while denying who He really is. This inescapable question demands an accurate and acceptable answer. "Who do people say that I am?"

There Is One Acceptable Answer (Mark 8:29-30)

Jesus shifts the question to His disciples.

Accurate declarations of who Jesus is have been given at the beginning of this Gospel by *Mark* the narrator: "Jesus Christ, the Son of God" (1:1); *God the Father:* "You are My beloved Son; I take delight in You!" (1:11); and *demons:* "the Holy One of God" (1:24), "You are the Son of God" (3:11), "Jesus, Son of the Most High God" (5:7). At the end of this Gospel, a Roman centurion will say, "This man really was God's Son!" (15:39).

At the center of Mark's Gospel, the voice of Peter is added: "You are the Messiah." This is the one and only acceptable answer. Peter and the Twelve reject the prevailing opinions of the crowds and religious leaders (note their negative evaluation in 3:22), and so must we!

Popular and trendy views of Jesus must always surrender to the clear and consistent witness of Scripture. James Edwards is right: "The categories of John the Baptist or Elijah or one of the prophets are no closer to the real Jesus than are the various 'Jesus' figures of historical criticism or Enlightenment rationalism or feminism or Aryan and racist theories or the Jesus Seminar or the various sociological models in our day" (*Mark,* 248). Resist the trends! Stand on the Word against these faulty assaults! Personally, publicly, and even proudly declare your allegiance to Jesus proclaiming He is the Son of God, the Messiah, the One and Only Savior of the world.

You Must Learn and Affirm the Ways of God and Not Man
MARK 8:31-33

Mark 1:1–8:30 has led to the confession "You are the Christ." Mark 8:31–16:8 will lead to the confession "You are God's Son" and reveal the kind of Messiah He will be—a suffering Messiah, something hinted at in 1:11 and 2:20 but now made plain.

The first half of Mark focuses on who He is. The Gospel tells us the King has come! Our response is to repent and believe. The first confession comes from an insider when Peter says, "You are the Messiah!" (8:29). The second half focuses on what He came to do. The Gospel tells us the King must die! Our response is to take up our cross and follow Him. The climactic confession comes from an outsider—a Gentile, a Roman Centurion: "This man really was God's Son!" (15:39) (Timothy J. Keller, unpublished notes).

A King who dies is not what they *expected* or *wanted*. It is, however, what they desperately *needed*.

God's Ways Are Often Hard but Clear (Mark 8:31-32)

Jesus begins a new chapter in the disciples' education. It is time for them to graduate, even if they are not ready.

Jesus is the Christ, the Davidic Son of Psalm 2, the apocalyptic Son of Man of Daniel 7. He will usher in an eternal kingdom over which He will rule as King and Lord. However, God's way will be different from what a world that exalts power would expect: He will suffer, be rejected, especially by the religious establishment, be killed, and rise three days later.

All of this *must* happen. It is necessary. It is what the Scriptures promised. This is why He came. This is what sin's payment demands and we cannot provide. This is where the law of God and the love of God will meet! This is where judgment and grace kiss! Rob the word "must" of its meaning, and you empty the gospel and the cross of its glory. God's ways are often hard but clear.

God's Will Is Often a Challenge but Perfect (Mark 8:32-33)

Peter was on board with Jesus as the Messiah. Peter was not on board with Jesus going to the cross. As Jesus rebuked the demons in 3:12, Peter now rebukes Jesus. Bad call! Peter quickly gets in return what he had just given and more!

Jesus treats Peter as if he were Satan or a demon-possessed man! It is harsh but justified and necessary. Like Satan at the temptation in the wilderness (Matt 4:9-11), Peter offers Jesus the crown without the cross. He thinks he has a better plan than God does.

Peter wants a Jesus who fits his agenda. He thinks he knows the kind of Messiah Jesus needs to be and attempts to reshape and redefine Him to fit his conception. Are we not often guilty of doing the same thing? "Give me a Jesus I can control, one I conjure up in my image and likeness!" No, you and I must learn and affirm the ways of God, not man. You may not fully understand it. It may not be easy or safe. It will, however, be best. In fact, it will be perfect (Rom 12:2).

You Must Understand and Accept That Jesus Calls You to Die
MARK 8:34-38

God's ways are often hard but usually clear. They are a challenge but always perfect. The passion of the Christ reinforces these biblical truths.

Confident that God's will is perfect, even if it might not be safe, we embrace the call of Jesus to follow Him and to die in order that we and others might truly live!

The Self-Centered Life Must Be Put to Death (Mark 8:34)

Jesus lays out the essence of "the normal Christian life," the basics of discipleship, which sadly in our day looks like "the radical Christian life." Being Jesus' disciple requires three essentials.

First, deny yourself. Give up the right to self-determination. Live as Christ directs. Treasure and value Jesus more than yourself, your comforts, your aspirations. Put to death the *idol of I!* Say no to you and yes to Jesus!

Second, take up your cross. Die! Luke 9:23 adds the word "daily" because that is what we must do. This is not *normal* or *natural*, but it is *necessary* to be Christ's disciple. And it is a slow, painful death.

Finally, follow Me! Are we willing to believe and obey Jesus? It will be radical, not comfortable, because it involves a death to the self-centered life.

The Safe Life Must Be Put to Death (Mark 8:35)

Verses 35-38 all have the word "for" in Greek (*gar*). Jesus is providing the basis for the challenge of verse 34.

If you save or treasure your life above all else, you will lose it. The one who plays it safe and considers his existence more important than Jesus will lose both Jesus and eternal life.

In contrast, the one who gives his life for Jesus and the gospel will actually save it! Following Jesus involves risking it all—safety, security, satisfaction in this world. But He promises us that it leads to a reward this world can never, ever offer.

There is a life worth *giving* for the glory of God *and the gospel!* It is a dying to self that others might live! It is not safe! But it is the normal Christian life! J. I Packer says, "There are, in fact, two motives that should spur us constantly to evangelize. The first is love to God and concern for His glory; the second is love to man and concern for his welfare" (*Evangelism*, 73). C. T. Studd (1860–1931), missionary to China, India, and Sudan, said,

"We will dare to trust our God . . . and we will do it with His joy unspeakable singing aloud in our hearts. We will a thousand times sooner die trusting only in our God than live trusting in man" (Platt, *Radical,* 178).

The Self-Serving Life Must Be Put to Death (Mark 8:36-38)

Your life is set free to live the normal/radical Christian life when you see death as reward, when you can say with Paul, "For me, living is Christ and dying is gain" (Phil 1:21).

Jesus asks, "For what does it benefit a man to gain the whole world yet lose his life?" The answer is *nothing.* He asks, "What can a man give in exchange for his life?" The answer is *nothing.*

On April 17, 1998, Linda McCartney, wife of Paul McCartney of the Beatles, died. *Newsweek* concluded its article on her death by saying, "The McCartney's had all the money in the world. . . . Enough to afford their privacy. Enough to give them a beautiful view. But all the money in the world wasn't enough to keep her alive" (Giles, "Lady McCartney," 64).

I appreciate the way John Piper puts it:

> What's the opposite of being ashamed of somebody? Being proud of them. Admiring them. Not being embarrassed to be seen with them. Loving to be identified with them.
>
> So Jesus is saying, "If you are embarrassed by me and the price I paid for you (and he's not referring to lapses of courage when you don't share your faith, but a settled state of your heart toward him)— if you're not proud of me and you don't cherish me and what I did for you—if you want to put yourself with the goats that value their reputation in the goat herd more than they value me, then that's the way I will view you when I come. I will be ashamed of you, and you will perish with the people who consider me an embarrassment." ("The Son of Man")

Dietrich Bonhoeffer (1906–1945) understood what the normal Christian life should look like. The way may be hard, but the path and the end are glorious.

> The cross is laid on every Christian. The first Christ-suffering which every man must experience is the call to abandon the attachments of this world. It is that dying of the old man which is the result of his encounter with Christ. As we embark upon discipleship we surrender ourselves to Christ in union with his death—we give over our lives to death. Thus it begins; the cross is not the terrible end to an otherwise god-fearing and happy life, but it meets us at the beginning of

our communion with Christ. When Christ calls a man, he bids him come and die. . . . But it is the same death every time—death in Jesus Christ, the death of the old man at his call. Jesus' summons to the rich young man was calling him to die, because only the man who is dead to his own will can follow Christ. In fact every command of Jesus is a call to die, with all our affections and lusts. But we do not want to die, and therefore Jesus Christ and his call are necessarily our death as well as our life. The call to discipleship, the baptism in the name of Jesus Christ means both death and life. (Bonhoeffer, *Cost*, 99)

May all of us learn how to die for Christ and the gospel, that we, and others, may truly live. May all of us learn what is, and how to live, the normal Christian life.

Reflect and Discuss

1. How is Jesus' call to discipleship "radical"? How have we made the normal Christian life less radical than what the Bible calls for?
2. Why is it inadequate to consider Jesus only a great moral teacher? Why is it inadequate to see Him as merely an example to follow?
3. In what way is it commendable to "proudly" declare that Jesus is the Messiah, the Son of God? How should we be cautioned regarding such an attitude?
4. What kind of King did the Jews of Jesus' day expect the Messiah would be? How do we sometimes expect Jesus to do the same for us?
5. How would you answer a child who asked, "Why does it say Jesus 'must' suffer, die, and rise again?" How would you answer a Muslim?
6. What do you suppose Peter was thinking when he rebuked Jesus (8:32)? What are man's concerns (8:33)?
7. How does the world entice you to live the self-centered life? How does giving up the right to self-determination counter those temptations?
8. Compare the sayings "The safe life must be put to death" and "The safest place to be is in the middle of God's will." What is the definition of *safe* in each case?
9. How would you argue that the death of the missionary Jim Elliot was not a great tragedy?
10. Discuss Bonhoeffer's statement: "In fact every command of Jesus is a call to die."

A Glimpse of Glory: The Transfiguration of Jesus

MARK 9:1-13

Main Idea: The transfiguration reveals the glorious true identity and deity of Jesus Christ.

I. **Look at the Glory of the Son of God (9:1-4).**
   A. He was God incognito (9:1-3).
   B. He is the fulfillment of the Law and the Prophets (9:4).
II. **Listen to the Voice of God the Father (9:5-8).**
   A. Our human perspectives are often foolish (9:5-6).
   B. The divine perspective is what we need (9:7-8).
III. **Learn from the Suffering of God's Servants (9:9-13).**
   A. God's Son Jesus was crucified but rose from the dead (9:9-10).
   B. God's servant John was mistreated but completed his assignment (9:11-13).

"Things are not always as they seem." "Looks can be deceiving." Never was this more true than when the Son of God left heaven and came to earth, when "the Word became flesh and took up residence among us" (John 1:14), when the fullness of deity came and dwelt in a body (Col 2:9), when the essence of God "did not consider equality with God as something to be used for His own advantage. Instead, He emptied Himself by assuming the form of a slave, taking on the likeness of men" (Phil 2:6-7). The transfiguration of Jesus confirms that, despite having the outward appearance of a mere mortal man, Jesus of Nazareth is in His nature and essence God—deity dressed in a body.

Although He is not the kind of Messiah Savior the nation of Israel was expecting, He is exactly the Messiah Savior they needed. He looks defeated, but He is actually victorious. He dies and is buried by men, but He will be raised and exalted by God. He looks like a regular dude, but in actuality He is deity!

The transfiguration is something of "a preview of coming attractions." It follows Peter's great confession (Mark 8:27-30), Jesus' prediction of His death (8:31-33), His call to radical discipleship (8:34-38), and His promise that some standing with Him will see the kingdom (9:1). These events are related.

What happened to Moses in the early stages of redemptive history pre-figured a greater Moses, a greater exodus, and a greater salvation. Note the following (adapted from Garland, *Mark*, 342):

MOSES	JESUS
Moses goes with three named persons plus 70 elders up the mountain (Exod 24:1,9).	Jesus takes three disciples up the mountain (Mark 9:2).
Moses' skin shines when he descends from the mountain (Exod 34:29).	Jesus is transfigured and His clothes become radiantly white (Mark 9:2-3).
God appears in veiled form in an over-shadowing cloud (Exod 23:15-16,18).	God appears in veiled form in an overshadowing cloud (Mark 9:7).
A voice speaks from the cloud (Exod 24:16).	A voice speaks from the cloud (Mark 9:7).
The people are afraid to come near Moses after he descends from the mountain (Exod 35:30).	The people are astonished when they see Jesus after He descends from the mountain (Mark 9:15).

A new and greater Moses has arrived, the long-awaited prophet He had promised (Deut 18:15-20). Yes, Jesus is God's eschatological prophet. He is also God's much-loved Son.

Look at the Glory of the Son of God
MARK 9:1-4

The call to follow Jesus in discipleship is not easy. It is a costly calling. It is also filled with encouragement and confirmation. Jesus provides just that when He says, "I assure you [Gk *amen*]: There are some standing here who will not taste death until they see the kingdom of God come in power."

Jesus was not in error. He was not talking about the climactic arrival of the kingdom. He was not talking, at least exclusively, about the coming of the Spirit at Pentecost (Acts 2). He was not talking about the fall and destruction of Jerusalem (AD 70). He was talking about the transfiguration, which immediately follows, and His glorious resurrection. Jesus' use of *amen* gives personal authority to His words. He says it. That settles it!

He Was God Incognito (Mark 9:1-3)

Jesus takes the inner circle of Peter, James, and John (cf. 1:16-20; 3:16-17; 5:37-43) up to a high mountain by themselves. Tradition says it was Mount Tabor, but Mount Hermon (9,000 ft.) in the far north of Galilee is more likely.

"He was transformed in front of them." "Transformed" means "changed," and here it speaks of a radical transfiguration that reveals His true essence in an outward visible manifestation. Even "His clothes became dazzling." Psalm 104:1 says, "My soul, praise Yahweh! LORD my God, You are very great; You are clothed with majesty and splendor." For a brief moment our Lord's true identity is allowed to shine forth in all its glory. Here is the Christ they will see when He triumphantly comes the second time, to establish His universal kingdom (Rev 19:11-16).

He Is the Fulfillment of the Law and the Prophets (Mark 9:4)

While His glory is being displayed in brilliant light, Elijah and Moses appear, talking to Jesus. Luke says in Luke 9:31 they "were speaking of His death." The word for "death" in the Greek text is "exodus"! Jesus would lead the people of God out of the bondage of sin in a new exodus through His death (a new Passover) and resurrection, and He would constitute a new people called the church.

Elijah and Moses represent the Law and the Prophets. They were both great deliverers. Together they represent the prophetic tradition that points to the Messiah. Their appearance draws from Malachi 4:4-6:

> Remember the instruction of Moses My servant, the statutes and ordinances I commanded him at Horeb for all Israel. Look, I am going to send you Elijah the prophet before the great and awesome Day of the Lord comes. And he will turn the hearts of fathers to their children and the hearts of children to their fathers. Otherwise, I will come and strike the land with a curse.

With their appearing, the Law and Prophets are signaled as being fulfilled in the coming of Messiah who has brought the kingdom of God near (cf. Mark 1:15).

This is not Mount Sinai all over again. No, this is a gospel mountain, not a law mountain. Here the law of God and the grace of God converge in the One who is God incarnate and the fulfillment of all the Old Testament promised. Look at Him and believe His gospel.

Listen to the Voice of God the Father
MARK 9:5-8

In these verses only two persons speak: Peter and God the Father. Jesus does not say a word. He doesn't need to! Peter's words we can set aside and even excuse in light of his fear (v. 6) and his being suddenly awakened from a nap (Luke 9:32). We must hear the Father's words and heed them. Our spiritual lives depend on it.

Our Human Perspectives Are Often Foolish (Mark 9:5-6)

The disciples understandably are amazed and "terrified" at the revelation of the glorified Christ. Peter says, "It is good we are here." You think?! He then suggests that this mountaintop summit should be continued and he, James, and John will gladly construct three tents for Jesus and the honored guests from the past.

Is Peter placing Jesus on equal standing with Elijah and Moses? Does he think that up on a mountain in isolation is where God wants His workers? Peter was so excited and scared he just had to say something. His mind would only catch up with his words after the cross and the resurrection. We will never understand the person and work of Christ apart from the cross and resurrection. Leave them out, and He is at best a moralist and at worst a self-destructive fool. Leave out the cross, and there is no atonement. Leave out the resurrection, and there is no victory over sin. In sinful weakness we would avoid the cross, stay on the mountain, and make ourselves comfortable. In contrast Jesus will embrace the cross, ascend Calvary's hill, and drink the cup of suffering filled with the wrath of God.

The Divine Perspective Is What We Need (Mark 9:7-8)

Suddenly a cloud, God's *shekinah* glory cloud, overshadows or envelops them (cf. Exod 40:35; 1 Kgs 8:10-11). We do not need man-made tents (v. 5). Rather, we need the presence of the living God, who now speaks words that thunder with authority and are pregnant with meaning: "This is My beloved Son; listen to Him!"

The statement recalls Jesus' baptism (1:11). It calls to mind Deuteronomy 18:15, where Moses says God will send His prophet and "You must listen to him." This is God's beloved, one-of-a-kind Son. We are to listen to Him and only Him. When the cloud disappears, Elijah and Moses vanish, and "Jesus alone" remains. Moses and Elijah were great revealers of truth along with all the other prophets, but the voice of God commands us to listen to His Son, Jesus. Give Him your ears. Have eyes only for Him (Heb 12:2). He can give you what neither Moses nor Elijah could ever give. This is God's perspective on the matter!

Learn from the Suffering of God's Servants
MARK 9:9-13

The three disciples have learned that despite His earthly, outward appearance, Jesus is God. The transfiguration has proven that beyond any reasonable question.

But might the transfiguration mean Jesus could triumph without the cross? Might the Messiah enter into His glory and establish His kingdom in power *now*, given the breathtaking display they had just witnessed?

Who says the cross must come before the crown? Jesus does. What He has just experienced has not weakened His resolve to go to Calvary. It has emboldened Him to go and drink the last drop of the cup of divine wrath in the place of unworthy and helpless sinners.

God's Son Jesus Was Crucified but Rose from the Dead (Mark 9:9-10)

The disciples are commanded to tell no one what they had seen "until the Son of Man had risen from the dead" (see 8:31). This is our Lord's last command to silence and the only one that receives a time limitation. After the resurrection, proclamation will be the order of the day!

The "Son of Man" title appeared only twice in the first half of Mark (2:10,28). Now it will occur with great regularity, especially in the context of His suffering (8:31; 9:9,12; 10:33,45; 14:21,41). The title hearkens back to the heavenly man of Daniel 7:13-14:

> I continued watching in the night visions, and I saw One like a son of man coming with the clouds of heaven. He approached the Ancient of Days and was escorted before Him. He was given authority to rule, and glory, and a kingdom; so that those of every people, nation, and language should serve Him. His dominion is an everlasting dominion that will not pass away, and His kingdom is one that will not be destroyed.

Jesus is the coming Lord of glory who will inherit a universal and everlasting kingdom. But first He will suffer and die.

The three disciples kept questioning one another about what "rising from the dead" meant. They had a place in their theology for such a doctrine, but it was expected to take place at the end of the age.

God's Servant John Was Mistreated but Completed His Assignment (Mark 9:11-13)

The presence of Moses and Elijah at the transfiguration, references to resurrection from the dead, and the recognition that Jesus is the Messiah would constitute a compelling argument that the end of the age is near. It prompts a question in the disciples' mind: "Why do the scribes say that Elijah must come first?"

Jesus makes a surprising connection. "'Elijah does come first and restores everything,' He replied. 'How then is it written about the Son of Man that He must suffer many things and be treated with contempt?'" Wow! They did not see that one coming! The same divine Scriptures that predicted the coming of Elijah prior to the Day of the Lord also predicted a suffering Messiah. How did they miss Psalms 16; 22; 110; Isaiah 52:13–53:12? Read the whole of the Old Testament in light of Genesis 3:15, and all of it unfolds from there. The Son of Man will suffer, be treated with contempt, be killed, and then rise from the dead.

As for Elijah, he has come in the person of John the Baptist (see Matt 17:12-13). They rejected his message and killed him. They will do the same with Jesus. John fulfilled the assignment given to him by God, and so would our Lord. God would faithfully see them through their suffering and greatest hours of trial! Might we not be able to trust Him to do the same for us?!

Conclusion

Why was Jesus gloriously transfigured? Why did the God who came incognito momentarily yet unmistakably reveal His true identity and nature?

- It was to reveal Jesus as God incarnate.
- It was to strengthen Christ as He began His march to the cross.
- It was to fortify the disciples in obeying the call to radical discipleship.
- It was to demonstrate that Messiah Jesus was the fulfillment of the Law (Moses) and the Prophets (Elijah) as God's final, complete, and climactic revelation.
- It was a confirmation of Peter's confession (8:29).
- It was to teach that the Messiah who was crucified is the same Messiah who will reign over His kingdom in glory.
- It was to encourage the disciples in light of Jesus' prediction of His passion (8:31-32).
- It fulfilled, at least in part, the promise of Mark 9:1.
- It reaffirmed the Father's love and delight in His Son (cf. 1:11).

Lessons Learned in the Fires of Failure

MARK 9:14-29

Main Idea: We will fail, but God uses these failures to deepen our dependence on Him, our faith in Christ, and our discipline in prayer.

I. **We Never Advance Beyond Our Need for Jesus (9:14-19).**
   A. We need Christ when criticized by our detractors (9:14-16).
   B. We need Christ when confronted with the demonic (9:17-18).
   C. We need Christ when corrected in our defeats (9:19).
II. **We Never Advance Beyond Our Need for Faith (9:19-27).**
   A. The key is direction (9:19-22).
   B. The key is dependency (9:23-27).
III. **We Never Advance Beyond Our Need for Prayer (9:28-29).**
   A. Failure should lead us to ask questions of ourselves (9:28).
   B. Failure should drive us to God in humility (9:29).

Failure is never fun and defeat is seldom something we take delight in. It can be painful, embarrassing, and humiliating. And our response can be life changing, altering our destiny. Failure can make us bitter, or it may make us better. We can take it as instructive and corrective and learn from it. Failure may show us, "Obviously I need to work harder if I want to succeed" or "As I move ahead I need help. I can't do this by myself."

It is this last lesson the disciples need to learn and so many of us need to learn as well. But there is another truth we must hold on to as well: "I can do all things through Christ who strengthens me" (Phil 4:13). I can do nothing that really matters without Him, but this drives me continually to Him for help. I need to let my weakness drive me to His strength. I need to let my impotence drive me to His omnipotence. I need to let my limitations drive me to His unlimited resources. I need to let my humility drive me to His sufficiency.

There is an old hymn by William C. Poole titled "Just When I Need Him Most." The fourth stanza says, "Just when I need Him, He is my all. Answering when upon Him I call; Tenderly watching lest I should fall" (William C. Poole, 1907). The disciples have a ways to go before they learn this lesson. A father with a suffering son, on the other hand, is about to plumb the depths of this marvelous truth.

We Never Advance Beyond Our Need for Jesus
MARK 9:14-19

Mountaintop experiences are wonderful, and we need them from time to time for spiritual nourishment and the recharging of our spiritual batteries. However, God never intended for us to stay there. He wants us "down here" preaching the gospel to and ministering among the hurting and suffering. He wants us living with and serving real people devastated by the ravages of the fall and of sin. As His agents of redemptive love, we go in His name and with the promise of His presence. To forget this is to open ourselves up to all sorts of difficulty, challenges, and even failure, as nine of His disciples discovered with pain and humiliation.

We Need Christ When Criticized by Our Detractors (Mark 9:14-16)

Peter wanted to stay on the mountaintop (9:5), but Jesus was headed to Jerusalem and the cross (cf. 8:31-32). He leads them down the mountain (9:9) to rejoin the other disciples and to minister to the hurting on the way to Jerusalem and His passion (9:30). As soon as He descends, Jesus finds the disciples surrounded by a great crowd, arguing with the scribes. Further, there is a demon-possessed child whom they were unable to help (v. 18).

No doubt the scribes were mocking the disciples over their failure to heal the boy. Probably they used the lack of success as an opportunity to question Jesus' authority. After all, "the messenger of a man is as the man himself" (Lane, *Mark*, 331). Thus their failure reflected badly not only on them but also on Jesus!

We never sin in a vacuum. We hurt ourselves, we hurt those we love, we hurt the gospel, and we hurt the reputation of Christ! When this happens, we do not need to look to ourselves but to Christ! Criticized by our detractors for our failures, we must point them to Christ, the One who does not fail—ever! We should encourage them to follow the example of the crowd in verse 15. They saw Him, they were amazed at Him, and they ran to Him.

Our detractors may accurately point out our flaws and failures. Such, however, will never be found in Jesus. Oh how we need Him when enemies are nipping at our heels, ready to devour us if they can!

We Need Christ When Confronted with the Demonic (Mark 9:17-18)

We are more fully informed concerning the cause of this dispute. Someone from the crowd yelled out the answer to Jesus' inquiry (v. 16), but it wasn't just anyone. It was the father of a demon-possessed boy. He called Jesus "Teacher" and informed Him that his son had a spirit that made him mute.

It caused violent seizures, and he had been like this since childhood. It regularly tried to destroy him. Thus, he came to Jesus' disciples, but he was greatly disappointed, for "they couldn't" help.

Many lessons are here. (1) We see that demons are real beings, not simply mythological creatures. Jesus clearly believes in the demonic. (2) Demons desire to inflict pain and death. (3) Demons are capable of inflicting physical suffering. This boy had symptoms resembling epilepsy (Matt 17:15). (4) In our own strength we are helpless against the supernatural powers of the demonic. (5) Spiritual victories in the past (cf. Mark 6:7-13) are no guarantee we will be victorious today, especially when we operate with faith in ourselves rather than in Christ. (6) When all human efforts have been exhausted, we can turn to Jesus. Counter to our sinfulness and weakness, He is where we should turn from the start.

We Need Christ When Corrected in Our Defeats (Mark 9:19)

Correction is seldom pleasant. Hard words may cut, but they also cure. Jesus is tough and direct in His rebuke of the disciples. First, He calls them a "faithless generation." I believe this epithet is directed toward the disciples. This word "generation" is normally used of Israel as an unbelieving nation and, in particular, its leaders (8:12,38). Second, by means of parallel rhetorical questions, He expressed His exasperation and weariness: "How long will I be with you? How long must I put up with you?" I appreciate the convicting words of William Lane: "The rhetorical questions . . . express the loneliness and the anguish of the one authentic believer in a world which expresses only unbelief" (*Mark*, 332). Sinclair Ferguson adds, "Mark vividly captures the pressures and frustrations of Christ's life in these verses. On the mountaintop he had been faced with the spiritual short-sightedness of his disciples. Here in the valley he was confronted by [their] unbelief" (*Mark*, 143).

Whenever the disciples are separated from Jesus, they get in trouble and experience a crisis. What a valuable lesson: we *never* advance beyond our need for Jesus!

We Never Advance Beyond Our Need for Faith
MARK 9:19-27

The author of Hebrews tells us, "Now without faith it is impossible to please God, for the one who draws near to Him must believe that He exists and rewards those who seek Him" (11:6). But how much belief—how much faith—do we need? A lot? Must it be perfect? No. Faith the size of a tiny little mustard seed will do just fine (Matt 17:20). The key is not the *depth* of our faith but the *direction* of our faith. What is important is not the *potency* of our faith but the *Person* our faith is in. A little faith in a great Savior gets amazing results!

The Key Is Direction (Mark 9:19-22)

The time for messing around is at an end. The demon certainly understands this because as soon as he saw Jesus, he "convulsed the boy."

This torture has gone on since childhood and has occasionally been nearly fatal. Out of sheer desperation the father now turns to the only possible source of hope and help: Jesus. He begs, "If you can do anything, have compassion on us and help us."

Though the man's faith is weak and small, he is at least looking in the right direction and asking the right Person for help. Unlike the leper in Mark 1:40-45, the father raised not a "would" question but a "could" question. The leper knew Jesus *could* help, but would He? The father believed Jesus *would* help, but could He? Well, he is about to find out!

The Key Is Dependency (Mark 9:23-27)

Jesus responds in surprise. If He can?! "Everything is possible to the one who believes." Divine ability is not the problem; human unbelief is. There is a reliable bridge between human weakness on the one hand and divine sufficiency and power on the other. It is called faith, trust, and dependency. Psalm 34:8 says, "Taste and see that the Lord is good. How happy is the man who takes refuge in Him!" This is what Jesus is calling this father to do. It is what He calls us to do. Taste! See! Take refuge!

The father responds, "I do believe! Help my unbelief." You have got to love his honesty and humility. He was effectively saying, "I know my faith is weak, partial, incomplete. Still, I trust You, Jesus, and only You. If You don't deliver my son, then he will not be delivered. Help me in spite of me!"

The crowd begins to build due to all the commotion. Seeing this, Jesus banishes the vile demon and places a "No Trespassing" sign over the child's soul. The demon has no choice except to obey, but as he leaves, he convulsed the boy again—"terribly" this time. The boy collapsed like a corpse, and most thought he had died.

However, Jesus took him by the hand. Literally the text reads, "Jesus raised him, and he was resurrected." Jesus here provides insight into the meaning of His own death and resurrection. Satanic powers bring death, but divine power brings resurrection life. This is what dependent faith can see!

We Never Advance Beyond Our Need for Prayer
MARK 9:28-29

The disciples might have learned a lot by contrasting the transfiguration with this healing.

TRANSFIGURATION	HEALING OF THE BOY
On the mountaintop	In the valley
The kingdom of God on display	The kingdom of Satan on display
A Son is radiantly glorified	A son is terribly demonized
A Father is honored in His Son	A father is horrified by his son
The disciples are confused and lack understanding	The disciples are defeated and lack power
A lesson about the future	A lesson about faith
A display of divine power	A directive for human prayer

What went wrong for the disciples? Why didn't their attempt at "binding the strong man" (3:27) work?

Failure Should Lead Us to Ask Questions of Ourselves (Mark 9:28)

Introspection is a healthy spiritual discipline when it causes us to examine our weaknesses and confront our limitations. Presumptuous self-sufficiency may be viewed as a great strength by the world, but it is deadly to our spiritual lives.

The disciples failed big time. It was public, brought ridicule, cast doubt on their Master and mission, and filled them with self-doubt. So when Jesus initiated reflection and debriefing, they asked, "Why couldn't *we* drive the demon out?" Their question betrays a sense of confidence in their own strengths and abilities. It suggests a spirit of pride rooted in past accomplishments (6:7-13) that they believed should have been sufficient for this encounter. They are saying, "We did it before and we will do it again. But it didn't work this time. Why?" Failure leads them to question themselves. This is a good thing.

Failure Should Drive Us to God in Humility (Mark 9:29)

Jesus responds with a powerful spiritual insight: "This kind can come out by nothing but prayer." The phrase "this kind" refers to casting out demons and all other spiritual conflicts of this nature. He is not saying some demon exorcisms require prayer but others do not. He is saying that whenever we take to the spiritual battlefield, if we go in our own strength, pride, and self-sufficiency, we have lost the battle before it begins. Faith bridges the gap between divine omnipotence and human weakness, and that faith is experienced and exercised through prayer. Could this be why prayer is one of the most difficult of the spiritual disciplines? Could this be why we don't see greater things in missions, our churches, and our personal lives? Is this why Paul says in 1 Thessalonians 5:17, "Pray without ceasing"?

The power of prayer is obviously not going to be experienced if we don't pray. Tim Keller observes that the prayer of the father is characterized by *honesty, helplessness, hopefulness, specificity,* and *passion* ("Mark," 112). These character traits of believing prayer can be summed up in one word: *humility.* It all depends on Jesus. If He acts, I'm delivered; if He doesn't, I am lost. Faith expressed in prayer says, "I would not have it any other way."

Conclusion

Lessons learned in the fires of failure may hurt us, but they can hurt us in a good way if they drive us to Jesus, increase our faith, and humble us in prayer. Today we do not have Jesus with us in the flesh, but through the gift of prayer, He is only a word, a thought, away. Remember what Jesus said to Thomas: "Because you have seen Me, you have believed. Those who believe without seeing are blessed" (John 20:29). We believe, Lord. Help us in our unbelief. Give us the shield of faith with which we will be able to extinguish all the flaming arrows of the evil one (Eph 6:16).

Reflect and Discuss

1. What has been your most profitable mistake—the one from which you learned the most valuable lessons?
2. Do you tend to berate others for making mistakes or encourage them to learn from mistakes?
3. How did witnessing the transfiguration prepare the disciples for this next lesson? How did this lesson bring them down to earth from their mountain-top experience?
4. How does our failure reflect badly on Jesus in the eyes of the world? What might we say when we have failed that would mitigate the damage done to His name?

5. How would you respond to someone who said the child's behavior probably represented epilepsy or some other natural disease rather than demonic forces?

6. Is our generation more or less of a "faithless generation" than the one Jesus confronted? In general, what causes people to change over generations?

7. How does turning to Jesus with questions and doubts demonstrate at least small faith rather than no faith at all? What would no faith look like?

8. Should our daily lives be divided into things we can do on our own and things we need Jesus' help to do? Explain.

9. What did the disciples do after their failure? How can failure be made profitable?

10. How does self-sufficiency express pride, while prayer and humility express "faith, trust, and dependency"?

The Road to True Greatness

MARK 9:30-50

Main Idea: The road to true greatness is found in following Jesus Christ.

I. **Obedience to the Will of God (9:30-32)**
    A. It is important to listen (9:30-31).
    B. It is important to understand (9:32).

II. **Service to Others (9:33-37)**
    A. We must overcome the desires of pride (9:33-34).
    B. We must overcome the desires for position (9:35).
    C. We must overcome the desires for prominence (9:36-37).

III. **Allegiance to Christ (9:38-41)**
    A. The one who is not against Christ is for Christ (9:38-40).
    B. The one who serves Christ will be rewarded by Christ (9:41).

IV. **Fear of Hell (9:42-50)**
    A. Learn the lesson of the great millstone (9:42).
    B. Learn the lesson of self-mutilation (9:43-48).
    C. Learn the lesson of good salt (9:49-50).

Tony Merida says, "The gospel frees us from our addiction to ourselves!" ("Twitter Post"). Before Christ redeems us and sets us free, we are like crack addicts addicted to ourselves. We are like alcoholics intoxicated with ourselves. We are not as interested in serving as in being served, in giving as in receiving, in pursuing God's way as in getting our way, in being the least as in being the greatest.

And we are certain the way to greatness is not by an obedience that leads to death (vv. 30-32), being last and servant of all (vv. 33-37), having others do what we can't (vv. 38-41), and pursuing a life of serious suffering (vv. 42-50). Yet this is exactly what Jesus says as He lays before us the road to true greatness—greatness as defined by God!

We are in the middle of Jesus' great discipleship discourse (Mark 8–10). Our Lord is turning upside down the value systems of this world. His teaching is radical and mind-blowing. No wonder "they did not understand." Ours is a world where everything is about me! Jesus died to free us from such slavery. He died to free us to serve and to walk a road of true greatness, the road He Himself walked as He "did not come to be served, but to serve, and to give His life—a ransom for many" (Mark 10:45; cf. Isa 53:10-12).

The road to true greatness is paved with four important truths, all of which begin in our mind and lead to concrete action.

Obedience to the Will of God
MARK 9:30-32

Jesus and the Twelve passed through northeast Galilee headed south to Jerusalem where our Lord will be brutally murdered on the cross. His heart and mind are set to obey the Father's will. He "must suffer many things" (8:31), and nothing will stop Him from fulfilling His divinely ordained destiny. Yet, as He focuses on the cross, He also takes time to continue instructing His disciples. They, like us, still have much to learn.

It Is Important to Listen (Mark 9:30-31)

Jesus wants to keep His movements a secret, "For He was teaching His disciples." It also explains what He was teaching them: The Son of Man (Dan 7:13-14), who is Jesus, is going to be handed over to men who will kill Him, and after three days He will rise. This is the second of three passion predictions (cf. 8:31-32; 10:32-34). His goal is to prepare them for what lies ahead.

Jesus says He "is being betrayed into the hands of men." This word "betrayed," *paradidotai*, is used of our Lord's betrayal by Judas (Mark 3:19; 14:41; Luke 24:7) but also of the Father's delivering up of His Son (Isa 53:6,12; Acts 2:23; Rom 8:32). Here I believe the implied agent is God. We must not forget: God purposefully killed His Son in order that He might not kill us! The way to the crown is by way of the cross. Salvation is ours by His suffering.

It Is Important to Understand (Mark 9:32)

As has been the case throughout our Lord's ministry, the disciples do not understand. We need to be fair to them—we know now what they did not know then. Only after the resurrection does it all make sense.

"A dying Messiah? I have no room for that in my worldview. A crucified Christ? I have no room for that in my theology. The glorious Son of Man of Daniel 7 is also the Suffering Servant of Isaiah 53? That just does not fit into my preconceived thinking of how God does things." Ouch!

They did not understand, and they were afraid to ask Him. In contrast we should understand with the help of the Holy Spirit, but if we don't, we should have no fear of asking Him anything. This Savior can be trusted. This Lord is approachable.

When He speaks, we need to listen. And when we know God's will for our lives, like Jesus we should obey because God's will is always perfect (Rom 12:2). Obedience to the will of God marks the road to true greatness.

Service to Others
MARK 9:33-37

Jesus and the disciples arrive in Capernaum on the Sea of Galilee. This will be His last visit here, and as He had done previously, He gives private teaching to the Twelve.

In spite of what He has taught them about self-denial, dying to self (8:34) and losing their lives for Christ and the gospel (8:35), they still aspire to be sovereigns and not servants. They remain deaf to what He has said about the road to true greatness. Serving others out of an overflow of "gospel gratitude" has still not sunk in. They had yet to embrace the truth that gripped the heart of missionary David Brainerd: "It is sweet to be nothing and less than nothing that Christ may be all in all" (source unknown).

We Must Overcome the Desires of Pride (Mark 9:33-34)

Jesus confronts them about what they had been talking about. They admit they had debated "with one another about who was the greatest" (v. 34).

Matters of rank and recognition were important to the Jews of Jesus' day. The nature of man and the times have not changed all that much. Pride and the cult of personality arise even among the people who follow after the lowly Jesus.

Let's take a "painful pride" test.

1. Am I upset if I am not praised for my work?
2. Do I like and even long to sit at the head table in the seat of honor?
3. Do I seek credit for what others have done?
4. Do honorary titles pump me up?
5. Is popularity crucial to my sense of self-worth?
6. Am I a name dropper of those I know (or pretend to know?!)
7. Do I think I have something valuable to say about almost everything?

Proverbs 11:2 says, "When pride comes, disgrace follows, but with humility comes wisdom." James 4:6 adds, "God resists the proud, but gives grace to the humble."

We Must Overcome the Desires for Position (Mark 9:35)

With a heart of pride comes a desire for position. Jesus, in grace and tenderness, gives the Twelve a simple proverbial maxim: "If anyone would be first, he must be last of all and servant of all."

Jesus does not repudiate greatness. He redefines it. Be great in things that matter to God not man. Plato said in *Gorgias* (491e), "How can man be happy when he has to serve someone?" (Edwards, *Mark*, 287). Jesus says you will only find real and lasting happiness (joy) when you do serve someone, not because you have to but because you get to and want to.

Jesus does say there is a position you should aspire to obtain: a *diakonos*, a waiter of tables, one who washes others' feet (John 13:1-20) or changes their soiled undergarments. The work is not glorious in man's eyes, but it is great in God's! Here is a posture and position worthy of heaven!

We Must Overcome the Desires for Prominence (Mark 9:36-37)

Jesus illustrates what it means to be a servant of all: He "took a child, [and] had him stand among them." However, He does not stop there but picks him and takes him in His arms. This would have been unusual. The ancients, with high infant mortality rates, did not exalt the merits of children as do many modern cultures. A little child was an excellent example of the last or least.

Jesus then startles the disciples by saying that if you receive one like this on My behalf, you receive Me. It gets even better: receive Me and you receive the One "who sent Me" (v. 37). Effectively, "Treat well those who have no standing in this world (children, lepers, AIDS victims, the mentally impaired, the physically disabled, the aged), and you will receive an audience with My Father!"

Jesus points the way to true greatness: Die to self, serve others, care for those no one else cares for. Receive them in Jesus' name, and you receive Jesus—and His Father too! The way up is down. The way to get is to give. The way to be first is to be last. This is the way of Jesus. This is the way to true greatness.

Allegiance to Christ
MARK 9:38-41

A. T. Pierson said, "The ideal missionary must have four passions: A passion for the *truth*; a passion for *Christ*; a passion for the *souls of men*; and a passion for *self-sacrificing*" (Pierson, "Speech," 122).

At this point the disciples just aren't there. Oh, they are zealous, but it is a misplaced zeal, myopic and self-centered. In fact it is downright sinful.

The disciples are about to learn that God's kingdom is bigger than their experience of it. It is so large that anyone who is for Christ is with us. Sinclair Ferguson says, "In the last analysis, it is more important that the servants of God are devoted to Christ than that they are to one of us" (Ferguson, *Mark*, 152).

The One Who Is Not Against Christ Is for Christ (9:38-40)

John came across someone casting out demons (something they failed at in 9:18!) in Jesus' name. They did not know him—he obviously was not part of the "in group" of their religious denomination—so they "tried to stop him, because he was not following us" (v. 38). Us?

If John expected a word of affirmation and approval, he was sadly mistaken. Jesus responds with a strong command, "Don't stop him." On the contrary, stop what *you* are doing! Why?

First, anyone doing these things in My name does so by the power of God. It is an evidence of My call on his life (cf. 1 Cor 12:3). No, do not try to hinder him. Help him. Don't try to restrain him. Rejoice in and with him.

Second, "For whoever is not against us is for us" (v. 40). Paul obviously understood this principle when he wrote,

> *Some indeed preach Christ from envy and rivalry, but others from good will. The latter do it out of love, knowing that I am put here for the defense of the gospel. The former proclaim Christ out of rivalry, not sincerely but thinking to afflict me in my imprisonment. What then? Only that in every way, whether in pretense or in truth, Christ is proclaimed, and in that I rejoice.* (Phil 1:15-18)

Against us/for us leaves no room for neutrality. And here is a nobody exalting Somebody while the somebodies are worried about who is following a bunch of nobodies! Who in these verses is on the road to true greatness?

The One Who Serves Christ Will Be Rewarded by Christ (Mark 9:41)

Verse 41 illustrates the point, undergirded by the authoritative amen, "I assure you."

- "Whoever" is all-inclusive.
- "Gives you a cup of water to drink because of My name"—he serves Me and shows his allegiance to Me by serving My servants.
- "He will never lose his reward"—I see and reward the smallest and humblest acts of service done to others in My name. You reflect the love and concern I have for the nations (11:17), for those I came to serve and give My life as a ransom (10:45).

Service to others frees us. It gets our eyes off of us and onto others who need the same Christ we need. An anonymous author said, "World Missions is God's major therapy for our sin of selfishness that eats the heart out of the local church" (source unknown). Allegiance to Christ will lead us to applaud and celebrate those on God's team, even if they are different from us!

Fear of Hell
MARK 9:42-50

These nine verses are a source of great interest. (1) They put front and center the cost and serious nature of radical discipleship. (2) They are grouped together and united by various catchwords: "downfall," various body parts, "hell," and "salt." (3) Several of these sayings are found in different contexts in the other Gospels (Matt 5:13,29-30; 18:8-9; Luke 14:34-35). Jesus taught these truths on more than one occasion, as any good teacher would.

Our Lord had the strongest possible view of judgment and hell: it is real and it lasts forever. In this context it serves as a warning and a motivation to follow Jesus in devotion and discipleship.

Learn the Lesson of the Great Millstone (Mark 9:42)

This is a hinge verse that brings to an end the themes found in verses 35-41 and then introduces what follows. It picks up on the theme of a child in verses 36-37 and those who belong to Christ in verse 41.

"Little ones" here does not refer to children but to those who follow Jesus, to disciples. If verse 41 speaks of doing good to them, verse 42 addresses just the opposite. If you cause just one disciple to "stumble" (Gk *skandalizein*), it would be better to be given a pair of cement shoes and hurled into the ocean.

I believe Jesus is still speaking to John, and the issue is still pride. God's wrath is great against it because it does so much harm. If we do not rid ourselves of the sin that took both Satan and Adam down, we will be a stumbling block to others, and God will hold us accountable.

Learn the Lesson of Self-Mutilation (Mark 9:43-48)

A saving faith is a fighting faith. It will engage the battle against sin with deadly seriousness. Out of gratitude for the new "life" (vv. 43,45) we have in Christ and the "kingdom of God" (v. 47) we now belong to, we pursue a holy agenda with passion and discipline.

Jesus launches three powerful hyperboles to warn us of sin's danger to others as well as to ourselves. We know they are hyperboles—not to be taken literally—because the Bible forbids bodily mutilation (Deut 14:1; 23:1; 1 Kgs 18:28; Zech 13:6). However, in no way does this diminish or negate the importance of what Jesus is saying. "Things we value supremely, like eyes, hands, and feet—should not stand in the way of eternal life" (Edwards, *Mark*, 294). Eyes, hands, and feet are all inclusive of what we see, what we do, and where we go. As important as they are, better to lose them than to let them prevent you from entering eternal life and God's kingdom.

Evil actions come from a heart that rejoices in sin rather than in Christ (Mark 7:20-23). But Sam Storms is correct, "Very little, if any, sin comes out of your heart that didn't first enter through your eyes." He then adds, "Our external members are but the instruments we employ to gratify the lust that emerges from within. What our Lord was advocating, therefore, [to quote John Stott], was not a literal physical self-maiming, but a ruthless moral self-denial. Not mutilation but mortification is the path of holiness he taught" (Storms, "Be Killing Sin").

Jesus said more about hell than anyone else in the Bible. "Hell" is the New Testament word used for the place of eschatological punishment (Matt 5:29-30; 10:28; Mark 9:43,45,47; Luke 12:5). The Greek word *gehenna* comes from the Hebrew *ge-hinnom*, "Valley of Hinnom," a valley south of Jerusalem where Kings Ahaz (2 Chr 28:3) and Manasseh (2 Chr 33:6) offered child sacrifices to the pagan god Molech. Declared unclean by Josiah (2 Kgs 23:10), it became the place to burn refuse and to dispose of corpses (Isa 66:24; Jer 31:40). The prophets proclaimed oracles of doom on it, and *gehinnom* became a symbol of final judgment (Isa 31:9; Jer 7:31-32; 19:6). It is a place of unquenchable fire (Matt 3:12; Mark 9:43), a lake of fire and brimstone (Rev 20:10,14-15), an eternal fire (Matt 18:8-9; 25:41), a furnace of fire (Matt 13:42), an outer darkness (Matt 8:12; 22:13; 25:30), and an eternal punishment (Matt 25:46). Only God has power to cast both body and soul into hell (see also Luke 12:5).

Learn the Lesson of Good Salt (Mark 9:49-50)

Picking up on the word "fire" in v. 48, Jesus affirms that "everyone will be salted with fire." "Salt" is a preservative. Thus all will be "salted with fire" in a manner consistent with their relationship to Christ. For unbelievers it will be the perpetual fires of final judgment in hell. For the disciple it will be the preserving and refining fires of trials and suffering that mark the road to true greatness. This saying is found only in Mark's Gospel. It must have held special significance for him and Peter.

Salt is good as long as it can serve its purposes. But if it loses its purifying and preserving value then it is worthless. Sinclair Ferguson helps clarify the intent of our Lord's words: "unless we maintain the purity of our own lives (plucking out the eye, etc.) and are purified by the flames of testing, and remain faithful to Christ, our lives will have no preserving influence on this corrupt world" (*Mark*, 155).

Perhaps in light of the disciple's argument about the greatest (v. 34) and John's opposition to another brother doing the work of the Lord (vv. 38-41), Jesus draws one simple application from having salt in yourselves: "Be at peace with one another." Be humble, and avoid stumbling or causing others to stumble. Don't fuss and fight over positions and status. Be a reflection of the God-given peace you have received from Jesus (Rom 5:1). Pull for your brothers and sisters in Christ, not against them. After all, though we may play different positions, all who follow Jesus as Lord are on the same team. Here is a path to true greatness where it really matters: in the eyes of our Savior.

Conclusion

One of the greatest servants of King Jesus, I believe, that has ever walked the earth was a short woman, thin haired in her last years, named Emma Lou. With only a high school education, she faithfully served her Lord until the end of her life, when the Alzheimer's disease destroyed the precious mind that cared so deeply for her Savior. When rational thought escaped her and moments of panic gripped her, she would repeatedly voice a simple prayer, "Help me, Jesus."

At her funeral her son-in-law would remark that he never heard Emma Lou say, "I want." Even if it was her birthday and you asked her where she would like to go out for dinner, her response was always the same: "Whatever you all want will be fine with me." Her daughter-in-law looked to her as if she were her own biological mother.

Her son had the honor of preaching her funeral and did so from Proverbs 31 because Emma Lou was a Proverbs 31 lady. And I have heard him on more than a few occasions recount how she worked a double shift for two weeks from 7:30 a.m. to 4:30 p.m. and from 10:00 p.m. to 2:00 a.m. so her son could go on a mission trip, a trip on which God called him to the gospel ministry.

I know so much about Emma Lou because she was my mother. Was she a great lady in the eyes of the world? No, not really. Was she a great lady in the eyes of our Lord? Without a doubt! When I get to heaven, I will see my mom. I suspect, however, that I will need some heavenly binoculars because she will be so close to the Lord's throne and I will be so far away. She understood and walked the road to true greatness as a simple and faithful follower of Jesus.

Reflect and Discuss

1. What evidence is manifest in our current culture that, before redemption, we are addicted to ourselves? How does that temptation persist even after we are saved?
2. Some skeptics contend that the disciples made up the resurrection story. How does 9:31-32 argue against this notion?
3. How is pride viewed in our current culture? Is this the same kind of pride that is condemned in the Bible, or is it different?
4. How does Jesus redefine aspiring to greatness and seeking a reward? How does this fit together with Him condemning pride and encouraging sacrificial service?
5. How does 9:39-40 support cooperation among Christian churches of various denominations? Do you tend to resist such ideas? Why?
6. What are some examples of giving a cup of water? How does doing it in Jesus' name and belonging to the Messiah further define this good deed?
7. Can hell still serve as a motivation for repentance, or should Christians avoid speaking about hell?
8. Why did Jesus use hyperbole to warn us about temptation and hell? Does this mean His words are not really, literally true?
9. What should Christian individuals do to be "salt" in their families and neighborhoods? What should the church as a body do to be salt in the world?
10. Do you know someone who is little known and unnoticed but who is probably a spiritual superstar in God's eyes? What aspects of that person's life are worthy of imitation?

Jesus, the Bible, Divorce, and Remarriage

MARK 10:1-12

Main Idea: Marriage is a sacred covenant that ideally is dissolved only by death.

I.   Divorce and Remarriage: A Look at the Key Biblical Texts with Theological Observations
II. Some Basic Observations About Divorce and Remarriage from a Survey of Scripture
III. Four Major Views on Divorce and Remarriage
IV. The Teaching of Paul on Divorce (1 Corinthians 7)
V.   A Summation of Evangelical Positions on Divorce and Remarriage (After Sexually Consummated Marriage)
VI. Conclusion
VII. A Premarital Wedding Covenant

Few issues have caused me more grief, soul searching, and study than what the Bible says about divorce and remarriage. In addition to the dozens of books and sermons I have on the subject, I have four, four-inch-thick files. With divorce being so common, many ministers avoid the subject to keep from hurting feelings and causing conflict. Some believe the Bible is no longer relevant to the issue in a world of no-fault divorce, the pill, "living together," and same-sex relationships.

The church has a dismal and embarrassing track record in this area. Many believers are as casual about divorce and remarriage as are their lost friends and neighbors. In a culture that bears proudly the motto "I have the right to be happy," "*serial* polygamy" is considered a right, as well as being normal. Never mind that bodies are strewn everywhere (especially the children), and happiness is even more elusive for those in subsequent marriages. Consider this poem penned by a little girl:

The Monster

The monster's here
The monster's there
The monster is just everywhere.
In my milk,
In my tea,

Doesn't it ever think of me?
Mom's here,
Dad's there,
And I'm just not anywhere!
How can I say this,
Without any force;
The monster is called
Divorce! (author unknown)

Divorce is even more traumatic than losing a spouse or parent. John Piper is right: "Death is usually clean pain. Divorce is usually dirty pain" ("What God Has Joined Together").

Kelly Clarkson, the first winner of *American Idol*, saw her parents divorce at age six. "I know people probably think I've been heartbroken, because of the stuff I've sung and written," she says. "I love my friends and my family. But I have never said the words 'I love you' to anyone in a romantic relationship. I shouldn't be a mother at all, because I'd be horrible. I'm not willing to be that selfless. I'm not keen on marriage. Men come and go." Clarkson acknowledges that she fears betrayal. "When it comes to certain parts of my life, I won't allow myself to be vulnerable at all. I have a lot of trust issues. I don't let many people in." Making a relationship work, she says, requires too much effort. "Love is something you work at. It doesn't come easily. There are going to be bad days. You are going to have to work at loving someone when they are being an idiot. People think they're just going to meet the right guy." She laughs. "Don't be ridiculous" (Djansezian, "Kelly Clarkson"). The effect of divorce can be seen in Clarkson's music, especially her blockbuster hit "Because of You," a reflection on the pain and fallout of divorce.

First we will see exactly what the Bible says about divorce and remarriage. Then I want us to note the different perspectives held by those who accept the full authority of the Bible. We will conclude with observations from Mark 10:1-12, as well as some practical points of application. This study demands our most careful and humble efforts. It is treacherous territory.

Two competing rabbinic schools of thought were present in Jesus' day:

1. The more conservative school followed Rabbi Shammai and said the only ground for divorce was adultery (sexual immorality).
2. The more liberal school followed Rabbi Hillel and said divorce could be granted for "*any* indecency."

The Pharisees in that day, for the most part, followed Rabbi Hillel, made divorce easy and wanted it to stay that way. So they come to Jesus "to test Him" (v. 2). Jesus was, therefore, thrust into a debate like many of us are today. The Pharisees wanted to talk about divorce, but Jesus wanted to talk about marriage and God's divine blueprint.

Divorce and Remarriage: A Look at the Key Biblical Texts with Theological Observations

Genesis 2:18-25 tells us,

> Then the LORD God said, "It is not good for the man to be alone. I will make him a helper as his complement." So the LORD God had formed out of the ground every wild animal and every bird of the sky, and brought each to the man to see what he would call it. And whatever the man called a living creature, that was its name. The man gave names to all the livestock, to the birds of the sky, and to every wild animal; but for the man no helper was found as his complement. So the LORD God caused a deep sleep to come over the man, and he slept. God took one of his ribs and closed the flesh at that place. Then the LORD God made the rib He had taken from the man into a woman and brought her to the man. And the man said:
>
> > This one, at last, is bone of my bone
> > and flesh of my flesh;
> > this one will be called "woman,"
> > for she was taken out of man.
>
> This is why a man leaves his father and mother and bonds with his wife, and they become one flesh. Both the man and his wife were naked, yet felt no shame.

Marriage is a good gift from a great God to be enjoyed. Sex is a part of this good gift. God's design is one man, for one woman, for a lifetime (unless separated by death; Rom 7:1-3). Marriage is the joining of two bodies, two wills, two minds, and two sets of God-given emotions. Marriage is sacred because it reflects the spiritual union of Christ and His church (Eph 5:21-33). As Jesus would never divorce His bride, a spouse should never divorce his or her mate. "The ultimate meaning of marriage is the representation of the covenant keeping love between Christ and His church" (Piper, "What God Has Joined Together").

In Deuteronomy 24:1-4 we see,

> If a man marries a woman, but she becomes displeasing to him because he finds something improper about her, he may write her a divorce certificate, hand it to her, and send her away from his house. If after leaving his house she goes and becomes another man's wife, and the second man hates her, and writes her a divorce certificate, hands it to her, and sends her away from his

house or if he dies, the first husband who sent her away may not marry her again after she has been defiled, because that would be detestable to the LORD. You must not bring guilt on the land the LORD your God is giving you as an inheritance.

Though the Bible never condones divorce, it does recognize the reality of divorce (see also Isa 50:1; Jer 3:1,8-9). The allowance of a divorce certificate provides regulations and is a *concession* for the *protection and welfare* of an innocent victim. Remarriage to one's former spouse after marrying another is strictly forbidden.

Ezra 10:2-3,10-12 states,

Then Shecaniah son of Jehiel, an Elamite, responded to Ezra: "We have been unfaithful to our God by marrying foreign women from the surrounding peoples, but there is still hope for Israel in spite of this. Let us therefore make a covenant before our God to send away all the foreign wives and their children, according to the counsel of my lord and of those who tremble at the command of our God. Let it be done according to the law." . . . Then Ezra the priest stood up and said to them, "You have been unfaithful by marrying foreign women, adding to Israel's guilt. Therefore, make a confession to Yahweh the God of your fathers and do His will. Separate yourselves from the surrounding peoples and your foreign wives." Then all the assembly responded with a loud voice: "Yes, we will do what you say!"

This appears to be a unique situation. (Nowhere does God give a direct command to divorce. The text may be recording their activity but not affirming it.) Some believe polygamy was an issue, though the text does not say this. In the best light this is an exceptional act eliminating the greater of two evils: defilement through mixed marriages, which led to idolatry.

In Malachi 2:13-16, we read,

And this is another thing you do: you cover the LORD's altar with tears, with weeping and groaning, because He no longer respects your offerings or receives them gladly from your hands.

Yet you ask, "For what reason?" Because the LORD has been a witness between you and the wife of your youth. You have acted treacherously against her, though she was your marriage partner and your wife by covenant. Didn't the one God make us with a remnant of His life-breath? And what does the One seek? A godly offspring. So watch yourselves carefully, and do not act treacherously against the wife of your youth.

"If he hates and divorces his wife," says the LORD God of Israel, "he covers his garment with injustice," says the LORD of Hosts. Therefore, watch yourselves carefully, and do not act treacherously.

Malachi wrote during the time of Ezra. God hates divorce. It is never His perfect will. (Is this perhaps a counter to the activity recorded in Ezra?) Matthew 19:3-12 says,

> *Some Pharisees approached [Jesus] to test Him. They asked, "Is it lawful for a man to divorce his wife on any grounds?"*
>
> *"Haven't you read," He replied, "that He who created them in the beginning made them male and female, and He also said:*
> *For this reason a man will leave his father and mother*
> *and be joined to his wife, and the two will become one flesh'?*
> *So they are no longer two, but one flesh. Therefore, what God has joined together, man must not separate."*
>
> *"Why then," they asked Him, "did Moses command us to give divorce papers and to send her away?"*
>
> *He told them, "Moses permitted you to divorce your wives because of the hardness of your hearts. But it was not like that from the beginning. And I tell you, whoever divorces his wife, except for sexual immorality, and marries another, commits adultery."*
>
> *His disciples said to Him, "If the relationship of a man with his wife is like this, it's better not to marry!"*
>
> *But He told them, "Not everyone can accept this saying, but only those it has been given to. For there are eunuchs who were born that way from their mother's womb, there are eunuchs who were made by men, and there are eunuchs who have made themselves that way because of the kingdom of heaven. Let anyone accept this who can."*

Jesus affirms God's original design for marriage. He states that divorce is the result of sin and the hardness of men's hearts. He says divorce is permitted in a case of sexual immorality (viewed only in a Jewish "betrothal" context by some). He seems to imply permission to remarry though this is not clearly stated (19:9-12).

Mark 10:1-12 parallels Matthew 19:1-12. There is an important omission of the words "except for sexual immorality." The omission is because either the betrothal view of Matthew 19 is correct and Mark (being written to Romans) would not need to address the exception, or Mark's account is simply a summation of Matthew's and assumes the exception.

Luke 16:18 states, "Everyone who divorces his wife and marries another woman commits adultery, and he who marries a woman divorced from her husband commits adultery." This is an even more concise account of the Matthew 19 and Mark 10 passages. The last point under Mark 10:1-12 also applies here.

According to Romans 7:1-3,

Since I am speaking to those who understand law, brothers, are you unaware that the law has authority over someone as long as he lives? For example, a married woman is legally bound to her husband while he lives. But if her husband dies, she is released from the law regarding the husband. So then, if she gives herself to another man while her husband is living, she will be called an adulteress. But if her husband dies, she is free from that law. Then, if she gives herself to another man, she is not an adulteress.

Paul reaffirms (like Jesus) God's original design for marriage. The death of a spouse is the only instance in which God advocates remarriage. This is stated in 1 Corinthians 7:8-16,39-40:

I say to the unmarried and to widows: It is good for them if they remain as I am. But if they do not have self-control, they should marry, for it is better to marry than to burn with desire.

I command the married—not I, but the Lord—a wife is not to leave her husband. But if she does leave, she must remain unmarried or be reconciled to her husband—and a husband is not to leave his wife. But I (not the Lord) say to the rest: If any brother has an unbelieving wife and she is willing to live with him, he must not leave her. Also, if any woman has an unbelieving husband and he is willing to live with her, she must not leave her husband. For the unbelieving husband is set apart for God by the wife, and the unbelieving wife is set apart for God by the husband. Otherwise your children would be corrupt, but now they are set apart for God. But if the unbeliever leaves, let him leave. A brother or a sister is not bound in such cases. God has called you to live in peace. For you, wife, how do you know whether you will save your husband? Or you, husband, how do you know whether you will save your wife?

. . .

A wife is bound as long as her husband is living. But if her husband dies, she is free to be married to anyone she wants—only in the Lord. But she is happier if she remains as she is, in my opinion. And I think that I also have the Spirit of God.

Paul affirms the positive nature of the single life. Paul says it is better to marry than to burn with lust (and possibly fall into sexual immorality). God's desire for troubled marriages is always reconciliation. God's desire for those separated in marriage is to be reconciled or remain separated. Desertion by an unbelieving spouse permits divorce and, it seems, grants permission for remarriage (some believe the summation of verses 39-40 rules out remarriage).

Some Basic Observations About Divorce and Remarriage from a Survey of Scripture

Our goal must be to be biblical and not emotional. We should also empha-size prevention and not be reactionary. The latter is difficult, especially for those who have experienced the pain of divorce in some way. One man joined to one woman for a lifetime is God's perfect will for every marriage (Gen 2:18-25).

God hates divorce (Mal 2:13-16). God's desire is that troubled mar-riages would always be reconciled. Divorce is never commanded or desired by God. Separation is sometimes wise (1 Cor 7:10-11).

I believe divorce may be biblically permissible in the cases of

1. sexual immorality,
2. desertion by an unbeliever, or
3. if the divorce was preconversion (2 Cor 5:17).

Where reconciliation is not possible, permission to remarry in the Lord may be allowed (though it is not expressly stated).

Divorce and remarriage are not sanctioned for reasons other than sex-ual immorality or desertion by an unbeliever. Some counter that it would be better to remarry than to commit sexual immorality (1 Cor 7:9) or to be unduly burdened and oppressed in a single state (Deut 24:1-4). However, God commends a single status (1 Cor 7). Single people look to God in faith to provide self-control and to meet their needs.

Four Major Views on Divorce and Remarriage

1. Patristic (Church Fathers) View: The exception clause "except for sexual immorality" (fornication, *porneia*) in Matthew 5:31-32 and 19:9-10 qualifies only the verb "divorces" and not the remarriage clause. Divorce is allowed for adultery only. No remarriage is allowed. Those holding this view note the lack of any expressed statement for remarriage, and the nearness of the early church fathers to the apostles.

2. Protestant-Evangelical View: The exception clause qualifies both "divorces" and "marries another." Divorce is allowed for adultery and desertion by an unbelieving spouse with no possibility of reconciliation. Remarriage to a believer is permissible for the innocent party. However, the reaction of the disciples in 19:10—"If the relationship of a man with his wife is like this, it's better not to marry!"—does not seem to be explained as well by this view. This is also an argument from silence.

3. Betrothal View: The exception clause means "premarital sexual intercourse" in the case of a betrothed couple. Jewish betrothal was a legal contract that could only be broken by divorce or death. It was more than an engagement but not a sexually consummated marriage. This view better explains the disciples' reaction. Divorce is allowed only for unfaithfulness during the betrothal period. If adultery was committed after the marriage, then divorce was not allowed for any reason.

However, the technical meaning given to the phrase "sexual immorality" as "premarital sexual intercourse" is unknown elsewhere in the Bible or in Greek literature. The context of Deuteronomy 24, which is the Old Testament passage forming the foundation of Jesus' statements in Matthew 5 and 19, implies a married wife. This view makes Matthew 19:7 and 8 refer to a married wife, while verse 9 is a betrothed wife. The context seems to point to a married wife in both cases.

4. Unlawful Marriage View: This view takes "sexual immorality" in the exception clause to refer to incestuous marriages. Divorce is allowed for those marriages within the prohibited degrees of kinship in Leviticus 18:6-18. Remarriage is usually not allowed, though there seem to be some differences of opinion. However, the technical meaning of "incest" given to "sexual immorality" does not fit the total context of the passage.

The Teaching of Paul on Divorce (1 Corinthians 7)

Jesus had already spoken on divorce for adultery. Paul takes up the Corinthians' questions on the subject of divorce for desertion.

In 1 Corinthians 7:10-11, Paul says that a husband and a wife who are both Christians are not to divorce, but if they do, they are not to remarry. In verses 12-16, Paul addresses the problem of a saved spouse who is married to an unsaved spouse. If the unsaved party departs, the saved party is "not bound" in such cases. "Not bound" can mean: (1) free to divorce, (2) free to divorce and remarry, or (3) free to separate but not allowed to divorce and remarry.

A Summation of Evangelical Positions on Divorce and Remarriage (After Sexually Consummated Marriage)

As a result of the above survey, several biblical positions on the subject of divorce are possible today:

1. Divorce is never permitted for any reason.
2. Divorce is permitted for adultery only, but remarriage is not allowed.

3. Divorce is permitted for adultery and desertion of an unbelieving spouse, but remarriage is not permitted.

4. Divorce is permitted for adultery or desertion of an unbelieving spouse, and remarriage to a believer is granted to the innocent party. (Those who believe the Bible allows for remarriage do so on the grounds of the exception clause in Matthew and the logic that if God grants divorce to the innocent party, by His grace He would also grant permission to remarry.)

5. Divorce is permitted in the case of an incestuous marriage.

6. Divorce is permitted in the case of the divorce taking place prior to one's conversion and there is no possibility of reconciliation (2 Cor 5:17 is the basis of this position).

Conclusion

Dogmatism and certainty are not appropriate in an area where good and godly students who affirm the infallibility and inerrancy of the Bible hold differing views. Still, there are some things we can affirm based on Jesus' words in Mark:

1. Marriage is a gift and work of God that receives its meaning and significance from Him.

2. God's design for marriage is exclusively heterosexual and unique among all human relationships (10:6-7).

3. God's plan from the beginning is that marriage would be permanent (10:9).

4. Jesus acknowledges that because we live in a fallen world and have hard hearts, divorce will occur (10:3-4). However, no divorce is ever necessary, though it may be occasionally permissible to those whose divorce is on biblical grounds.

5. To divorce one's mate (without a biblical cause?) and remarry another is to commit the sin of adultery (10:11-12).

Now, to these clear statements in Mark 10:1-12, what else can we say about divorce and remarriage that is both prophetic and pastoral, instructive and redemptive?

1. Where the sin of adultery and/or divorce has taken place, forgiveness is possible and available to those who repent and confess their sin (1 John 1:9).

2. If we are in an unbiblical marriage, we should not attempt to get out of it. Seek forgiveness for the sin of adultery, and then work

hard to glorify God and be a blessing to the mate with whom you are married.

3. In the church we should emphasize the value and dignity of marriage while eliminating the shame and stigma of the divorced. We "mingle the call to obedience with the tears of compassion" (Storms, "Divorce and Remarriage").

4. We should acknowledge that divorce is a sin that is far more hurtful and destructive than many other sins.

5. "An ounce of prevention is worth a pound of cure." No minister should perform a wedding without requiring extensive premarital counseling and the signing of a premarital wedding covenant.

Reflect and Discuss

1. How has the world changed in the last 50 years with regard to relationships and divorce? What were the social trends behind those changes? What can the church do to improve society?

2. What aspects of Genesis 2:18-25 point to God's prescription for the ideal marriage?

3. What is the definition of *marriage*? What is the purpose of marriage? How does this affect our view on the legal definition of marriage?

4. What is the difference in the Bible between regulating or reporting divorce, on the one hand, and sanctioning or affirming divorce on the other?

5. Why is it difficult not to let feelings enter into the determination of what is the biblical truth about divorce? For a Christian leader, what is the place of compassion with regard to divorce?

6. How has the fall influenced God's ideal for marriage? How does it affect the way a Christian might counsel couples?

7. How would you respond to someone who says, "I'll just get divorced and remarried, then I'll ask God to forgive me"?

8. Why are there so many different Christian opinions on divorce and remarriage? How does this uncertainty affect the way a Christian leader might counsel a couple? What do we know for sure?

9. What interest does the church have in defining and regulating secular marriage?

10. What can the church do to help prevent divorce before it happens? What can individuals do?

A Premarital Wedding Covenant

The decision to marry is the second most important decision one will ever make. (The first is whether one will commit to Jesus Christ as Savior and Lord.) Keeping this in mind, we commit to God, our minister, and each other to do the following:

1. Seek God's will for our lives personally and together by following biblical principles for Christian living and marriage.
2. Don't engage in premarital sex.
3. Do everything possible to build a Christian marriage and home. This means that both of us have a personal relationship with Jesus Christ and that we desire growth for that relationship over the entire course of our lives by being obedient to His Word.
4. Read and listen to all premarital material provided by our minister.
5. Be active in a Bible-believing church beginning now and throughout our marriage.
6. Buy and read *His Needs, Her Needs* by Willard Harley, *The Act of Marriage* by Tim LaHaye, *God on Sex* by Danny Akin, and *A Promise Kept* by Robertson McQuilkin.
7. Maintain total openness and honesty with our minister and with each other both now and after our wedding.
8. Postpone or cancel the marriage if, at any time between now and the wedding, either one of us comes to believe this marriage is not right.
9. Never allow the word *divorce* to enter the realm of our relationship. We are in this together for the duration of our lives. Divorce is not an option for us!
10. Seek competent Christian counsel if we encounter any difficulty in our marriage.

With the above commitments made, we believe God will be honored and the prospects for a meaningful and happy marriage enhanced. With God's help we will seek to honor God with our lives and marriage all the days of our lives.

Husband: _____

Wife: _____

Witness: _____

Jesus Loves the Little Children
(Why I Believe Children Who Die Go to Heaven)
MARK 10:13-16

Main Idea: Jesus loves all children, and He lovingly calls all people to become like dependent children if they are to enter His kingdom.

I. **We Should Bring Children to Jesus (10:13-14).**
   A. Love them to Jesus (10:13).
   B. Lead them to Jesus (10:14).
II. **We Should Learn from Children About the Kingdom of God (10:14-16).**
   A. We come helpless and hopeful (10:14).
   B. We come trusting and dependent (10:15).
   C. We come for affection and blessing (10:16).

I grew up in a Christian home and began attending church nine months before making my public arrival into this world. I then continued to attend church multiple times every week, and I fell in love with many Christian children's songs. "Jesus Loves Me" is still my favorite song of all time. Its basic biblical truth is simple yet profound.

> Jesus loves me this I know,
> For the Bible tells me so.
> Little ones to Him belong,
> They are weak but He is strong.
>
> Yes, Jesus loves me,
> Yes, Jesus loves me,
> Yes, Jesus loves me,
> The Bible tells me so. (Anna B. Warner and William B. Bradbury, "Jesus Loves Me," 1862)

A second song I quickly grew fond of was "Jesus Loves the Little Children."

> Jesus loves the little children,
> All the children of the world;
> Red and yellow, black and white,
> They are precious in His sight,
> Jesus loves the little children of the world. (Clare Herbert Woolston and George Frederick Root, "Jesus Loves the Little Children," c. 1895)

Jesus does indeed love the little children of the world. Sadly many people do not share Jesus' love. In Jesus' day children often were viewed as a liability until they could contribute to society. Some people today treat children as little more than a commodity to be used and discarded.

Throughout history the intrinsic value of children has often been ignored. Biblical examples of dishonoring children as image bearers include Herod's killing of babies during Jesus' day, mirroring the Pharaoh in Exodus. In general children were not held in high esteem by Romans. By Jesus' time Romans had a trash heap beside many homes where people could leave unwanted children. If other people wanted the children, they would pick them up. Sometimes these kids were raised to be prostitutes, gladiators, or slaves.

Unfortunately, the world is not much safer for today's children. On February 23, 1992, John Piper preached a sermon entitled "Receiving Children in Jesus' Name":

> If you leave out the heartache of miscarriages and the genocide of abortion, the statistics are painful. Fourteen million children who reach the age of birth die each year before the age of five. If we could all put a face on each of those children and hear the wheezing and the cries and feel the final limp silence, what an ocean of grief would fill the world. I always marvel at the awesome emotional depth and complexity of God that enables him to empathize with the grief of millions and millions of parents all the time, and yet rejoice with those who rejoice with him.
>
>   Of these fourteen million, about ten million die from five conditions: about five million from diarrhea; about three million from measles, tetanus, and whooping cough; and about two million from respiratory infections, mainly pneumonia. Most of these could be saved by simple Oral Rehydration Therapies for the diarrhea; a five-dollar injection for the measles, tetanus, and whooping cough; and a fifty-cent antibiotic for the respiratory problems.
>
>   . . .
>
> America is one of the most violent countries in the world against its children. Not only do we kill a million and a half pre-born children a year, but 22% of the children in America live in poverty; one out of every four girls under eighteen has probably been sexually abused by someone close to her; possibly as high as 30% of all mental retardation may be owing to fetal alcohol syndrome; one study of 36

hospitals showed that in 10% of the pregnancies mothers used illegal drugs during pregnancy; and 89% of school teachers surveyed report that abuse and neglect of children are a problem in their education. The American home is increasingly an unsafe place for children to be. And there is no better place. The family is God's will. (Piper, "Receiving Children")

On the other hand, especially in American culture and even sometimes in Christian homes, children can be turned into idols to be pampered and coddled. They are placed at the center of a universe they will gladly occupy.

The only way to have a balanced view of children is to have a biblical view, to see them as God sees them: they are His gifts to parents (Ps 127:3-5); they provide an illustration as to how we enter the kingdom of God (Mark 9:14-15).

Chapter 10 divides into five major sections: Jesus teaches on *marriage* in verses 1-12 and on *children* in verses 13-16. Then He addresses the perils of *possessions* (vv. 17-31) and the glory of sacrificial *service* (vv. 32-45). Finally, Jesus responds to the *faith* of a blind man (vv. 46-52). The concern and love our Savior has for children is crystal clear.

We Should Bring Children to Jesus
MARK 10:13-14

Jesus had a special affection for children. What *is* surprising is that the disciples didn't! Jesus loves children for who they are: a work of His sovereign Father. He also loves them for what they teach: how someone enters the kingdom of God. One would have a difficult time finding in ancient literature concern for children comparable to that shown by Jesus (Edwards, *Mark*, 306).

Love Them to Jesus (Mark 10:13)

The text says, "They were bringing children to Jesus." "They" might mean both Dad and Mom, and extended family and friends as well. They wanted these little ones to meet Jesus and to be "touched by Him." In contrast, the disciples thought it was a waste of time and "rebuked" them. As Jesus' "political handlers," they sought to restrict the access of those who would love children to Jesus. Their attitude and actions are a replay of their exclusivism and elitism toward the exorcist in 9:38.

Are you like those who want to love children to Jesus, or are you like the disciples who have no time for babysitting? Will you work in the nursery, with preschoolers, with schoolchildren, at VBS, or with children in sports?

Will you stand up and be heard on the evils of abortion, sex-trafficking, and child poverty? Will you love children toward Christ?

Lead Them to Jesus (Mark 10:14)

When Jesus saw the disciples fussing at the folks for bringing children to Him, He wigged out! This is the only time Jesus is said to be "indignant." His righteous anger was aroused, and He publicly rebuked them. James Edwards says, "The object of a person's indignation reveals a great deal about the person. Jesus' displeasure here reveals his compassion and defense of the helpless, vulnerable, and powerless" (*Mark*, 306). Jesus is affirming that children are worth His time, and they should be worth our time!

There are several ways we can consistently and actively lead children to Christ. We can evangelize them with a gospel-saturated home. We can disciple them with a Bible-saturated home. We can pray with them in a prayer-saturated home. We can encourage them, bless them, and challenge them. We absolutely must model for them a "Christ-intoxicated life," letting them see that living for Jesus is the natural and normal ebb and flow of life.

We Should Learn from Children About the Kingdom of God
MARK 10:14-16

There is something about a child that is essential for entrance into the kingdom of God. It is not their *innocence*, for they are not innocent! They are little sinners just like we are big sinners. Nor is it their *purity* or that they are *sweet*. Again, they are sinners with Adam and Eve's and your and my DNA running throughout their being.

Still, for some reason, Jesus says children are a better example of how to enter the kingdom than are adults. "We tell children to behave like adults, but Jesus tells the adults to model themselves after the children" (Wiersbe, *Be Diligent*, 99)!

We Come Helpless and Hopeful (Mark 10:14)

Jesus says children are the kind of people who obtain "the kingdom of God." Children teach us something. We see them coming to Jesus with the help of others, no doubt having some degree of hope and expectation, small though it may be. Children are helpless. Their lives are in the hands of another. Yet, even at a tender age, they seem to be filled with hope and expectation. They don't know all they need, but they know they need the help of another, and they are hopeful they will receive it. They come small, helpless, and powerless. They have no clout or standing, and they bring nothing but empty hands. This is appropriate since only empty hands can be filled!

We Come Trusting and Dependent (Mark 10:15)

Jesus says the kingdom of God is received not earned. It is received like a little child, or it is not received at all. By their display of trust and absolute dependence on another, children point the way to entrance into God's kingdom. Children have the capacity to enjoy a lot but explain little. They live by faith and dependence. They must trust another to survive.

We Come for Affection and Blessing (Mark 10:16)

Jesus picked up the children. What a picture of amazing gospel grace! He is tender and affectionate to those who bring nothing to Him but their need. He even "laid His hands on them and blessed them." There were several components of the Hebrew blessing: a *meaningful touch, a spoken word, attaching high value, picturing a special future,* and *an active commitment* (Trent and Smalley, *The Blessing, passim*). Christ fulfilled these components. He picked up and held these children, spoke a word of blessing over them, and attached high value to their intrinsic worth. He might have spoken prophetic words for future service in God's kingdom. And He made an active commitment to see the blessing fulfilled. Calvary and the cross say it all.

Conclusion

So Jesus loves the little children. But what happens to those who die in infancy, die young, or never reach an age of moral discernment (often called the "age of accountability")? As the subtitle of this message states, I believe children who die go to heaven.

Few things in life are more tragic and heartbreaking than the death of a baby or small child. The grief can be overwhelming. Many console themselves that the child is now in a better place. Some believe the rather popular myth that small children who die become angels. However, sentimentalism and emotional hopes and wants are not sufficient for those who live under the authority of the Word of God. We must ask, Do we really know that those who die in infancy go to heaven? What biblical evidence is there?

The church has not been of one mind on this issue. Some church fathers remained silent on the topic. Ambrose said unbaptized infants were not admitted to heaven but have immunity from the pains of hell.

Augustine basically affirmed the damnation of all unbaptized infants, but taught they would receive the mildest punishment of all. Gregory of Nyssa believed infants who die immediately mature and are given the opportunity to trust Christ. Calvin affirmed the election of some infants to salvation and was open to the possibility that all infants who die are saved. Commenting on this narrative, he said, "Christ receives not only those who, moved by holy desire and faith, freely approach unto Him, but those who are not yet of age to know how much they need His grace" (Calvin, *Harmony*, 1:389). Zwingli, B. B. Warfield, and Charles Hodge all taught that God saves all who die in infancy. This perspective has become the dominant view of the church today.

Yet a popular evangelical theologian chided Billy Graham when, at the Oklahoma City bombing memorial service, he said, "Someday there will be a glorious reunion with those who have died and gone to heaven before us, and that includes all those innocent children that are lost. They're not lost from God because any child that young is automatically in heaven and in God's arms." The theologian scolded Dr. Graham for offering what he called "a new gospel: justification by youth alone" (Sproul, "Comfort"). There are good reasons biblically and theologically for believing God saves all who die and do not reach a stage of moral understanding and accountability. Scripture does not speak to this issue directly, yet there is evidence that can be gleaned that would lead us to affirm on biblical grounds that God receives into heaven all who have died in infancy.

First, the grace, goodness, and mercy of God would support the position. This is the strongest argument. God is love (1 John 4:8) and desires that all be saved (1 Tim 2:4). His concern for children is evident when Jesus says, "Your Father in heaven is not willing that any of these little ones should be lost" (Matt 8:14). People go to hell because they choose in willful rebellion and unbelief to reject God and His grace. Children are incapable of this kind of conscious rejection of God. Where such rebellion and willful disobedience are absent, God is gracious to receive.

Second, when the baby boy who was born to David and Bathsheba died (2 Sam 12:15-18), David did two significant things. He confessed his confidence that he would see the child again, and he comforted his wife Bathsheba (2 Sam 12:23-24). David must have been confident that his little son was with God.

Third, in James 4:17, the Bible says, "So it is a sin for the person who knows to do what is good and doesn't do it." The Bible is clear that we are all born with a sin nature as a result of being in Adam (Rom 5:12), called "original sin." However, the Scriptures make a distinction between original sin and actual sins. Infants are incapable of actual sins because they are incapable of moral discernment. Original sin is why infants die physically. Actual sins committed with knowledge and understanding are why people die spiritually and eternally if they die without Christ (2 Cor 5:10; Rev 20:12-13).

Fourth, Jesus affirmed that the kingdom of God belonged to little children (Mark 10:13-16; Luke 18:15-17). Jesus says that saving faith is a childlike faith, but He also seems to be affirming the reality of children populating heaven.

Fifth, Scripture affirms that the number of saved souls is great (Rev 7:9). Since most of the world has been and is still non-Christian, might it be the untold multitude who have died prematurely or in infancy make up a majority of those in heaven? Charles Spurgeon said, "I rejoice to know that the souls of all infants, as soon as they die, speed their way to paradise. Think what a multitude there is of them" (Spurgeon, "Defense").

Sixth, some in Scripture are said to be chosen or sanctified from the womb (1 Sam 1:8–2:21; Jer 1:5; Luke 1:15). This affirms the salvation of some infants and refutes the view that only baptized babies are assured of heaven.

Seventh, Deuteronomy 1:35-39 is helpful. After the children of Israel rebelled against God in the wilderness, God sentenced that generation to die in the wilderness. But God specifically exempted young children and infants from this sentence and explained, "Your little children, whom you said would be plunder, your sons who don't know good from evil, will enter there" (Deut 1:39). God specifically exempted from the judgment those who "don't know good from evil" because of their age. These "little children" would inherit the promised land and would not be judged on the basis of their fathers' sins. This passage bears directly on the issue of infant salvation and implies that the accomplished work of Christ has removed the stain of original sin from those who die in infancy. Knowing neither good nor evil, these children are incapable of committing sins in the body—are not yet moral agents—and die secure in the grace of our Lord Jesus Christ. John Newton, who wrote the hymn "Amazing Grace," was certain of this. He wrote to close friends who had lost a young child, "I hope you are both well reconciled to the death of your child. I cannot be sorry for the death of infants. How many storms do they escape! Nor can I doubt, in my private judgment, that they are included in the election of grace" (Newton, *Works*, 4:340–41).

Anyone who is saved is saved because of the grace of God, the saving work of Jesus Christ, and the undeserved and unmerited regenerating work of the Holy Spirit. Like all who have ever lived, except for Jesus, infants need to be saved. Only Jesus can take away their sin, and if they are saved, it is because of His sovereign grace and abounding mercy. Abraham said, "Won't the Judge of all the earth do what is just?" (Gen 18:25). For those incapable of willful acts of sin, we can rest assured God will, indeed, do right. Precious little ones are the objects of His saving mercy and grace.

On September 29, 1861, Charles Spurgeon chastened some critics who had "wickedly, lyingly, and slanderously said of Calvinists that we believe that some little children perish" ("Infant Salvation"). Spurgeon affirmed that God saved little ones without limitation and without exception. He concluded the message with an evangelistic appeal to parents:

> Many of you are parents who have children in heaven. Is it not a desirable thing that you should go there too? . . . Mother, unconverted mother, from the battlements of heaven your child beckons you to Paradise. Father, ungodly, impenitent father, the little eyes that once looked joyously on you, look down upon you now and the lips which had scarcely learned to call you "Father" ere they were sealed by the silence of death, may be heard as with a still, small voice, saying to you this morning, "Father, must we be forever divided by the great gulf which no man can pass?" . . . If thou wilt think of these matters, perhaps the heart will begin to move, and the eyes may begin to flow and then may the Holy Spirit put before thine eyes the cross of the Savior . . . if thou wilt turn thine eye to Him, thou shalt live. ("Infant Salvation")

Little ones are precious in God's sight. If they die, they go to heaven. Parents who have trusted Jesus and have lost a little one can be confident of a wonderful reunion someday. Are you hopeful of seeing again that little treasure God entrusted to you for such a short time? Jesus has made a way.

Reflect and Discuss

1. In what way do children have intrinsic value, not just potential value?
2. What is the greatest danger to children in the U.S.? in Sub-Saharan Africa? in China? in Thailand? What can you do about these issues?
3. At what age can a person typically leave the nurturing environment and fend for himself or herself in the world? How might this expand the discussion of the "age of viability"?
4. What reasons might some people have today for restricting the access of children to Jesus? Who among non-Christians and Christians might suggest that children shouldn't be brought to church? Why?
5. What opportunities do you have to bring your children to Jesus? to bring other children? How can you participate and assist in these ministries?
6. What do children do that demonstrates they are sinners? How do they show they are helpless and hopeful? Trusting and dependent?
7. Did you receive a blessing from your parents? Have you given your blessing to your children? Why is this formal tradition meaningful and powerful?

- It calls us to trust and follow the One and only Son who is "the image of the invisible God" (Col 1:15) and the "radiance of God's glory" (Heb 1:3). In Jesus and Jesus alone we can behold the glory and greatness of God and live!

The British preacher Martyn Lloyd-Jones said, "The Son of God became man that the children of men might become children of God" (*God the Father*, 265). Jesus Christ is the hero of the Bible—God in a body, the Savior of sinners, the final sacrifice, and the glory of God made flesh. He took the three disciples up a mountain for a glimpse of glory. He wants to take you and me up to heaven to glory forever. Will you follow Him? Will you trust Him? You become what you behold! May we all behold Jesus now and forever.

Reflect and Discuss

1. What were some of the mistaken impressions the disciples, Jews, and Gentiles had of Jesus?
2. What mistaken impressions do people have of Jesus today? How can a proper understanding of the incarnation help people avoid these misconceptions?
3. What is the meaning of the word *amen* at the beginning of Jesus' statement (9:1)? How is it encouraging?
4. In what sense was Jesus changed in the transfiguration, and in what sense was He unchanged?
5. How did Jesus fulfill the promises Moses and Elijah embodied?
6. What would you say to someone who argued that the disciples only dreamed Jesus was transfigured?
7. What do you suppose Peter was thinking or feeling when he suggested building three shelters?
8. How does the command to listen to Jesus alone, and not Moses or Elijah, affect our view of the prophets, priests, and kings of the Old Testament?
9. How would the transfiguration have given Jesus greater resolve to continue on His path to the cross?
10. Was there a moment in your life when Jesus suddenly was revealed to you as glorious and holy God? Share that moment with someone this week.

8. What have you heard expressed about the fate of children who die? Were these statements based on wishful thinking or anchored in biblical truth?
9. Why would an appeal to God's mercy and love be insufficient by itself as an argument in favor of the salvation of children?
10. Which of the seven arguments in favor of the salvation of infants do you consider the strongest? Why?

What Must I Do to Inherit Eternal Life? (Will You Leave Everything and Follow Jesus?)

MARK 10:17-31

Main Idea: Following Jesus may involve great personal cost, but it always results in great eternal gain.

I. **It Is Easier Than You Think (10:17-22).**
   A. Go to the right Person (10:17).
   B. Ask the right question (10:17).
   C. Get the right answers (10:18-21).
   D. Give the right response (10:22).
II. **It Is Harder Than You Think (10:23-27).**
   A. One thing can cost you salvation (10:23-25).
   B. Only God can provide you salvation (10:26-27).
III. **It Is Better Than You Think (10:28-31).**
   A. Leave a little and get a lot (10:28-30).
   B. Be last and come in first (10:31).

Who am I? Why am I here? What is my purpose in living? Where will I go when I die? These are what we sometimes refer to as the "ultimate questions" of life. Everyone thinks about them. These questions go to the heart of what it means to be human. They address our significance, importance, and destiny. And think about this: The questions do connect. How you answer one will influence how you answer the others.

One day a fine and respected man of the community came to Jesus. He was interested specifically in his destiny. "What must I do to inherit eternal life?" In the process of answering that question, Jesus also gave him insight concerning what or who really matters most in life. And what you decide now will determine where you go later. The questions connect, and so do the answers.

This text addresses the important question, Who or what should have first place in my life? Jesus demands that people give Him first place in their lives above all else and all others (Col 1:18).

John Mark wrote the second Gospel about AD 65–68, making great use of an eyewitness, the apostle Peter. He wrote to a Roman audience facing severe persecution during the reign of Nero. He challenged them concerning true discipleship in 8:31–10:52. This section contains three passion predictions (8:31-33; 9:30-32; 10:32-34), each followed by instruction on what it means to be a disciple of Jesus. In 10:13-16, Jesus says we must receive the kingdom of God like a little, helpless child. The account of the rich young ruler raises the question, Will someone with great wealth and standing receive the kingdom like a little child?

So the question is, What must I do or, better, whom must I trust to inherit eternal life?

It Is Easier Than You Think
MARK 10:17-22

Jesus was continuing His journey toward Jerusalem. Our Savior is engaging the disciples in teaching about true discipleship and His forthcoming crucifixion and resurrection. They are struggling students who can't grasp what He is saying. Jesus has just told them that those who enter the kingdom of God must be like a little child (10:13-16). All must come to Jesus with nothing, in total dependence on Him. No one can earn the kingdom. The requirement is the same for all: simple, childlike reliance on Jesus. It is that easy. It is in the context of this teaching that one who is the opposite of a helpless child approaches Jesus.

Go to the Right Person (Mark 10:17)

A man ran up to Jesus. The man had great wealth ("many possessions"). Luke 18:18 calls him a ruler. Matthew 19:22 says he is young. Thus we call him "the rich young ruler." He was a man of power, affluence, and influence. Evidently he had heard Jesus teach and was impressed with what he heard. He did not walk to Jesus, he ran to Him. He was eager to get to Him because Jesus "was setting out on a journey." He may not have another opportunity to talk to this man whose teachings were unlike any he had ever heard. With remarkable respect he "knelt down before Him." He saw Jesus as a distinguished rabbi and paid Him honor reserved for the great teachers of the law. He certainly had come in the right way (with humility) and to the right person (Jesus).

And Jesus will readily identify with the rich young ruler. After all, He was about 30 years of age Himself. And He, too, was rich—far richer than this man could possibly imagine. As the Son of God, Jesus had lived for all of eternity in the glory, wealth, love, and sweet fellowship of His Father. What He was about to ask this man to do was not unfamiliar to Him! He had already left it all behind. Paul says it perfectly in 2 Corinthians 8:9, "Though He was rich, for your sake He became poor, so that by His poverty you might become rich."

"And [Jesus would say] I am going into a poverty deeper than anyone has ever known. . . . I am giving it all away. Why? For you. Now, [get ready, I am going to ask] you [to] give away everything to follow me. If I gave away my 'big all' to get you, can you give away your 'little all' to follow me? I won't ask you to do anything I haven't already done. I'm the ultimate Rich Young Ruler who has given away the ultimate wealth to get you. Now, you need to give away yours to get me" (Keller, *King's Cross*, 136). Jesus is the right person.

Ask the Right Questions (Mark 10:17)

This man then calls Jesus *good*. "Good teacher, what must I do to inherit eternal life?" This was an astounding tribute indicating the impression Jesus had made on him. The Jews referred to God as good but never spoke this way of one another except in a derivative or qualified sense (see Prov 12:2; 14:14; Eccl 9:2; Matt 12:35). Only God is good in the absolute sense of the word. Jesus' response in verse 18 bears this out. The rich young ruler was awed by Jesus, and he had an extremely important question to ask Him. This question is one of the most significant in the whole Bible and for all humanity: How do I get eternal life? In the Bible the gift of the life of God is called eternal life (10:17), entering the kingdom of God (10:23,25), having treasure in heaven (10:21), and enjoying the age to come (10:30). It is the life *of* God and life *with* God. It is the privilege of being a member of God's kingdom, and it must be received with faith in Jesus and the reliance of a little child in Jesus. We do not know whether the young ruler had heard Jesus say this or not. His question, though by no means a bad one, implies he believes eternal life is something you work for. "What must I *do*?" All religions of the world can be categorized under "do" or "done." I am saved by what I *do* or by what another has *done*. Christianity is a *done* religion/relationship. Eternal life is not achieved; it is received as a gift (John 1:12) based on what Jesus has done for us (John 3:16). So the young ruler must have both a change of theology and a change of heart if he is to inherit eternal life.

Get the Right Answers (Mark 10:18-21)

Jesus answers the young ruler's question with a theological question: "Why do you call Me good? . . . No one is good but One—God." Jesus does not return the young man's flattering greeting as might have been expected. Jesus puts the focus of the issue where it must be: on God. The young man's starting point was wrong because it was himself. "What must I *do*?" The rich young ruler was no doubt a "good man" by the standards of his day. He saw in Jesus another good man whose insight into spiritual matters could perhaps solve some lingering questions that plagued his soul. Jesus forced him to look to God for any hope of genuine goodness and eternal life. Furthermore, Jesus implicitly confronted the young ruler with his evaluation of Jesus. To call Him good is to call Him God. Is that what he meant? If Jesus is not God, then He, like the rest of humanity, is a sinner and therefore not good in the supreme sense. On the other hand, if He *is* God, it would be appropriate to call Him good. It would also be appropriate to worship Him, follow Him, and obey Him. He challenges the young ruler to think clearly and choose his words carefully, a challenge each one of us should accept.

Jesus does not wait for a response. "You know the commandments." Jesus cites the last six commandments, which address our human relationships with one another. "Do not defraud" may be a rewording or application of the last commandment against covetousness or may even be an application of commandments eight and nine. The young ruler wanted to know, "What must I do to inherit eternal life?" Jesus says, "I'll tell you what you must do: obey the will of God, which is revealed in His perfect, holy, and moral law. Obey this in the *good* sense (perfect)—in the same way God is *good*—and eternal life is yours."

The young man responds, "Teacher, I have kept all these from my youth." The young man had conducted his life according to the law of God. He had honored it and obeyed all of it! In an external sense what he said was probably true. Like the apostle Paul he was faultless (Phil 3:6) with respect to the outward demands of the law as taught by the religious teachers of Israel. From his *Bar Mitzvah* to this day, he had worked for God's approval, and his record was spotless! Verse 21 is one of the most touching and tender verses in the Bible, just as verse 22 is one of the most tragic. "Then, looking at him, Jesus loved him" (v. 21). There was a sincerity and earnestness about this young man that moved the heart of our Lord. His divine heart of love reached out because this man made in His image was so very near to the kingdom. Jesus then said, "You lack one thing: Go, sell all you have and give to the poor, and you will have treasure in heaven. Then come, follow Me" (v. 21).

Having addressed the last six commandments, Jesus now addresses the first (Exod 20:3). God must be God in our lives. No one and nothing can stand between Him and us. The particular demand Jesus puts on the rich young ruler is not a general command for all persons. It was specific to him, though it could be specific to some of us too! His wealth occupied the place that only God should have in his life. It was his idol, his god. He may have obeyed, relatively speaking, those commands that address human relationships, but he lived in perpetual disobedience, sin, and idolatry when it came to the first and foundational commandment: "Do not have other gods besides Me." You come up short in your life in one crucial area, Jesus was saying: what will be first? Jesus offers Himself as a substitute for the man's wealth. Only when he gives it all away will he become like a small, vulnerable child. Only then will he actually possess everything!

The call to discipleship is a call to radical trust and commitment to Jesus. Jesus challenges all of us to put away anything that is an obstacle to our following Him. You cannot love your wealth supremely and love Jesus supremely.

Give the Right Response (Mark 10:22)

Verse 22 records the tragic end of their encounter—"stunned." A cloud of gloom and sorrow moved in. "He went away grieving." Why? "Because he had many possessions." His gold would remain his god. Jesus' difficult demand was met with a "no." He got the right answer to his question. He just did not give the right response. James Edwards insightfully notes, "A person who leads an exemplary life—who even endears himself to the Son of God—can still be an idolater" (Edwards, *Mark*, 313).

It Is Harder Than You Think
MARK 10:23-27

The rich young ruler had come to the right person: Jesus. He had asked the right question: How do I inherit eternal life? He had received the right answer: Honor God and follow Jesus in complete trust like a little child. Sadly he did not respond correctly, and he walked away from the only true source of eternal life. "When Jesus called this young man to give up his money, the man started to grieve, because money was for him what the Father was for Jesus. It was the center of his identity. To lose his money would have been to lose himself" (Keller, *King's Cross*, 132).

One Thing Can Cost You Salvation (Mark 10:23-25)

Jesus told His disciples, "How hard it is for those who have wealth to enter the kingdom of God!" Jesus was not condemning wealth and commending poverty. This is not a call for asceticism. The point is, wealth breeds confidence in one's self, and it has an addictive quality. Scripture addresses its dangerous attraction (see Matt 6:19-21,24; Luke 12:13-21; 16:19-30; 1 Tim 6:17). It becomes life's priority and the things of God go by the wayside.

The disciples could not believe their ears! So Jesus said it again: "Children, how hard it is to enter the kingdom of God! It is easier for a camel to go through the eye of a needle than for a rich person to enter the kingdom of God!" Jesus prefaced His statement with a term of tenderness: "Children." The camel was one of the largest animals found in that part of the world. The thought of trying to squeeze it, humps and all, through the eye of a needle would strike His disciples as funny, and also impossible. "I guess salvation is harder than we thought," they said. And it takes only one thing like wealth to keep you out of God's kingdom. They did not see that coming. Jesus turns the value system of the world on its head.

Only God Can Provide You Salvation (Mark 10:26-27)

The Twelve were "even more astonished." They asked, "Then who can be saved?" Judaism was guilty of its own "prosperity theology." Wealth and riches were seen as an evidence of God's favor (see Job 1:10; 42:10; Ps 128:1-2; Isa 3:10). Jesus corrected their bad theology. Actually, wealth can build a barrier to the one thing necessary to enter the kingdom: helpless, childlike trust in Jesus (v. 15).

His answer to their question is one of the great theological affirmations in the Bible: "With men it is impossible, but not with God, because all things are possible with God." Salvation is something man cannot accomplish. Left to himself, he will never make it into God's kingdom and inherit eternal life. Salvation is, has always been, and will always be a divine accomplishment through the perfect atonement and sacrificial death of God's Son. *Done*, not *do*!

With men, entering God's kingdom and receiving eternal life is impossible, and no one will be saved. With God all things are possible, and anyone can be saved! If you desire for Christ to be your Savior, you have to replace what you have been looking to as a savior. We all have something. What's yours? That is an excellent "life question" to consider.

It Is Better Than You Think
MARK 10:28-31

We could suspect that the disciples would have lots of questions. They needed to think things over. Peter expresses a perplexed but heartfelt plea.

Leave a Little and Get a Lot (Mark 10:28-30)

Peter, the ever-ready spokesman for the disciples, picks up on the words of Jesus and says, "Look, we have left everything and followed You." Jesus affirms that whatever you might lose or give up in this present age (or life) for Jesus and the gospel, you will not fail to receive a hundred times as much "now at this time" and in the age to come "eternal life." The things Jesus notes we may have to give up are precious things: home or brothers or sisters or mother or father or children or lands. It costs to follow Jesus. However, the blessings far outweigh the losses. In God's kingdom the benefits and blessings are simply too great to imagine.

One surprising "blessing" is "persecutions." Its inclusion strikes a sobering note of realism for the person who would follow Jesus. To be a member of Christ's kingdom means to share in all that is His. This includes suffering on His behalf, a momentary light affliction when seen against the promise of eternal life (2 Cor 4:17).

John Piper specifically applies these verses to missionaries—and all of us are called to be missionaries:

This text does not mean that you get materially rich by becoming a missionary—at least not in the sense that your own private possessions increase. It means mainly that if you are deprived of your earthly family in the service of Christ, it will be made up a hundredfold in your spiritual family, the church. But even this may be too limiting. What about the lonely missionaries who labor for years without being surrounded by hundreds of sisters and brothers and mothers and children in the faith? Is the promise not true for them? Surely it is.

Surely what Christ means is that *he himself makes up for every loss.* If you give up a mother's nearby affection and concern, you get back one hundred times the affection and concern from the ever-present Christ. If you give up the warm comradeship of a brother, you get back one hundred times the warmth and camaraderie from Christ. If you give up the sense of at-homeness you had in your house, you get back one hundred times the comfort and security of knowing that your Lord owns every house and land and stream and tree on earth. Isn't what Jesus is saying to prospective missionaries just this:

I promise to work for you and be for you so much that you will not
be able to speak of having sacrificed anything. That's the way Hudson
Taylor took it, because at the end of his 50 years of missionary labor
in China he said, "I never made a sacrifice." (Piper, "Missions")

So, leave a little and get a lot.

Be Last and Come in First (Mark 10:31)

Verse 31 is another hinge verse connecting and contrasting the rich young
ruler (10:17-31) with the Servant of the Lord, Jesus (10:32-45; cf. 9:35).
Again the value system of this present evil age is turned on its head.

"But many who are first will be last, and the last first" is one of those sayings Jesus probably repeated on numerous occasions (cf. Matt 19:30; 20:16).
In Christ's kingdom there is a grand reversal of every earthly standard of
position, rank, and importance. God does not evaluate things in the same
way fallen humanity does. As citizens of His kingdom, His children should
think more like Him than like the world.

To the general public, the rich young ruler stood first and the poor
disciples stood last. But God saw things from the perspective of eternity—and the first become last while the last become first. Those who
are first in their own eyes will be last in God's eyes, but those who are
last in their own eyes will be rewarded as first! What an encouragement for true disciples! (Wiersbe, *Be Diligent*, 103)

Tim Keller says, "The heart of the gospel is all about giving up power,
pouring out resources and serving . . . the Center of Christianity is always
migrating away from power and wealth" (Keller, *King's Cross*, 124).

Jesus said to the rich young ruler, "I want you to imagine life without
money. All you have is Me. Am I really enough?" Do you truly believe the
person who has Jesus plus nothing actually has everything? That is the question Jesus puts before this man. It is the same question He puts before us.
How will you respond?!

Reflect and Discuss

1. At what age did you begin to ponder the ultimate questions of life? What
   questions have you thought about the most?
2. How does the context of Jesus welcoming the little child set the stage for
   this instruction?
3. Why is (1) coming to Jesus (2) with respect and (3) in humility necessary
   for salvation? Why is it not sufficient?
4. How do churchgoing Christians sometimes make it look like our religion is
   based on what we do? How can we change this perception?

5. Is it possible for a person to keep the last six commandments? How do Matthew 5:22,28 and 22:36-40 raise the bar for perfection?

6. Why did Jesus make this particular demand of the rich young ruler? What demand might He make of you? (What is your identity? What is your savior?)

7. Is wealth evidence of God's favor? How can it also be an impediment to salvation? What determines your opinion about money: your culture or the Bible?

8. Are there some people who have the gift of managing money for the kingdom and others who do not? What are the characteristics of this gift? Do you have the gift?

9. Is it wrong to seek a reward? How is the reward of discipleship better than anything the world has to offer?

10. Why did Jesus mention "persecutions" (v. 30) among the rewards of discipleship? Does this kind of frank disclosure seem like a good policy for evangelism?

Sent to Serve
(Why Did Jesus Come?)
MARK 10:32-45

Main Idea: Our Savior came calling us to serve others just as He served us.

I. Consider the Cost of Being a Servant (10:32-34).
  A. The road of service invites misunderstanding (10:32).
  B. The road of service involves a mission (10:32-34).

II. Consider the Challenge to Being a Servant (10:35-40).
  A. Being a servant goes against our human inclinations (10:35-37).
  B. Being a servant is ordained by divine revelation (10:38-40).

III. Consider the Conflict in Being a Servant (10:41-44).
  A. You must say no to the ways of the world (10:41-43).
  B. You must say yes to the work of a slave (10:43-44).

IV. Consider Christ when Being a Servant (10:45).
  A. Follow Christ in service.
  B. Follow Christ in sacrifice.

In 2006 John Piper wrote the book *Fifty Reasons Why Jesus Came to Die.* Among those 50 reasons:

1. To Absorb the Wrath of God
2. To Please His Heavenly Father

3. To Achieve His Own Resurrection from the Dead
4. To Show the Wealth of God's Love and Grace for Sinners
5. To Show His Own Love for Us
6. For the Forgiveness of Our Sins
7. To Take Away Our Condemnation
8. To Make Us Holy, Blameless, and Perfect
9. To Give Us a Clear Conscience
10. To Obtain for Us All Things That Are Good for Us
11. To Heal Us from Moral and Physical Sickness
12. To Give Eternal Life to All Who Believe on Him
13. To Free Us from the Slavery of Sin
14. To Enable Us to Live for Christ and Not Ourselves
15. To Make His Cross the Ground of All Our Boasting
16. To Enable Us to Live by Faith in Him
17. To Create a People Passionate for Good Works
18. To Unleash the Power of God in the Gospel
19. To Show That the Worst Evil Is Meant by God for Good

Three are particularly relevant to the text before us:

1. To Become a Ransom for Many
2. To Call Us to Follow His Example of Lowliness and Costly Love
3. To Ransom People from Every Tribe and Language and People and Nation (Piper, *Fifty Reasons*)

Mark 8–10 is the most sustained and specific teaching on discipleship in the New Testament. In each chapter there is

1. a passion prediction of our Lord's death and resurrection (8:31-32; 9:30-31; 10:32-34);
2. a foolish response by the disciples (8:32-33; 9:32-34; 10:35-41);
3. and a lesson on discipleship, service, and true spiritual greatness (8:34-38; 9:35-37; 10:42-45).

Our Lord's instruction on spiritual greatness reaches its climax in 10:45: "For even the Son of Man did not come to be served, but to serve, and to give His life—a ransom for many." This is the key verse of Mark's Gospel, the ultimate reason Jesus came. This gets at the heart of the gospel, the pattern for all who would follow Christ. We are sent to serve, even laying down our lives if God ordains it, just as He ordained it for His Son.

In grateful response to the One who came and gave His life as a ransom for many, just what will the gospel make of us? It will make us lowly, humble servants just like the Savior. However, before we surrender to serve, we must consider the issue of servanthood: What is its nature? What do we see and learn from the greatest servant of all, King Jesus?

Consider the Cost of Being a Servant
MARK 10:32-34

"They were on the road, going up to Jerusalem." We might have expected Jerusalem is where His passion will occur, but now it is plainly stated.

Jesus the Savior leads the way, His face set for the destiny that awaits Him. He has counted the cost, and nothing will stop Him on His march to the cross. I believe the Servant Song of Isaiah 50:4-11 was in our Lord's mind as He marched on to Calvary: "The Lord God will help Me; therefore I have not been humiliated; therefore I have set My face like flint, and I know I will not be put to shame."

The Road of Service Invites Misunderstanding (Mark 10:32)

He leads the way, and it unnerves them. He knows where He is going and what He will do, but they do not. They watch our Lord in amazement and fear, even though they have no idea what is happening and what awaits Him. That may have contributed to their fear.

Jesus knew, and He knew fully. He considered the cost even as others misunderstood. Know that it will be the same with us.

The Road of Service Involves a Mission (Mark 10:32-34)

Privately, with the Twelve Jesus provides the most detailed and precise prophecy of His passion. His words reflect texts like Psalm 22:6-8 and the mocking of the Righteous Sufferer; and Isaiah 50:6, one of the Servant Songs, and the Suffering Servant of the Lord.

Eight specific aspects of His passion and His mission are delineated in verses 33 and 34. God sovereignly and providentially has laid out the road He will walk, the plan He will accomplish.

Again, *it is no different with us.* God orchestrates the steps of our lives, down to the *final* detail, the *last* breath of life. There are no accidents, no surprises with our God.

Family and friends may misunderstand. "*Ministry?* Are you kidding? What a waste of talent and education! *Missions?* Have you lost your mind? Do we need to get you on medication and into counseling?"

God has a plan for your life crafted to the *last detail,* the *last breath,* the *last beat of your heart.* He was sent to serve. He sends us to serve. Count the cost!

Consider the Challenge to Being a Servant
MARK 10:35-40

Being a servant doesn't come easily, especially for those who have been trained to lead and especially for those who dream of being served. Of course there is also the battle we must engage with the flesh. There is a voice in our head from our fallen sinful nature that can whisper persuasively, "The Lord takes care of those who take care of themselves." Just enough truth to *deceive* us, and just enough heresy to *derail* us.

James and John get one thing right but everything else wrong. They are correct that Jesus is headed for glory. But as for how the glory would come, they don't have a clue. They still don't get it. They need a discipleship lesson on a *cup* and a *baptism.*

Being a Servant Goes Against Our Human Inclinations (Mark 10:35-37)

Matthew 20:20-21 reveals James and John had their mother do their dirty work. She was possibly Jesus' aunt, which would make James and John His cousins. Peter is cut out, along with the rest of the disciples.

Their request reveals their complete lack of comprehension of what Jesus has just said. It also reveals their selfishness. Jesus had promised the 12 apostles that they would sit on 12 thrones with Him in the kingdom (Matt 19:28). That, however, was not enough. They wanted the two most honored thrones!

Their request is for the best seats in the house, in the kingdom. Their request reveals: (1) their superficial understanding of what it means to follow Jesus, to be His disciple; (2) their inflated opinion of their own importance, something those who are called to lead are especially susceptible to; and (3) their wrongheadedness on how God measures greatness (cf. Mark 9:34-36). Being a servant goes against our human inclinations. It often is counter to our opinion of ourselves. We know who we are, what we have done, and what we deserve. Being a servant after the pattern of Jesus is a divine enablement, not a human inclination.

At the time of our Lord's greatest glory, there were indeed men on His right and left. They were not two apostles on thrones; they were two criminals on crosses!

Being a Servant Is Ordained by Divine Revelation (Mark 10:38-40)

Jesus is gentle but firm, gracious but direct in His response. He compares His approaching suffering and death to drinking a *cup* and experiencing a *baptism*. These are interesting and powerful metaphors.

Drinking a cup with someone speaks of sharing in that person's fate, experiencing his destiny. The cup was also a common picture of the wrath of God in judgment (Ps 75:8; Isa 51:17-23; Jer 25:15-17; Ezek 23:28-34).

Similarly, Jesus' passion and death were a baptism—His being overwhelmed, flooded, and immersed in the destiny planned for Him by His Father (cf. Gen 6; Ps 69:2,15). His cross was a divine appointment!

Jesus understood this was the will of God for His life. Still, He struggled with the weight of it. What did He pray in the garden of Gethsemane? "Take this cup away from Me. Nevertheless, not what I will, but what You will" (Mark 14:36). And in Luke 12:50 He said, "But I have a baptism to be baptized with, and how it consumes Me until it is finished!"

Their all-too-quick answer (Mark 14:39) makes plain that James and John did not understand. Jesus reveals that they are indeed ordained for a similar destiny (v. 34). James would be the first of the apostles to be martyred (Acts 12:1-2). John would experience, alone, the great persecution of Domitian and be exiled to Patmos (Rev 1). But to choose who sits on His right or left is a decision reserved for His Father. And it is not the kind of question those who will sit in those chairs would ask!

Sadly, James and John fail to see that the pathway to glory is always the pathway of suffering. Before the crown there is a cup of suffering. Before the blessings that flow there is a baptism that overwhelms and drowns.

Consider the Conflict in Being a Servant
MARK 10:41-44

The ten are angry at the two because of their request and probably because they had not thought of it first (cf. 9:33-34 and their lust for position as well). Jesus steps in again and uses the occasion for His most powerful lesson on being a servant, on being great in God's kingdom. It is a hard lesson to learn. It just doesn't seem to make sense. By earthly standards self-promotion is right. By heavenly standards it could not be more wrong!

You Must Say No to the Ways of the World (Mark 10:41-43)

The lost world is driven by selfish ambition and a lust for raw power and position. They "dominate" and "exercise power over" them. In the world, the more important you are, the more are the people who serve you. Jesus says, "But it must not be so among you" (v. 43). In His world the more important you are, the more people you serve. Jesus opposes the mind-set of the world and so must we (Rom 12:2).

You Must Say Yes to the Work of a Slave (Mark 10:43-44)

You want to be great, do something great for God? You want to please and honor the Lord Jesus with your life? Then become a *diakonos* (servant; v. 43), a *doulos* (slave) of all (v. 44). Become a table waiter, a household servant. Become a slave. Such a person will have the mind of Christ, esteeming others better than himself, not giving attention to their own interests, but to those of others (Phil 2:3-5).

Jesus reverses all ideas of greatness, turning the world's philosophy on its head. So, who will we say "yes" to? It will be a battle. To many it will not make sense. Be a servant? Why?

Consider Christ When Being a Servant
MARK 10:45

Jesus has told us He will die in Jerusalem. Now He tells us *why*. Jesus makes a promise no other religious leader in the world has made or could make. He came to serve you and me not just as our example but as our ransom!

William Lane said, "The reversal of all human ideas of greatness and rank was achieved when Jesus came, not to be served, but to serve" (*Mark*, 383). John Piper says, "Mark 10:45 is what turns Christianity into gospel" ("The Son of Man").

Before we unwrap this extraordinary verse, we need to make a couple of important theological observations. There is no thought in the Bible that the ransom was paid to Satan. At the cross Satan received only one thing: his defeat and ruin. Also, the price Christ paid was not taken from Him. He freely and, as Hebrews 12:2 says, joyfully gave it. He was the great giver and not the pitiful victim. John 10:18 says it perfectly, "No one takes [My life] from Me, but I lay it down on My own. I have the right to lay it down, and I have the right to take it up again. I have received this command from My Father."

Follow Christ in Service

"For even" emphasizes the remarkable humility and service of One who should by all rights be honored and served. The "Son of Man" title (Dan 7:13) is wed to "ransom for many" language (Isa 53:12), which radically redefines who and what Messiah would be. He is a suffering Messiah, a servant Messiah. The man for all men, the Man from heaven, the Son of Man came not to be served but to serve.

This is what Christmas is all about! It's about the Son of God, who existed eternally with the Father as "the radiance of God's glory and the exact expression of His nature," taking on human nature (Heb 1:3). It's about the birth of a man by a virgin conceived miraculously (not sexually) by the Holy Spirit so that He is the Son of God in an utterly unique way (Luke 1:35). It's about the coming of a man named Jesus in whom "all the fullness of deity was pleased to dwell" (Col 2:9). It's about the coming of the "fullness of time" (Gal 4:4) that had been prophesied by the prophets of old that

- a Ruler would be born in Bethlehem (Mic 5:2);
- a child would be born called Wonderful Counselor, Mighty God, Eternal Father, Prince of Peace (Isa 9:6);
- a Messiah, an anointed One, a shoot from the stem of Jesse, a son of David, a King would come (Isa 11:1-4; Zech 9:9); and
- the Son of Man would come, who "did not come to be served, but to serve, and to give His life—a ransom for many" (Mark 10:45).

That's what Christmas is about! If He serves, we must serve! If He gives, we must give! If He stoops down, we must stoop down!

C. J. Mahaney says, "Ultimately our Christian service exists only to draw attention to *this* source—to our crucified and risen Lord who gave Himself as the ransom for us all" (*Humility*, 48).

Follow Christ in Sacrifice

In verse 45, we see the term "come." Tim Keller rightly says this "is a strong giveaway that he existed before he was born" (*King's Cross*, 140).

He came to "give His life"—no one takes it. Jesus did not have to die despite God's love. He died because of God's love. The cross is the self-substitution of God for sinful humanity.

He came to "give His life [as] a ransom." This is what theologians often call "the wonderful exchange." "Ransom" means to deliver by purchase. It means a payment, usually of money, required to release someone from punishment or slavery. We needed a ransom because we had all gladly and willingly sold ourselves into the bondage of slavery to sin. When He purchased us, our slave masters—sin, death, hell, and Satan—had to set us free! First Peter 1:18-21 says,

> *For you know that you were redeemed from your empty way of life inherited from the fathers, not with perishable things like silver or gold, but with the precious blood of Christ, like that of a lamb without defect or blemish. He was chosen before the foundation of the world but was revealed at the end of the times for you who through Him are believers in God, who raised Him from the dead and gave Him glory, so that your faith and hope are in God.*

Here ransom speaks of Jesus' substitutionary atonement: His sacrificial death on the cross purchased the release from bondage of those sinners who would believe in Him. Again the ransom was not directed to the Devil but the Father. *Righteousness* demanded it. *Love* provided it. We were then adopted into a new family. "When the time came to completion, God sent His Son, born of a woman, born under the law, to redeem those under the law, so that we might receive adoption as sons" (Gal 4:4-5). We had run away like fools and sold ourselves to Satan and slavery. Jesus sees our pitiful and hopeless situation, pays the ransom, redeems us out of slavery, and brings us into the Father's house!

> Guilty, vile, and helpless we,
> Spotless Lamb of God was He!
> Full atonement! Can it be?
> Hallelujah, what a Savior! (Bliss, "Hallelujah," 1875)

The greatest and best person who ever lived and walked on this earth was a humble servant. He got down low so that He might lift others up. He, as Philippians 2:3 says, "consider[ed] others as more important than [Himself]," all the way to the death of the cross. And now He calls us, those who follow Him, to do the same.

Francis Schaeffer understood what our Savior calls us to do, and he also understood the challenge that confronts us.

> Christ taught his disciples that they were not to be called "Rabbi" or "Master" (Mt. 23:8, 10) and that the greatest among them would be the servant of all (Mk. 10:44). Doesn't each of us tend to reverse this, following our natural inclinations as fallen men while ignoring the Word of God? Don't we like the foremost place? . . . Seeking the highest place is in direct contradiction to the teaching of the Lord. . . .
> If we are going to do the Lord's work in the Lord's way, we must take Jesus' teaching seriously: He does not want us to press on to the greatest place unless he himself makes it impossible to do otherwise. . . .
> If we have the world's mentality of wanting the foremost place, we are not qualified for Christian leadership. This mentality can lift us into ecclesiastical leadership or fit us for being a big name among men, but it unfits us for real spiritual leadership. To the extent that we

want power we are in the flesh, and the Holy Spirit has no part in us. (Schaeffer, *No Little People*, 67–68)

Sent to lead? Perhaps. Sent to serve? No doubt.

Reflect and Discuss

1. How would you answer someone who asked you, "Why did Jesus have to die?" Can you give three reasons?
2. What have you done for the sake of your commitment to Jesus that was misunderstood by the people around you?
3. How is it comforting to know that God has a plan for your life? Does the plan guarantee freedom from suffering? What is the comfort and encouragement in this?
4. How does servanthood go against human nature? How does it compare with what advertisers compel us to think of ourselves?
5. How do we put away the mind-set of the world and adopt the mind-set of Christ? Where does the power and help come from to do this? How long does it take?
6. Does being a slave imply working for salvation? Why not?
7. How are a "servant" and a "slave" the same? How are they different? Which best describes various aspects of the Christian life?
8. In what ways was Jesus an example for us in service and humility and sacrifice? What is the limitation of building a theology around "Jesus is my example"?
9. How would you explain substitutionary atonement in two sentences?
10. How would you answer someone who asked if Jesus had to pay a ransom to Satan in order to obtain our souls?

Loving Someone Enough to Stop and Help

MARK 10:46-52

Main Idea: Jesus demonstrates the love of God through extending grace and mercy to those in need.

I.   **People Are All Around Us Who Are Hurting and Need Our Love (10:46-48).**
     A.   There are crowds who are often insensitive (10:46,48).
     B.   There is the one who needs our help (10:47-48).
II. **We Should Never Be So Busy We Cannot Stop and Help (10:49-51).**
     A.   Hear the cries of the hurting (10:49).
     B.   Listen to the cries of the hurting (10:50-51).

III. Never Be Surprised at How the Most Undesirable Respond to Grace (10:52).
   A.   There is healing grace that saves.
   B.   There is following grace that sanctifies.

On Thursday, October 20, 2011, a little two-year-old girl named Yue Yue was struck by a van in a hit-and-run accident in China. Then at least 18 people passed by, some going out of their way to avoid her. She was then struck by a second van that also did not stop. She was finally helped by a trash collector. It was, tragically, too late. She was declared brain-dead at a local hospital and declared dead early the next day. The whole incident was caught on video, shocking the moral sensibilities of the world and bringing shame to the proud Chinese nation.

One of the passersby later said, "This wasn't my child. Why should I bother?" Journalist Lijia Zhang would shout at her own people, "Shame on us Chinese!" ("How Can I?"). Chai Ling, a leader of the Tiananmen Square student protest and author of *A Heart for Freedom*, would dig even deeper while expressing a measured degree of hope:

> Yue Yue's untimely and inhumane death has caused an ever greater stir in regards to the value of little girls in Chinese society and the responsibility of families and society to care for them than any video in all of history. And this has happened in a country that appears to care less about girls than boys—China has 37 million more men than women and is eliminating girls through prenatal sex-selection, infanticide and abandonment after birth. If one video of a small toddler on a side street in China can cause millions of people around the world to stop and rethink their own morals, and spur others to craft legislation that may save lives in the future, what sort of change is possible if we can capture the larger-scale, mass killing of girls on video? What if there were videos of women crying, being dragged into abortion centers while others look on? What if there were videos of girls being born and immediately drowned or strangled because they're not boys, while others witnessed the crime? And what [if] there were videos of a family leaving its newborn daughter in a box outside the city because they can have only one child and they don't want a daughter? Would this cause a similar commotion and stir a comparable amount of action? (Ling, "Can Video?")

All of this requires each one of us to ask, "Would I have cared enough to take the time to stop and help little Yue Yue?" Jesus would have. And Jesus did: a poor blind beggar named Bartimaeus experienced it himself. In the process Jesus shows us what it means to "be a slave to all" (v. 44) and to serve those who cannot do a single thing in return for your loving them enough to stop and help.

People Are All Around Us Who Are Hurting and Need Our Love
MARK 10:46-48

Jesus has arrived at Jericho. There were two Jerichos in Jesus' day, the ancient city and the new Herodian location. Matthew mentions two blind men, whereas Mark and Luke only mention one. Mark alone tells us that one man's name is Bartimaeus. This does not mean that any of the accounts is inaccurate but rather that Mark and Luke chose to focus only on the more vocal and active of the two men. Matthew and Mark say the miracle occurred as Jesus was leaving Jericho, while Luke says it happened "as He drew near to Jericho" (Luke 18:35). This may be because Matthew and Mark use the new Jericho as their point of reference, whereas Luke is talking about the old Jericho, or vice versa. It may also be that Bartimaeus called out to Jesus as they entered the city, but the healing was not performed until they were leaving (Wilkins, "Study Notes," 1864).

So Jesus makes a visit to Jericho, the last major city on the edge of the Judean wilderness. He will soon make the 3,500-foot climb to Jerusalem where He will give His life as a ransom (10:45) for the sins of the world. But first, He must stop and help someone who is hurting, someone needing a little—no, a lot—of love.

There Are Crowds Who Are Often Insensitive (Mark 10:46,48)

"Mob mentality" or "herd behavior" is the tendency to act together in unison, sometimes in morally reprehensible and unimaginable ways. Gang rape, gang beatings, even the extermination of an entire people group are tragic examples of a "mob mentality."

A poor blind beggar named Bartimaeus suffered because of a "mob mentality" during the days of Jesus. Bartimaeus literally means "son of honor." However, he was the recipient of anything but respect from the crowd that was attracted to Jesus. He was marginalized and sidelined!

Bartimaeus is no longer noticed by most. They do not see him or hear him. He sits by the road, day after day, begging to survive. Some give him a little, but most give him nothing. Hearing that Jesus is passing by, he begins to shout loudly with Messianic respect, "Jesus, Son of David, have mercy on me!" (10:47-48). The response of the mob was less than helpful: "Many told him to be quiet" (10:48). I would paraphrase this: "Shut up, you fool! You are embarrassing us!"

Perhaps this was the first time in a long time that anyone even took notice of him. On this occasion they did notice him, but not in love, only in scorn. They were insensitive. In their minds he did not matter. He was a taker and not a contributor. They just did not care. No one cared but Jesus.

There Is the One Who Needs Our Help (Mark 10:47-48)

No doubt the crowd was loud and boisterous, yet Mark tells us it is one solitary person who gains the attention of the Savior. He refers to Jesus as, "Son of David," a messianic title that looks back to God's promise to David in 2 Samuel 7:12-16 where we read,

> When your time comes and you rest with your fathers, I will raise up after
> you your descendant, who will come from your body, and I will establish his
> kingdom. He will build a house for My name, and I will establish the throne of
> his kingdom forever. I will be a father to him, and he will be a son to Me. . . .
> My faithful love will never leave him as I removed it from Saul; I removed him
> from your way. Your house and kingdom will endure before Me forever, and
> your throne will be established forever.

Solomon was the immediate and partial fulfillment of this prophecy. Jesus would be the final and climactic fulfillment!

The blind man pleads with Jesus, "Have mercy on me!" He acknowledges without apology his helpless and hopeless condition. He cannot give himself sight. He cannot make himself wealthy. He is all alone and completely dependent on others, and he boldly and publicly declares he will stake his dependency on Christ and Christ alone, the Son of David.

Like Jesus, Christians should avoid getting so caught up with the masses that we miss the one. *Pray* for one at a time. *Evangelize* one at a time. *Feed* one at a time. *Clothe* one at a time. *Disciple* one at a time. *Adopt* one at a time. *Love* one at a time. There is always one who needs our help. Do you see that one? Do you hear that one?

We Should Never Be So Busy We Cannot Stop and Help
MARK 10:49-51

Jesus is on the way to Jerusalem—on the way to die. He is determined to fulfill His destiny. His mind must be racing; His heart is filled to overflowing with sorrow for what awaits Him. We could certainly understand if He just moved on this one time without stopping to help a poor blind man. He had more important things on His mind. He is about to give His life for the sins of the world! But He "stopped." He brought this caravan of pilgrims to a screeching halt so that He might minister to just one. Jesus taught His disciples *the art of stopping*.

Hear the Cries of the Hurting (Mark 10:49)

Jesus hears the cries of a man who is hurting. The crowd wants to prevent this man from coming to Jesus, much like the disciples wanted to block the children (10:13). Still, Jesus heard his cry of desperation and stopped. With compassion He said, "Call him" (10:49). The crowd responded in obedience to this greater Son of David. They called the blind man, told him to "take heart" and "get up." Jesus has heard his cry, and He will stop and meet this man at his point of need, his *greatest* need!

Listen to the Cries of the Hurting (Mark 10:50-51)

It is one thing to hear. It is another thing to listen. Some of us are good at neither! Some of us are good at hearing but not listening. Our Lord Jesus is great at both!

Jesus then asked Bartimaeus a straightforward question, "What do you want Me to do for you?" (10:51). This is the same question He has just asked James and John in verse 36. They asked for the best seats in the kingdom. Bartimaeus, in radical and stark contrast, has a much more humble request: "I want to see!" James Edwards says it so well: "The Sons of Thunder asked for extraordinary glory, Bartimaeus asked only for ordinary health" (*Mark*, 330).

Jesus heard his cry just like He hears ours. Jesus listened to his request just as He listens to ours. Psalm 17:6 says, "I call on You, God, because you will answer me; listen closely to me; hear what I say." Psalm 54:2 says, "God, hear my prayer; listen to the words of my mouth." And Psalm 71:2 says, "In Your justice, rescue and deliver me; listen closely to me and save me."

The Lord indeed heard his request, which is actually a prayer to God! And our Lord will respond in glorious salvation—yes, *salvation*.

Never Be Surprised at How the Most Undesirable Respond to Grace
MARK 10:52

Job 42:5 says, "I had heard rumors about You, but now my eyes have seen You." Job was addressing God as the awesome Creator. Bartimaeus could

now voice those same words to God his Savior! As he comes face-to-face with
his Creator, Bartimaeus cries out for mercy. Here comes the answer, and oh
what a wonderful answer it is!

There Is Healing Grace That Saves

Jesus simply and quickly responds to the cry for grace and mercy from the
blind beggar, "Go your way . . . your faith has healed you." When Jesus
refers to the man's faith, Jesus is not saying that the man has earned anything. *Grace* is the divine hand that extends healing. *Faith* is the human
hand that reaches out and receives it. And the object of our faith is crucial.
Exhortations to "keep the faith!" or "just have faith" are nonsensical and
vacuous statements. Bartimaeus did not have empty faith. No, Bartimaeus
directed his faith to the only One who could heal, the only One who could
save!

The word for "healed" is also the word for "saved." It can have both
a physical and a spiritual dimension. Here, it no doubt has both! Would
Bartimaeus be healed physically? Yes! Would he be healed spiritually? An
even better yes! How do we know?

There Is Following Grace That Sanctifies

"Immediately he could see." Instantaneous healing! No medical treat-
ment! None of this is necessary when the Great Physician is at work. But
Bartimaeus was not an ungrateful recipient of grace. He "began to follow
Him on the road." Bartimaeus is now a disciple, a follower of King Jesus.
Where He goes, Bartimaeus will go. What He asks, Bartimaeus will do.
Gospel gratitude will inspire us to follow, at any and all cost, the One who
has so freely dispensed His grace. I see! I've been saved! I will joyfully follow
King Jesus wherever He leads. John Grassmick says, "Bartimaeus pictured
discipleship clearly. He recognized his inability, trusted Jesus as the One to
give him God's gracious mercy, and when he could 'see' clearly he began to
follow Jesus" ("Mark," 155).

Some early church traditions say Bartimaeus would follow Jesus all
the way to His passion and later become a major figure in the church at
Jerusalem. Personally, that is an easy thing for me to imagine!

Conclusion

This is the last healing miracle in the Gospel of Mark. It began with His
healing a blind man (8:22-26), and it closes with His healing a blind man
(10:46-52).

But then like Bartimaeus we were all blind until Jesus gave us sight. We were poor beggars until He saved us as our ransom. We brought to Him nothing but our weakness and need, and He graced us with His power and blessing. Praise God Jesus stopped and had time for Bartimaeus. Praise God Jesus had time for you and me!

Nothing has changed in two thousand years. Jesus still stops for anyone who calls on His name. And like poor, blind Bartimaeus, no one is disappointed in what He does! Yes, there is hope for anyone who, in faith, looks to Jesus.

Reflect and Discuss

1. What thoughts, attitudes, or worldview allowed people to walk by the child Yue Yue after she was hit by a car?
2. Do the differences in details in the accounts of this miracle in Matthew, Mark, and Luke mean that the Gospels are unreliable? Explain.
3. Do you remember any unfortunate cases of "mob mentality" from your school days? What makes it difficult to resist or put a stop to such behavior?
4. Why is it sometimes easy to overlook individuals while we are trying to do great things for the kingdom? How does pride play a part?
5. How do the busyness of our culture and "the tyranny of the urgent" make it hard to stop and help individuals? How do we learn to stop?
6. What is the significance of Bartimaeus referring to Jesus as *Rabbouni*, "my Teacher"?
7. Why did Jesus ask this blind man what he wanted—wasn't it obvious? What else might a blind beggar ask for from passersby? How did Bartimaeus's request demonstrate faith in Jesus? What have you asked Jesus to do for you?
8. Why did Bartimaeus follow Jesus? How do his reasons compare with the reasons we might have?
9. Previously when Jesus healed a blind man (8:22-26), He touched him, applied saliva, and accomplished it in two stages. Here Jesus simply speaks and it is done. Why did Jesus do the same thing in two different ways? What point was He making?
10. In what sense are we all blind until Jesus heals us?

Here Comes Our King
(The Triumphal Entry of Jesus)

MARK 11:1-11

Main Idea: Delight and be satisfied in the King who has come.

I.   Worship the One Who Is Always in Control (11:1-3).
II. Worship the One Who Submits to the Word of God (11:4-7).
III. Worship the One Who Embodies Humility (11:7-8).
IV. Worship the One Who Alone Can Save (11:9-10).
V.   Worship the One Who Always Acts Justly (11:11).

Steve Lambert is a Christian brother who lives in Washington, D.C., and is a member of Capitol Hill Baptist Church. He reflects on the differences between Christianity and Islam:

> In no other manner are the differences between Muslims and
> Christians more sharply contrasted than in the difference between
> the characters and legacies of their prophets. Perhaps the contrast
> is best symbolized by the way Mohammad entered Mecca and Jesus
> entered Jerusalem. Mohammad rode into Mecca on a warhorse,
> surrounded by 400 mounted men and 10,000 foot soldiers. Those
> who greeted him were absorbed into his movement; those who
> resisted him were vanquished, killed, or enslaved. Mohammad
> conquered Mecca, and took control as its new religious, political,
> and military leader. Today, in the Topkapi Palace in Istanbul, Turkey,
> Mohammad's purported sword is proudly on display. . . .
>   Jesus entered Jerusalem on a donkey, accompanied by his 12
> disciples. He was welcomed and greeted by people waving palm
> fronds—a traditional sign of peace. Jesus wept over Jerusalem
> because the Jews mistook him for an earthly, secular king who was to
> free them from the yoke of Rome, whereas, Jesus came to establish a
> much different, heavenly kingdom. Jesus came by invitation and not
> by force. (Dever, *It Is Well*, 65)

Mark 11–16 record the final week of our Lord's earthly life. Mark devotes more than one-third of his Gospel to "Passion Week." Some have referred to Mark's Gospel as a passion narrative with an extended introduction (Stein, *Mark*, 33). It will be a busy week culminating in His death on the cross and His glorious resurrection.

The week begins with Jesus' arrival in Jerusalem during Passover. Traditionally we call it "the triumphal entry." It is an unambiguous declaration of His kingship. The event is so important it is recorded in all four Gospels (Matt 21; Mark 11; Luke 19; John 12). With His arrival the die is cast! There will be no turning back. The Lamb who was slain before the foundation of the world (1 Pet 1:20) will now be slain in space and time. The atonement for sin, ordained in eternity past, now becomes historical for all to behold.

Jerusalem would be abuzz with activity. During Passover the population could swell to three times its normal size as pilgrims from all over the world descended on it. However, this Passover would be unlike any other had been or ever would be. As Paul would write in 1 Corinthians 5:7, "For Christ our Passover has been sacrificed."

Worship the One Who Is Always in Control
MARK 11:1-3

Jesus and the disciples, as they drew near to Jerusalem, came to Bethany on the Mount of Olives. Bethany was the home of Mary, Martha, and Lazarus whom Jesus raised from the dead (John 11:38-44). It will be the place where Jesus will stay during the final week of His life (Mark 11:11).

Our Lord then sent two unnamed disciples to a local village telling them as they entered they would find a colt tied up, on which no one had ever sat. As the ark of the covenant needed an unyoked carrier (1 Sam 6:7; cf. Num 19:2; Deut 21:3), so the true ark of the covenant, the Lord Jesus, required an unridden animal. It is bringing the Holy One into Jerusalem.

Jesus has planned everything out to the last detail and is in complete control. From the moment He enters Jerusalem, the prerogatives of deity are present. Jesus is "Lord" and Master of every detail of His divine destiny. Sinclair Ferguson is spot on when he says, "His majesty and authority began to shine through from the moment of his entry into Jerusalem" (*Mark*, 180).

The Mount of Olives rises about two hundred feet higher than Mount Zion. Its crest is less than a mile directly east of Jerusalem. It is known for its many olive trees. Its slopes were the path of David's retreat from Jerusalem to escape capture by Absalom (2 Sam 15:30-32). On this mount Solomon grieved God by erecting idols for his foreign wives to worship (1 Kgs 11:1-10). Ezekiel witnessed the glory of God on the Mount of Olives (Ezek 11:23). Jesus, the Son of David, made his royal entry into Jerusalem from here (Mark 11:1-10; see Matt 21:1-10; Luke 19:28-40; John 12:12-13). On this mount Jesus wept over the disobedience and blindness of Jerusalem (Luke 19:41-44). The disciples witnessed Jesus' ascension into glory on this mount (Luke 24:50-51; Acts 1:9-12).

In Acts 1:10-11 Jesus said He would come again in the same way they had watched Him go. Zechariah 14:4-5 tells us what will happen when those holy feet touch down once again where He left:

> On that day His feet will stand on the Mount of Olives, which faces Jerusalem
> on the east. The Mount of Olives will be split in half from east to west, forming
> a huge valley, so that half the mountain will move to the north and half to
> the south. You will flee by My mountain valley, for the valley of the mountains
> will extend to Azal. You will flee as you fled from the earthquake in the days of
> Uzziah king of Judah. Then the LORD my God will come and all the holy ones
> with Him.

Worship the One Who Submits to the Word of God
MARK 11:4-7 (CF. ZECH 9:9-17; MATT 21:4-5; JOHN 12:14-15)

The two disciples went and found things as Jesus said. They brought the colt to Jesus, they threw their cloaks on it (for Him to sit on), and Jesus sat on it to ride into Jerusalem. But there is so much here between the lines! Jesus has walked everywhere else in His ministry throughout Israel except for those occasions when He was riding in a boat. This is the one and only time He rides an animal, a small donkey.

All of this is highly symbolic in light of Old Testament prophecy, expectations, and allusions! The phrase "The Lord needs it" (Mark 11:3) uses the same phrase as in 2:25 to justify David's eating "the sacred bread" when he and his men were hungry. David's greater Son is here! His riding in on a donkey also is a declaration of His kingship and a fulfillment of Zechariah 9:9, as Matthew 21:4-5 and John 12:14-15 make clear. Zechariah 9—which, as is often the case with Old Testament prophecy, does not make a clear distinction between our Lord's first and second coming—surely would have been in the minds of those watching all of this unfold:

> Rejoice greatly, Daughter Zion! Shout in triumph, Daughter Jerusalem! Look,
> your King is coming to you; He is righteous and victorious, humble and
> riding on a donkey, on a colt, the foal of a donkey. I will cut off the chariot
> from Ephraim and the horse from Jerusalem. The bow of war will be removed,
> and He will proclaim peace to the nations. His dominion will extend from
> sea to sea, from the Euphrates River to the ends of the earth. As for you, also,
> because of the blood of your covenant, I will release your prisoners from the
> waterless cistern. Return to a stronghold, you prisoners who have hope; today I
> declare that I will restore double to you. . . . The LORD their God will save them

on that day as the flock of His people; for they are like the jewels in a crown, sparkling over His land. (Zech 9:9-12,16)

Our Lord lived His life from beginning to end in total submission to the Word of God. His life, death, and resurrection were the unfolding of the drama of redemption. No wonder He would say in John 5:39, "You pore over the Scriptures because you think you have eternal life in them, yet they testify about Me."

Worship the One Who Embodies Humility
MARK 11:7-8

Jesus mounts the young colt and begins the parade into Jerusalem. Here is deity on a donkey! The prophecy in Zechariah 9:9 beautifully makes a connection to His riding in on a donkey and His humility. He had no need to break it in—this donkey knew its Creator, its Master! Yes, He is bringing righteousness and salvation. And yes, He comes humble and mounted on a donkey.

In response, "Many people spread their robes on the road, and others spread leafy branches cut from the fields." It was a festive time of celebration as they welcomed this King (cf. 2 Kgs 9:12-13). Coming in this way our Lord now proclaims openly what He has forbidden until this moment: I am your King! Jesus with purpose and intentionality presents Himself as the Messiah, knowing that it will provoke the Jewish leaders resulting in His crucifixion. Nevertheless, His declaration also is bathed in gracious humility.

The paradoxical kingship of Jesus shines so bright at this moment! He is royalty and deity wrapped in a single person, yet He moves forward in His declaration to be King in lowliness, weakness, and service. He does not come in pomp, but in meekness and lowliness; He comes in humility and simplicity. I absolutely love the way Sinclair Ferguson captures the moment:

Think, for a moment, what Mark's record would convey to those who read it first—the Christians in Rome. No doubt many of them had seen generals enter Rome in triumph to receive the accolades of victory. How stark the contrast between Roman glory and Jesus' humility must have seemed. How mighty and powerful the sword and political power by contrast with King Jesus! Yet we know that his kingdom was established, while the glory that was Rome disappeared into oblivion. We know that what Jesus did in Jerusalem established a kingdom which would outlast all the kingdoms of this world and break in pieces every man-centered kingdom which sets itself against it. Jesus

had come to take his throne—but had committed himself to begin
his reign from a cross. (Ferguson, *Mark*, 181)

Worship the One Who Alone Can Save
MARK 11:9-10

I am fascinated by the shouts of the crowd. Their words could not be truer,
but they could not have been more misunderstood by those who were shout-
ing them. Only Jesus knew the full significance of what they were saying.

"Hosanna" means literally, "Save, I pray." It draws from Psalm 118:25-26
(from the Egyptian Hallels; Pss 113–118) which says, "Lord, save us! Lord,
please grant us success! He who comes in the name of the Lord is blessed.
From the house of the Lord we bless you." Passover celebrated the Hebrew
people's deliverance out of Egypt. Now the nation of Israel anticipates a
messianic liberation and deliverance from Rome.

"Blessed" draws from Numbers 6:24-27 which says, "May Yahweh bless
you and protect you; may Yahweh make His face shine on you and be gracious to you; may Yahweh look with favor on you and give you peace. In this
way they will pronounce My name over the Israelites, and I will bless them."
The One who is blessed, or better, who will be the blesser, is (1) He who
comes in the name of the Lord, and (2) He who is "bringing the coming
kingdom of David!"

- 2 Samuel 7:12-16 is being fulfilled!
- Isaiah 9:1-7 is being fulfilled!
- Isaiah 11:1-10 is being fulfilled!
- Jeremiah 23:5-8 is being fulfilled!
- Ezekiel 34:23-24 is being fulfilled!
- Micah 5:2-4 is being fulfilled!

But prophecy was not being fulfilled in the way they thought, hoped,
and believed it would be. They are right. He is their King. But He is not
here to purge Israel of foreign domination. No, He is here to purge His
people of their sin! They are looking and longing for a temporal, political, and military Savior. He, however, is bringing what only He can bring: a
complete and eternal salvation of body and soul! They want and expect a
Savior only for Jews, but He is a Savior for the whole world, for any and all
who will believe on His Name. John 1:12 says it so well: "But to all who did
receive Him, He gave them the right to become children of God, to those
who believe in His name." John 3:16 says it so well: "For God loved the world
in this way: He gave His One and Only Son, so that everyone who believes

in Him will not perish but have eternal life." John 14:6 says it so well: "Jesus told him, 'I am the way, the truth, and the life. No one comes to the Father except through Me.'" Acts 4:12 says it so well: "There is salvation in no one else, for there is no other name under heaven given to people, and we must be saved by it." First Timothy 2:5 says it so well: "For there is one God and one mediator between God and humanity, Christ Jesus." Christ's salvation and triumph would be the victory of life over death, salvation over sin, truth over error, love over hate, forgiveness over condemnation. They cried out for salvation that day. Have you cried out to Him to save you? He is the only One who can.

Worship the One Who Always Acts Justly
MARK 11:11

This day ends rather uneventfully. Tomorrow will be a different day (11:12-25). Jesus enters Jerusalem, goes to the temple, looks things over carefully, sees that it is "late" (late for the temple?), and leaves with the disciples for Bethany.

I wonder if Jesus' mind returned to the first time He saw the temple as a 12-year-old boy (Luke 2:41-52). He must have been impressed at that young and tender age. Not anymore—not knowing what He knows now and what will transpire in the coming days and years. Jesus does not come to the temple as a tourist or gawking pilgrim caught up in the fanfare of Passover and enamored by the spectacular beauty of the temple. No, He makes a commanding survey of the situation and goes away to return the next day. Then He will curse something—the temple—that should have been bringing the nations to God (Mark 11:17) but in reality was driving them away.

It would seem that this would have been the moment for Him to claim and receive His Messianic throne and kingdom. Amazingly, not one thing happens. The enthusiastic crowds have mysteriously vanished. Was He only "King for a day"? Jesus, with no fanfare whatsoever, leaves with the Twelve.

However, Malachi 3:1-2, a text Mark cites at the beginning of this Gospel, is lurking in the prophetic shadows:

> *"See, I am going to send My messenger, and he will prepare the way before Me. Then the Lord you seek will suddenly come to His temple, the Messenger of the covenant you desire—see, He is coming," says the LORD of Hosts. But who can endure the day of His coming? And who will be able to stand when He appears? For He will be like a refiner's fire and like cleansing lye.*

The refining fire has arrived to purify that which is putrid. The cleansing lye has arrived to cleanse that which is filthy. He will *start* His work with the *temple.* He will *finish* His work on the *cross.* He acts justly when He judges. He is so worthy of our worship!

Our King has come, and our King is coming again. And what a difference there will be in His first and second advents.

THE FIRST COMING OF JESUS	THE SECOND COMING OF JESUS
He came to die.	He will come to reign.
He came on a little donkey.	He will come on a warrior horse.
He came as a humble servant.	He will come as an exalted King.
He came in weakness.	He will come in power.
He came to save.	He will come to judge.
He came in love.	He will come in wrath.
He came as deity veiled.	He will come as deity revealed.
He came with 12 disciples.	He will come with an army of angels.
He came to bring peace.	He will come and make war.
He was given a crown of thorns.	He will receive a crown of royalty.
He came as the Suffering Servant.	He will come as the King of kings and the Lord of lords.

Few bowed before the great King the first time He came. However, every knee will bow when He comes again (Phil 2:9-11). Are you looking? Are you waiting? Are you ready?

> Jesus shall reign where e'er the sun
> Doth his successive journeys run;
> His kingdom stretch from shore to shore,
> Till moons shall wax and wane no more.

> Blessings abound where e'er He reigns:
> The prisoner leaps to lose his chains,
> The weary find eternal rest,
> and all the sons of want are blest.

> Let every creature rise and bring
> Peculiar honors to our King;

Angels descend with songs again,
And earth repeat the loud Amen. (Watts, "Jesus Shall Reign," 1719)

Reflect and Discuss

1. How were Mohammed's entrance into Medina and Jesus' entrance into Jerusalem symbolic of the movements they initiated?
2. What are some other fundamental differences between Christianity and Islam?
3. Some scholars contend that Jesus had arranged ahead of time for the donkey and colt to be available. Does this possibility affect the meaning of the text?
4. Did it seem like events were in control or out of control during Passion Week? How is it encouraging to know that Jesus was in control of those events?
5. What aspects of this fulfillment of prophecy could have been achieved by any ordinary man who set his mind to do so? What aspects could only have been miraculously fulfilled by the Son of God?
6. What leaders do you know who like to make a grand entrance? Do you know any leaders who arrive humbly? Which kind is the better leader?
7. Why didn't Jesus use His power and growing popularity to make a grand entrance? How might His ultimate mission have failed if He had done so?
8. What kind of Messiah did the people expect and want? What kind of savior do people want today—what do they want relief from? How does Jesus exceed those expectations?
9. Do you think you would have been among those who welcomed Jesus to Jerusalem with shouts of "Hosanna!"? Do you think you would have shouted "Crucify Him!" a few days later?
10. What would Jesus see if He came to your church and looked around?

A Savior for All Nations

MARK 11:12-25

Main Idea: Jesus is a Savior for all nations, without barriers.

I. **Jesus Will Curse Those Who Put On a Show but Do Not Produce (11:12-14).**
   A. Our Savior curses hypocrisy (11:12-13).
   B. Our Savior curses unfruitfulness (11:13-14).
II. **Jesus Will Condemn What Promises One Thing but Delivers Another (11:15-19).**
   A. Our Lord will deal with our wickedness (11:15-16).

B.   Our Lord will judge concerning our witness (11:17-19).
III. **Jesus Will Challenge Us to Believe in God, but He Understands Doubt (11:20-25).**
A.   Put your faith in this Savior (11:20-24).
B.   Be forgiving like this Savior (11:25).

As I survey the landscape of the modern church, my own denomination, and my own soul, I am certain of a critical truth. We continually, definitely, and desperately need a "heart change." We need an inward transformation that will result in an outward metamorphosis that will result in our churches on earth looking more like the church in heaven! We need churches that gladly proclaim Jesus as a Savior for all nations!

As of this moment my own denomination remains a mostly middle-class, mostly white network of mostly declining churches in the southern United States of America. Those are the undeniable facts, and that must change or we will die. Even more importantly, we must change, or God will judge us for neglecting and even hiding the truth that we have "a Savior for all nations!" God judged His people Israel for this sin. Why would we think He would deal with us any differently?

We must embrace the "temple theology of the Bible." God once had a physical temple located in Jerusalem. He now has a perfect temple located in heaven. That temple is *Jesus*, as He Himself said in John 2:18-22. He now has a spiritual temple, which is the *church* (1 Cor 3:16). He now has a personal temple scattered all around the world as a witness that He is indeed a Savior for all nations. That temple is *you* and *me* (1 Cor 6:19-20). Indeed that temple is *anyone* who recognizes that they are not their own, for they were bought with a price, the precious blood of "Christ our Passover" (1 Cor 5:7), "a lamb without defect or blemish" (1 Pet 1:19).

Jesus has made His triumphal entry into Jerusalem (Mark 11:1-10). He then went to the magnificent temple (v. 11), which would not be completely finished until AD 64. Sadly it would be totally destroyed just six years later. Here in the spring of AD 33, Jesus looks around at everything (v. 11). It would soon be evident that Jesus did not like what He saw. A people and a place that was meant to be a light to the nations had become "a den of thieves" (v. 17), a hideout for religious outlaws. The status quo was not acceptable.

How would our Lord respond to those who, though recipients of His grace and goodness, had failed in the assignment and calling He had given them? How will He respond to us today if we are likewise disobedient?

Jesus Will Curse Those Who Put On a Show but Do Not Produce
MARK 11:12-14

The day after the triumphal entry and His visit to the temple, our Lord and the disciples leave Bethany and head back to the temple. The text says, "He was hungry." This will set the stage for one of the most controversial miracles performed by our Lord, the cursing of a fig tree. Joseph Klausner wrote it was "a gross injustice on a tree which was guilty of no wrong" (Klausner, *Jesus*, 269). T. W. Manson said, "It is a tale of miraculous power wasted in the service of ill-temper (for the supernatural energy employed to blast the unfortunate tree might have been more usefully expended in forcing a crop of figs out of season) and as it stands is simply incredible" (Garland, *Mark*, 433). William Barclay said, "The story does not seem worthy of Jesus. There seems to be a petulance in it" (Hughes, *Mark*, 85). And the atheist philosopher Bertrand Russell accused Jesus of "vindictive fury" and wrote of our Lord's character, "I cannot myself feel that either in the matter of wisdom or in the matter of virtue Christ stands quite as high as some other people known to history" (Russell, *Why*, 17–19). Jesus, however, was not acting like a spoiled brat who did not get His way. There is no anger, no malice, no temper tantrum. It is (as we will see) an object lesson, an acted-out parable of our Lord's judgment on Israel and on those who claim to be one thing but are actually another, who put on a show but do not produce. It is a curse on the temple and the nation of Israel. By application it could be a curse on you and me and on our churches.

Our Savior Curses Hypocrisy (Mark 11:12-13)

Walking from Bethany to Jerusalem, Jesus sees in the distance a fig tree in leaf (v. 13). Though it is not yet "the season for figs" (v. 13), the presence of the leaves would indicate this tree would have fruit on it—if not full figs, at least *paggim*, small green figs (*knops*). Though not all that tasty, they were edible and could relieve His hunger.

However, the tree bore no fruit. Its leaves promised one thing, but it had not produced. It was a hypocritical fig tree. The outward appearance, said, "Come here! I have fruit that will meet your needs." However, when you arrive, you realize you have been deceived. It was a show with no substance.

Sadly this is what Israel had become, especially the temple and the religious leaders (the Sanhedrin) who oversaw its operation. They gave an outward appearance of great spirituality and devotion to God but proved to be hypocrites. Gentiles were denied the opportunity to come close to

God, being restricted to the outer court. The poor were exploited by money changers and merchants. The temple culture had grown big and impressive, but it was all a sham, and Jesus cursed them for it (v. 14). There was no gospel and no God to be found by those needing salvation. Once a beacon of light, it was now only a faint flicker that was about to be extinguished.

If our Lord did that then to "His own people" (John 1:11), what makes us think He would not do it to us today? Professing the fruit of righteousness and devotion to God, could it be we are nothing more than the dry and dying leaves of sterile religion, ritualism, and profession? Charles Spurgeon well said, "The great majority of persons who have any sort of religion at all bear leaves, but they produce no fruit" ("Nothing but Leaves"). We may say, "Oh, my denomination may not be much, but we are the best God has!" "Oh, we may be in decline, but at least we are not losing ground like the other denominations." "Oh, don't forget, we have the best mission force in the world." You don't have to ask; we will be glad to tell you. Never mind that we are in decline in financial support, total numbers, and especially men! Hypocrisy always keeps company with self-deception. We think we are one thing when we are actually another. And our Savior curses hypocrisy.

Our Savior Curses Unfruitfulness (Mark 11:13-14)

The prophets often spoke of Israel by the symbol of a fig tree (Jer 8:13; 29:17; Hos 9:10,16; Joel 1:7; Mic 7:1-6). Jeremiah 8:13 especially stands out, and I wonder whether this was in the mind of Jesus:

> "How can you claim, 'We are wise; the law of the LORD is with us'? In fact, the lying pen of scribes has produced falsehood. The wise will be put to shame; they will be dismayed and snared. They have rejected the word of the LORD, so what wisdom do they really have? . . . From prophet to priest, everyone deals falsely. They have treated superficially the brokenness of My dear people, claiming, 'Peace, peace,' when there is no peace. Were they ashamed when they acted so abhorrently? They weren't at all ashamed. They can no longer feel humiliation. Therefore, they will fall among the fallen. When I punish them, they will collapse," says the LORD. I will gather them and bring them to an end. This is the LORD's declaration. There will be no grapes on the vine, no figs on the fig tree, and even the leaf will wither. Whatever I have given them will be lost to them.

Jesus arrived at the fig tree to find "nothing but leaves." Mark informs us that "it was not the season for figs," but the tree with its leaves said, "Come to me. Others may be barren but not me. I have fruit for you." Jesus responded, "May no one ever eat fruit from you again!" And "His disciples heard it." They were there as eyewitnesses. This is no myth or legend conjured up only to make a theological or moral point.

There is a point without a doubt. Fruitlessness *now* may result in fruitlessness *forever*. Lose your usefulness for Jesus, and He may curse you and move on! It is not He who needs us, it is we who desperately need Him. We need Him to save us. We need Him to make us useful and fruitful. Turn His church into a religious club of hypocrisy and unfruitfulness, and you will receive not His blessing but His curse. Regionalism and ethnocentrism are abominations in His eyes. He sees it all. His eyes, which are a flame of fire (Rev 19:12), will expose you for who and what you really are.

Jesus Will Condemn What Promises One Thing but Delivers Another
MARK 11:15-19

On September 6, 1520, Martin Luther wrote in *An Open Letter to Pope Leo X*, "The Roman church, once the holiest of all, has become the most licentious den of thieves, the most shameless of all brothels, the kingdom of sin, death and hell. It is so bad that even Antichrist himself, if he should come, could think of nothing to add to its wickedness" (Garland, *Mark*, 446).

We call what we read in verses 15-19 "the cleansing of the temple." It is actually its condemnation. It is Jesus' critique of false religion. It is not too strong to say He hates it. I am inclined to believe there were actually two cleansings: one early in His public ministry (John 2:13-22) and one at the end of His ministry (Matt 21:12-16; Mark 11:15-19; Luke 19:45-47). The acted-out parable of the cursing of the fig tree now finds its fulfillment and reality in our Lord's assault on those He identifies as a "den of thieves" (Mark 11:17), a hive of spiritual robbers!

Our Lord Will Deal with Our Wickedness (Mark 11:15-16)

Jesus enters the temple (the 35-acre outer court of the Gentiles) and wreaks havoc on those who sold the animals for sacrifice (specifically mentioning "pigeons," the sacrificial animal for the poor) and exchanged money. Further, He blocked the thoroughfare that may have become a sort of "short-cut" for those who wanted to get from one side of the temple mount to the other without having to go the long way around. They had no respect. No reverence.

People come to Jerusalem to celebrate the Passover in the spring. The population would grow to 10 times its normal size. Hundreds of thousands were there with no hotels. Family, friends, and fields would be their accommodations. The Jewish historian Josephus tells us that in one Passover year (AD 66), 255,000 lambs were bought, sold, and sacrificed in the temple courts (Edwards, *Mark*, 341).

Pilgrims were requested to bring an acceptable (perfect!) sacrifice that had to pass a rigorous inspection. Most chose—were really forced—to buy an approved animal certified by the mafia of temple priests backed by the powerful and corrupt Sanhedrin. The markup was shameful and immoral. Some estimate they charged 16 times the normal price (two pigeons normally sold for $0.25 now sold for around $4.00). Moneychangers would exchange foreign currency, which was unacceptable for transaction in the temple, into Jewish currency, again for an outrageous fee.

Jesus saw extortion, bribery, greed, and dishonesty in this religious bazaar. He got physical in righteous rage and indignation, and He cleaned house! Burning with passion and purity, He restored, at least for a moment, the temple of God to its rightful purpose. Here is God's greatest High Priest exercising His rightful authority over His temple.

> According to v. 15, He "drove out" the merchants. The word is the same used often of exorcising or expelling demons. Jesus suddenly became a bouncer! He grabbed them by the scruff of the neck, kicked them in the seat of the pants, overturned their tables, and knocked them from their perches. When the time comes for His crucifixion, He will permit them to lay hands on Him and carry Him off. But not now! (Storms, "Figs")

All wickedness is an abomination to our Lord. But as for religious wickedness in His name, He finds it especially detestable. And He will deal with it.

Our Lord Will Judge Concerning Our Witness (Mark 11:17-19)

Verse 17 brings us to the heart of our Lord's anger over what His temple has become. The text says by His actions and His words, "He began to teach them." He then quotes from Isaiah 56:7, "My house will be called a house of prayer for all the nations." However, now citing Jeremiah 7:11, He declares, "But you have made it a den of thieves!" So much is here!

Only Mark includes the crucial phrase "for all the nations." Consider the context of Isaiah 56:7, beginning with verse 3:

> *No foreigner who has joined himself to the Lord should say, "The Lord will exclude me from His people." . . . And the foreigners who join themselves to the Lord minister to Him, love the name of Yahweh and become His servants, all who keep the Sabbath without desecrating it and who hold firmly to My covenant—I will bring them to My holy mountain and let them rejoice in My*

house of prayer. Their burnt offerings and sacrifices will be acceptable on My
altar, for My house will be called a house of prayer for all nations.

God's temple is to be a house of prayer, a place of worship that attracts
and blesses all the nations! It is not a shrine to be admired and praised. It
is to exhibit no geographical, national, racial, or ethnic segregation or discrimination. I love the way John Piper puts it:

> Over and over, Jesus shows that the people of God will no longer be
> defined in an ethnic way. . . . The new people that he is calling into
> existence is defined not by race or ethnicity or political ties, but by
> "producing the fruit of the kingdom." This will mean a new global
> family made up of believers in Christ from every ethnic group on
> the planet. And it will mean that those who love that vision will work
> toward local manifestations of that ethnic diversity. Jesus is the end
> of ethnocentrism—globally and locally. Not color but faith in Christ
> is the mark of the kingdom. But it is a mighty long journey. And the
> price is high. Jesus was on the Calvary road every step of the way. He
> knew what it would finally cost him. It would cost him his life. But his
> heart was in it. To the end. (Piper, *Bloodlines*, 119)

Israel missed this, and too many of our churches do as well—both at
home and in their concern for the nations. And as the chief priest was
mainly at fault, so are many pastors today. A genuine revival in this area will
succeed or fail on the back of our religious leaders.

The context of Jeremiah 7:11 is painfully instructive. Jesus is declaring the
fulfillment of that ominous prophecy by His symbolic act on this very day. It
is a long passage, but Jeremiah 7:1-29 is worth reading.

It was popularly believed that when the Messiah came He would purge
the temple *of* Gentiles. Instead, Jesus comes and cleanses the temple *for*
Gentiles. Israel's religious show with all its glitz and fanfare was an empty
embarrassment. Instead of bringing people into God's presence they
obscured it until no one could find Him. Jesus effectively said, "Enough!
Your charade is over."

Jesus' protest caught the attention of the Sanhedrin (v. 18; see also v.
27)! He had called them out. Little wonder that the religious elite wanted
to destroy Him. And the stakes are now much higher. It was one thing for
Jesus to antagonize the country lay preachers, the Pharisees. It is something
else to take on the chief priest and the powerful Sanhedrin. A showdown
is on the horizon. However, fear paralyzed them on this day. As for the
crowds, they were "astonished," not sure what to make of all this teaching.

Jesus would, with sadness and grief, leave and go home to Bethany (v. 19). Tomorrow would bring another day of teaching. He would press on.

Jesus Will Challenge Us to Believe in God, but He Understands Doubt
MARK 11:20-25

Andrew Murray well said, "Christ actually meant prayer to be the great power by which His church should do its work and the neglect of prayer is the great reason the church has not greater power over the masses in Christian and heathen countries. . . . The power of the church to truly bless rests on intercession: asking and receiving Heavenly gifts to carry to men" (Murray, *Ministry of Intercession*, 12–13).

Mark concludes the fig tree/temple story with lessons on faith, prayer, and forgiveness, the very things the people should have found through God's temple. The fig tree event brackets and interprets the temple story. Jesus did not just cleanse the temple, He cursed it. It had failed in the divine assignment, and it would be destroyed. With no fruit, its use was at an end. God would remove it: in less than a generation (AD 70), the Romans destroyed Jerusalem and the temple.

Jesus uses all of this as an opportunity to teach His disciples two more valuable spiritual truths.

Put Your Faith in This Savior (Mark 11:20-24)

When they passed the fig tree the next day, it was dead (v. 20). Any sympathy for a soulless tree in our day is badly misplaced and says much about our sloppy, sentimental culture and its tragic perversion of real values. God had told Jonah to weep over lost *people*, not a *plant* (Jonah 4:10-11)! Jesus says to weep over a dead *temple*, not a dead *tree*.

Peter, an eyewitness to all that has happened, remembers our Lord's words (v. 14) and notes they have come to fruition immediately (v. 21): "Rabbi, look! The fig tree that You cursed has withered." John 15:6 warns us, "If anyone does not remain in Me, he is thrown aside like a branch and he withers. They gather them, throw them into the fire, and they are burned." Sinclair Ferguson is spot on: "The question of our spiritual fruitfulness is one of immense seriousness which we ignore at our peril. . . . Jesus means what He says!" (*Mark*, 185).

Jesus' response at first glance seems out of place:

> *Jesus replied to them, "Have faith in God. I assure you: If anyone says to this mountain, 'Be lifted up and thrown into the sea,' and does not doubt in his*

heart, but believes that what he says will happen, it will be done. Therefore I
tell you, all the things you pray and ask for—believe that you have received
them, and you will have them."

"Have faith in God." The great missionary Hudson Taylor said, "God
uses men who are weak and feeble enough to lean on Him." He is faithful
when the religious establishment and its institutions fail. Trust the One who
judges hypocrisy with severity and extends amazing grace to those who seek
it in faith.

Have mountain-moving faith that does not doubt but asks in prayer.
The "mountain" is a hyperbole. It represents what appears to be impos-
sible, immovable, beyond our finite ability. Good! This is where faith begins.
Believing faith taps into God's power to accomplish His purpose. Again hear
Andrew Murray: "We have a God who delights in impossibilities" (Cowman,
Streams, 336).

True and believing prayer is not attempting to get God to change His
will to fit our plans. It is a passionate pursuit to see God's plans accomplished in us! Prayer is not conjuring God up like some "genie in a bottle"
obligated to grant us whatever we wish. Read Matthew 6:9-10; Mark 14:36;
John 14:13-14; 15:7; 16:23-24; and 1 John 5:14-15 before you draw such a
foolish theological conclusion.

When we pray with mountain-moving faith, our God will give us what
we need to glorify His name. Here is a "house of prayer" you can bring your
petitions to! In one of his hymns, John Newton said,

> Thou are coming to a King!
> Large petitions with thee bring!
> For His grace and power are such—
> none can ever ask too much! (Newton, "Come, My Soul," 1779)

So when we pray, we trust not only in His power to give us what we ask but
also in His wisdom to give us what we need! I trust Him enough to have
Him turn me down if that is what He chooses. That means "we may receive
answers we do not want, find things we are not looking for, and have doors
opened [and closed] we do not expect" (Garland, *Mark*, 449).

Be Forgiving like This Savior (Mark 11:25)

We can forgive because we have been forgiven through the atoning work of
Jesus on the cross. Forgiveness so freely and graciously extended to us can
now be graciously and freely extended to others. The theme of prayer finds
its contextual connection in the fact that God's temple, which is what we

now are, is to be "a house of prayer for all nations." Jesus is such a temple, for as Hebrews 7:25 says, "Therefore, He is always able to save those who come to God through Him, since He always lives to intercede for them." And we are to be such a temple extending the same forgiveness that we have received from the God we now call Father (Mark 11:25). By means of the temple named Jesus and through millions of temples called Christians— who are unrestricted by geography—pagans and unclean Gentiles can find the Savior for all nations and receive the forgiveness so freely offered from the Father who is watching over all the earth.

Are you a barren fig tree? Am I? Are our churches? Let me be specific: Can you forgive those you once hated and who have wronged you, and can you to get the gospel to them? Can you? Can we? Can you remove any and all barriers that would keep them from a genuine face-to-face encounter with the Savior for all nations? Can you? Will we? Will we pay any price necessary that all the nations might hear of King Jesus?

The missionary C. T. Studd said, "Some wish to live within the sound of a chapel bell. I want to run a rescue shop within a yard of hell!" Now that is a great place to plant a temple! That is a great place to plant a life with a sign that reads, "A Savior for All Nations! Come on in! All are welcomed! None will be turned away!"

Reflect and Discuss

1. What are the main shortcomings of your denomination?
2. How was the magnificent temple in Jerusalem insufficient for the ultimate plan of God? How can the church overcome those deficiencies?
3. How would you respond to someone who said Jesus was being unreasonable or even petulant when He cursed the fig tree?
4. How were the fig tree and the temple alike? Does your church or your denomination exhibit any of those characteristics?
5. If hypocrisy always involves self-deception, how can a person find out if he is a hypocrite? If his church or denomination is hypocritical?
6. What is the definition of *fruitlessness* in regards to a Christian? a church? a denomination? What "fruit" does God see in you and your church?
7. Which is worse, a secular rip-off or a religious rip-off? Why?
8. How are your church and denomination doing with regard to including all nations?
9. Why do you think the chief priests and scribes did not apprehend Jesus immediately? Were these valid and commendable reasons?
10. In what way is asking in prayer and forgiving in faith the opposite of what was taking place in the temple? Are your church and denomination exercising this kind of faith?

Three Reasons People Are Not Willing
to Follow Jesus

MARK 11:27-33

Main Idea: People refuse to trust Jesus not because He is not worthy but because of the hardness of their own hearts.

I. **They Do Not Want to Submit to His Authority (11:27-28).**
II. **They Refuse to Examine Honestly the Evidence (11:29-32).**
III. **They Fear Men More than They Fear God (11:32-33).**

In Matthew 23:37-39 (also in Luke 13:34-35) we find some of the saddest words found in the whole Bible:

> *Jerusalem, Jerusalem! She who kills the prophets and stones those who are sent to her. How often I wanted to gather your children together, as a hen gathers her chicks under her wings, yet you were not willing! See, your house is left to you desolate. For I tell you, you will never see Me again until you say, "He who comes in the name of the Lord is the blessed One!"*

The phrase "you were not willing" has the feel of a clock when it strikes midnight. Time has run out.

Jesus has just cleansed and cursed the temple for its corruptions and abuse (Mark 11:12-25). In response, the religious leaders were "looking for a way to destroy Him" (11:18). You would think Jesus would avoid the public eye, but He does nothing of the sort! He returns to Jerusalem and the temple with courage, looking for a fight—not a physical confrontation, but a spiritual one that will place His claims and identity front and center.

Mark 11:27–12:44 records five temple controversies in Jerusalem that parallel five earlier controversies in Galilee (cf. 2:1–3:6). In both cases His opponents are the religious leaders. Now that He is in Jerusalem, the stakes are much higher and the intensity of the conflict much stronger. Things are moving to an inevitable climax: the cross.

In this first of five temple controversies, we will see some common reasons people are not willing to come and follow Jesus. Not much has changed in two thousand years. The same kinds of reasons cause people to refuse Him today.

They Do Not Want to Submit to His Authority
MARK 11:27-28

Jesus "came again to Jerusalem." At some point the religious authorities show up—the Sanhedrin, the Jewish high court, who exercised both political and religious authority in Israel. It consisted of 71 men led by the acting high priest. Their power was enormous. They were supersensitive to anything that could threaten their authority, and Jesus was clearly a threat.

They question Him regarding His authority, which clearly they reject. The immediate context of their interrogation is His actions during the previous day in the temple. In essence they are asking, "Who gave you the right to wreak havoc in our temple?" However, this is not the first time the issue of authority has come up:

> *They were astonished at His teaching because, unlike the scribes, He was teaching them as one having authority.* (1:22)

> *Then they were all amazed, so they began to argue with one another, saying, "What is this? A new teaching with authority! He commands even the unclean spirits, and they obey Him."* (1:27)

> *"But so you may know that the Son of Man has authority on earth to forgive sins," He told the paralytic, "I tell you: get up, pick up your mat, and go home."* (2:10-11)

This man teaches with authority, casts out demons with authority, and heals with authority. He does what only God can do! But they request His ordination papers. They are not motivated by a willingness to know who He is, and they have no interest in bringing their lives under His authority. Their goal is to ensnare Him, embarrass Him, and discredit Him. If He admits He has no religious credentials and that He is acting on His own authority, He will probably lose the respect and following of the people, and they can be finished with this troublemaker. On the other hand, if He makes a claim to divine authority, then they could charge Him with blasphemy, arrest Him, and start the process for His destruction. Either way, this "hick from the sticks" would be finished.

The question of authority is important. We all have a source of authority in our lives, someone or something that guides us and drives us, something that rules. For most of us, like the Sanhedrin, it is ourselves. We are not really interested in surrendering that rule to anyone else.

Aldous Huxley noted that part of what drove him to atheism was a desire for emotional liberation in the area of his sex life: "We objected to the morality [imposed by God] because it interfered with our sexual freedom"

(Huxley, *Ends and Means*, 273). Huxley died on the same day as both John F. Kennedy and C. S. Lewis. The latter's perspective was radically different from Huxley's. In *Mere Christianity*, Lewis wrote,

> The more we get what we now call "ourselves" out of the way and let [Christ] take us over, the more truly ourselves we become. . . . In that sense our real selves are all waiting for us in Him. It is no good trying to "be myself" without Him. The more I resist Him and try to live on my own, the more I become dominated by my own heredity and upbringing and surroundings and natural desires. . . . What I call "My wishes" become merely the desires thrown up by my physical organism or pumped into me by other men's thoughts or even suggested to me by devils. . . . I am not, in my natural state, nearly so much of a person as I like to believe: most of what I call "me" can be very easily explained. It is when I turn to Christ, when I give myself up to His Personality, that I first begin to have a real personality of my own. . . . Sameness is to be found most among the most "natural" men, not among those who surrender to Christ. How monotonously alike all the great tyrants and conquerors have been: how gloriously different are the saints.
>
> But there must be a real giving up of the self. You must throw it away "blindly" so to speak. Christ will indeed give you a real personality: but you must not go to Him for the sake of that. As long as your own personality is what you are bothering about you are not going to Him at all. The very first step is to try to forget about the self altogether. Your real new self (which is Christ's and also yours, and yours just because it is His) will not come as long as you are looking for it. It will come when you are looking for Him. . . . Give up yourself, and you will find your real self. Lose your life and you will save it. Submit to death, death of your ambitions and favorite wishes every day and death of your whole body in the end: submit with every fiber of your being, and you will find eternal life. Keep back nothing. Nothing that you have not given away will ever be really yours. Nothing in you that has not died will ever be raised from the dead. Look for yourself, and you will find in the long run only hatred, loneliness, despair, rage, ruin, and decay. But look for Christ and you will find Him, and with Him everything else thrown in. (Lewis, *Mere Christianity*, 225–27)

Here is an authority worth submitting to. What a tragedy that so many say no.

They Refuse to Examine Honestly the Evidence
MARK 11:29-32

This question asking for "board certification" is on one level understandable and even wise. After all, we are seldom helped in spiritual matters by religious "nut cases" running around and stirring up trouble. However, when there is insurmountable evidence that would indicate they are the "real deal," we reject the evidence at our own spiritual peril.

Jesus would have been a masterful chess player. He brilliantly makes a counter move: "Jesus said to them, 'I will ask you one question; then answer Me, and I will tell you by what authority I am doing these things. Was John's baptism from heaven or from men? Answer Me.'" Jesus' counterquestion was a common debating technique among rabbis in that day, and it exposed their hearts and motives.

Jesus basically says, "Let's look at the evidence of the one who paved the way for My coming and with whom I closely aligned Myself: the ministry of John the Baptist." Those who come to Jesus with hostile intentions never receive a direct answer. The response forces them to think. Jesus twice commands them, "Answer Me." The implication is they lack the courage to give an honest answer.

Like Jesus, John came preaching a message of repentance. And, like Jesus, he bypassed the temple and the official religious authorities. If Jesus was a hick from the sticks, John was a "wilderness wacko" in the opinion of the temple mafia. Not so, however, among the common people, hence the dilemma of the religious leaders. "They were afraid of the crowd because everyone thought John was a genuine prophet" (v. 32).

They do not deny the evidence as they huddle up to draft their response. They struggle with how to set it aside. John was popular with the people, and his ministry was universally believed to have been given to him by God. So what if he had no human credentials, he had God's! Yet in spite of the evidence, the religious leaders rejected him and did not lift a finger when he was unjustly murdered by Herod (6:14-29).

Jesus' question is pure genius. He is not being evasive. His argument is basically this:

> My claim to authority is based on the possibility of a divine authoritative ministry given directly by God without human endorsement. John the Baptist is a perfect example universally affirmed by the people. Now, if you are unwilling to grant My premise and accept the evidence I have put before you, then we are at an impasse, and we

have nothing further to talk about. If you cannot judge the ministry of John based on the evidence, then you are not qualified to judge Me either! Your willful blindness condemns you.

When Mark began his Gospel, he cited Malachi 3:1 and Isaiah 40:3, linking the ministries of John and Jesus to prophetic promise. The evidence is there, but the hearts of these men will not embrace it. They may attempt to put forth a rational argument against Jesus, but in the end it is an emotional reaction rooted in a fear of losing control, losing their position, and losing their way of life.

For so many people the real problem is not the evidence. The problem is internal: it is us and our sin. The idols of the heart are the real issue. If I accept that Jesus is the Son of God who died for my sins and was raised from the dead, then my life will never be the same. But I like my life. With eyes shut and ears plugged, I do not want to talk about this anymore. As Abraham says to the rich man in hell in Luke 16:31, "If they don't listen to Moses and the prophets, they will not be persuaded if someone rises from the dead."

They Fear Men More than They Fear God
MARK 11:32-33

Few things in life are more paralyzing than fear. According to a recent Gallup Poll, more American adults—51 percent—fear snakes than any other common possibility the pollsters suggested, including heights, flying, storms, the dark, or going to the doctor (Brewer, "Snakes"). Women, in particular, are terrified by the slinky slitherers. And what else are Americans afraid of?

Public speaking	40%
Heights	36%
Being enclosed in a small space	34%
Spiders and insects	27%
Needles or shots	21%
Mice	20%
Flying	18%

In this text God's Word addresses a fear that is common to all people: the fear of man. Proverbs 29:25 says, "The fear of man is a snare, but the one who trusts in the Lord is protected" (cf. 1 Sam 15:24; Luke 12:4-5).

Mark 11:32 lays bare what is at the core of the religious authorities' being: "They were afraid of the crowd, because everyone thought that John was a genuine prophet." And so they beg off: "We don't know." Jesus shuts them down: "Neither will I tell you by what authority I do these things," although the parable of the wicked tenant farmers that follows will give them a big hint (see 12:1-12, esp. v. 12).

It's sad, isn't it? What was expedient and safe was more important to them than what was true and right. "We don't know" was a lie motivated by fear. They would rather keep their position and live a lie than submit to Christ and walk in the truth. They had neither sincere motives nor an open mind. Cowardice instead of courage now registers on their barometer.

Conclusion

So here is a question for all of us to consider, especially if you have never trusted in Christ and submitted your life to His authority: What is holding you back? Is it your desire to be the lord of your own life? Is it your refusal to honestly consider His claims? Is it that you fear men more than you fear God? Is it really that you have not been given good answers to your questions? Is it really that Jesus is not sufficiently good and glorious and true and kind and loving? Or is it that you are paralyzed from moving forward for the same reason these religious leaders were?

Twice in this section of Mark, it says the religious leaders were afraid of the people. The fear of man hindered their movement toward Jesus. Their fear of what others would think paralyzed them. Their fear of losing face, of losing power and position and prestige, condemned them.

Be honest with yourself today. How much of your hesitation and alleged doubts and unanswered questions are really a mask to hide your fear of what faith in Christ might cost you socially, culturally, relationally, and financially? Look once more into the face of this Jesus. Listen once more to the words He speaks. Watch once again how He loves the unlovely. Ponder once more His claim to be God. Be willing to come to Jesus. The end result will not disappoint you.

Reflect and Discuss

1. What gave Christ the courage and boldness to confront the religious leaders in the temple? How can we have the same courage and boldness to confront the enemies of God today?
2. On what basis did the Sanhedrin claim their own authority? Are there religious leaders today who claim the same basis for authority?
3. Where should genuine Christian leaders derive their authority? How can the church and its members investigate and validate the authority of leaders?
4. Why do people naturally question and resist authority? What is the connection to the fall in Genesis 3?

5. What is the challenge in submitting to Christ's authority? What are the rewards?
6. What makes it hard for people to consider evidence fairly? Can a person be won to Christ through persuasive arguments based on good evidence?
7. How does the fear of man affect someone who is considering repenting and following Christ? What can cruel people do to that person? Is there anything worse than that?
8. How does the fear of man affect a Christian layperson? What does a fearless disciple look like?
9. How does fear of man affect Christian leaders? What can cruel people do to a leader? How can you encourage your leader not to be swayed by fear of man?
10. In which cases should a pastor rely on the votes or polls of the church members, and in which cases should he stand against popular opinion?

God Sent His Son and We Killed Him

MARK 12:1-12

Main Idea: To reject the Son is to reject the Father who sent Him.

I. **God Is Patient When Sinners Resist His Wooing (12:1-5).**
   A. God has given us many gifts (12:1).
   B. God has sent us many faithful messengers (12:2-5).
II. **The Father Sent the One He Loves and We Should Honor (12:6-8).**
   A. The Father sent His Son as an act of grace (12:6).
   B. Sinners murdered His Son in an act of insanity (12:7-8).
III. **God's Judgment Will Certainly Come (12:9-12).**
   A. Our response to the Son will decide our eternal destiny (12:9).
   B. The rejection of the Son results in a glorious reversal (12:10-12).

In the Holy Scriptures we need to keep together a number of biblical truths to keep them in balance. For example, we best understand the reality and the beauty of *heaven* against the backdrop of the horrors of *hell*. We see *mercy* more wonderfully when contrasted with the severity of *judgment*. *Grace* will be better loved and appreciated when we see it in contrast with *wrath*.

This is especially important when it comes to two central moments in the life of Jesus Christ: His *incarnation* and His *crucifixion*. Christmas must always be celebrated in light of Easter. The *cradle in a stable* providing a resting place for the little Baby must always be viewed in tandem with the bloody Man hanging on a *cross at Calvary*.

In "the parable of the wicked tenants," Jesus tells a story of judgment and mercy, grace and wrath, Christmas and Easter. The meaning can scarcely be doubted: God sent His Son, and we killed Him.

Jesus has recently entered Jerusalem to the shouts and applause of the people (11:1-11). A couple of days later He enraged the religious leaders by cleansing the temple (11:15-19). The tension grew worse as He embarrassed them in a public showdown over the source of John the Baptist's ministry and His own (11:27-33). Now He will inflame their hatred even more with a parable that will expose their evil hearts and their long-intended goal: to "destroy Him" (3:6; cf. 11:18; 14:1-2).

The story Jesus tells is really an allegorical parable drawn from Isaiah 5:1-7. In Mark the identity of the central characters is plain. The *man* who plants the vineyard is God the Father. The *vineyard* is Israel. The *tenants* are the religious leaders of Israel. The *servants* are the faithful prophets. The *beloved son* is Jesus.

God Is Patient When Sinners Resist His Wooing
MARK 12:1-5

Once more Jesus speaks to the people, and in particular to the religious leaders (cf. 11:27), in a parable. This one is a "judgment parable" or "prophetic parable" portraying the Christ event from God's perspective. It resembles the clever trap Nathan set for King David in 2 Samuel 12:1-15. Like David, the religious leaders will snare themselves.

It is a story of Israel's relationship to the Son of God. It is a reminder of the extraordinary restraint of a God who, as 2 Peter 3:9 teaches, "Is patient with [us], not wanting any to perish but all to come to repentance."

Wealthy absentee landlords and tenant farmers would have been familiar to those listening. It is the turn at the end that will entrap and infuriate the religious leaders because they would readily have identified with the landowners until Jesus identified them as the wicked tenants! They understood His meaning. Like David they knew their guilt. Unlike David they did not repent.

God Has Given Us Many Gifts (Mark 12:1)

Psalm 73:1 says, "God is indeed good to Israel." God planted Israel as a special and elect vineyard. He cared for her and provided for her, and He put in place leaders to protect her and enable her to prosper for His glory and her good. Yet, "He expected it to yield good grapes, but it yielded worthless grapes" (Isa 5:2). He went to great expense on behalf of the vineyard and had every right to expect a bountiful harvest. However, the vineyard failed in its assignment.

God Has Sent Us Many Faithful Messengers (Mark 12:2-5)

The landowner had made an agreement with the tenant farmers whom he believed would be reliable caretakers. They would work the vineyards, benefit from the produce, and pay a percentage as rent. However, as C. H. Dodd said, these particular tenants "pay their rent in blows" (*Parables*, 93).

The landowner sends a servant to collect what rightly belongs to him. They beat him and send him away empty-handed. He sends another, who is treated even worse. They strike him on the head and treat him "shamefully." The word means to insult or dishonor. The gracious and longsuffering landowner sends yet a third servant, and the response of the tenants escalates—they kill him. And so it goes with many others. Some they beat; some they kill.

These faithful servants represent the faithful prophets (see Jer 7:25-26; 25:4-7). Hebrews 1:1 reminds us that "long ago God spoke to the fathers by the prophets at different times and in different ways." Hebrews 11:35-38 sadly records the reception many of them received:

> *Some men were tortured, not accepting release, so that they might gain a better resurrection, and others experienced mockings and scourgings, as well as bonds and imprisonment. They were stoned, they were sawed in two, they died by the sword, they wandered about in sheepskins, in goatskins, destitute, afflicted, and mistreated. The world was not worthy of them. They wandered in deserts and on mountains, hiding in caves and holes in the ground.*

Jeremiah was beaten and put in stocks (Jer 20:2). Isaiah, tradition says, was sawed in two. Zechariah was stoned to death in the temple (2 Chr 24:21). Nehemiah 9:26 says, "But they were disobedient and rebelled against You. They flung Your law behind their backs and killed Your prophets who warned them in order to turn them back to You." And in recent days John the Baptist had been beheaded. Jesus will address this tragic reality:

> *This is why I am sending you prophets, sages, and scribes. Some of them you will kill and crucify, and some of them you will flog in your synagogues and hound from town to town. So all the righteous blood shed on the earth will be charged to you, from the blood of righteous Abel to the blood of Zechariah, son of Berechiah, whom you murdered between the sanctuary and the altar.* (Matt 23:34-35)

God's gracious patience was extended repeatedly, but rebellious sinners like you and me resisted His wooing. We took His good things and turned them into god things thereby making them bad things. We took what was His and in rebellion said it was ours!

The Father Sent the One He Loves and We Should Honor
MARK 12:6-8

The parable takes a remarkable turn. It continues the theme of the amazing patience of God with humanity. It also testifies to the amazing grace of a God who would send His only Son to reconcile rebellious sinners who commit horrible crimes, do not seek God, and have no fear of God.

I understand Jesus is talking at this moment to the religious leaders of Israel, and yet, I must confess, I see all of us in this crowd as well.

The Father Sent His Son as an Act of Grace (Mark 12:6)

In one final attempt to receive from the tenants what is rightly his, he sends "a beloved son." Certainly, he says, "They will respect my son."

The phrase "beloved son" is filled with biblical and theological significance. It was idiomatic for "an only son." A. T. Robertson is most certainly correct when he says, "Jesus evidently had in mind the language of the Father to him at his baptism (Mark 1:11)" (*Word Pictures*, 1:365). We hear this term of endearment also in 9:7 at Jesus' transfiguration.

It recalls the language of Genesis 22:2 when God says to Abraham, "Take your son, your only son Isaac, whom you love." It draws us to that most wonderful verse in the Bible, John 3:16. It even echoes that magnificent messianic prophecy, Isaiah 9:6-7:

> *For a child will be born for us, a son will be given to us, and the government will be on His shoulders. He will be named Wonderful Counselor, Mighty God, Eternal Father, Prince of Peace. The dominion will be vast, and its prosperity will never end. He will reign on the throne of David and over his kingdom, to establish and sustain it with justice and righteousness from now on and forever. The zeal of the LORD of hosts will accomplish this.*

Take note of this last line. We will hear its echo at the end of our text.

As James Edwards notes, there are several significant differences between the mission of the servants who go first and the son who follows:

SERVANTS	SON
Many	Unique
Hirelings	Heir
Forerunners	The last One

If verses 1-5 convey the *hope* of God for His people, verse 6 conveys the *faithful love* of God for His people. The Father sent His Son as an act of grace.

Sinners Murdered His Son in an Act of Insanity (Mark 12:7-8)

In the parable, seeing the son may have led the tenants to wrongly conclude that the landowner was dead. They surmised that if they assassinate the son, then they could claim his property as their own. The phrase "Come, let's kill him" is used by Joseph's brothers in Genesis 37:20.

I appreciate David Garland's insight:

Covetousness makes humans want what they should not have. It makes them think that this desire should be fulfilled at all cost. Other persons become things to exploit, and our desires become our gods. . . . Do humans think that by erasing God from their lives they can take control of their earthly and eternal destinies? Apparently so . . . [Here] is the utter foolishness of sinful rebellion against God. (Garland, *Mark*, 456, 459)

Three days later we would see all of this unfold in what the religious leaders of Israel did to God's Son. Throwing the landlord's son out may allude to Jesus' crucifixion outside the city walls. They would murder Him, an astonishing offense. In God's sending His Son we are reminded of Christmas, the incarnation, the gift of God, and His amazing love. In the killing of the Son, we are reminded of Easter, the crucifixion, the grace of God, and His amazing sacrifice. John 1:11 rings in our ears: "He came to His own, and His own people did not receive Him."

Charles Spurgeon said, "If you reject Him, He answers you with tears. If you wound Him, He bleeds out cleansing. If you kill Him, He dies to redeem. If you bury Him, He rises again to bring us resurrection. Jesus is love manifest." But he then adds:

Let us see for a minute who this Messenger is. *He is one greatly beloved of His Father* and in Himself *He is of surpassing excellence.* The Lord

Jesus Christ is so inconceivably glorious that I tremble at any attempt to describe His Glory. Assuredly, He is very God of very God, co-equal and co-eternal with the Father and yet He deigned to take upon Himself a human form! He was born an infant into our weakness and He lived as a carpenter to share our toil. . . . He took upon Himself the form of a Servant and yet in Him dwells all the fullness of the Godhead bodily! He is the Prince of the kings of the earth and yet He took a towel and washed His disciples' feet! . . .

Because of His Godhead you must not dare to harden your hearts. He is God's Well-Beloved and if you are wise, He will be yours. Do not turn your back on Him whom all the angels worship! Beware, lest you reject One whom God loves so well, for He will take it as an insult to Himself—He that despises the Anointed of God has blasphemed God Himself! You put your finger into the very eye of God when you slight His Son! In grieving the Christ you vex the very heart of God—therefore do not do it. I beseech you, then, by the love which God bears to His Son, to listen to this matchless Messenger of mercy who would persuade you to repent. (Spurgeon, "The Pleading"; emphasis in original)

To reject the Son is to reject the One who sent Him. It is nothing less than an act of spiritual insanity.

God's Judgment Will Certainly Come
MARK 12:9-12

Romans 11:22 says, "Note then the kindness and the severity of God." To slight and reject the Son is to invite the "wrath of the Lamb" into your life (Rev 6:16). Again the great London preacher Charles Spurgeon says it so well:

Remember, once more, that if you do not hear the well-beloved Son of God, you have refused your last hope. *He is God's ultimatum.* Nothing remains when Christ is refused. No one else can be sent. Heaven, itself, contains no further messenger. If Christ is rejected, hope is rejected! . . . I should like every person here that is uncon-verted to remember that there is no other Gospel and no more Sacrifice for sin. I have heard talk of "a larger hope" than the Gospel sets before us—it is a fable, with nothing in Scripture to warrant it! Rejecting Christ, you have rejected all—you have shut against yourself the one door of hope! Christ, who knows better than all pretend-ers, declares that "He that believes not shall be damned." There remains nothing but damnation for those who believe not in Jesus! (Spurgeon, "The Pleading"; emphasis in original)

The One rejected and murdered will be vindicated, and how we now respond to this radical change of events could not be more important.

Our Response to the Son Will Decide Our Eternal Destiny (Mark 12:9)

Jesus provides the answer to His parable, one the religious leaders would be forced to concede. In the process they condemned themselves, and they condemn us as well. The owner will destroy those who refuse his son!

Historically, God judged Israel for their rejection of His Son. In AD 70 Jerusalem was destroyed, and the nation was brought to ruins. Today that same judgment falls on all who have "trampled on the Son of God, regarded as profane the blood of the covenant by which he was sanctified, and insulted the Spirit of grace" (Heb 10:29). It is indeed "a fearful thing to fall into the hands of the living God" (Heb 10:31).

The Rejection of the Son Results in a Glorious Reversal (Mark 12:10-12)

Jesus quotes from Psalm 118:22-23, changing the metaphor to a building. It is the same psalm shouted by the people at His triumphal entry. It is clearly messianic. He knows who He is and why He has come!

The stone rejected would become a symbol for the Messiah and an explanation for how the Jewish people rejected Jesus (Luke 20:17; Acts 4:11; Rom 9:33; 1 Pet 2:6-8). They cast the stone aside as worthless. God, however, in a marvelous reversal, takes what man rejects and makes it the cornerstone (lit. "the head of the corner"), the stone most important to the whole structure, ensuring its stability and symmetry. It refers to the capstone atop a column, keystone in an arch, or cornerstone of a foundation.

The rejection, humiliation, and crucifixion of Jesus is an apparent tragedy, but God will use it all for a greater purpose that can only be described as, "This came from the Lord and is wonderful in our eyes."

Sadly, the religious leaders are blind to all of this. Knowing He told the parable against them, they were conniving to seize Him. They move ahead with their plan to murder the Son sent by God. Like the demons who recognize Jesus as a threat to their very existence (Mark 1:24), they refuse to submit to His lordship and plot how they might destroy Him. Mark 12:12 is a disappointing summation of their response: "Because they knew He had said this parable against them, they were looking for a way to arrest Him, but they were afraid of the crowd. So they left Him and went away." As Paul would later explain, all of this is foolishness and a stumbling block to them; for us, however, it is the power of God unto salvation (1 Cor 1:18-25).

Calvin was right: "Whatever may be the contrivances of men, God has at the same time declared, that in setting up the kingdom of Christ, His power will be victorious" (*Calvin's Commentaries*, 17:34). God will win even when, for a fleeting moment, it seems He has lost. An empty tomb proves it is so. Redemptive history reaches a glorious climactic victory in this beloved Son, this rejected stone.

Conclusion

In *The Last Battle* by C. S. Lewis, Queen Lucy says to Lord Digory, "In our world too, a stable once had something inside it that was bigger than our whole world" (Lewis, *The Last Battle*, 161). To this we might add, "In our world there was also a cross, and hanging on it was someone greater and more wonderful than our whole world." It was the Lord's doing. And it is marvelous in our eyes!

Reflect and Discuss

1. How does the world view Christmas? What do they think of Easter? How does Easter help Christians to properly understand Christmas?
2. Why did Jesus use parables as a teaching method? Why did He use a parable in this particular case?
3. God blessed Israel, but that nation did not honor God. Can the same be said of mankind in general? of the country you live in? of your church or your denomination?
4. Israel killed the prophets God sent. In what way are we guilty of killing the prophets? of crucifying Christ?
5. If your attempts to get people to fulfill their contractual obligations had been violently refused, what would you do? What was the logic of the father in the parable in sending his only son? What was the motivation for God to send His only Son?
6. What did the tenant farmers think they would gain from killing the landlord's son? What did the Jewish leaders hope to gain by killing Jesus? What did they in fact accomplish?
7. What do sinners think they can have and keep if they reject repentance? Why do Christians resist radical obedience? What does each of these in fact obtain, and what do they miss out on?
8. What do secular people say when asked about judgment and hell? What do you think is necessary for them to accept the truth? Do you know any logical arguments that might be compelling?
9. How did the Jewish leaders react when they lost their debate with Jesus? What persons or organizations do you know of that, when faced with the truth claims of Christianity, respond with hatred or violence?

10. The Sanhedrin postponed their persecution of Jesus because they feared the crowd (12:12). How does this expose faulty reasoning on their part? What should be the basis of our decision on how to respond to Jesus' demands? How might this observation be employed during evangelism?

Should Christians Obey the Government?

MARK 12:13-17

Main Idea: Followers of Jesus should obey the government and the Lord according to what each is due.

I.   **The Trap: Be Careful When Approached by Strange Bedfellows (12:13).**
II. **The Setup: Beware of Flattering Words (12:14).**
III. **The Question: Watch Out for Either/or Scenarios (12:14).**
IV. **The Answer: Give to Each What They Rightly Deserve (12:15-17).**
  A.   Obey the government as long as you can.
  B.   Worship God as long as you live.

It is one of those questions Christians have discussed and debated for two thousand years. Regardless of one's political loyalties and commitments, the question must be faced by every believer: "Should I, as a Christian—a devoted follower of Jesus Christ my King—obey the government?"

This question, of course, is much easier to answer when you live in a democracy or when the winds of governmental laws and policies are blowing in your direction. But what if you live in a totalitarian context? What if you are subjected to a cruel and tyrannical dictatorship? Or, even within a free democracy, what do you do when asked to violate Scripture or conscience?

This text appears in the midst of a series of controversies between Jesus and the religious leaders in Jerusalem. Mark 11:20–13:37 is one long day. There are five confrontations altogether:

1. The question of His authority by the Sanhedrin (11:27-33)
2. The question of paying taxes by the Pharisees and Herodians (12:13-17)
3. The question of the resurrection by the Sadducees (12:18-27)
4. The question of the greatest command by the scribes (12:28-34)
5. The question of whose Son is the Christ by Jesus Himself (12:35-37)

Here we ask, Should we obey the government and pay taxes, especially if we do not recognize its legitimacy, disdain its policies, and are subjected by its oppression? Do we feed the monster that is eating us? Within the context of this dispute with those who will be the authors of His death, Jesus provides the answer. He also provides some practical and basic wisdom when we are confronted by those devoted to our destruction.

The Trap: Be Careful When Approached by Strange Bedfellows
MARK 12:13

It is Passover, a week of national celebration for Israel. During this celebration the Sanhedrin (see 11:27; 12:1,12) sends to Jesus some Pharisees and Herodians. We have seen these strange bedfellows before (3:6). And as before, they are up to no good.

The Pharisees were the conservatives, the right-wingers of that day. The Herodians were the liberals, the left-wingers, advocates of big government. The Pharisees hated Jesus because He was messing with their religious agenda. The Herodians opposed Him because He was threatening their political advantage. Amazingly, Jesus brought them together! They both wanted to destroy Him.

Jesus knew they were up to something. They came "to trap Him by what He said." The word "trap" means to capture by hunting or fishing. The idea is violent pursuit of prey. They hope to trap Him in a slip of the tongue, a public gaffe that will take Him down. "They watched closely and sent spies who pretended to be righteous, so they could catch Him in what He said, to hand Him over to the governor's rule and authority" (Luke 20:20).

When you see sworn enemies allied as they approach you, be on guard! It is almost certain they do not have your best interest at heart.

The Setup: Beware of Flattering Words
MARK 12:14

The Bible has a lot to say about flattery. None of it is good!

For there is nothing reliable in what [the wicked] say; destruction is within them; their throat is an open grave; they flatter with their tongues. (Ps 5:9)

A lying tongue hates those it crushes, and a flattering mouth causes ruin. (Prov 26:28)

A man who flatters his neighbor spreads a net for his [own] feet. (Prov 29:5)

We see this sin on display when the Pharisees and Herodians attempted to "trap" Jesus. They call Him "teacher," a title of respect, even though they had no respect for Him. They tell Him they know He is "truthful," even though they will crucify Him as a blasphemer. They tell Him they know He is impartial, and they conclude that He teaches "truthfully the way of God."

Even though their flattery is insincere, what they say is actually true! And since it is true, He will not be snared by their words. His ego will not inflate; pride will not cause Him to lower His guard. No, Jesus, the "wisdom of God" (1 Cor 1:30), will not be tripped up by the foolishness of men.

The Question: Watch Out for Either/or Scenarios
MARK 12:14

This trap is now sprung with a question that had been carefully crafted. Its brilliance is in its simplicity: "Is it lawful to pay taxes to Caesar or not? Should we pay, or should we not pay?"

Wow! What a question for that day! The stakes are high, and the issue at hand is volatile. And it requires a yes or no answer. They have Him! Regardless of which way He goes, He loses.

The context of the question bears this out. The Greek word for taxes is *kenson*, a transliteration of the Latin word *census*. It refers to an imperial Roman tax. The Jews despised it because it was a constant reminder of their subjection to pagan Rome. So, if Jesus said to pay it, the people would turn on Him as a traitor, and He would be finished. On the other hand, if He said not to pay it, He could be arrested and tried by the Romans for sedition and insurrection. Silence was not an option. His enemies have trapped Him on the "horns of a dilemma," or so they thought.

I like "yes or no" options. However, we should never allow ourselves to be backed into such a corner. "Have you stopped beating your wife?" That is a lose-lose predicament, the classic unfair question.

Jesus recognized their evil intent (11:15) and would not be manipulated by their game.

The Answer: Give to Each What They Rightly Deserve
MARK 12:15-17

The moment of truth has arrived. All eyes were on Jesus, and people held their breath to see what He would say.

He begins by exposing their hypocrisy, something He was well aware of (11:15), with a question: "Why are you testing Me?" This is the same word Mark used in 1:13 when Satan "tempted" our Lord in the wilderness. There is demonic intent in their motivation to destroy Jesus, like the efforts of the Devil to get Him off track from His mission. And as Satan failed in the wilderness, the Pharisees and Herodians will fail in the temple.

Obey the Government as Long as You Can

Jesus asked for a denarius, the required tax and a day's wage for a typical laborer in Israel. Ironically, He does not have one, but they do! He then asks, "Whose image and inscription is this?" They said to Him, "Caesar's." On one side of the coin was a bust of Tiberius Caesar with the inscription, "Tiberius Caesar Augustus, Son of the Divine Augustus." The other side had an image of Tiberius's mother Livia with the words, "*Pontifex Maximus*," meaning "High Priest." The Jews found this to be idolatrous: a man claiming to be a god and a woman a priest—blasphemy!

Jesus then said some of the most significant words in history. Their impact on Western civilization is mammoth: "Give back to Caesar the things that are Caesar's, and to God the things that are God's." They never saw it coming!

By His reply Jesus acknowledges the legitimacy of human government. He is no anarchist. God has ordained the *family*, the *church*, and *human government*. It has the right to levy taxes, and we have the responsibility to pay. It has the right to make laws, and we have the responsibility to obey. Other writers in the New Testament, especially Paul and Peter, reaffirm and expand on this statement of Jesus, even though they lived when the lunatic Nero (AD 54–68) was emperor. Note the following:

> *Everyone must submit to the governing authorities, for there is no authority except from God, and those that exist are instituted by God. So then, the one who resists the authority is opposing God's command, and those who oppose it will bring judgment on themselves. For rulers are not a terror to good conduct, but to bad. Do you want to be unafraid of the authority? Do what is good, and you will have its approval. For government is God's servant for your good. But if you do wrong, be afraid, because it does not carry the sword for no reason. For government is God's servant, an avenger that brings wrath on the one who does wrong. Therefore, you must submit, not only because of wrath, but also because of your conscience. And for this reason you pay taxes, since the authorities are God's public servants, continually attending to these tasks. Pay your obligations to everyone: taxes to those you owe taxes, tolls to*

those you owe tolls, respect to those you owe respect, and honor to those you owe honor. (Rom 13:1-7)

First of all, then, I urge that petitions, prayers, intercessions, and thanksgivings be made for everyone, for kings and all those who are in authority, so that we may lead a tranquil and quiet life in all godliness and dignity. (1 Tim 2:1-2)

Submit to every human authority because of the Lord, whether to the Emperor as the supreme authority or to governors as those sent out by him to punish those who do what is evil and to praise those who do what is good. For it is God's will that you silence the ignorance of foolish people by doing good. As God's slaves, live as free people, but don't use your freedom as a way to conceal evil. Honor everyone. Love the brotherhood. Fear God. Honor the Emperor. (1 Pet 2:13-17)

Christians have legitimate responsibilities to the government, and as long as those obligations do not interfere with our ability to honor and worship God, we are to fulfill them. It is our Christian duty.

Worship God as Long as You Live

Jesus also said, "Give back . . . to God the things that are God's." He refused to be trapped by an either/or proposition. Once more He "amazed" them with His teachings.

If the coin has Caesar's image on it, then it belongs to him. So give him what is rightfully his. However, as humans, you all bear the image of God (Gen 1:26-27). You must give to God what is rightfully His—your entire life. We have a duty to the government, but we have an even greater duty to God, who has created us and redeemed us. As 1 Corinthians 10:31 says, "Therefore, whether you eat or drink, or whatever you do, do everything for God's glory."

In Acts 4:19-20 Peter and John say, "Whether it's right in the sight of God for us to listen to you rather than to God, you decide; for we are unable to stop speaking about what we have seen and heard." And again in Acts 5:29, "But Peter and the apostles answered, 'We must obey God rather than men.'"

Kent Hughes says, "The statement by our Lord was not only astounding the instant it was uttered, but is even today universally acclaimed to be the single most influential political statement ever made in the history of the world" (*Mark*, 2:103). With one simple maxim Jesus put everything in proper perspective. He put Caesar in his place, and He placed God where He rightfully belongs in our lives as well. All the people could do was stand back and look on in amazement!

Conclusion

Adopting something of a manifesto, I think we can say at the very least the following:

> As a devoted follower of King Jesus, my Lord, my Savior, and my sovereign God, I pledge the following to the governing authorities, which are ordained by God:

1. I will be a good citizen living in subjection to governmental authority, even a pagan one (Rom 13:1-7; 1 Pet 2:13-17). I will responsibly engage the political process. If allowed, I will vote, seeking to bring my Christian convictions into the public arena (see Prov 14:34).
2. I will live internationally like Joseph in Egypt, Daniel in Babylon, and Jesus Himself on earth. My ultimate allegiance is to Christ and His kingdom.
3. I will obey the state but worship only God. And I will thank God for all the good He does through the government, praying always for all who are in authority (1 Tim 2:1-5).
4. I will acknowledge that all governmental authority is established by and comes from God (Mark 12:17; Rom 13:1,4,6).
5. I will acknowledge that all government serves in some measure the purposes of promoting good and punishing evil (Rom 13:3-4). Bad government is almost always better than no government.
6. I will pay all taxes levied upon me by my government, recognizing its right to do so (Mark 12:17; Rom 13:6-7).
7. I will engage in "civil disobedience" only when my government prohibits me from doing what the Bible commands, or when it commands me to do what the Bible prohibits.

This last point, while true, needs some further clarification. (1) The law being resisted must be unjust and immoral, clearly contrary to the will of God, and not just inconvenient or burdensome. (2) Legal means of changing the unjust situation must have been exhausted. Civil disobedience is a method not of first resort, but of last resort. (3) The act of disobedience must be public rather than secretive or hidden. (4) There should be some hope of success, as my intent is to produce changes in laws and institutions. (5) As I consider civil disobedience, I must be willing to accept the penalty for breaking the law.

Mark Dever says it precisely: "The legal establishment of Christianity for many nations, centuries after the apostles, reflected an already distorted understanding of the gospel and led to terrible confusion as the church wielded the sword" ("Jesus Paid Taxes"). The Christian has only one God: Jesus. The Christian longs for only one kingdom: the kingdom of God. The Christian has only one sword: the Word of God.

So, as a devoted follower of Jesus, I will say yes to obeying the government and paying taxes to Caesar, but I will say no to disobeying the Word of God and worshiping a man or institution. Independence Day for the Christian is not marked by a flag. No, our independence day is Easter, marked by a cross and an empty tomb.

Reflect and Discuss

1. On what points do you disagree with the government of your country? How does your situation compare with the Jews under Roman rule?
2. What groups are there in your country that can't agree about much, but they agree to oppose Christianity?
3. What was the motive of those who asked Jesus this question? Have you encountered people who have this motive in their questions? How can you deal with them?
4. Did Jesus expect to change the mind of the Pharisees and Herodians with His answer? How do you think the crowd responded when Jesus delivered such a wise answer?
5. What is the difference between compliments and flattery? Would it be fair to say that flattery is a form of lying?
6. How can those who perform surveys bias the results by the way they formulate the questions? How can one person in a debate try to win a point by defining the nature of the question at hand?
7. How can Christians be encouraged when they hear someone deliver a well-crafted answer to a skeptic? Is the skeptic still responsible for his motives and his refusal to repent?
8. What is the legitimate purpose of human government? What are the responsibilities of citizens?
9. What are the responsibilities of humanity, made in the image of God?
10. Is there a danger in your country for its citizens to worship the political leaders? to worship the government? to worship the country? How can you balance patriotism with Christianity?

Will There Be Sex in Heaven?

MARK 12:18-27

Main Idea: Those who are in Christ are promised a future resurrection and fullness of life in the presence of King Jesus.

I. The Hypothetical Problem from Skeptics (12:18-23)
II. The Perfect Plan for Heaven (12:24-25)
III. The Divine Power to Do What God Promises (12:26-27)

There is a playful saying that teachers of the Bible will often cite: "If you want to build a big crowd, teach on *sex* or teach on *the end times*. And if you want to build a really big crowd, teach on *sex in the end times*!" That very issue was raised by a group of religious leaders who did not even believe in the end times, in life after death—the Sadducees.

The question of life after death has always fascinated humans. Every religion has some perspective on the issue, though they vary widely. Recent surveys point out that 80 percent of Americans believe in some form of life after death, with another 9 percent saying they are not sure.

Christians have always had a strong doctrine concerning life after death. After all, we build our understanding of the future, end times, and eternity from the teachings of Jesus, an empty tomb, and a resurrected and living Savior. But we have to admit to a good bit of mystery on the precise details. The Bible tells us a lot, but it does not tell us everything.

Jesus countered the troubling riddle of the Sadducees and demolished their doctrine of annihilation. Additional Scriptures and theological reflection help us craft a healthy perspective on what we can expect for the future. For those who trust Christ for salvation, one thing is certain: it is all good!

The Hypothetical Problem from Skeptics

MARK 12:18-23

The parade of opponents continues. The chief priests, scribes, and elders took their shot in 11:27–12:12 and went down in flames. The Pharisees and Herodians took Him on in 12:13-17, and He shut their mouths. Now the Sadducees come with a trick question they had probably used to frustrate the Pharisees. They will now try it out on Jesus.

A small sect of the priestly families, the Sadducees were wealthy aristocrats with significant political and temple influence. They dominated the
Sanhedrin (Acts 5:17). They were sympathetic to Hellenism, the Herods,
and Rome. They considered only the books of Moses (the Pentateuch) as
authoritative. In a sense this made them theological conservatives. They
also had a strong doctrine of human free will and did not believe in angels
and demons (Acts 23:8). They did not believe in the immortality of the
soul or in a future bodily resurrection. Josephus said, "The doctrine of the
Sadducees is this: souls die with bodies" (*Antiquities*, 18:1, 4). Because of
their truncated Scriptures, they were not looking for a Messiah King from
David's line. With the total destruction of their center of power—Jerusalem
and the temple (AD 70)—their political influence came to an end, and they
vanished from history.

Their trick question was grounded in the issue of "levirate [Latin for
'brother-in-law'] marriage" mentioned in Genesis 38:8-10 and in the book
of Ruth. It is explained in Deuteronomy 25:5-6:

> *When brothers live on the same property and one of them dies without a son,*
> *the wife of the dead man may not marry a stranger outside the family. Her*
> *brother-in-law is to take her as his wife, have sexual relations with her, and*
> *perform the duty of a brother-in-law for her. The first son she bears will carry*
> *on the name of the dead brother, so his name will not be blotted out from Israel.*

God made a provision for a family to be raised up in name and property
rights for a husband who dies with no male heir.

The Sadducees created what we call a *reductio ad absurdum* argument,
reducing things to the absurd or the ridiculous. A man marries a woman,
and he dies. He has six brothers who can fulfill the levirate obligation. She
married each one, and tragically all seven died without bearing a child.
The Pharisees and most rabbis believe the world to come is basically an
improved and better version of this world, which therefore would include
things like marriage. Assuming monogamy (which they would have), to
whom then will she be married in the world to come?

The Sadducees argue such a scenario is absurd, and it shows the foolishness of believing in a future resurrection. Look at all the problems it
could potentially cause. No, God is too smart for that, and the books of
Moses (which are the undisputed Word of God) do not mention a future
resurrection. Therefore, it must not exist.

Jesus has already spoken of His own resurrection three times (Mark
8:31; 9:31; 10:34). The Sadducees think they have Him cornered.

The Perfect Plan for Heaven
MARK 12:24-25

Theological error must be confronted quickly and clearly. That is exactly what Jesus does. He says they do not know "the Scriptures or the power of God."

Jesus tells them plainly that they are "deceived," in error.[6] Jesus accuses the theological elite of His day of error in their area of expertise! What they claim to know best, the Torah, they actually know least. And because they misunderstand the Bible, they also misunderstand God! Misinterpreting the Scriptures inevitably leads to a distorted view of God. It always leads to your god being too small and impotent to be the God of the Bible!

Jesus begins correcting them in verse 25. The world of resurrection is different from the world we live in. There is continuity, to be sure. I will be me, and you will be you, but we will live for all of eternity in an entirely new reality. In Revelation 21:1, it is called a "new heaven and a new earth." Why? Because "the first heaven and the first earth had passed away."

Jesus addresses the Sadducees' question. (1) There will be a resurrection. (2) There will be no marriage relationship as we know it in this life. (3) We will become "like angels," probably in the sense that we will no longer procreate and we will never die. Therefore marriage will not be necessary, at least for that purpose.

This leads to the key question, "Will there be sex in heaven?" While the Bible does not pose this question in exactly this way, I think we can safely shed light on the answer. We will exist as glorified bodies in heaven but will maintain our unique identities. There will be, in one sense, sex in heaven because sex identifies us in terms of gender. But whatever physical, sensual, and sexual pleasure we enjoy in this life will be transcended beyond our imagination in the life to come.

Jonathan Edwards (1703–1758) says it so well: "[In heaven] the glorified spiritual bodies of the saints shall be filled with pleasures of the most exquisite kind that such refined bodies are capable of. . . . The sweetness and pleasure that shall be in the mind, shall put the spirits of the body into such a motion as shall cause a sweet sensation throughout the body, infinitely excelling any sensual pleasure here" (*Works*, 13:351).

No one will be disappointed in any way when they get to heaven! No one will be deprived of one thing that is necessary for maximum joy, optimal

---

[6] The Greek word here is *planan*, from which we get our English word *planet*. It means "to wander off course, to go astray."

happiness, and complete satisfaction. Our relationship with Jesus and with all of our brothers and sisters will be so intense and so filled with love and affection that all earthly marital bliss will seem shallow and small in comparison. Heaven is indeed God's perfect plan for His children who have come to Him through His Son Jesus.

The Divine Power to Do What God Promises
MARK 12:26-27

Jesus defeats the Sadducees on their own turf, the books of Moses. The doctrine of resurrection finds Old Testament support in places like Job 19:25-27; Psalm 16:9-11; and Daniel 12:2. Jesus in grace meets the Sadducees where they are and takes them to the "burning bush" story found in Exodus 3:6. There God speaks to Moses in the present tense: "I am . . . the God of Abraham, the God of Isaac, and the God of Jacob." Though they died physically, they are alive spiritually right now! It is not "I was their God" but "I am their God." Further, being their God implies covenant, and it is inconceivable that the eternal God does not maintain an eternal covenant with His people, which is exactly what we find in the covenant God made first with Abraham (Gen 12) and later with David (2 Sam 7).

Tim Keller explains,

> Notice that Jesus does not hang the hope of life after death (like the Greeks did) on the idea of an immortal part of us. Rather, He rests in the commitment of God to us ("I am the God of Abraham, Isaac, and Jacob"). This is a very powerful argument for life after death. We have a God who cannot, at our death, scrap that which is precious to Him! (Keller, "Mark," 161)

Thus the matter ends. God is not God of the dead but of the living. The Sadducees are wrong. Jesus has silenced His critics once again.

Conclusion

We would expect a great God to prepare a great heaven! The Bible does not tell us everything we want to know, but it tells us more than enough to make us long for that glorious destiny.

WHAT WILL HEAVEN BE LIKE? SEVENTEEN OBSERVATIONS	
1. Heaven is being prepared by Christ Himself.	John 14:3
2. Heaven is only for those who have been born again.	John 3:3
3. Heaven is described as a glorious city.	Rev 21:11,18
4. Heaven will shine with and be lighted by God's glory.	Rev 21:11,23; 22:5
5. Heaven's gates will never be shut.	Rev 21:25
6. Heaven has the water of life for everlasting life.	Rev 22:1
7. Heaven has the tree of life for abundant life.	Rev 2:7; 22:19
8. Heaven has the throne of God at its center.	Rev 4:2; 22:1-2
9. Heaven is a place of holiness.	Rev 21:27
10. Heaven is beautiful.	Ps 50:2
11. Heaven is a place of unity.	Eph 1:10
12. Heaven is a place of perfection.	1 Cor 13:10
13. Heaven is joyful.	Ps 16:11
14. Heaven is a place for all eternity.	John 3:15; Ps 23:6
15. Heaven has no night.	Rev 21:25; 22:5
16. Heaven is filled with singing.	Isa 44:23; Rev 14:3; 15:1-3
17. Heaven is a place of wonderful service.	Rev 7:15; 22:3 (Barton, *Mark*, 347)

WHAT WILL OUR BODIES BE LIKE? NINE OBSERVATIONS	
1. They will be recognizable.	1 Cor 13:12
2. They will be like Christ's body (glorified).	1 John 3:2
3. They will not be limited by space.	Luke 24:31; John 20:19,26
4. They will be eternal.	2 Cor 5:1-5
5. They will be glorious.	Rom 8:18; 1 Cor 15:43
6. They will not have pain.	Rev 21:4
7. They will not die.	1 Cor 15:26; Rev 21:4
8. They will not hunger or thirst.	Rev 7:16
9. They will not sin.	Rev 21:27 (Barton, *Mark*, 351)

Now you know why we can sing with Eliza Hewitt (1851–1920) that wonderful refrain,

> When we all get to heaven,
> what a day of rejoicing that will be!
> When we all see Jesus,
> we'll sing and shout the victory. ("When We All Get to Heaven")

The issue is really not, "Will there be sex in heaven?" The real issue is, "Will you be in heaven?" It will be wonderful beyond words. Won't you join us?

Reflect and Discuss

1. Why do you think belief in life after death is the majority opinion? How do Christians defend this opinion with facts and evidence?
2. Have you met anyone who seems to have a standard "trick question" ready for a Christian? What was the question? Have you prepared a good answer in case you hear that question again?
3. How did the law of levirate marriage address issues important to the ancient Near Eastern culture? How should your culture address issues of widowhood and inheritance?
4. What are some mistaken ideas about what heaven is going to be like? Why do people project such ideas onto the concept of heaven?
5. Some people are indifferent about heaven because they think it will be boring. How would you respond to that attitude?

6. When Jesus debated the Sadducees, He used evidence from one of the five books of Moses. Why? How should His example affect the way we debate Jews? Should it determine how we debate atheists?
7. Jesus' argument hinges on the tense of a verb. What does this say about the accuracy of the Bible? What does it teach us about the importance of studying the Word closely?
8. Which biblical description of heaven is most often overlooked, ignored, or mistaken?
9. Which biblical description of heaven is the most encouraging for you? Why?
10. Which biblical description of our bodies in heaven is most encouraging for you? Why?

Two Great Commands/Two Great Loves

MARK 12:28-34

Main Idea: Citizens of Christ's kingdom are called to love God supremely and to love their neighbor unselfishly.

I. **We Are Commanded to Love God Supremely (12:28-30).**
   A. Love God for who He is (12:29).
   B. Love God with all you are (12:30).
II. **We Are Commanded to Love Others Genuinely (12:31-34).**
   A. Such love is legitimately selfish (12:31).
   B. Such love is a true sacrifice (12:32-33).
   C. Such love is crucial to salvation (12:34).

Humans love to ask what I call "mega" or "greatest" questions. What was the greatest empire in world history: Greek? Roman? Ottoman? American? Who was the greatest leader: Jesus? Mohammed? Moses? Augustus Caesar? Who was the greatest American leader: Washington? Lincoln? Roosevelt? Reagan? We do the same thing in sports. Who is the greatest baseball player ever: Babe Ruth? Willie Mays? Ted Williams? Ty Cobb? Hank Aaron? Who is the greatest football player ever: Jim Brown? Jerry Rice? Joe Montana? Walter Payton? Who is the greatest basketball player: Michael Jordan? Magic Johnson? Larry Bird? Wilt Chamberlain? Bill Russell? Kareem Abdul-Jabbar? LeBron James?

The questions keep coming: cars, movies, books, musicians. We want to know who or what is the greatest. And interest in these "mega" questions is not new. It goes back even to the time of Jesus, when a religious leader asked our Lord about "the most important" of the commands. Our Lord did not give him one. He gave him two, telling him, "All the Law and the Prophets depend on these two commands" (Matt 22:40). Both commands are grounded in our responsibility to love. We are to love God supremely and love our fellow humans genuinely.

Our response to these two commandments exposes our hearts, lays bare our souls, and reveals what matters most to us. What do you cherish? What is of supreme value in your life?

We Are Commanded to Love God Supremely
MARK 12:28-30

A scribe, a religious lawyer, had come to Jesus. He had overheard our Lord's disputes with the other Jewish leaders and saw that Jesus "answered them well." So, without malice, this man asked Jesus a question that was often batted around in religious circles: "Which command is the most important of all?" This is not as easy as it sounds. The rabbinic tradition had identified 613 commands in the first five books of the Bible. Of these, 365 were negative, and 248 were positive. Some were "light," making less demand, while others were viewed as "heavy," with severe repercussions for disobedience. So this scribe asked Jesus to "declare Himself." Our Lord gladly obliges, and His answer takes us to the core of what really matters in life.

Love God for Who He Is (Mark 12:29)

Jesus quotes what Israel called the "Shema," found in Deuteronomy 6:4-5: "Listen, Israel: The LORD our God, the LORD is One. Love the LORD your God with all your heart, with all your soul, and with all your strength." This confession was recited by every devout Jew morning and evening. Edwards explains, "It was and is as important to Judaism as is the Lord's Prayer or the Apostles' Creed to Christianity" (Edwards, *Mark*, 371).

"The LORD [*Yahweh*] our God [*Elohim*], the LORD [*Yahweh*] is One." Here is the heart and soul of the Hebrew faith, yes, of Christianity. *Yahweh* is God's covenant name declared to His people. Yahweh is our God and our only God. Yahweh is One. He is unified and unique in essence and existence. He alone is God; there is no other.

This is a powerful statement of uniqueness and exclusivity. Our God is God alone, and our worship, love, devotion, and allegiance must be exclusively to God or He will not accept it. Teachers and theologians could debate all they want, but Jesus begins by bringing them back to the fundamentals, the nonnegotiables of the faith. We should love this God because of who He is: He is our God.

What kind of God is He? Exodus 34:6-7 describes Him as perfect in His gracious love and His pure justice.

Furthermore, the context of the Shema is instructive. To love God is to obey His commandments and statutes "all the days of your life" (Deut 6:2). To love God means you will teach these commandments to your children and grandchildren (Deut 6:2), when you sit, walk, lie down, and rise up throughout the day (Deut 6:7), remembering He is the God "who brought you out of the land of Egypt, out of the place of slavery" (Deut 6:12). To love God supremely means you must "not follow other gods, the gods of the peoples around you, for the LORD your God [*Yahweh* your *Elohim*], who is among you, [because Yahweh] is a jealous God" (Deut 6:14-15).

Love God with All You Are (Mark 12:30)

The repetition of the word "all" (four times in Mark 12:30) emphasizes the comprehensive nature of how we are to love *Yahweh* our *Elohim*, the Lord our God. It calls for a total response of love and devotion to God. Indeed heart, soul, mind, and strength are not intended as a "psychological analysis of human personality" (Hiebert, *Mark*, 304), but a call to love God wholly and completely. Kent Hughes says, "It does not take much of a man to be a believer, but it takes all there is of him!" (*Mark*, 2:115).

The *heart* speaks to our emotions, the real me on the inside (see Exod 20:3). The *soul* speaks to the spirit, the self-conscious life (see Ps 42:1-2). The *mind* speaks to our intelligence and thought life (see 2 Cor 10:3-5). *Strength* speaks to our bodily powers, perhaps even the will (see Rom 12:1). There is overlap in these categories, but as Sinclair Ferguson says, "God is never satisfied with anything less than the devotion of our whole life for the whole duration of our lives" (*Mark*, 200).

Comparing a man's love for his wife gives insight into his love for his God.

1. Is the Lord the all-consuming passion of my life?
2. Do I have a deep, intense, and abiding affection for my Lord?
3. Am I loyal to my God with an exclusive love?
4. Do I resist and even oppose anything or anyone that seeks to do my Lord harm?
5. Am I zealous to defend, with grace, my Lord's name and honor?
6. Do I enjoy spending time with my Lord?
7. Do I do things that please my Lord and increase His joy?

8. Do I brag on my Lord to others?
9. Do I tell my Lord that I love Him?
10. Do I talk with my Lord as much as I can? (Storms, "I Love You")

Remember, these are not things I do to get God to love me. They are things I do because I am loved by Him and because I love Him. I love Him because He first loved me (1 John 4:10).

We Are Commanded to Love Others Genuinely

MARK 12:31-34

As is so often the case, Jesus gives us more than we ask for! The religious lawyer asks which command is the most important. Jesus tells him there are two that go together. How you respond to the first (loving God) will determine how you respond to the second (loving your neighbor). When you obey the second, it shows that you have embraced the first.

> Jesus shows us that love actually defines the lawful life, [and] He shows us that the law actually defines the loving life. . . . When Jesus says all the laws boil down to "love God and neighbor," He is saying we have not fulfilled a law by simply avoiding what the law prohibits, but we must also do and be what the law is really after—*namely* love. (Keller, "Mark," 163; emphasis in original)

Such Love Is Legitimately Selfish (Mark 12:31)

Jesus adds Leviticus 19:18 to complement Deuteronomy 6:4-5. Growing out of my love for God, I love those who have been created by God in His image. "Neighbor" is not used here in a restrictive sense. All of humanity, even my enemies, are in view (see Luke 10:25-29).

Some wrongly think Jesus, the unselfish One, actually tells me to selfishly love myself. How do we make sense of this? (1) There is a healthy kind of self-love that recognizes we are the objects of both the "creating" and the "redeeming" love of our God. To hate myself is an offense to God and calls into question His wisdom and goodness. (2) The love a person naturally has for himself is now "turned out" toward others (cf. Phil 2:3-5). (3) The fact that this is a command makes clear that the primary focus is on our actions and not our feelings. (4) There is certainly a mysterious paradox, for the same Jesus who tells us to love ourselves also tells us to deny ourselves and die to ourselves (Mark 8:34). The more I rightly love myself, the more I will deny myself and love others. I will serve the needs of others with all the energy, passion, and zeal with which I attempt to meet my own needs. However, only by loving my God supremely will I be able to love others—all others—genuinely. And as I do so, I demonstrate that I love my God supremely. No wonder Jesus said, "There is no other command greater than these."

In a sermon preached at Southeastern Baptist Theological Seminary in February 2012, Don Carson helped us see what it means to love others genuinely. He encouraged us to examine the context surrounding Leviticus 19:18, showing that loving your neighbor as yourself means that you will

- care for the poor (19:10),
- not steal (19:11),
- not lie (19:11),
- be fair in business dealings (19:14),
- care for the deaf (19:14),
- care for the blind (19:14),
- deal justly with all (19:15),
- avoid slander (19:16),
- not "jeopardize" the life of your neighbor (19:16),
- not "harbor hatred against your brother" (19:17),
- rebuke your neighbor when necessary for his and your good (19:17), and
- not take revenge or bear a grudge against others (19:18).

Wow! God does not leave it to our imaginations as to what He means when He tells us to love our neighbors as ourselves.

Such Love Is a True Sacrifice (Mark 12:32-33)

The scribe responds with delight. He affirms Jesus' creedal confession of the exclusive monotheism of the one true God, affirms the comprehensive love, devotion, and worship our God is worthy to receive, and adds an insight that drew the praise and applause of Jesus.

To love God supremely and our neighbor genuinely "is far more important than all the burnt offerings and sacrifices." Real religion ultimately is a matter of the heart. Religious rituals always must give way to the superiority of a right relationship with God and others. Indeed rituals have no real meaning unless they are expressions of our love for Jesus and others. Such spiritual insight finds its echo in the Old Testament at numerous points.

> *Then Samuel said: Does the Lord take pleasure in burnt offerings and sacrifices as much as in obeying the Lord? Look: to obey is better than sacrifice, to pay attention is better than the fat of rams.* (1 Sam 15:22)

Doing what is righteous and just is more acceptable to the Lord than sacrifice. (Prov 21:3)

For I desire loyalty and not sacrifice, the knowledge of God rather than burnt offerings. (Hos 6:6)

Such Love Is Crucial to Salvation (Mark 12:34)

Jesus was pleased with the scribe's answer. He told the man, "You are not far from the kingdom of God." What did Jesus mean by this? It is not, "You are close, so try harder!" Rather, the man has come to see that entering the kingdom of God is a matter of heart devotion not hard duty. Obeying rules and regulations will never get me into the kingdom because I can never measure up to God's perfect standard. No, I need a new me. I need a new heart (Ezek 36:26). I need the grace and mercy of my God who can make me a new creation in Christ (2 Cor 5:17). I need to draw near to Jesus, who has brought the kingdom of God near (Mark 1:15). One draws near and enters the kingdom not by religion but by a relationship with Jesus, a relationship that results in loving God supremely and others genuinely.

Conclusion

The cross tells us that Jesus loves God supremely. It tells us He loves us genuinely. This is why the Holy Spirit moved John to write,

> *Dear friends, let us love one another, because love is from God, and everyone who loves has been born of God and knows God. The one who does not love does not know God, because God is love. God's love was revealed among us in this way: God sent His One and Only Son into the world so that we might live through Him. Love consists in this: not that we loved God, but that He loved us and sent His Son to be the propitiation for our sins. Dear friends, if God loved us in this way, we also must love one another. No one has ever seen God. If we love one another, God remains in us and His love is perfected in us.* (1 John 4:7-12)

To love God is to love others. To love others is to love God. Two great commands. Two great loves.

Reflect and Discuss

1. Why do people like to discuss "greatest" questions? How are such questions valuable? When do such questions become trivial or even harmful?
2. Which of the Ten Commandments do you consider the most important? Why?
3. Books and movies often tell us that love is the supreme virtue. How does their definition of love often fall short of the Bible's emphasis?

4. Why is it important that God is "One"? Why did this cause the Jews to resist Jesus' claims to be divine?
5. In what way is the command to love God completely more difficult than the Ten Commandments?
6. What do "heart, soul, mind, and strength" represent individually and collectively?
7. How would you respond to the person who says, "Jesus is telling us we need to learn how to love ourselves first and then to love others"?
8. How is obedience to these two great commands different from observance of religious ritual? How do you explain that God commanded Israel to observe sacrificial rituals?
9. What is the connection between these two great commands and the concept of a relationship with God through Christ?
10. How was Jesus an example of absolute love for God? How was He an example of perfect love for His neighbor?

Turning Theologians on Their Heads

MARK 12:35-40

Main Idea: Jesus' identity as the true God-Man demands genuine devotion and obedience rather than hypocritical piety.

I. **The Coming of Jesus Reveals a Greater David (12:35-37).**
    A. The Christ is David's Son and therefore human (12:35).
    B. The Christ is David's Lord and therefore divine (12:36-37).
II. **The Coming of Jesus Results in a Greater Accountability (12:38-40).**
    A. Beware of those who put on a show (12:38-39).
    B. Beware of those who take advantage of others (12:40).
    C. Beware of those who make a pretense of their piety (12:40).
    D. Beware of the judgment of God that awaits us all (12:40).

We like to engage in "theological wrestling," seeing who can come out on top. Who can make the sharper and better theological argument? Subjects can include Is Jesus God? What must I do to be saved? How do you explain the problem of evil? Does God exist? How do you know? Within the family of orthodox Christianity we "box" over our view of the end times, divine sovereignty, free will, old earth creation versus young earth creation, and the nature of spiritual gifts. It is one thing for you and me to question one another about theology. It is something altogether different when Jesus is asking the questions!

Jesus has just answered the question on the greatest command (12:28-34). Prior to that He had addressed His authority (11:27–12:12), paying taxes (12:13-17), and the reality of the resurrection (12:18-27). Jesus answered these questions so well that "no one dared to question Him any longer" (12:34).

It is now Jesus' turn to ask a question, and in doing so He turns the theologians upside down. And He did not ask just any question; He asked the most important question. He asked the question concerning the identity of the Messiah, the Christ, the Savior of the world.

The Coming of Jesus Reveals a Greater David
MARK 12:35-37

Jesus is teaching in the temple. The Pharisees were present (Matt 22:41), and "a large crowd was listening to Him" (Mark 12:37). Jesus has been on the receiving end of the questions all day long; now it is His turn.

I don't think it would be a stretch to say it is "the question of the ages." It is the question of the identity of the Messiah. What our Lord had raised privately with the disciples at Caesarea Philippi (8:27) He now takes public. He knows this raises the stakes. He also knows the cross is just three days away. A moment of truth has arrived.

The Christ Is David's Son and Therefore Human (Mark 12:35)

Jesus begins simply enough by establishing that the Christ will be the son of David. No problem here. The Davidic sonship of the Messiah was a common and almost universally accepted belief throughout Israel in Jesus' day. For example, in John 7:42 we read, "Doesn't the Scripture say that the Messiah comes from David's offspring and from the town of Bethlehem, where David once lived?" It is still a popular belief today among orthodox Jews.

Indeed the Davidic sonship of the Messiah is firmly and widely established in Old Testament Scripture.

> *Your house and kingdom will endure before Me forever, and your throne will be established forever.* (2 Sam 7:16)

> *The LORD said, "I have made a covenant with My chosen one; I have sworn an oath to David My servant: 'I will establish your offspring forever and build up your throne for all generations.'"* (Ps 89:3-4)

The people walking in darkness have seen a great light; a light has dawned on those living in the land of darkness. . . . For a child will be born for us, a son will be given to us, and the government will be on His shoulders. He will be named Wonderful Counselor, Mighty God, Eternal Father, Prince of Peace. The dominion will be vast, and its prosperity will never end. He will reign on the throne of David and over his kingdom, to establish and sustain it with justice and righteousness from now on and forever. The zeal of the LORD of Hosts will accomplish this. (Isa 9:2,6-7)

Then a shoot will grow from the stump of Jesse, and a branch from his roots will bear fruit. The Spirit of the LORD will rest on Him—a Spirit of wisdom and understanding, a Spirit of counsel and strength, a Spirit of knowledge and of the fear of the LORD. His delight will be in the fear of the LORD. He will not judge by what He sees with His eyes, He will not execute justice by what He hears with His ears, but He will judge the poor righteously and execute justice for the oppressed of the land. . . . An infant will play beside the cobra's pit, and a toddler will put his hand into a snake's den. None will harm or destroy another on My entire holy mountain, for the land will be as full of the knowledge of the LORD as the sea is filled with water. (Isa 11:1-4,8-9)

"The days are coming"—this is the LORD's declaration—"when I will raise up a Righteous Branch of David. He will reign wisely as king and administer justice and righteousness in the land. In His days Judah will be saved, and Israel will dwell securely. This is what He will be named: Yahweh Our Righteousness." (Jer 23:5-6)

They will serve the LORD their God and I will raise up David their king for them. (Jer 30:9)

In those days and at that time I will cause a Righteous Branch to sprout up for David, and He will administer justice and righteousness in the land. In those days Judah will be saved, and Jerusalem will dwell securely, and this is what she will be named: Yahweh Our Righteousness.

For this is what the LORD says: David will never fail to have a man sitting on the throne of the house of Israel. . . . The hosts of heaven cannot be counted; the sand of the sea cannot be measured. So, too, I will make the descendants of My servant David and the Levites who minister to Me innumerable. (Jer 33:15-17,22)

I will appoint over them a single shepherd, My servant David, and he will shepherd them. He will tend them himself and will be their shepherd. I, Yahweh, will be their God, and My servant David will be a prince among them. I, Yahweh, have spoken. (Ezek 34:23-24)

Afterward, the people of Israel will return and seek the LORD their God and David their king. They will come with awe to the LORD and to His goodness in the last days. (Hos 3:5)

In that day I will restore the fallen booth of David: I will repair its gaps, restore its ruins, and rebuild it as in the days of old. (Amos 9:11)

Bethlehem Ephrathah, you are small among the clans of Judah; One will come from you to be ruler over Israel for Me. His origin is from antiquity, from eternity. Therefore, He will abandon them until the time when she who is in labor has given birth; then the rest of His brothers will return to the people of Israel. He will stand and shepherd them in the strength of Yahweh, in the majestic name of Yahweh His God. They will live securely, for then His greatness will extend to the ends of the earth. He will be their peace. (Mic 5:2-5)

The Messiah, the Christ, the Anointed One of God, will be a human descendent of David. On this they could all agree.

The Christ Is David's Lord and Therefore Divine (Mark 12:36-37)

Jesus now extends the question by taking His audience to Psalm 110. Jesus both ascribes this psalm to David and says that David was inspired by the Holy Spirit. Here is a wonderful description of what the Bible is. It is words written by men who were moved and empowered by the Holy Spirit (2 Pet 1:21). It is uniquely a divine-human book.

Psalm 110 is the most quoted psalm in the New Testament. The first verse reads, "This is the declaration of the LORD to my Lord: 'Sit at My right hand until I make Your enemies Your footstool.'" So Jesus asks, "David himself calls Him 'Lord'; how then can the Messiah be his Son?"

Here is a problem no one had seen until Jesus raised it. The Messiah is both David's Son and David's Lord at the same time. Think about it. What father would ever call his son or great-grandson his Lord? The Messiah is not simply David's Son; He is David's Sovereign. He is God's Son who reigns as King seated at His heavenly Father's right hand. David's words will not work if Messiah is just a human being. He must be more. This is where Jesus is trying to take them. This is what they had failed to see. Tragically, many still don't see it.

Jesus will cite this text again when the high priest asks Him, "Are You the Messiah, the Son of the Blessed One?" (Mark 14:61). "'I am,' said Jesus, 'and all of you will see the Son of Man seated at the right hand of the Power and coming with the clouds of heaven'" (v. 62). Yes, He is the Messiah. He is also the Son of the Blessed. He indeed is the God Man.

The Pharisees no doubt scoffed and fumed at His words. In contrast, "the large crowd was listening to Him with delight." Don Carson says, "The teacher who never attended the right schools (John 7:15-18) confounds the greatest theologians in the land" (Carson, "Matthew," 468).

The Coming of Jesus Results in a Greater Accountability
MARK 12:38-40

"Revelation brings responsibility. The more you know, the greater is your accountability." Where does this come from? It comes from Jesus (12:40; Matt 11:20-24).

One of the most dangerous vocations in life is being a theologian. One of the most dangerous places you can go is to a Bible-believing church that faithfully proclaims the gospel. Each time you hear God's Word taught, your accountability before Him increases. Tragically, those who often receive God's revelation and traffic in His truth become deaf, even hardened. Rather than walk humbly, they become proud. Having drawn so near to Jesus, they think and act nothing like Jesus. God will not overlook such hypocrisy and sin.

Mark warns the "large crowd" of verse 37 to "beware" of the teachers of the law. Why? Seven reasons are given.

Beware of Those Who Put On a Show (Mark 12:38-39)

First, the scribes craved recognition as they walked about in their full-length prayer shawls with showy tassels. They were not interested in seeing the needs and hurts of others. Rather they wanted others to see and admire them! "Bling" is not new! Neither is religion exempt from its lure.

Second, they demanded acknowledgment of status. They expected people to rise and honor them with titles fitting their significance and importance. Such titles included "rabbi," "master," and even "father" (Matt 23:7-10).

Third, they demanded people pay attention to their rank and position of authority. No back rows for these boys. They were to sit up front looking down on the commoners in the congregation.

Fourth, they expected "the places of honor at banquets." They insisted on sitting near the host. Jesus addressed this plainly: "The greatest among you will be your servant. Whoever exalts himself will be humbled, and whoever humbles himself will be exalted" (Matt 23:11-12). These religious elite would have none of this.

Beware of Those Who Take Advantage of Others (Mark 12:40)

Jesus provides a fifth warning to the people concerning their religious leaders. "They devour" and take advantage of the vulnerable, who in this context were the widows. Like some televangelist and religious charlatans in our day, they preyed on the weak. "There is money to be made in ministry" was their philosophy. The prophets condemned in the strongest terms those who took advantage of widows and orphans (Isa 10:2; Amos 2; Mic 3). Had they not read Leviticus 19, especially verse 18?! Did they not hear Jesus when He spoke of the two great commands, the two great loves?

Beware of Those Who Make a Pretense of Their Piety (Mark 12:40)

Sixth, the religious hirelings were experts in pseudo-piety. They could "say long prayers" in public while their private prayer closet fell into disuse. Their public prayers were eloquent, but Jesus judged them empty. Better a few fumbling words from a humble heart than a marvelous oration from a proud heart.

Beware of the Judgment of God That Awaits Us All (Mark 12:40)

The Bible says, "Much will be required of everyone who has been given much" (Luke 12:48). The greater our revelation, the greater our accountability. To know what is right and not do it invites "the harsher punishment" in judgment. No wonder James would write in James 3:1, "Not many should become teachers, my brothers, knowing that we will receive a stricter judgment."

Heaven will not be equally delightful for all, though all will be fully satisfied. And hell will not mete out equal punishment for all, though all will be punished. Indeed God will judge with special severity hypocritical religious leaders who strut like peacocks, abuse the less fortunate, and traffic in false worship that is all show with no substance. Such wickedness in motive and action makes plain they never embraced the greatest servant of all, the greater Son of David, Jesus the Christ.

Conclusion

In his classic *Mere Christianity*, C. S. Lewis takes us to the heart of our faith when he addresses the identity of Jesus Christ and the response we all must give. The "trilemma" of "Liar, Lunatic, or Lord" has become famous and rightfully so. He explains,

I am trying here to prevent anyone saying the really foolish thing
that people often say about Him: "I'm ready to accept Jesus as a great
moral teacher, but I don't accept His claim to be God." That is the
one thing we must not say. A man who was merely a man and said the
sort of things Jesus said would not be a great moral teacher. He would
either be a lunatic—on a level with the man who says he is a poached
egg—or else he would be the Devil of Hell. You must make your
choice. Either this man was, and is, the Son of God: or else a madman
or something worse. You can shut Him up for a fool, you can spit at
Him and kill Him as a demon; or you can fall at His feet and call Him
Lord and God. But let us not come with any patronizing nonsense
about His being a great human teacher. He has not left that open to
us. He did not intend to. (Lewis, *Mere Christianity*, 55–56)

It is so clear, isn't it? Jesus is both David's Son and David's Savior. Jesus is
both David's Son and God's Son. Jesus is both human and divine. Jesus is
both man and God.

So now you know who He is. There is no sitting on the fence. You must
decide for Him or against Him. Your accountability has never been greater.
To say no now is only to invite greater judgment when you stand before God
and explain to Him why you rejected His Son. Please make sure you choose
wisely. Your eternal destiny is at stake!

Reflect and Discuss

1. What is the value of publicly debating theological questions? Is there value
   even if none of the participants change their views?
2. Why is the teaching method Jesus uses here—asking a question—often
   effective?
3. What is the theological significance that Jesus is the Son of Mary? the
   descendant of David?
4. How would you respond to those who argue that none of the Psalms were
   actually written by David but were only written in his honor or in his style?
5. Explain the conundrum in Psalm 110:1 in your own words. What is the
   meaning of the first "LORD" in small capital letters? Of the second "Lord"?
6. What part does the authorship and inspiration of the Psalms play in Jesus'
   argument?
7. Have you heard Christians joke about spiritual matters or treat God lightly?
   How did you feel or respond? Can familiarity with spiritual matters bring
   about disrespect? How can we avoid this?
8. How can a pastor or other leader receive the respect and honor he or she
   deserves without "pulling rank"?
9. Why do spiritual leaders face "stricter judgment" (Jas 3:1)? Is this fair?
10. How would you respond to someone who says, "I believe Jesus was a great
    moral teacher, but that's all"?

The Poor Woman Who Gave All She Had

MARK 12:41-44

Main Idea: Biblical giving is a voluntary act flowing from a thankful heart, which involves giving of one's self and all that one has.

I. **Jesus Sees What We Give (12:41-42).**
   A. Some give a lot because they have a lot (12:41).
   B. Some give their all though they have little (12:42).
II. **Jesus Knows Why We Give (12:43-44).**
   A. Sacrificial giving honors Christ even if the amount is small (12:43-44).
   B. Comfortable giving honors no one even if the amount is large (12:43-44).

A long with her unnamed spiritual sister in Mark 14:3-9, the poor widow of 12:41-44 has been immortalized wherever the gospel of Jesus Christ has been proclaimed. Why? Because in both instances the women gave what they could to honor the Lord. One's gift was actually large and costly. The other's was small and worth almost nothing. Yet the issue in both instances is not *what* they gave but *why* they gave. In both instances the issue is the heart.

On the topic of money, two truths are certain: the Bible has a lot to say about it, and most people don't like to hear what the Bible says about it. Yet we desperately need to hear it because, as Jesus said, "Where your treasure is, there your heart will be also" (Matt 6:21). Clearly the poor widow of this text had her heart in the right place. Unfortunately, many others did not. We will note two overarching truths. Then we will construct a biblical theology of what I love to call "the grace of giving."

Jesus Sees What We Give

MARK 12:41-42

The preceding paragraph mentioned widows as the object of religious exploitation (v. 40). The simple piety of this "poor widow" stands in stark contrast to the self-centered ambition of the scribes. She also must be contrasted with the rich young ruler (10:17-31) who loved his money more than he loved God. In this lady we find a marvelous example of one who "love[s] the Lord [her] God with all [her] heart, with all [her] soul, with all [her] mind, and with all [her] strength" (12:30). Further, "The elevation of the simple woman to such an exemplary place captures the essence of Jesus' words that in God's judgment 'many who are . . . last [will be] first' (10:31)" (Hurtado, *Mark*, 207).

The scene has shifted to the court of the women and the temple treasury where 13 shofar chests were located for the various offerings. Jesus takes a seat and watches.

Some Give a Lot Because They Have a Lot (Mark 12:41)

Jesus "watched how the crowd dropped money into the treasury," into the trumpet-like receptacles. The more you gave, the bigger the noise you would make, and of course the greater the attention you would draw.

Jesus watched as "many rich people were putting in large sums." The rich, the powerful, and the influential gave a lot because they had a lot. No doubt the crowds watching would have been impressed. But what about Jesus?

Some Give Their All Though They Have Little (Mark 12:42)

Our Lord always has an eye for the individual. He hears the cry of the blind beggar Bartimaeus when no one else does (10:46-52). Now He sees the generous and sacrificial gift of a poor widow when no one else sees a thing.

No doubt she came alone, quietly hoping no one would notice her. Being poor and a widow and a woman, she was the least of the least in the cultural context of the day. All she deposited into the treasury were "two tiny coins worth very little." The "coins" (Gk *lepta*) were the smallest bronze coin in circulation in Palestine. Two of them equaled 1/64 of a Roman denarius, a day's wage for a typical laborer. As far as what her gift could purchase, she might as well have given nothing. However, as 1 Samuel 16:7 reminds us, "Man does not see what the Lord sees, for man sees what is visible, but the Lord sees the heart." Jesus knew (supernaturally) that she gave all she had! And even though it was little in man's eyes, it was a lot in God's eyes!

Jesus Knows Why We Give
MARK 12:43-44

With piercing divine insight Jesus saw both the *gift* and the *heart*, both the *act* and the *motive* behind the act. He knew those who gave only because others were watching, and He knew those who would have given if no one was watching. And then He once again turns the value system of the world on its head.

Sacrificial Giving Honors Christ Even If the Amount Is Small (Mark 12:43-44)

Jesus calls the disciples; it is teaching time again! Our Lord prefaces His remarks with *amen*, "I assure you," a word appearing 13 times in Mark. It adds weight and importance to what Jesus is about to say. It has the ring of divine authority!

He begins and ends by commending not the rich but the poor. Why? Because "she out of her poverty has put in everything she possessed—all she had to live on." She had two coins, so she could have kept one, but she didn't. She gave her all. The amount was not large, but the sacrifice was great.

Comfortable Giving Honors No One Even If the Amount Is Large (Mark 12:43-44)

Jesus had not failed to see the others. It was simply that the others "gave out of their surplus" (v. 44). Their giving was not sacrificial, it was comfortable. Did they truly give God their best? No, they gave to an institution (and a corrupt one at that) what was easy and convenient. Jesus was not impressed. Warren Wiersbe captures it well: "The rich made a big production out of their giving (see Matt 6:1-4), but Jesus rejected them and their gifts. It is not the portion but the proportion that is important: the rich gave out of their abundance, but the poor widow gave all she had. For the rich, their gifts were a small contribution, but for the widow, her gift was a true consecration of her whole life" (Wiersbe, *Be Diligent*, 120).

William Kelly said, "The test of liberality is not what is given, but what is left" (Hiebert, *Mark*, 363). The poor widow's sacrificial giving was a foreshadowing of Jesus' own: she gave all she had, and so would He!

Now, I want to be practical and helpful as we consider what the Bible has to say about money. I hope this overview will inspire both faith and generosity! I am especially indebted to pastors John MacArthur and John Morgan for much of what I have learned in this area.

First, what is God's purpose for money? All of our needs are purposed by God to help us experience spiritual growth in Christlikeness. Money is used by God in supplying our needs. Therefore, God's ultimate purpose for money is spiritual growth. Note the following six purposes God has for money.

1. God wants to grow us spiritually by growing our faith (Luke 6:38; Phil 4:19).
2. God wants to finance His earthly ministry through us for His glory and our good (Mal 3:10).
3. God wants to unite Christians who have needs with those who have surplus (2 Cor 8:14-15).
4. God wants to reveal clearly His infinite power (Deut 8:18).
5. God wants to help give direction in our lives (Prov 3:5-6).
6. God wants to fulfill His promise to supply our needs (Matt 6:31-33; Phil 4:19).

Christian financial advisor Ron Blue helps us see the impact of embracing God's purposes for money:

> Very few Christians would argue with the principle that God owns it all, and yet if we follow that principle to its natural conclusion, there are three revolutionary implications. First of all, God has the right to whatever He wants whenever He wants it. . . .
>
> If I really believe that God owns it all then when I lose any possessions, for whatever reason, my emotions may cry out, but my mind and spirit have not the slightest question as to the right of God to take whatever He wants whenever He wants it. Really believing this also frees me to give generously of God's resources to God's purposes and His people. All that I have belongs to Him.
>
> The second implication of God's owning it all is that not only is my giving decision a spiritual decision, but *every spending decision is a spiritual decision*. . . . As a steward, I have a great deal of latitude, but I am still responsible to the Owner. Someday I will give an accounting of how I used His property.
>
> The third implication of the truth that God owns it all is that *you can't fake stewardship*. . . . A person who has been a Christian for even a short while can fake prayer, Bible study, evangelism, going to church, and so on, but he can't fake what his checkbook reveals. (Blue, *Master*, 22–23; emphasis in original)

Second, what is financial bondage? When even the smallest area of our financial life obstructs God's will in our life, we enter into financial bondage and the sin of idolatry. You are in financial bondage when

1. you have more faith in your material goods than in your eternal God (Job 31:24-28; Matt 6:19-20);
2. you place any desire or motive above those of God (1 Tim 6:8-9);
3. you have a burning desire to get rich quick (Prov 28:20,22);

4. you have to delay paying due bills (Prov 22:7);
5. you compromise your Christian ethic and fail to honor a moral obligation (Jas 5:4);
6. you fail to make investments for future needs (Matt 25:14-30);
7. you force your wife to work in order to provide basic needs (1 Tim 5:8);
8. you do not give from a willing and cheerful heart (2 Cor 9:7).

Third, exactly what is "The Grace of Giving"? Giving of our resources to the work of the Lord, in gratitude for all God has given us in Christ, is a wonderful privilege. It is simply giving in response to God's grace. Grace giving allows us to

1. demonstrate our *love* and *devotion* to the Lord Jesus and His church;
2. acknowledge that all we are and have is the result of His gracious activity in our lives;
3. testify to our faith in God that as we give out of our God-given resources, He will bless us and meet every need that we may perform His perfect will.

Grace Giving

Giving is an act of worship. In the Word of God, numerous truths are set forth to help us in our understanding of grace giving (what also can be called Christian stewardship):

I. Grace Giving Is Guided by a Proper Perspective.

A. *All that I am belongs to God (1 Cor 6:19-20).* We are not only dependent on God but also owned by Him. The price He paid to purchase us was the precious blood of His Son, the Lord Jesus.

B. *All that is belongs to God (Pss 24:1; 50:10-12; Hag 2:8).* We are accustomed to thinking and speaking of "our" possessions. The things we possess are not really ours; they are God's.

C. *God has entrusted His possessions to me (1 Cor 3:21-23; 4:1-2; 9:17).* The custodial nature of our stewardship of God's possessions suggests that they should ultimately be transferred to another trustworthy steward (either an individual or an institution) so that they can continue to be used for God's purposes.

D. *God's possessions entrusted to me have a purpose.* (1) God's assets meet personal needs (Phil 4:13,19). They are intended for our support, as well as for those dependent on us. Paul warned, "But if any one does not provide for his own, that is his household, he has denied the faith and is worse than an unbeliever" (1 Tim 5:8).

(2) God's assets build and glorify God's kingdom through me (Col 3:23-24). How we apply them is a matter of individual judgment and prayer since we alone are accountable to the Lord. Our accountability also extends into eternity.

As stewards, we have been given the privilege of arranging for God's assets to flourish well beyond our years. We can stand with Abel, who "offered to God a better sacrifice than Cain did. By faith he was approved as a righteous man, because God approved his gifts, and even though he is dead, he still speaks through faith" (Heb 11:4).

II. Grace Giving Is to Be Guided by Proper Principles.

A. *Giving is to be viewed as investing with God (Matt 6:19-21; Luke 6:38).* We get a return that will last eternally. When we invest money in what is perishable, we are consumed with maintaining what we have. But when we invest with God, it unburdens us and deepens our relationship with Him.

B. *If you cannot handle money, you will not be able to handle spiritual riches either (Luke 16:11).* How we manage money is usually a reflection of our spiritual maturity and faith in God. God has said He will meet our needs when we give (Phil 4:14-20). If we don't give, then we in essence call God a liar, which is a much more serious spiritual problem.

C. *Giving is to be sacrificial (Mark 12:42-44; 2 Cor 8:1-3).* Jesus noticed the woman who truly gave sacrificially, for she gave all she had. The essence of giving is sacrifice (cf. Gen 22). What does this teach us? Should we give one-tenth? No, we are to give sacrificially. True sacrificial giving is when we do without something we would otherwise have so that God's work will be advanced.

D. *Giving is not just a matter of what we have (Luke 16:10).* Faithfulness is what pleases God. You do not have to possess a large amount to be sacrificial.

E. *Each individual determines the amount to give (Luke 19:8).* Giving is to be a worshipful and happy action of love and gratitude to a wonderful God. It is not the keeping of some law or tradition. Some people rigidly and mechanically give 10 percent. Others give only in a token fashion with no real thought. This is not God's way. Your giving should be done in an attitude of prayer and spiritual contemplation, asking the Father what He would have you to do each and every time.

F. *Giving can be in response to a need (spontaneous and special; Acts 2:42-47; 11:27-30; 1 Cor 16:1-2; Phil 4:14-20).* If a man comes to you with a need and you can help meet it, it is your Christian responsibility to do so. Give to the

Lord regularly out of gratitude and joy, but also give in response to specific needs.

G. *Giving should demonstrate love, not law (2 Cor 8:8).* Love and gratitude to God for *who* He is and *what* He has done is the fountain out of which grace giving is to flow.

H. *Giving should be planned (1 Cor 16:1-2; 2 Cor 8:6-7).* Giving should not be haphazard but planned in an orderly fashion. We are to give regularly so that churches can meet needs as they arise, rather than always pleading for additional money through special offerings. Giving is to be done *systematically, proportionately, faithfully,* as you have determined in your heart. You are to *plan, pray,* and *prepare.*

Some people say they give their time and talent to the church rather than their money. It is a fine and right thing to give those, but it does not replace giving money. It is God's way of teaching you stewardship each week of your entire life.

I. *Giving is to be generous (2 Cor 8:2-3; Phil 4:14-20).* As Christ has given to us, so should we give. Bow your knee, look to the cross, and then give.

J. *Giving is to be joyful (2 Cor 9:7).* Our *attitude* in giving is as important to our Lord as the *act* of giving itself. The absence of joy in giving is evidence of a deeper spiritual problem, which invalidates our offering.

K. *Giving is to be complete (2 Cor 8:5).* Total discipleship extends far beyond our financial giving to God. The New Testament clearly teaches total commitment in all areas of our lives. Overemphasizing the tithe has caused us to miss this important truth.

L. *Giving biblically always results in God's blessings (Acts 20:35; 2 Cor 9:6-11; Phil 4:19).* Being obedient to the Word of God will always open the way for His blessings to be experienced.

III. Grace Giving Is to Be Guided by Proper Practice.

Faith must have feet! We must act in obedience to see God work in our lives. If you have been delinquent in the past, remember: it is never too late to begin doing the right thing!

Conclusion

Biblical and spiritual giving is the act of giving one's self and all that one has completely to God by a voluntary act that flows out of a thankful and grateful heart. It is motivated by a sincere understanding that everything belongs to God and that He is the source of every blessing (1 Chr 29:14; Ps 50:9-12). It is also motivated by gratitude for what God has done for us in Christ (2 Cor 8:8-9; 9:15). By returning a portion of that blessing to God, the believer acknowledges that he has received God's blessing and that he is truly grateful.

The times of Israel's greatest spiritual fervor and the church's greatest impact on society are the times of their greatest sacrificial giving. This indicates that there is a correlation between the spiritual state of true believers and their willingness to be involved in sacrificial giving. In practice, the tithe (10 percent) is a good place to begin one's financial service and worship unto God. It is, however, a bad place to stop. God wants us to grow in all areas of our Christian life, including giving. As we look to Him in faith, as we look to the cross and give, He will, in this area, do through us and for us far beyond that which we could ever hope or imagine. In light of God's indescribable gift of His Son Jesus (2 Cor 9:15), it is hard to imagine doing anything less. God gave His all. He gave His best. So should we.

Reflect and Discuss

1. Why does the Bible have a lot to say about money and our attitude toward it?
2. What is the significance that the focus of Jesus' attention was a poor widow?
3. What is the purpose of giving an offering? Who are the various parties that benefit? Does your pastor's salary each week have any connection to the amount of the offering?
4. What is the danger in focusing on what benefit you can receive by giving an offering? What is the counterfeit benefit, and what is the true benefit?
5. How would you respond to a preacher or teacher who told you there was a certain percentage that you should give in order to receive a blessing?
6. How can knowing God's purposes for money help us to avoid loving money?
7. Does sacrificial giving obligate God to bless us? Does faithfulness?
8. Which is the first priority: providing for oneself and one's family, or supporting God's work? In what scenario might these things come into conflict?
9. How might a person who gives 10 percent every week fail to please God?
10. What part does faith play in giving and in the blessing received? What part does gratitude play?

What Did Jesus Say About the End Times? Part 1

MARK 13:1-23

Main Idea: We should be on guard so that we are not deceived or anxious about the end times.

I. Deception Is Coming, so Do Not Be Led Astray (13:1-8).
II. Persecution Can Be Expected, but Do Not Be Anxious (13:9-13).
III. Tribulation Will Be Intense, so Be on Guard (13:14-23).

Few subjects spark greater interest than the study of eschatology, the "end times." Christians and non-Christians alike are fascinated by the issue, even if they are skeptical about much of what they see. Unfortunately, much of this skepticism is warranted when you consider the spectacularly erroneous predictions of so many pseudo-prophets and prognosticators.

No one has swung and missed more than the Jehovah's Witnesses, whose false predictions currently stand at nine (1874, 1878, 1881, 1910, 1914, 1918, 1925, 1975, and 1984). In 1988, many evangelical Christians looked rather foolish when they were seduced by Edgar Whisenant's *88 Reasons Why the Rapture Is in 1988*. Not to be outdone, New Age advocates cited Mayan calendars and predicted the end would come on December 21, 2012. They of course were wrong too. I could continue down this tragic trail for quite some time.

Jesus addressed issues related to the end times in what is often called "the Olivet Discourse," delivered on the Mount of Olives overlooking Jerusalem (Matt 24:1-25,46; Mark 13:1-37; Luke 21:5-36). We do not find Jesus encouraging us to set dates or identify the Antichrist, the False Prophet, or the Four Horsemen of the Apocalypse. Rather, He admonishes us to be on guard (Mark 13:9,23,33) and stay awake (vv. 33,35,37). No one but God knows when the end will come (vv. 32-37). However, since the end will come—and suddenly (v. 36)—we must remain constantly faithful in our service to our Master (v. 35). It will not be easy, but "it will be worth it all when we see Jesus."

Now, Mark 13 is a difficult text to interpret, with faithful, Bible-believing teachers differing on the details. Some are convinced Jesus is only addressing the destruction of Jerusalem, which took place in AD 70. Others are equally certain He only has in view the end of the age. I, personally, think there is a third and better understanding. Jesus does indeed address the *imminent* destruction of the temple and Jerusalem. And in doing so, He provides a preview of *distant* attractions: His Second Coming and the end of the age. John Grassmick says,

> Jesus predicted the destruction of the temple in Jerusalem (13:2) which prompted the disciples to inquire about the timing of "these things" (v. 4). Apparently they associated the destruction of the temple with the end of the Age (cf. Matt 24:3). In reply Jesus skillfully wove together into a unified discourse a prophetic scene involving two perspectives: (a) the near event, the destruction of Jerusalem (AD 70); and (b) the far event, the coming of the Son of Man in clouds with power and glory. The former local event was a forerunner of the latter universal event. In this way Jesus followed the precedent of Old Testament prophets by predicting a far future event in terms of a near future event whose fulfillment at least some of His hearers would see (cf. Mark 9:1,12-13). (Grassmick, "Mark," 168)

Jesus will employ no less than 19 imperatives in verses 5-37 as He instructs us on how to be prepared for the end times. Many will be surprised both by what He says and by what He does not say.

Deception Is Coming, so Do Not Be Led Astray
MARK 13:1-8

Jesus leaves the temple for the last time. The glory of the Lord has departed (cf. Ezek 11:23). One of the disciples draws attention to the magnificent splendor of the temple, one of the great architectural wonders of the world. Built with large white stones and lavishly decorated with gold, it was blinding when struck by the sunlight. The Jewish people believed it to be the very sanctuary of God and therefore virtually indestructible until the end of time. Thus, Jesus' response could not have been more shocking: "Do you see these great buildings? Not one stone will be left here on another that will not be thrown down!"

Verse 3 now locates them on the Mount of Olives "opposite the temple." It is 2,700 feet above sea level and two hundred feet above the temple complex. The inner circle of Peter and James and John and Andrew approach Him privately. They want to know, "When will these things happen? And what will be the sign when all these things are about to take place?" The disciples are thinking about the final consummation of history. They did not expect a long interval between the destruction of the temple and the end of the age. But Jesus does not address the issue of *timing*, though He does use the soon coming destruction of the temple and Jerusalem as a *type* or foreshadowing of end-time events. The imminent destruction of the temple is the lens through which we should view the distant destruction of this present evil age and the return of the Son of Man, the Lord Jesus (13:24-27).

Jesus begins with a warning that is applicable to any believer at any time: "Watch out that no one deceives you." Why?

1. "Many will come in My name, saying, 'I am He,' . . ." This is literally "*ego eimi*" (I AM), and a claim to deity. They will say, "I am from God, and I am God."
2. "They will deceive many." Simon the magician typifies what Jesus is talking about (Acts 8:9-11). First John 2:18 describes the parade of false christs who will come prior to the climactic false Christ: "Children, it is the last hour. And as you have heard, 'Antichrist is coming,' even now many antichrists have come."
3. You will hear of "wars and rumors of wars," but "do not be alarmed." Why? The evidences that we live in a broken world will continue until the end.
4. Nations and kingdoms will fight one another, and earthquakes and famines will take place. These types of events set the stage for the finale. What we experience now, almost daily, will intensify as history draws to a close (Rev 6–18).

Human history is headed toward the birth of a new Messianic Age and kingdom, of that we can be sure. But before it comes, we can expect times of worldwide trouble and tribulation. Like the labor pains of a woman that grow in intensity before the blessed birth of the baby, distress will increase before the glorious end. This was true leading up to the destruction of the Jewish temple in AD 70. It especially will be true as the curtain on world history comes down.

Persecution Can Be Expected, but Do Not Be Anxious
MARK 13:9-13

Not only will there be trouble on a *global* level; there will also be trials and persecutions on a *personal* level. Jesus again challenges His disciples to "be on your guard" (the same word as in verse 5). This is also a present imperative, a word of command. Why does He issue a second challenge to watchfulness? Difficult times are to be expected for faithful followers of King Jesus.

You can expect that "they will hand you over to Sanhedrins" just like your Lord. You also will be publicly flogged in the synagogues and viewed as false teachers and traitors to the nation of Israel. This is all part of God's plan for gospel proclamation! "You will stand before governors and kings because of Me, as a witness to them." We see this unfold in the book of Acts (4:1-22; 5:17-42; 12:1-19; 21:27–28:31). Further, "the good news must first be proclaimed to all nations." All the *ethne*, all the people groups of the world, must hear this gospel before the end comes. So do not get discouraged. This is God's plan. Just be faithful to speak of Jesus and His gospel "in that hour. . . . For it isn't you speaking, but the Holy Spirit." Wow! Praise the Lord! He will empower you and enable you to say the right thing in the right way at just the right time.

Opposition from governmental and legal authorities will be harsh. Rejection by family and friends will be heartbreaking, but it will happen, so get ready. "Then brother will betray brother to death, and a father his child. Children will rise up against parents and put them to death." The word "death" occurs twice, emphasizing the extent of the betrayal and persecution some will face. We will be arrested, beaten, betrayed, put to death, and even "hated," all for the sake of King Jesus. While this may sound surreal and unfathomable in America, it is the experience of millions of brothers and sisters around the world today and throughout church history. One can consult the famous *Fox's Book of Martyrs* to read the stories of faithful believers who sealed their witness with their blood. Church tradition informs us that all the apostles, with the possible exception of John, died as martyrs. Some have estimated that more than 70 million Christians have given their lives for their witness to Jesus, 45 million in the twentieth century alone (ZENIT.org, "20th Century"). In the last decade "there were on average, 270 new Christian martyrs every 24 hours," or approximately one million in the last 10 years (Weigel, "Christian Number").

Yes, we will be hated for our faithful witness to our Master, but Jesus tells us to be encouraged: "The one who endures to the end will be delivered." Perseverance is the proof that our profession is real. It may be tough, but our Lord will be faithful to keep us by His power.

Vance Havner used to say, "Faith that fizzles before the finish was faulty from the first." This is especially true when we experience severe persecution. It was certainly true in the first century, it is true in the twenty-first century, and it will be true in the future as history moves toward its climactic end with the return of King Jesus.

Tribulation Will Be Intense, so Be on Guard
MARK 13:14-23

Verse 14 introduces us to one of the most cryptic and difficult phrases in the Bible: "the abomination that causes desolation." The phrase occurs three times in the book of Daniel:

> *He will make a firm covenant with many for one week, but in the middle of the week he will put a stop to sacrifice and offering. And the abomination of desolation will be on a wing of the temple until the decreed destruction is poured out on the desolator.* (Dan 9:27)

> *His forces will rise up and desecrate the temple fortress. They will abolish the daily sacrifice and set up the abomination of desolation.* (Dan 11:31)

> *From the time the daily sacrifice is abolished and the abomination of desolation is set up, there will be 1,290 days.* (Dan 12:11)

Jesus connects the phrase with meaning of indescribable suffering and tribulation, "the kind that hasn't been from the beginning of the world" (v. 19). Let me do my best to simplify the complex.

First, the initial fulfillment of Daniel's prophecy (particularly 11:31-32) was the desecration of the temple in 167 BC by the Syrian Antiochus Epiphanes when he sacrificed a pig on the altar of burnt offerings and set up an altar to Zeus. This act of idolatry and insult so incensed the Jewish people they would soon rise up in what history calls the Maccabean Revolt.

Second, given the context of the passage and Jesus' instructions, it appears He has in mind another fulfillment in the destruction of Jerusalem in AD 70. When the abomination of desolation is "standing where it should not"—perhaps a reference to the Roman General Titus entering the temple in September AD 70—then "those in Judea must flee to the mountains" (v. 14). Further, everyone was to act with a sense of urgency. James Edwards said, "People on their flat-roofed Palestinian house must flee by the outside staircase without going inside (v. 15) . . . and the field worker will have no time to fetch his outer cloak (v. 16). Worst of all will be the fate of pregnant women and nursing mothers (v. 17; see Luke 23:29-31), and anyone fleeing in winter when the wadis—the ravines and gorges—are swollen and impossible to cross (v. 18)" (Edwards, *Mark*, 397). All of this took place in Judea in AD 70.

Third, the tragic events of 167 BC and AD 70 anticipate a climactic event of horrible destruction and desecration just prior to our Lord's second coming. Jesus is speaking of the eschatological end through the eyes of the imminent destruction of the temple. Again, the precise explanation of

James Edwards is excellent, especially as he makes a connection with other crucial New Testament texts:

> "The abomination that causes desolation" refers to "the man of lawlessness" as conceived in 2 Thess 2:3-4, who will exalt himself in the temple as God. . . . The agreements of 2 Thessalonians 2 with v. 14 are [close]. The "man of lawlessness" corresponds to the man *standing* (masculine participle) in v. 14; and the description of him parodying God in the temple correlates with "'the abomination that causes desolation standing where he *does not belong*.'" Both texts depict a blasphemous Antichrist who will do a scandalous deed that will trigger the return of the Lord. Both texts also warn disciples against mistaken eschatological assumptions, especially against being deceived by signs and wonders. . . .
>
> [Verse] 14, like 2 Thessalonians 2, indicates that Jesus foresaw the rise of a terrible antagonist, an Antichrist, who at some future time will unleash a severe tribulation on the people of God, which in turn will usher in the return of the Lord. Mark relates this abominable event only cryptically and suggestively to the destruction of the temple. In so doing he imputes both historical and eschatological value to the same event. V. 14 is thus the hinge of Mark 13 that links "these things," relating to the destruction of Jerusalem in A.D. 70, with "those days" of the End. "The abomination that causes desolation" alludes to the destruction of the temple in A.D. 70, but it is not exhausted by it. The "abomination" is a mysterious (2 Thess 2:7!) double referent, a historical medium that anticipates an ultimate fulfillment in the advent of the Antichrist and the final tribulation before the return of the Son of Man. Titus's destruction of Jerusalem is like a scouting film: it gives an authentic picture of one's future opponent; but there is, of course, a great deal of difference between clashing with players in the stadium as opposed to simply watching them on film. (Edwards, *Mark*, 388–89)

John Grassmick adds of the man "standing where he should not" of verse 14, "This person is the end-time Antichrist (Dan 7:23-26; 9:25-27; 2 Thes. 2:3-4,8-9; Rev 13:1-10,14-15)" ("Mark," 170).

Verse 19 informs us "those days" (cf. v. 24) will be unequalled in all of human history. As horrible as AD 70 was, that event will pale in comparison to the end-time "tribulation." Indeed, no one would be delivered from death if those days were allowed to continue. However, in grace, God places a divine limitation on the time of tribulation. Even in His wrath, God remembers mercy (Hab 3:2).

Jesus concludes this section with a warning about "false messiahs and false prophets" (v. 22). Count on it that they will come on the scene and "perform signs and wonders" (cf. Rev 19:20). If possible—but praise God they can't—they would "lead astray the elect." Since we are safe, do we grow complacent? No! "Watch!" This is the third time Jesus has warned them. In fact He concludes, "I have told you everything in advance."

Conclusion

Teaching on the end times can be both comforting and troubling. In our broken and fallen world we can expect trials, tribulations, and troubles until Jesus returns. While we wait, should we be working out a prophetic schedule of events? Not at all. Instead, listen to what Jesus says and not to others who wish to lead you astray. Instead, do not be surprised by the catastrophes of nature, the wars throughout history, or the sufferings of God's people. Instead, realize that when Jesus talks about the future, "his words are meant to change the way we live in the present" (Ferguson, *Mark*, 218). Instead, do as Paul encouraged in Titus 2:13 and look for "the blessed hope and appearing of the glory of our great God and Savior Jesus Christ." Instead, do as John urged in Revelation 22:20 and pray, "Come Lord Jesus." And as you watch and pray, be on your guard and don't worry. Jesus already told you all about what to expect!

Reflect and Discuss

1. Do you remember hearing any predictions of the end of the world? What did you think at the time?
2. How was Jesus' prophecy a prediction of both imminent events and distant events? What Old Testament prophecies also had near and far fulfillments?
3. Why did the Jews think the temple could not possibly be destroyed? Do we feel the same way about certain buildings, institutions, or denominations?
4. What is discouraging about Jesus' predictions of end times? What is encouraging about having the predictions before the events happen?
5. What recent and current events appear to be fulfilling this prophecy? What should we do in light of these events?
6. How can persecution of Christians result in the spread of Christianity? What are some recent examples? How is this encouraging?
7. In what context should you not "worry beforehand what you will say"? Does this mean we should not practice our testimony, study apologetics, or prepare for hypothetical theological debates?
8. When we see that "death" is a possible result of persecution, what should be our Christian attitude toward death? Why is this sometimes difficult to take to heart?

9. What are the indications in this text that God is completely in control of events all the way to the end of time? How is this encouraging?
10. What value is there in studying current events and analyzing whether they are fulfilling the prophecies of the end of time? What should we be doing with our time and talents while we wait?

What Did Jesus Say About the End Times? Part 2

MARK 13:24-37

Main Idea: Although we don't know the exact moment, we do know with certainty that Jesus will come again, and therefore we must be alert.

I. Jesus Will Come Again to Gather His People (13:24-27).
II. Jesus Will Come Again, and the Time Is Near (13:28-31).
III. Jesus Will Come Again, but Only God Knows When (13:32-37).

I have been asked my opinion of a man named Harold Camping, who had predicted that Christ would come again and the world would end on May 21, 2011. When the end did not come, Camping revised his prediction to October 21, 2011. That day also came and went without our Lord's return. Fortunately, Mr. Camping has acknowledged his error and says he is retiring from date setting. While some would say these are the musings of an old man out of touch with reality, others recognize that real damage can be done by these false predictions. When interviewed, I was able to say, "When we engage in this kind of wild speculation, it's irresponsible. It can do damage to naïve believers who can be easily caught up, and it runs the risk of causing the church to receive sort of a black eye" (Associated Press, "End of the World").

Many have predicted that our Lord's literal second coming will occur on a specific date, only to be disappointed. Others, however, go in a completely different direction by redefining the event and explaining it away in order to satisfy a modernist mind-set. The liberal pastor and theologian Harry Emerson Fosdick (1878–1969), who for many years pastored the influential Riverside Church in New York, said,

> Christ is coming! They say it with all their hearts; but they are not
> thinking of an external arrival on the clouds. They have assimilated
> as part of the divine revelation the exhilarating insight which these

recent generations have given to us, that development is God's way of working out his will. . . .

And these Christians, when they say Christ is coming, mean that, slowly it may be, but surely, His will and principles will be worked out by God's grace in human life and institutions. (Fosdick, "Fundamentalists")

These perspectives do not find one ounce of support in the teachings of Jesus. If they are right, then He was wrong. However, our Lord clearly, confidently, and boldly declares He is coming again to "gather His elect from the four winds, from the end of the earth to the end of the sky" (v. 27). So, "Watch! Be alert! For you don't know when the time is coming" (v. 33).

Jesus Will Come Again to Gather His People
MARK 13:24-27

Jesus employs end-times, or eschatological, vocabulary and imagery in these verses. That Jerusalem is not mentioned is a death knell for those who would apply these verses to its destruction in AD 70. Jesus says, "In those days." What days? The days "after that tribulation" (v. 24). After those days cosmic, apocalyptic signs will occur: (1) the sun will be darkened (see Rev 6:12), (2) the moon will not give its light (see Rev 6:12), and (3) the stars (perhaps meteorites) will be falling from heaven, and the powers in the heavens will be shaken (see Rev 6:13-14). Ultimate cosmic upheaval and universal cataclysmic judgment will signal that the end has come. In heaven and on earth, the cosmos will be rocked and shaken as God prepares to come in judgment in the person of the Son (cf. Isa 13:9-10; 34:4-5; Ezek 32:7-9,15).

"Then . . ." (v. 26)—what a wonderful word of anticipation. "They will see the Son of Man," the great eschatological figure described in Daniel 7:13-14, "coming in clouds with great power and glory." Edward Adams well says, "It is highly likely that Mark would want his readers to understand this reference to the coming of the Son of Man in the light of the previous mention at 8:38. The Old Testament allusions and associations in 13:24-27 fit a picture of the advent of God, with Jesus as the Son of Man in the main role" (Adams, "Coming," 57).

"He will send out the angels" (v. 27) who will harvest the work done by suffering saints who have "proclaimed [the good news] to all nations" (v. 10). These will be gathered from every corner of the globe as well as heaven. Revelation 7:9-10 tells us,

After this I looked, and there was a vast multitude from every nation, tribe, people, and language, which no one could number, standing before the throne

and before the Lamb. They were robed in white with palm branches in their hands. And they cried out in a loud voice: "Salvation belongs to our God, who is seated on the throne, and to the Lamb!"

Our labor of love for our Lord is not in vain.

Jesus will come again to gather His people. What a day of celebration that will be. Our Lord, the Son of Man, will bring to the earth the kingdom He has received from the Father, the Ancient of Days.

Jesus Will Come Again, and the Time Is Near
MARK 13:28-31

Jesus moves to amplify what He has just taught with an illustration from a fig tree. There is nothing complicated until He gets to the end, then a theological Pandora's box is opened! Branches with developing leaves tell us summer is on the way. From this Jesus makes a theological affirmation, "In the same way, when you see these things happening, know that He is near—at the door!" The events of chapter 13, especially verses 14-25, tip us off that affairs in world history are moving toward a climactic end. These signs warn us "He," that is Jesus, the Son of Man, "is near," ready to storm the citadels of sin, Satan, death, hell, and the grave. Antichrist (v. 14) and his false prophets (v. 22) are about to meet their doom (cf. Rev 19:19-21). Imminence is clearly an essential component of biblical eschatology.

Jesus drops an interpretive bomb in verse 30: "I assure you: This generation will certainly not pass away until all these things take place." The question is, Who is "this generation"? The answer is not a simple one, and how you understand and interpret other parts of Mark 13 will influence how you answer the question. What are the major options?

1. The contemporary generation of Jesus' day who would see the destruction of Jerusalem in AD 70
2. The eschatological generation that will be alive at the end of history who will see all these things because they occur in close proximity to one another
3. The Jewish people, with the word "generation" being understood to mean "race"—a particular race of people
4. The generation of Jesus' day who would see the coming of the kingdom

If Jesus intended number 4, unfortunately He was in error and was killed in the process of trying to bring in the kingdom. Of course, that scenario is unacceptable. Though dogmatism is unwarranted, I believe the best understanding is number 2. "This generation" refers to those who will see all these things occur in rapid-fire succession just before Jesus comes again. I believe the future tribulation (v. 24) will be a period of seven years. There is support for this in Daniel 9:27; Revelation 7:14; 11:3; 12:4,6; 13:5. If this is true, then the eschatological generation will witness these events in less than a decade.

The phrase "pass away" is repeated in v. 31. The temple will fall to ruin. History will come to an end. This present heaven and earth will give way to "a new heaven and a new earth" (see Rev 21:1). But God's words will never pass away. Nothing is so true, stable, permanent, and abiding as the word of our Lord. Here is a firm foundation on which we can stand forever. No wonder the prophet Isaiah was inspired to write, "The grass withers, the flowers fade, but the word of our God remains forever" (40:8; cf. 51:6).

Jesus Will Come Again, but Only God Knows When
MARK 13:32-37

Jesus is clearly speaking of His coming again (vv. 26-27). He plainly states that "no one knows" when it will happen, "neither the angels in heaven nor the Son—except the Father." It is that phrase "nor the Son" that gives us pause. As orthodox, Bible-believing Christians, we affirm the full and undiminished deity of God the Son. As God, He possesses all the attributes of deity, including omniscience. Yet here He clearly states there is a body of knowledge of which He is, dare I say, ignorant: the day and hour of His own second coming. This statement makes no sense apart from the incarnation. In taking on a human nature and entering into the time-space reality, the Son of God did not surrender His deity, but He did lay aside His glory (John 17:5; see also Phil 2:6-11). In doing so, our Lord for a time relinquished the free exercise of His divine attributes such as omniscience. In the mystery and beauty of the incarnation, the all-knowing sovereign Son could temporarily lay aside or suspend the free exercise of His "God attributes" so that He might live an authentic human life in submission to His Father and in dependence on the Holy Spirit. This also explains why our Lord could be hungry, experience thirst, grow tired, and be killed. And here lies another indictment for those caught up in prophetic speculation and date setting. *NO ONE KNOWS BUT GOD!*

We may not know *when* Jesus will return. However, we do know *what* we should be doing until He does. "Watch! Be alert!" Why? "For you don't know when the time will come." Three times our Lord affirms what I like to call "human eschatological agnosticism" (vv. 32,33,35). Like a man on a journey, our Lord has left the house, but only for a while. We, His servants, have been put in charge with a task: proclaim the gospel "to all nations" (v. 10). We each have our work (v. 34). So be faithful, be ready, and "be alert."

> Stay awake! Stay awake! It could be in the evening.
> Stay awake! Stay awake! It could be at midnight.
> Stay awake! Stay awake! It could be when the rooster crows.
> Stay awake! Stay awake! It could be in the morning.

Bottom line, "He might come suddenly." His coming is imminent. It could happen at any time, including today. You don't want Him to find you asleep, unprepared. Not doing the work He has given you. Oh, how tragic it would be for our Lord to return and find His church asleep at the wheel, neglecting her assignment, squandering her resources, deceiving herself into thinking He won't come today. How tragic to say, "Tomorrow, I will get busy serving Him," only to discover tomorrow is never coming. So again Jesus sounds the warning "to everyone: Be alert!" If He said it once, that should be sufficient. That He says it four times should really get our attention. "Be alert" and serve Him today. Tomorrow may never arrive!

Conclusion

Leila Naylor Morris (1862–1929) wrote more than a thousand gospel songs. I cannot help wondering if our text was a source of inspiration for Leila Morris when she penned the words to the song, "What If It Were Today?" (1912).

> Jesus is coming to earth again, what if it were today?
> Coming in power and love to reign, what if it were today?
> Coming to claim His chosen Bride, all the redeemed and purified,
> Over this whole earth scattered wide; what if it were today?
>
> Satan's dominion will then be o'er, O that it were today!
> Sorrow and sighing shall be no more, O that it were today!
> Then shall the dead in Christ arise, caught up to meet Him in the skies,
> When shall these glories meet our eyes? What if it were today?
>
> Faithful and true would He find us here, if He should come today?
> Watching in gladness and not in fear, if He should come today?
> Signs of His coming multiply; morning light breaks in eastern sky.
> Watch, for the time is drawing high; what if it were today?
>
> > Glory, glory! Joy to my heart 'twill bring.
> > Glory, glory! When we shall crown Him King.

Glory, Glory! Haste to prepare the way.
Glory, Glory! Jesus will come someday.

Jesus is coming again! So "be alert, since you don't know when the master of the house is coming."

Reflect and Discuss

1. How does a failed prediction of the rapture harm the church? How does the false doctrine that Jesus will never physically return harm the church?
2. What is the significance of the upheaval in the heavens before the second coming?
3. What is the work we Christians are assigned to do between now and the second coming? What is the attitude we should be in while we wait?
4. How would you respond to those who say that Jesus hasn't returned for two thousand years, so any talk of His "imminence" or "coming soon" should be rejected.
5. How would you explain to a class of adults what "this generation" refers to in Mark 13:30?
6. What aspect of the "words" of God will not pass away at the end of the world (13:31): His spoken words (His promises), the incarnate Word (Jesus), or the written Word (the Bible)?
7. Why is it important to say that Jesus *voluntarily* laid aside omniscience when He took on mortal flesh?
8. How would you respond to someone who says he knows the precise date when Jesus will return?
9. How would you respond to someone who says that Jesus could not come tomorrow because the things that are supposed to occur first have not happened?
10. What is your favorite song that celebrates Jesus' second coming?

A Sacrifice of Extravagant Love

MARK 14:1-11

Main Idea: True followers of Jesus will not hesitate to worship Him with great love and great sacrifice.

I. **Extravagant Acts of Love Will Be Public (14:1-3).**
II. **Extravagant Acts of Love Will Often Be Criticized (14:4-5).**
III. **Extravagant Acts of Love Will Be Remembered (14:6-9).**
IV. **Extravagant Acts of Love Will Be Contrasted with Acts of Betrayal (14:10-11).**

Have you in your life as a follower of King Jesus ever made a sacrifice of extravagant love? Can you recall a time when you did something that really cost you? A time when you actually went without something you really wanted because of a sacrifice of extravagant love for Jesus? I believe I did. Once. Yes, to my shame, only once.

Sadly, we are good at giving Jesus our leftovers and hand-me-downs. I served a church once whose student building was filled with old, worn, ratty couches. Sweet folks in our church had bought new couches for their homes and so they donated their old, worn couches to the church and in the process got a tax break and felt good that they had done something noble. But had they really? I must confess one of the couches in the youth center had been given by me. It was no longer worthy of being in my house, but it was good enough for Jesus.

In Mark 14:1-11 we see something altogether different: a sacrifice of extravagant love by a woman Mark allows to remain anonymous. And we also see two lives that could not stand in greater contrast when it comes to devotion to our Lord: an unnamed woman who gave her best and a man named Judas who betrayed the Son of God. Of the woman Jesus said, "Wherever the gospel is proclaimed in the whole world, what this woman has done will also be told in memory of her" (v. 9). Of the man our Lord said, "It would have been better for that man if he had not been born" (v. 21).

Extravagant Acts of Love Will Be Public
MARK 14:1-3

The backdrop of this story is the Jewish feast of Passover and Unleavened Bread in Jerusalem. It was a time of thanksgiving for God's miraculous deliverance of the Hebrews from Egyptian bondage (Exod 12). This Jewish "Independence Day" included the slaughter of the Passover lamb, whose blood on the doorpost 1,400 years earlier had caused the "death angel" to pass over each home where he saw it, sparing the life of the firstborn in that family.

In the shadows of secrecy, the Sanhedrin ("the chief priest and the scribes") were seeking to arrest Jesus and kill Him. Mark says they hoped to arrest Him in "a treacherous way" but not until after the feast. Jesus was popular with the people so they would wait until the crowds had gone. However, things would proceed on God's timetable, and Christ the Passover Lamb would be sacrificed for us right on time (1 Cor 5:7).

The scene shifts to Bethany, to Simon's home. Jesus apparently had healed him of leprosy (Matt 26:6). John 12:1 tells us the event happened "six days before the Passover," so Mark's account is a flashback. The lady here was Mary, the sister of Martha and Lazarus, the latter of whom Jesus had raised from the dead (John 12:2). Simon may have been their father.

As Jesus was "reclining at the table, a woman came with an alabaster jar of pure and expensive fragrant oil of nard. She broke the jar and poured it on His head" (Mark 14:3). Nard was a sweet-smelling perfume from a rare plant found only in India. Mary broke the flask, making it no longer usable, and poured its full contents out on Jesus, both His head and His feet; then she wiped His feet with her hair (John 12:3). Each time we see Mary, she is at Jesus' feet (Luke 10:39; John 11:32; 12:3). A woman normally would not approach a man in this public-meal setting except to serve him food. Mary cared not one whit for cultural conventions. Jesus was her Lord and Master. She deeply loved Him and would have done anything for Him. She wanted everyone to know the inestimable value she placed on Jesus. So she went public! No one could deny or doubt where her loyalty lay. Can the same be said for you and me?

Extravagant Acts of Love Will Often Be Criticized
MARK 14:4-5

The critics would have no part in praising what this woman had done. Some began to talk among themselves, and they were indignant. Led by Judas (John 12:4ff) and in self-righteous pride, they questioned both her motive and her action. While she worshiped, they expressed their anger and displeasure, snorting at her.

Observe: (1) The disciples not only demeaned the woman; they also demeaned Jesus. To honor Christ in this manner, they said, was a waste. They did not believe He was worthy of such a sacrifice of extravagant love. (2) Some are willing to be poor in their possessions in order to be rich in their devotion to Jesus; others are not. The latter are usually the critics. (3) The world, and sadly many in the church, will never have a problem with moderate, measured devotion to Christ. They will have little or no problem with too many possessions and a pursuit of a comfortable and convenient Christianity. But walk away from a "real career," and you will be marked as foolish, living a "wasted life." Walk away from Mom and Dad to serve the Lord in an inner city in America among the poor and hurting, and you will be deemed silly and impractical. Walk away from family and friends to head out to the mission field among an unreached people group (7,055 as of May 5, 2012), taking your small children with you, and you will be chided as reckless, radical, even imbalanced and in need of serious counseling (and maybe even drugs!).

Yes, you may be criticized here, but in heaven you have a Master who applauds your love for Him! Paul puts it all in perspective in Galatians 1:10: "For am I now trying to win the favor of people, or God? Or am I striving to please people? If I were still trying to please people, I would not be a slave of Christ." George Whitefield, the evangelist of the First Great Awakening, said, "Oh for a thousand lives to be spent in service for Christ!" However, we only get one!

Extravagant Acts of Love Will Be Remembered
MARK 14:6-9

Acts 7:54-60 records the stoning of Stephen, the first Christian martyr. Stephen sees the Lord Jesus "standing at the right hand of God." Our Savior stands to receive His faithful martyred servant into glory. Here in Mark 14:6-9 we see our Lord in effect standing up for another faithful servant, a woman who has showered Him with a sacrifice of extravagant love only to be ridiculed by those who should have known better.

"Leave her alone," Jesus commands them (v. 6). Don't harass her or give her a hard time. She has done something wonderful and singularly important to Jesus.

Some readers misread verse 7, supposing Jesus to be insensitive toward the poor. We should do good for the poor. Jesus believed and taught that. The issue here is between "always" and "not always." The poor are always there, but Jesus would not be. The opportunity to show Him this kind of personal love and affection would soon be gone. Further, Jesus is God, and the first of the great commands always trumps the second (Mark 12:30-31). Jesus indeed asserts His preeminence above all others (cf. Col 1:18). This might help: Put these words in the mouth of any other human person, and they sound scandalous, self-centered, even narcissistic. Put them in the mouth of the Son of God who "for your sake . . . became poor, so that by His poverty you might become rich" (2 Cor 8:9), and they make all the sense in the world. Care for the poor, but worship the Savior!

Jesus makes three striking observations about Mary. (1) "She has done what she could." She held nothing back! (2) Her act of extravagant love had prophetic and symbolic significance: "She has anointed My body in advance for burial." Did she fully understand what was about to happen? Probably not. Did she have greater insight into our Lord's coming passion than the

12 apostles? Of this I have little doubt. (3) Jesus makes a promise that her sacrifice of extravagant love will never be forgotten as the gospel advances throughout "the whole world." The fact I am sharing this story now is a validation of what Jesus promised.

Extravagant Acts of Love Will Be Contrasted with Acts of Betrayal
MARK 14:10-11

Some people find Jesus useful because of what they think they can get from Him. Others find Jesus beautiful because they get Him. This woman found Jesus beautiful and gave all she had to Him. In contrast, Judas found Jesus useful and sought to get all he could in exchange for Him. Judas was "one of the Twelve" (14:10). He was so close to Jesus, yet he missed Him.

Amazingly, Judas takes the initiative in going "to the chief priest to hand [Jesus] over to them" (v. 10). Luke (22:3) and John (13:2,27) inform us that Satan moved him to betray the Lord. Still, he made a freewill choice to do so.

Verse 11 is simple and tragic all at once. The leaders of the Sanhedrin were glad to hear this and promised Judas money: 30 pieces of silver (Matt 26:15; cf. Zech 11:12-13), "the value of a slave accidentally gored to death by an ox (Exod 21:32). That Jesus is lightly esteemed is reflected not only in his betrayal but in the low sum agreed on by Judas and the chief priest" (Carson, "Matthew," 593). Judas then "started looking for a good opportunity to betray Him." It would come much sooner than he expected but with results he would find deathly disappointing.

What a contrast we see in Mary and Judas:

MARY	JUDAS
A woman with no real standing	A man, one of the apostles
Gave what she could to Jesus	Took what he could get for Jesus
Blessed her Lord	Betrayed his Lord
Loved her Lord	Used his Lord
Did a beautiful thing	Did a terrible thing
Served Him as her Savior	Sold Him like He was his slave
Notable forever for her devotion	Notorious forever for his betrayal

Oh, how I want to be like Mary. But oh, how often Judas so readily appears in the mirror. Only the gospel of my Savior can heal my sin-sick soul.

Conclusion

If Mary, the unnamed woman of Mark 14, were alive today, and we were to interview her and ask her, "What is your favorite Christian hymn?" I strongly suspect she would say, "When I Survey the Wondrous Cross." It was written in 1707 by Isaac Watts. Charles Wesley reportedly said he would give up all his other hymns to have written this one. We know he wrote at least six thousand! I agree: it is that good! Stanzas 1 and 4 are especially meaningful to me.

> When I survey the wondrous cross
> On which the Prince of glory died,
> My richest gain I count but loss,
> And pour contempt on all my pride.
>
> Forbid it, Lord, that I should boast,
> Save in the death of Christ, my God;
> All the vain things that charm me most—
> I sacrifice them to His blood.
>
> See, from His head, His hands, His feet,
> Sorrow and love flow mingled down;
> Did e'er such love and sorrow meet,
> Or thorns compose so rich a crown?
>
> Were the whole realm of nature mine,
> That were a present far too small;
> Love so amazing, so divine,
> Demands my soul, my life, my all.

Reflect and Discuss

1. What was the costliest offering you have ever made to Jesus?
2. What is the value of celebrating feasts and festivals? What are the most important celebrations for Christians?
3. What is the value of honoring Jesus in public? How do we avoid doing so with wrong motives?
4. Mary did not care about social taboos or personal embarrassment when she worshiped Jesus. How can we follow her example today?
5. Mary's critics said that the value of her gift exceeded the limit of what should be spent on Jesus. How are we today similar to those critics?

6. How was Mary's willingness to make a radical, extravagant sacrifice threatening to her critics?
7. What is the balance between practical, responsible stewardship and radical, extravagant giving? How do we avoid using the former as an excuse to escape the latter?
8. Did Jesus dismiss His followers from taking care of the poor? What is the biblical evidence for your answer?
9. In Luke 14:27-28 Jesus says a person should "calculate the cost" of becoming a disciple. Here we learn that true love never calculates the cost. How do these two lessons fit together?
10. In what ways do some people today look for what they can get for Jesus? How do people try to profit from going to church?

The King Prepares for His Passion

MARK 14:12-25

Main Idea: Jesus is both the Suffering Servant of the Lord and the Sacrificial Lamb of God, who would die for the sins of the world according to the will of God.

I. **Jesus Was in Control of the Events Leading to His Death (14:12-16).**
II. **Jesus Was Not Caught by Surprise by His Betrayal (14:17-21).**
III. **Jesus Prepared a Last Supper That Was Actually a First Supper (14:22-25).**

In 1906 Albert Schweitzer published his groundbreaking work, *The Quest of the Historical Jesus.* He believed Jesus saw Himself as a first-century eschatological prophet who believed His ministry would usher in the apocalyptic end of history. Unfortunately, Jesus was mistaken. Things got out of hand, and He was brutally put to death in the process. Schweitzer wrote,

There is silence all around. The Baptist appears, and cries: "Repent, for the Kingdom of Heaven is at hand." Soon after that comes Jesus, and in the knowledge that He is the coming Son of Man lays hold of the wheel of the world to set it moving on that last revolution which is to bring all ordinary history to a close. It refuses to turn, and He throws Himself upon it. Then it does turn; and crushes Him. Instead of bringing in the eschatological conditions, He has destroyed them. The wheel rolls onward, and the mangled body of the one immeasurably great Man, who was strong enough to think of Himself as the spiritual ruler of mankind and to bend history to His purpose, is hanging upon it still. That is his victory and His reign. (Beilby and Eddy, *Historical*, 20)

This perspective, still popular among some liberal and skeptical scholars, fails with a fair and honest reading of the Gospels. There we see our Savior in total control—down to the last detail—as He makes His way to the cross to die for the sins of the world (John 1:29). He will indeed be crushed, not by the "wheel of the world," but by the will of His Father (Isa 53:10), a will our Lord both understood and embraced. "Jesus is not a tragic hero caught in events beyond his control. There is no hint of desperation, fear, anger, or futility on his part. Jesus does not cower or retreat as plots are hatched against him. He displays, as he has throughout the Gospel, a sovereign freedom and authority to follow a course he has freely chosen in accordance with God's plan" (Edwards, *Mark*, 419). Our King knows exactly where He is going and what will happen. Sovereign grace will use even human evil to accomplish its saving purposes. Our Lord will be certain everything goes according to plan.

Jesus Was in Control of the Events Leading to His Death
MARK 14:12-16

"The first day of Unleavened Bread, when they sacrifice the Passover lamb" (v. 12) was Thursday. The disciples want to know where the memorial meal will take place, that they might make preparation. Jesus provides precise instructions in verses 13-15 (cf. 11:1-6). He sent two disciples into the city. He tells them they will meet a man carrying a jar of water (this was normally something women or slaves would do). They were to follow him to a specific house. They were to tell the master of the house that "the Teacher" wants to know where the guest room is, that He may eat the Passover with His disciples. Jesus informed them that the master would "show [them] a large upper room furnished and ready" (v. 15). That is where they were to make preparation.

Amazingly but not surprisingly, verse 16 records, "the disciples went out, entered the city, and found it just as He had told them." It is possible Jesus knew the man carrying the water and the master of the house, yet the details suggest His supernatural knowledge of what would happen.

The two disciples did as they were instructed. They also would have prepared the Passover lamb that symbolized their deliverance from slavery and redemption out of Egypt. Little did they know that an even greater Passover was unfolding as Jesus prepared Himself to be sacrificed as our Passover

Lamb (1 Cor 5:7). John the Baptist had declared, "Here is the Lamb of God, who takes away the sin of the world" (John 1:29). Jesus is indeed this Passover Lamb, and He is in complete control of the events leading to His death. The cross did not catch Him off guard. No, it was a divine appointment scheduled, as Peter would write, "before the foundation of the world" (1 Pet 1:20). Jesus knew down to the last detail what was happening, and He joyfully embraced it (Heb 12:2). Such confidence in God's will should inspire us to trust Him even when the road of life may be difficult, painful, even deadly. Our God is in control!

Jesus Was Not Caught by Surprise by His Betrayal
MARK 14:17-21

If Jesus was in complete control of all the events leading up to His death, then He was not surprised by His betrayal. Was He heartbroken and disappointed? Certainly yes—the betrayer was a close and trusted friend. Mark focuses on two events: our Lord's betrayal (vv. 17-21) and Jesus' institution of what we call "the Lord's Supper" (vv. 22-25).

While they are reclining at the table and eating, the normal posture for having a meal in that day, Jesus utters words that must have shocked all and sent a chill through the room: "I assure you: One of you will betray Me—one who is eating with Me." How He knew this we are never told, but He knew. Psalm 41:9 says, "Even my friend in whom I trusted, one who ate my bread, has raised his heel against me." Did He draw from that text? Jesus clearly applies that Davidic psalm to this moment.

Our Lord's words provoke grief and soul searching, as they should. Each of the disciples ask Him, "Surely not I?" But Jesus narrows the list of possible betrayers to the 12 apostles, His most intimate and trusted companions.

Jesus then makes one of the most profound and theologically significant statements in the whole Bible. He says, "For the Son of Man will go just as it is written about Him, but woe to that man by whom the Son of Man is betrayed! It would have been better for that man if he had not been born" (v. 21). Observe: (1) Jesus, as Daniel's "Son of Man" (Dan 7:13-14), was predestined to be betrayed and crucified. Once again Jesus weds Daniel's apocalyptic figure to Isaiah's "Suffering Servant" (Isa 52:13–53:12; also Ps 22). (2) The one betraying the Lord Jesus was pitied in spite of his unconscionable deed ("woe to that man"). Jesus loved and cared even for Judas. (3) The future judgment for Judas will be so terrible it would have been better "if he had not been born." Again, we see the truth that "revelation brings responsibility." (4) Even though Judas' betrayal was ordained according to

God's plan, he is morally responsible for his freewill action. Jesus will be betrayed and crucified according to God's predetermined will, but this in no way relieved Judas of his responsibility and guilt. In a divine mystery we will never completely comprehend in this life, we embrace the truth and tension that divine sovereignty never cancels out human freedom and moral responsibility. Both are true. We affirm them both.

The answer to each disciple's question—Is it I?—requires an answer of yes from each and every one of us. Yes, Judas betrayed Jesus, but by morning all the disciples would betray Him. Judas betrayed Him for greed (vv. 10-11), but the rest would betray Him from weakness (vv. 37-42), fear (vv. 50-52), and cowardice (vv. 66-72). But what about you and me? Each one of us is a Judas because every sin against Jesus is a personal act of betrayal. Yet this is where the grace of the gospel shines so bright: even those who betray this great King and glorious Savior can experience immediate and complete forgiveness through simple repentance and confession of sin (1 John 1:9). Godly repentance will grieve over the terrible thing it has done, but then it flees to Jesus who took that sin on Himself at the cross. In grace God forgives, and He provides the strength to move forward in the "family of the forgiven." What a great family that is! If only Judas had repented of his sin.

Jesus Prepared a Last Supper That Was Actually a First Supper
MARK 14:22-25

Dietrich Bonhoeffer said, "He who would learn to serve must first learn to think little of himself." And he quoted Thomas à Kempis as saying, "This is the highest and most profitable lesson, truly to know and despise ourselves" (Bonhoeffer, *Life Together*, 94). Jesus has already served His disciples on their last night together by washing their feet (John 13:1-20). Now He serves them again as He institutes what we call "the Last Supper" (cf. Matt 26:26-29; Luke 22:18-20; 1 Cor 10:14-22; 11:17-34).

However, we could also refer to it as "the First Supper," as it inaugurates the "new covenant" (Jer 31:31-34; Luke 22:20), which God made with us through the Lord Jesus, the true Passover Lamb who had been sacrificed for us (1 Cor 5:7). His death made possible a new and greater exodus (see Luke 9:31), as we are set free from our slavery to sin.

The Passover meal was the proper occasion for the Lord's Supper to be instituted:

> It included four points at which the presider, holding a glass of wine,
> got up and explained the Feast's meaning. The four cups of wine

represented the four promises made by God in Exodus 6:6-7. These promises were for rescue from Egypt, for freedom from slavery, for redemption by God's power, and for a renewed relationship with God. The third cup came at a point when the meal was almost completely eaten (Keller, *King's Cross*, 164–65).

This third cup, I believe, is the one in verse 23.

The Passover meal is proceeding as usual when suddenly Jesus departs from the normal script. What He says are the words of a madman unless He is the Son of God and the true Passover Lamb. Breaking the bread and blessing it, He says, "Take it; this is My body." He takes the cup, blesses it, and "they all drank from it." Then He says, "This is My blood that establishes the covenant; it is shed for many" (v. 24). The new covenant, like the old covenant, is a "blood covenant." That it is "shed for many" informs us that the new covenant, promised in Jeremiah 31:31-34, is made possible by the death of Isaiah's "Suffering Servant of the Lord" who "bore the sins of many and made intercession for the transgressors" (Isa 53:12). Hebrews 8:1-13 speaks of the new covenant in greater detail.

Jesus told His disciples that each time they gathered in the future to celebrate this meal, they were to do it "in remembrance of Me" (Luke 22:19; 1 Cor 11:24). It is almost impossible to overstate how shocking these words are. Sam Storms helps us grasp the massive significance of what Jesus said:

> *What Jesus requested, indeed commanded, His followers and friends to do subsequent to His death is nothing short of shocking!* It's one thing to desire that your memory be preserved by your loved ones and that they continue to honor and esteem you throughout the remainder of their lives. . . .
>
> But it is altogether something else to command that your friends, family, and followers gather together regularly at a meal not only in your name but with you as the sole and exclusive focus. . . . Jesus commanded His followers, every time they broke bread together, to make Him the central point of their celebration and to recall and re-tell His life and death.
>
> Were anyone to make this request of me prior to their death, I would probably conclude that the proximity of their demise had afflicted them with delusions of grandeur and megalomania. Yet, this is precisely what Jesus commanded that each of His followers do in memory of Him! (Storms, "Passover Lamb"; emphasis in original).

Jesus brings things to a close by refusing to drink the fourth and final cup. It is the cup of consummation and life in the promised land of God.

For that cup He will wait. First, He must drink to the last drop the cup of God's wrath and justice. Apart from it, no cup of blessing would be possible.

Conclusion

In 1991 Christian songwriter and vocalist Twila Paris penned a song to accompany the observance of the Lord's Supper by the Lord's people. It has powerful words for reflection and celebration as we consider the King, His supper, and His passion.

> How beautiful the hands that served
> The wine and the bread and the sons of the earth
> How beautiful the feet that walked
> The long dusty roads and the hill to the cross
>
> *Chorus*
> How beautiful, how beautiful
> How beautiful is the body of Christ
>
> How beautiful the heart that bled
> That took all my sin and bore it instead
> How beautiful the tender eyes
> That chose to forgive and never despise
>
> *Chorus*
>
> And as He laid down His life
> We offer this sacrifice
> That we will live just as He died
> Willing to pay the price
> Willing to pay the price
>
> How beautiful the radiant bride
> Who waits for her groom with His light in her eyes
> How beautiful when humble hearts give
> The fruit of pure lives so that others may live
>
> *Chorus*
>
> How beautiful the feet that bring
> The sound of good news and the love of the King
> How beautiful the hands that serve
> The wine and the bread and the sons of the earth
>
> *Chorus* (Paris, "How Beautiful")

Reflect and Discuss

1. What is the danger in saying, "Jesus was a good, well-intentioned man who thought He was the Son of God, but He was mistaken"? Couldn't we still learn from His example?
2. How does the way Jesus sent the disciples to find the upper room give evidence that Jesus was in charge of the whole situation?
3. How does Jesus' control of events surrounding His passion encourage you when you face difficulties?
4. What might the disciples have thought when Jesus said that one of them would betray Him? Do you think you would have suspected your own heart if you had been there?
5. How does this passage express the tension between free will and the sovereignty of God?
6. In what way did all the disciples betray Jesus? In what way has every person betrayed Him and put Him on the cross? How can that betrayal be forgiven?
7. Why might the Last Supper also be called the First Supper? What did Jesus inaugurate?
8. Has the Lord's Supper sometimes become so familiar for you that it is no longer amazing? What did Jesus mean by saying, "This is My body" and "This is My blood"?
9. How would you like people to remember you after you die? How does this compare with Jesus' command?
10. Which lines of the song "How Beautiful" touch you the most? Why?

The King Who Suffers Alone

MARK 14:26-52

Main Idea: Jesus is the righteous King who endured betrayal and shame for the sake of sinners.

I. **The King Would Be Abandoned and Left Alone (14:26-31).**
II. **The King Would Agonize over His Passion Alone (14:32-42).**
III. **The King Would Be Arrested and Forsaken Alone (14:43-52).**

Jesus drank the cup of God's wrath that we might drink the cup of salvation (Ps 116:13). Jesus submitted Himself in the garden of Gethsemane that He might save sinners on the cross. Jesus is the King who suffers alone for His people.

Jesus has celebrated Passover with the disciples and in so doing instituted the "Lord's Supper," a memorial that pictures His bloody atonement and anticipates the coming of the kingdom of God in all its glory. The evening, however, has a dark cloud hanging overhead: one of His closest friends will betray Him. Jesus will suffer at the hands of His enemies who have been plotting His death for some time (Mark 3:6). He also will suffer at the betrayal of His friends who fail Him in His hour of need (14:37,40-41), sell Him out (vv. 44-45), abandon Him (v. 50), and deny Him (vv. 66-72). And He will suffer at the hands of His Father, whose will it was that He should drink the cup of divine wrath that each of us should have drunk (vv. 35-36,39). Yes, to the amazement of angels and the wonder of sinners saved by grace, "the Lord was pleased to crush Him severely" (Isa 53:10). It was the will of the Father to kill His beloved Son (Mark 1:11; 9:7) so that He would not have to kill you and me.

The suffering of this great King is multifaceted: personal, physical, mental, and most of all, spiritual. Jesus saw His loving Father's hand in it all. He trusted Him in His most trying hour, an hour our finite human minds can never fully comprehend. Our text highlights three aspects of the solitary suffering of the Savior King.

The King Would Be Abandoned and Left Alone
MARK 14:26-31

As they finished the Passover dinner, the Lord and His disciples probably sang one of the final Hallel psalms (Pss 115–118) and then "went out to the Mount of Olives." On the way Jesus again shakes up the Twelve. He tells them that not only will one of them (Judas) betray Him, but also they "will all fall away." This prediction is grounded in the Old Testament prophecy of Zechariah: "Strike the shepherd, and the sheep will be scattered" (Zech 13:7). This prophecy referred to the "martyrdom of the eschatological prophet" (Edwards, *Mark*, 428). The Father will strike His Son, the Good Shepherd (John 10). His suffering and death is divinely ordained and sanctioned. Using the evil intentions and actions of sinful men, God will work the greatest possible good in saving sinners. The disciples will scatter like frightened mice, but hope will not be lost. Jesus assured them, "After I have been resurrected, I will go ahead of you to Galilee" (14:28). Where He first called them, there He will meet them again. There He will return, reclaim, and recommission them for the work of taking the gospel to the nations.

Proverbs 16:18 painfully reminds us, "Pride comes before destruction, and an arrogant spirit before a fall." We often forget these words and suffer the consequences. Peter joins us: hearing Jesus predict their defection, he steps up and with arrogance and bravado announces, "Even if everyone runs away, I will certainly not!" (Mark 14:29). Wow, what a declaration of fidelity! But in making this bold pronouncement, Peter, in essence, calls Jesus a liar. Jesus says they will fall away. Peter responds, "No I won't!" Our Lord responds, and though His words contain a rebuke, I cannot help but imagine they were delivered with compassion and kindness: "I assure you . . . today, this very night, before the rooster crows twice, you will deny Me three times."

You would think our Lord's words would silence Peter, but not so. In fact he raises the stakes: "If I have to die with You, I will never deny You!" (v. 31). Apparently the rest of the disciples got caught up in this frenzy of loyalty because "they all said the same."

All of us would like to think we would have succeeded where Peter and the disciples failed. We would also hope to exhibit greater humility and a more controlled tongue! But if we are honest, we probably would have said the same thing and acted the same way. But we would also be the recipients of our Savior's gracious forgiveness and restoration. Jesus accepted that He would be abandoned and left alone so that you and I would never be abandoned or left alone. Hebrews 13:5 rings more precious than ever: "I will never leave you or forsake you."

The King Would Agonize over His Passion Alone
MARK 14:32-42

These verses constitute sacred, holy ground. We will never know the depths of agony and pain our Savior endured that night alone for love of sinners like us. Jesus takes the disciples to a place called Gethsemane. He would often go there with the disciples, probably to pray. He told the disciples to "sit here while I pray." This is the third and final time Mark records our Lord praying alone (cf. 1:35; 6:46). Each occasion was a time of significant importance, but none more than this one.

Jesus was "deeply distressed and horrified" (v. 33). James Edwards says, "'My soul is overwhelmed with sorrow to the point of death' echoes the haunting lament of the downcast and dejected soul of Pss. 42:6,12 and 43:5." Yet, "Nothing in all the Bible compares to Jesus' agony and anguish in Gethsemane—neither the laments of the Psalms, nor the broken heart of Abraham as he prepared to sacrifice his son Isaac (Gen 22:5), nor David's grief at the death of his son Absalom (2 Sam 18:33)" (Edwards, *Mark*, 432).

Jesus asked Peter, James, and John to stay and watch (v. 34). Sadly they will stay and sleep (vv. 37,40-41). He left them and went a little farther away, fell to the ground under the massive burden He was carrying, and asked His Father that "if it were possible, the hour might pass from Him" (v. 35). The intensity and intimacy of the request is staggering: "Abba, Father! All things are possible for You. Take this cup away from Me. Nevertheless, not what I will, but what You will." He would pray the same prayer again (Matt 26:44 informs us He prayed it a third time as well).

In spite of the exceptional trauma of the moment and the certain future that lay ahead, He trusted in God as His loving Father and in His will. What's more, the "cup" that He prayed might be removed was not the physical pain He would endure on the cross. Indeed many Christian martyrs have gone to their death with thanksgiving and joy with no evidence whatsoever that they wished to avoid the hour of their martyrdom. No, the cup that so distressed and troubled Him was the spiritual suffering He would endure as He would bear the sins of the world and drink to the last drop the fierce wrath of God as our substitute. Tim Keller says,

> In the garden of Gethsemane, he turns to the Father and all he can see before him is wrath, the abyss, the chasm, the nothingness of the cup. . . . Jesus began to experience the spiritual, cosmic, infinite disintegration that would happen when he became separated from his Father on the cross. Jesus began to experience merely a foretaste of that, and he staggered. (Keller, *King's Cross*, 176)

The anguish and pain of the cross was not what concerned His soul. It was knowing that He would be abandoned by and separated from His Father as He answered "for every sin and crime and act of malice and injury and cowardice and evil in the world." That is what brought Him to His knees and moved Him to make His poignant plea (Edwards, *Mark*, 433).

As Jesus struggles for the souls of men, His closest friends sleep soundly some distance away. The tone of our Lord's chastening was, no doubt, mild and full of grace. He encourages them to be watchful and prayerful. Temptation is always lurking nearby, and redeemed spirits are still attached to sinful flesh. The flesh's weakness actually acts with great power to take us where we do not want to go. Jesus knew they wanted to be strong for Him. He also knew they would fail.

Jesus has agonized over His passion, and He has done it alone. He wakens them: "Enough! The time has come." The issue is settled! Jesus' will and His Father's are united! For the joy that is set before Him, He will endure the cross and all that it entails (Heb 12:2).

Gethsemane was "hell" for Jesus, but I am so thankful He went through it. You see, if there is no Gethsemane, there is no Calvary. It there is no Calvary, there can be no empty tomb. And if there is no empty tomb, there is only hell for us.

The King Would Be Arrested and Forsaken Alone
MARK 14:43-52

While Jesus is talking, Judas, "one of the Twelve," comes with an armed crowd from the Sanhedrin—the "temple police," though they may have been accompanied by Roman soldiers (cf. John 18:3,12). By prearranged plan, Judas gives Jesus a greeting of respect and plants kisses of betrayal and death on His cheek, identifying clearly the One they came to arrest. The religious Gestapo springs into action: "Then they took hold of Him and arrested Him" (v. 46). No charges were made. Following legal protocol is not on their agenda this night!

The disciples may have been taken by surprise, but one of them "drew his sword, struck the high priest's slave, and cut off his ear." It was Peter who struck the man, whose name was Malchus, probably a servant of the high priest Caiaphas (John 18:10-14). Jesus healed Malchus (Luke 22:51).

Jesus rebukes the mob for their extreme methods (Mark 14:48-49). He is no robber or political revolutionary. Day after day He taught in the temple. They knew who He was. They could have arrested Him at any time. Arresting Him late at night in a quiet, secluded location showed their cowardice. It was shameful. It was also a fulfillment of Scripture, for the prophet Isaiah had prophesied of the Suffering Servant, "He was despised and rejected by men" (53:3); "He was taken away because of oppression and judgment" (53:8); He "was counted among the rebels" (53:12).

Mark 14:50-52 records the sad defection of the disciples—all of them! Those who had a short time earlier boasted that they would die for Him now are nowhere to be found. An anonymous "young man" was nearly captured but was able to escape. However, his "linen cloth" was captured and so he "ran away naked." Church tradition says the young man was Mark, the author of our second Gospel. So again, as it was in the garden of Eden, our nakedness is exposed as we desert the God who loves us and has graced us so abundantly with His kindness and good gifts.

And Jesus? He is arrested, and He is forsaken. He is all alone to face the wrath of men and the wrath of God. He will receive all that we deserve, that we might receive all that He deserves. The "Great Exchange" has begun.

Conclusion

Gethsemane is the prelude to Calvary. Before He could surrender His body to be beaten and crucified on the cross, He must first surrender His will to His heavenly Father in the garden. In the first garden, the garden of Eden, Adam said to the Father, "Not Your will but mine be done," and all of creation was plunged into sin. In this second garden, the garden of Gethsemane, Jesus, the second Adam, says, "Not My will but Yours be done," and the redemption and salvation of all creation begins! Eden brought death. Gethsemane begins new life.

Stuart Townend and Keith Getty penned a hymn titled "Gethsemane Hymn." The words beautifully capture what this King who suffered alone did on our behalf:

> To see the King of heaven fall
> In anguish to His knees;
> The Light and Hope of all the world
> Now overwhelmed with grief.
> What nameless horrors must He see,
> To cry out in the garden:
> "Oh, take this cup away from Me,
> Yet not My will but Yours;
> Yet not My will but Yours."
>
> To know each friend will fall away,
> And heaven's voice be still,
> For hell to have its vengeful day
> Upon Golgotha's hill.
> No words describe the Saviour's plight—
> To be by God forsaken
> Till wrath and love are satisfied,
> And every sin is paid,
> And every sin is paid.
>
> What took Him to this wretched place?
> What kept Him on this road?
> His love for Adam's cursed race,
> For every broken soul.
> No sin too slight to overlook,
> No crime too great to carry,
> All mingled in this poisoned cup,
> And yet He drank it all;
> The Saviour drank it all;
> The Saviour drank it all.

Reflect and Discuss

1. Do you regularly ponder and meditate on Jesus Christ and what He has done for you? What thoughts have produced the most serious meditation? What thoughts have led to the most joyous praise?

2. How would you respond to someone who said that Judas had no choice because he was destined to betray Jesus? How would you respond to the argument that Judas was not guilty because he did just what God needed him to do?
3. In what areas of temptation might you be susceptible to pride and say, "I would never do that"? How do Proverbs 16:18 and 1 Corinthians 10:12 address this attitude?
4. In what circumstances are you most tempted to fall away? How can you best prepare to stay true to God?
5. Imagine finding out that in 24 hours you would die violently and painfully. How would you handle that knowledge? How would you spend those hours? What did Jesus do?
6. Have you ever been determined to pray, but you fell asleep? What causes this? How might you improve your ability to "stay awake and pray" (14:38)?
7. How would you explain to a non-Christian what caused Jesus such agony as He prayed in the garden?
8. Why do you suppose Judas chose a kiss as the sign identifying Jesus to the police?
9. Why did the Jewish leaders not arrest Jesus in the temple in the daylight?
10. Why is it significant that it might have been Mark, the author of this Gospel, who "ran away naked" after Jesus was arrested (14:52)?

The Beginning of the End for the Great King

MARK 14:53-72

Main Idea: Even amid the falling away of all His followers, Jesus remained faithful to His calling.

I. **Jesus Makes the Faithful Witness as to Who He Is (14:53-65).**
    A. A false witness will find ways to lie no matter the facts (14:53-59).
    B. A true witness will tell the truth no matter the consequences (14:60-65).
II. **Peter Models the Unfaithful Witness as to Who He Is for (14:66-72).**
    A. Some say of Jesus, "I do not know what you are talking about" (14:66-68).
    B. Some say of Jesus, "I do not belong to Him" (14:69-70).
    C. Some say of Jesus, "I do not even know Him" (14:70-72).

If you were to ask my four sons what were some of their dad's favorite sayings, I am sure one would be, "Life is not fair." Most of us would readily agree with this proverb.

In the case of our Savior, not only was life unfair; His final hours were unjust and illegal. Jesus endured six hearings in a matter of hours—three ecclesiastical trials before the Jewish religious authorities and three civil trials before the Roman political authorities (Matt 26–27; Mark 14–15; Luke 22–23; John 18–19). It is difficult to count up all the violations of Jewish law. For example, in capital cases like Jesus', trials at night were forbidden. In cases where a guilty verdict was reached, a second day and session were required to ensure a fair trial. Such a trial should not convene on a Sabbath or festival. In addition, a charge of blasphemy could not be sustained unless the defendant cursed God's name, and then the penalty was to be death by stoning, not crucifixion. In Jesus' case no formal meeting of the Sanhedrin ever took place in the temple precincts, which was the proper location for a trial. Nor was Jesus provided or even offered a defense attorney.

These violations are not without their explanations. Pastor Sam Storms has noted that "contrary to the opinion of some, rabbinic law actually insists that the execution of a rebellious teacher take place on one of the three primary feast days to serve as a more visible example and deterrent to the people" (Storms, "Truth"). Furthermore, His trial was at night because criminals could not be executed on the Sabbath. If Jesus was arrested on Thursday night, things had to move swiftly if He was to be killed and buried by dusk on Friday, before the start of the Sabbath. Regarding the time of the trial, "an all-night session of the Jewish authorities was demanded by the fact that Roman officials like Pilate worked early in the morning and then refused to take on new cases for the rest of the day. If Jesus could not be presented to Pilate early Friday morning, the case would drag on till after the Sabbath—along with mounting risks of mob violence" (Carson, *Matthew*, 550).

Other irregularities are easily understandable once we remember that many of the legal procedures in rabbinic law were theoretical and were rarely put into practice. Also, these religious leaders were motivated by expediency. Judicial procedure was of little concern to them when the hour demanded quick action. When there is a will to quickly remove an undesirable enemy, a way will be found!

So it is the beginning of the end for the great King. Religious and political authorities will conspire to put Him to death. And His closest companion will draw near only to deny that he ever knew Him. He is all alone. How will things go for Him?

Jesus Makes the Faithful Witness as to Who He Is
MARK 14:53-65

In Revelation 1:5 the risen and glorified Christ is called the "faithful witness." Under exceptional duress and persecution, Jesus will stand up and speak out, bearing clear testimony concerning who He is and what He will do (Mark 14:62). He knows it will seal His fate. He knows it is what He must do. Our very souls and eternal destiny hang in the balance!

A False Witness Will Find Ways to Lie No Matter the Facts (Mark 14:53-59)

Jesus was taken to the high priest, a man named Joseph Caiaphas. He succeeded his father-in-law, Annas, who had been removed by the Romans but still wielded enormous influence. The soldiers took Jesus to Annas first (John 18:12). Then the 71-member Sanhedrin quickly convened for a night session to deal with Jesus (Mark 14:53).

Peter, apparently alone, "followed Him at a distance, right into the high priest's courtyard." He certainly deserves some credit at this point. Soon, that will not be the case.

The kangaroo court of the chief priest and Sanhedrin sought witnesses against Jesus but struck out! The false witnesses they were able to enlist "did not agree" with one another (vv. 56,59). Some accused Him of saying He would destroy and rebuild the temple in three days (vv. 57-58). Jesus had indeed said something like this, but He was speaking metaphorically of His body and the resurrection (John 2:19-21). No wonder their testimony did not agree (Mark 14:59). Destruction of a worship place was a capital offense, but the Scriptures require agreement from at least two witnesses for a conviction (Deut 17:6; 19:15; Num 35:30). Still, as far as this tribunal was concerned, Jesus was guilty until proven innocent, and He was not going to be found innocent. The Mishnah said, "A Sanhedrin which as often as once in seven years condemns a man to death, is a slaughterhouse" (Keller, "Mark," 195). Nevertheless, on this night they were determined to slay their victim.

A True Witness Will Tell the Truth No Matter the Consequences (Mark 14:60-65)

The trial has not gone as planned. The case is unraveling and headed for disaster from the perspective of the religious leaders. But then the high priest Caiaphas rises and begins to interrogate Jesus. Any idea of judicial impartiality flies out the window. He asks Jesus to respond to the charges of the false witnesses, "But He kept silent and did not answer anything" (v. 61). Once more Isaiah 53 is fulfilled: "He was oppressed and afflicted, yet He did not open His mouth. Like a lamb led to the slaughter and like a sheep silent before her shearers, He did not open His mouth" (Isa 53:7).

No doubt full of frustration by now, the high priest addresses Jesus again and asks Him (under oath, Matt 26:63), "Are You the Messiah, the Son of the Blessed One?" (Mark 14:61). "Blessed One" is a title for God (cf. 2 Sam 7:11-16; Ps 2). James Edwards notes the irony of the question:

> The effect is to put a full christological confession into the mouth of the high priest! . . . His arch-prosecutor confesses his name! How ironic that in the Gospel of Mark the two most complete christological confessions from humans occur in the mouth of those responsible for Jesus' death: the high priest in 14:61 and the centurion at the cross in 15:39. (Edwards, *Mark*, 446)

Numerous times in Mark's Gospel, Jesus asked those who followed Him and those He healed to be silent concerning His identity. The time for the "messianic secret" has now come to an end. Called, under divine oath, to bear witness to His true identity, He directly and openly affirms, "I am." He also identifies the Messiah with Daniel's apocalyptic Son of Man: "And all of you will see the Son of Man seated at the right hand of the Power [God] and coming with the clouds of heaven" (v. 62). Jesus weds Daniel 7:13-14 with Psalm 110:1 in identifying Himself as the Messiah and God's Son (cf. Mark 12:35-37). Today I stand before you, but there is coming a day when you will stand before Me in judgment! A great reversal is coming!

Jesus' words set the high priest off in an uproar of self-righteous indignation. As far as they are concerned, Jesus has condemned Himself with His own words. The high priest rules He is guilty of blasphemy, a capital offense, and first says that no other witnesses are needed and second asks what the verdict of the Council will be. "And they all condemned Him to be deserving of death."

Things move from unjust to shameful. (1) They begin to spit on Him, an act as insulting then as it is today (cf. Num 12:14; Deut 25:9; 30:10; Isa 50:6). (2) They cover His face, blindfolding Him for further mockery and abuse. (3) They begin to strike Him with their fists, taunting Him to "prophesy" as to who His attackers are (cf. Isa 11:2-4), and once more our Lord remains silent (cf. Isa 53:7). (4) "The temple police also took Him and slapped Him." They join the party and beat and slap the innocent, kind, loving man who, as Acts 10:38 says, "went about doing good and healing all who were under the tyranny of the Devil, because God was with Him." It is hard to put into words the severity of this miscarriage of justice. And it will get much worse.

Peter Models the Unfaithful Witness as to Who He Is For
MARK 14:66-72

"I've got your back" is a popular saying. Basically the idea is, "I am your friend, and I am watching out for what's behind you as you are busy looking ahead. You can trust me to look out for you, to even 'take a bullet for you' if necessary." It is a pledge of devotion, loyalty, and true friendship. Such friends are few and should be cherished as precious gifts.

Just a few hours earlier Peter had pledged, "Even if all the other disciples fall away, I won't" (v. 29). And in verse 31 he said, "If I have to die with You, I will never deny You." Well, in verse 50 Peter had run away just like everyone else when Jesus was arrested. Now, however, we find him, and only him, drawing close to the place where our Lord is being held. Maybe he does have Jesus' back.

Some Say of Jesus, "I Do Not Know What You Are Talking About" (Mark 14:66-68)

Peter is said to be "in the courtyard below," indicating Jesus was in a large upper room in the substantial home of the high priest, a man who had profited through religion. A servant girl noticed Peter and said, "You also were with that Nazarene, Jesus" (v. 67). Given his earlier promise of fidelity, we are confident Peter will step up and declare his loyalty. We and, more importantly, Jesus are sadly disappointed.

Peter blatantly rejected her accusation: "I don't know or understand what you're talking about" (v. 68). To avoid further scrutiny, Peter moved out into the entryway, "and a rooster crowed" (see v. 30)! Apparently, this had no impact on Peter. He was too busy claiming ignorance and trying to go undetected. This "rock" is beginning to crack!

Some Say of Jesus, "I Do Not Belong to Him" (Mark 14:69-70)

This servant girl was persistent and unrelenting in her (or God's!) pursuit of Peter. She, along with others (cf. Matt 28:71; Luke 22:58), began to say, "This man is one of them" (Mark 14:69). James Edwards well says, "A change in place is no substitute for a change of heart. Like a guilty conscience, the servant girl accuses Peter a second time" (*Mark*, 450).

Peter is now on the spot, in the hot seat, in front of others. Here is his chance to "man up," regain his courage, and take a stand for the Jesus for whom he had expressed undying loyalty. Unfortunately, "again he denied it" (v. 70). The tense of the verb he used means he kept on denying that he belonged to Jesus. It was not a one-time slip of the tongue. The fracture of this rock is growing.

Some Say of Jesus, "I Do Not Even Know Him" (Mark 14:70-72)

Peter failed the Lord three times in the garden of Gethsemane (vv. 37-42). Now he fails Him three times in the courtyard of the high priest. Initially, he failed Him by sleeping when he should have been praying. Now he fails Him by denying Him when he should have confessed Him. The rock named Peter crumbles and is pulverized under the pressure.

Again the bystanders call to Peter, "You certainly are one of them, since you're also a Galilean" (v. 70). This was all Peter could take. He puts himself under a divine curse. "If I am lying may God strike me dead" is a modern idiom that captures Peter's sentiment. "I don't know this man you're talking about!" Peter will not even mention Jesus' name, thereby distancing himself even further from this now convicted capital criminal.

"Immediately, a rooster crowed a second time" (v. 72). Peter then "remembered" that Jesus had predicted his denial. This broke him, and he, overwhelmed by this betrayal and cowardice, "began to weep." At the very moment he was voicing his third denial, Jesus "turned and looked at Peter" (Luke 22:61). Sinclair Ferguson says, "That look was to be his salvation, for he saw in those eyes not condemnation but compassion. That was the turning point in his life. . . . Now, in this most painful and memorable of ways, Peter saw himself as he really was, repented, and was remade into the great apostle" (*Mark*, 252).

Peter would repent, turn to Christ for forgiveness, and receive a full pardon. By contrast Judas would only feel regret, run to the religious leaders to try to make amends, and go out and hang himself (Matt 27:5). If only he had turned again to the Lord Jesus like Peter. Though his sin was great, he would have discovered that God's grace was even greater.

Conclusion

Balthasar Hubmaier has been called "the Simon Peter" of the evangelical Anabaptists of the sixteenth century. The movement's greatest theologian, he would see six thousand believers baptized at Nikolsburg in 1526–27. And because of severe persecution, he would compromise and deny his commitment to Christ on at least two different occasions. Yet, like Peter, he would be brought by God to deep repentance. In a work titled *Short Apology*, he would write, "O God, pardon me my weakness. It is good for me that you have humbled me" (Estep, *Anabaptist*, 63).

On what appears to be a third occasion of torture, Hubmaier, with uncompromising fortitude, remained true to Jesus. One week later, on March 10, 1528, Hubmaier was burned at the stake. As he faced the fire, he shouted loud for the onlooking crowd to hear, "O my gracious God, grant me grace in my great suffering." As the flames engulfed his beard and hair, his last words were simple: "O my heavenly Father! O my gracious God! . . . O Jesus!" Witnesses said that in his death "he appeared to feel more joy than pain." Such is the grace of God poured out on any sinner, no matter what the sin, who flees to Jesus in repentance, who flees to God in his hour of need. The great King in His passion has made it possible. Praise His name!

Reflect and Discuss

1. Why do people get upset when they perceive that something is not fair?
2. Have you ever been in a situation where normal procedures were set aside for the sake of expediency? When is this warranted? How was the Sanhedrin reasoning with regard to expediting Jesus' trial?
3. What was the Sanhedrin looking for in the witnesses who were called? In what situations do we sometimes look for evidence to support preconceived conclusions? How do we avoid this error?
4. What was the significance of Jesus' using the phrases "I am" and "Son of Man" in His answer?
5. Have you ever trusted a friend to defend you and then been disappointed? Were you able to forgive that person and restore the friendship?
6. In what situations are you tempted to make excuses in order to avoid being identified as a Christian? Are there other situations where you tend to simply lie low and avoid the subject?
7. Was there a time in your past where you denied knowing Jesus? Was there a time when you were not confronted, but still you could have spoken up and did not?
8. Do you feel shame and remorse over situations where you could have stood up for Jesus? Ask forgiveness from God, go back and correct your witness to that person where possible, and resolve, with God's help, to be courageous in the future.
9. How were Judas's and Peter's sins similar? How were their responses to guilt different?
10. How did Peter's experiences on that night prepare him for his ministry? What experiences have you had that help you communicate grace and compassion to others?

Jesus the Great King: The Sacrifice for Sinners
MARK 15:1-20

Main Idea: Jesus suffered in our place as the sacrifice for sinners.

I.   Our Great King's Silence: The Accusations and Amazement (15:1-5)
II. Our Great King's Substitution: The Injustice and Insult (15:6-14)
III. Our Great King's Suffering: The Pain and Shame (15:15-20)

When you consider the passion of the Christ, the suffering and death of Jesus, what do you see? What do you think? Is He simply a martyr dying for what He believed in like a Socrates, Savanorola, Michael and Margaretha Sattler, Mahatma Ghandi, or Martin Luther King Jr.? Was He a fool who believed He was actually the Son of God and was put to death amid His delusions of grandeur? Was He a blasphemer and false Messiah who was a threat to the well-being of Israel? Was He a political revolutionary that Rome wisely extinguished before His flame blazed out of control? Did He simply suffer the misfortune of irritating the religious leaders, who out of envy (15:10) appealed to the political pragmatism of Pilate to get rid of Him?

Or was He actually the sinless Son of God (1:1; 15:39), the God Man, who suffered in our place, took the beating we deserved, and died the death we should have died? Is He indeed the great King, the sacrifice for sinners?

It is early Friday morning. Our Lord has been betrayed, abandoned, interrogated, beaten, spit on, and denied throughout the night with no rest. He will soon be beaten nearly to death by Roman scourging (15:15) and crucified. He will die around 3:00 p.m. on Friday afternoon (15:33-37). What sinful man did to the Son of God can only make us weep. What the sinless Son of God did for man can only make us shout with joy for a "Savior King" who would suffer everything He suffered for you and for me.

Our Great King's Silence: The Accusations and Amazement
MARK 15:1-5

The Sanhedrin needs to move quickly to get the "Jesus case" before Pilate. They want Him executed before the Sabbath begins on Friday evening at sundown.

Pilate was the Roman procurator (imperial magistrate or governor) of Judea from AD 26–36. This information is helpful in dating Jesus' public ministry and is further confirmation of the Bible's historical accuracy. Pilate was a cruel and harsh governor who despised the Jews and enjoyed antagonizing them. He was also an expedient ruler who would gladly make compromises to keep the peace and stay in the good graces of Rome. Apparently Pilate held Jesus' fate in his hands.

Only one accusation concerned Pilate, so he asked Jesus, "Are you the King of the Jews?" (v. 2). This title has obvious political overtones for Pilate and Rome. Pilate, like the high priest (14:61), is an accurate, though ignorant, confessor of the Christ.

Jesus responds in a cryptic fashion to his question: "You have said so." This is neither a direct affirmation nor a denial. I think Jesus' intention is something like, "Yes, I am a king, but not the kind of king you are thinking of." As Jesus said, "My kingdom is not of this world" (John 18:36).

At this point the chief priests "began to accuse Him of many things" (Mark 15:3). Luke 23:2 provides the specifics: "We found this man subverting our nation, opposing payment of taxes to Caesar, and saying that He Himself is the Messiah, a King."

Pilate again turned to Jesus: "Are you not answering anything? Look how many things they are accusing you of!" (Mark 15:4). To his amazement, "Jesus still did not answer anything" (v. 5). Pilate would try to wash his hands of Jesus and send Him to Herod Antipas (Luke 23:6-12). Jesus would not say a single word to this evil murderer of John the Baptist. He does not toss His pearls before pigs (Matt 7:6). Once more the prophecy of Isaiah 53:7 is being fulfilled: "He was oppressed and afflicted, yet He did not open His mouth." Here is the great King's silence in the face of His accusers. Sinful men can only watch in amazement. No defense. Not a word. He will see to it that He goes to the cross.

Our Great King's Substitution: The Injustice and Insult
MARK 15:6-14

The true Son of the Father, sinless and innocent, will be beaten and crucified. The other "son of the Father," Barabbas, sinful and guilty, will be set free because Jesus became his substitute! The sovereign providence and plan of God could not be more clearly on display.

At Passover, Pilate was in the habit of releasing a prisoner, a condemned man, to gain the support and goodwill of the people. He apparently let them "make the call." Incarcerated was a notorious rebel, a "freedom fighter" and murderer named Barabbas. His name actually means "son of the father"! He was awaiting his execution. He might be a national hero to the common people, but he was a revolutionary that Rome and Pilate would gladly put to death.

The people began to petition Pilate for his annual Passover amnesty gift (v. 8). Pilate saw this as a way out of a tough situation. He had already told the Jewish leaders concerning Jesus, "I find no grounds for charging Him" (John 18:38). Further, his wife had warned him, "Have nothing to do with that righteous man, for today I've suffered terribly in a dream because of Him!" (Matt 27:19). He also knew the chief priests had only arrested Jesus out of envy (Mark 15:10). So Pilate asked the crowd, "Do you want me to release the King of the Jews for you?" (v. 9). If the people went with his option, he could release an innocent man and stick it to the Sanhedrin as well.

Things did not go as he hoped, though we know God's plan is proceeding exactly as He intended. It is easy to suspect that the religious leaders thought Pilate might pull such a stunt. They were ready. They "stirred up the crowd so that he would release Barabbas to them instead" (v. 11). Pilate then asked what he should do with Jesus (v. 12). He may have thought they would ask for him to release both Barabbas and Jesus. Again they shouted their wishes: "Crucify Him!" Pilate made one last overture: "Why? What has He done wrong?" (v. 14). The crowd became even more boisterous: "Crucify Him!"

Pilate has had enough. He publicly washes his hands, while the crowd accepts responsibility for executing the King (Matt 27:24-25). Jesus was innocent but declared to be guilty. Barabbas was guilty but was treated as though he were innocent. Jesus died in his place. He also died in our place, that in an amazing reversal we might truly become sons and daughters of the heavenly Father. Sinclair Ferguson says,

> Without knowing it, the religious leaders and Pilate and Barabbas were all part of a tapestry of grace which God was weaving for sinners. Their actions spoke louder than their words, louder than the cries of the crowds for Jesus' blood. Jesus was not dying for His own crimes, but for the crimes of others; not for His own sins, but the sins of others. He did not die for Himself, he died for us!

Ferguson then asks a most important question: "Have you ever seen what they were all too blind to notice?" (*Mark*, 257).

Our Great King's Suffering: The Pain and Shame
MARK 15:15-20

In the Gospel's record of the passion of the Christ, the emphasis does not fall on the physical suffering of Jesus—as great as it was. Mocking is clearly highlighted, but the focus is much more on the spiritual and psychological agony. Still, we would be negligent if we passed over too quickly the scourging and physical abuse He suffered.

In verse 15, Mark simply says, "And after having Jesus flogged, he handed Him over to be crucified." William Lane details what being "flogged" entailed:

> A Roman scourging was a terrifying punishment. The delinquent was stripped, bound to a post or a pillar, or sometimes simply thrown to [the] ground, and was beaten by a number of guards until his flesh hung in bleeding shreds. The instrument indicated by the Marcan text, the dreaded *flagellum*, was a scourge consisting of leather thongs plaited with several pieces of bone or lead so as to form a chain. No maximum number of strokes was prescribed by Roman law, and men condemned to flagellation frequently collapsed and died from the flogging. Josephus records that he himself had some of his opponents in Galilee scourged until their entrails were visible (*War* II.xxi.5), while the procurator Albinus had the prophet Jesus bar Hanan scourged until his bones lay visible (*War* VI. v. 3). (Lane, *Mark*, 557)

Following this life-threatening beating, "they called the whole company together." This would number about six hundred hardened Roman soldiers. (1) They clothed Him in a purple cloak, probably a faded military garment serving the purpose of a mock robe of royalty (v. 17). (2) They twisted together a mock crown, one made of thorns, and pressed it down on His head. The crown of thorns pictured God's curse on sinful humanity now being put on Jesus (Gen 3:17-18). (3) They began to mock Him again, this time with derisive salutes: "Hail, King of the Jews!" (v. 18). As the Romans would hail Caesar, so these soldiers sarcastically hailed King Jesus. (4) They hit Him again with a stick, a mock scepter (v. 19; cf. Matt 27:29-30). (5) They continued spitting on and insulting Him in this manner. (6) They knelt down in mock worship. (7) When they had finished ridiculing Him, they "led Him out to crucify Him."

Completely alone, humiliated, naked, and beaten nearly to death, our Savior endured yet again ridicule, shame, and pain at the hands of sinful men, at the hands of those He came to save. Oh, how heaven must have looked on in disbelief! Perhaps the angels wept. The Father sent His beloved

Son to rescue and redeem a rebel race. Look at what they have done to our Lord! But look, and never forget, what our Lord has done for us!

Conclusion

One of the majestic hymns of the faith begins, "Crown Him with many crowns, the Lamb upon His throne" (Thring and Bridges, "Crown Him, " 1851). This song rightly looks to heaven. However, here we see the Lamb on a different throne, the throne of His cross. He is crowned with a "crown of thorns" (15:17), a reminder of the curse from which He has redeemed us (Gen 3:15-18).

"Christ has redeemed us from the curse of the law by becoming a curse for us, because it is written: Everyone who is hung on a tree is cursed" (Gal 3:13; see Deut 21:23). Jesus suffered the injustice and insult I should have suffered. Jesus experienced the shame and pain I should have experienced. Jesus bore the guilt and curse I should have borne. The shepherd was struck that the sheep might be saved. The great King was tortured and killed that His people might live.

I truly "stand amazed in the presence of Jesus the Nazarene, and wonder how He could love me, a sinner condemned unclean! He bore my sin and my sorrow and made them His very own. He bore my burden to Calvary and suffered and died alone" (Gabriel, "Amazed," 1905). Jesus is the great King, the sacrifice for sinners!

Reflect and Discuss

1. Name some martyrs from history. What did they accomplish by their deaths? How does Jesus' death compare with that of these martyrs?
2. If Jesus had been primarily interested in avoiding execution, what defense might He have offered before Pilate? Why did He remain silent?
3. What were Pilate's concerns regarding Jesus' trial?
4. What did the Sanhedrin hope to accomplish at Jesus' trial?
5. What role did the Sanhedrin's instigation of the crowds play? Have you ever been in a situation where a group did something the individuals in it later regretted? How did this get started? How could it be avoided?
6. "Substitutionary atonement" sounds complicated. How would you explain it to a children's Sunday school class? What would you call it?
7. Jesus was (1) psychologically ridiculed, (2) physically beaten, (3) spiritually abandoned by God, and (4) mortally executed. How do these torments compare?
8. As a sinner for whom Christ suffered and died, what is your complicity in each of His torments?

9. What is the value in contemplating the appalling enormity of Jesus' suffering? Did the movie *The Passion of the Christ* (2004) go too far in its depiction of His physical suffering? Explain.
10. What does your church currently do to commemorate the arrest, trial, and crucifixion of Christ? How should it be commemorated?

The Murder of the Great King

MARK 15:21-47

Main Idea: Jesus was crucified, died, and was buried for sinners.

I. Jesus Was Crucified to Save Others, Not Himself (15:21-32).
    A. The great King was crucified naked (15:21-24).
    B. The great King was crucified with sinners (15:25-27).
    C. The great King was crucified amid ridicule (15:29-30).
    D. The great King was crucified to save others (15:31-32).
II. Jesus Died Forsaken Even Though He Was God's Son (15:33-41).
    A. The great King died in darkness (15:33).
    B. The great King died alone (15:34-36).
    C. The great King died and opened the way to God (15:37-39).
    D. The great King died with women looking on in love (15:40-41).
III. Jesus Was Buried Because He Was Dead (15:42-47).
    A. The great King was buried in a rich man's tomb (15:42-46).
    B. The great King was buried, and women saw where He was laid (15:47).

The crucifixion of Jesus Christ, the Son of God, was not an accident of human history. It was a divine appointment prophesied in Scripture. As Isaiah 53:10 says, "The LORD was pleased to crush Him severely." And it was the fulfillment of numerous prophecies that had anticipated a day that was both tragic and glorious all at the same time:

1. **Psalm 69:21**	**Mark 15:23 (also 15:36)**
For my thirst they gave me vinegar to drink.	They tried to give Him wine mixed with myrrh.

2. **Psalm 22:18**
They divided my garments among themselves, and they cast lots for my clothing.

Mark 15:24
Then they . . . divided His clothes, casting lots for them.

3. **Isaiah 53:12**
He . . . was counted among the rebels.

Mark 15:27
They crucified two criminals with Him, one on His right and one on His left.

4. **Psalm 22:6-8**
But I am a worm and not a man, scorned by men and despised by people. Everyone who sees me mocks me; they sneer and shake their heads: "He relies on the LORD; let Him rescue him; let the LORD deliver him, since He takes pleasure in him."

Mark 15:29-32
Those who passed by were yelling insults at Him, shaking their heads, and saying, "Ha! The One who would demolish the sanctuary and build it in three days, save Yourself by coming down from the cross!" In the same way, the chief priests with the scribes were mocking Him to one another and saying, "He saved others; He cannot save Himself! Let the Messiah, the King of Israel, come down now from the cross, so that we may see and believe."

5. **Psalm 22:16**
They pierced my hands and my feet.

Mark 15:24
Then they crucified Him.

6. **Amos 8:9**
And in that day—this is the declaration of the Lord GOD—I will make the sun go down at noon; I will darken the land in the daytime.

Mark 15:33
When it was noon, darkness came over the whole land until three in the afternoon.

7. **Psalm 22:1**
My God, my God, why have you forsaken me?

Mark 15:34
My God, My God, why have You forsaken Me?

8. **Isaiah 53:9**
They made His grave with the wicked and with a rich man in His death.

Mark 15:43,46
Joseph of Arimathea, a prominent member of the Sanhedrin . . . bought some fine linen . . . and wrapped Him in the linen. Then he placed Him in a tomb cut out of rock.

What King Jesus endured on the cross took place right on schedule, exactly according to divine plan. The horror of it is also the glory of it. Jesus is dying the death we should have died that we might live now and forever.

He is our Substitute. Jesus died our death. He is the Passover lamb (Exod 12) who *saves* us with His blood. He is the covenant keeper (Exod 24) who *seals* us with His blood.

He is our Propitiation. Jesus endured our condemnation and bears the full wrath of God on our behalf. The "cup" of the cross is not primarily *physical* suffering: it is mainly *spiritual* suffering (Mark 14:36; Ps 75:8; Isa 51:17). Jesus was not a *martyr* on the cross; He was a *Savior* who experienced divine wrath and satisfied the holiness and justice of God. "Before the cross, we were *afraid* of God; because of the cross, we are now *friends* of God" (Platt, "Centerpiece").

He is our Reconciliation. Jesus suffered our separation that we might be brought back to God. The cry on the cross is a cry of physical agony, spiritual anguish, and most of all *relational alienation* from His Father. The curse of the cross is this: Jesus was cut off from the Father's favorable *presence*; He endured the full penalty of our *disobedience* (2 Cor 5:21). Before the cross, we were separated from God's presence; because of the cross, we are now given access into God's presence (Mark 15:38).

Jesus Was Crucified to Save Others, Not Himself
MARK 15:21-32

Crucifixion was the cruelest, most painful, most humiliating form of capital punishment in the ancient world. And Rome had perfected the technique to ensure maximum suffering. The shame of such a death was so great that the Roman orator Cicero said, "The very word 'cross' should be far removed not only from the person of a Roman citizen but from his thoughts, his eyes, and his ears . . . the mere mention of them, that is unworthy of a Roman citizen and a free man" (*Defense*, 5, 16).

Two thousand years of church history have unfortunately domesticated and sanitized the cross for modern persons. The horror is gone. And our Gospels contain few details. Why? First, people in Jesus' day were fully familiar with the gruesome rood; they had seen it. Second, it was not the suffering that was important but the One who was suffering—the Son of God taking away the sins of the world (John 1:29).

The Great King Was Crucified Naked (Mark 15:21-24)

Normally, a man condemned to crucifixion would carry the cross beam. It could weigh as much as one hundred pounds. Jesus began by carrying it (John 19:17), but He apparently fell and needed help. A man named

Simon, from Cyrene in North Africa (see Acts 2:10), was enlisted to give aid. It is possible he was a black man.

Jesus was taken to a place called Golgotha, meaning "place of a skull." This would have been outside the city walls and along a public highway. The Romans wanted to show how they handled criminals.

They offered Jesus "wine mixed with myrrh" (Mark 15:23; cf. Ps 69:21), a primitive drug that would dull the pain. Jesus refused; He would face the agony to come with full control of His mental faculties.

They stripped our Lord of His clothing and gambled to see who would go home with these meager prizes (cf. Ps 22:18). It is possible our Savior died completely naked. Maybe He was allowed to retain His loincloth. Either way, He was humiliated. John Calvin captures something of the theological import: "The Evangelists portray the Son of God as stripped of His clothes that we may know the wealth gained for us by this nakedness, for it shall dress us in God's sight. God willed His Son to be stripped that we should appear freely, with the angels, in the garments of his righteousness and fullness of all good things" (Calvin, *Harmony*, 194).

The Great King Was Crucified with Sinners (Mark 15:25-27)

Jesus was crucified at the third hour, that is, around 9:00 a.m. As an act of further mockery, they nailed the charge against Him above His head: "The King of the Jews."

"They crucified two criminals with Him, one on His right and one on His left." As Isaiah 53:12 had promised, He "was counted with the rebels." Ironically, James and John had asked to be on Jesus' right and left "in Your glory" (Mark 10:37). Jesus informed them they did not know what they were asking. This is the hour when the Father will glorify the Son and the Son will glorify the Father (John 17:1). This is not the glory James and John had in mind.

The Great King Was Crucified amid Ridicule (Mark 15:29-30)

Jesus is again subjected to mockery and verbal abuse. Those walking past Him or hanging around for the show "were yelling insults at Him" continuously. They were also "shaking their heads" at Him in ridicule and sarcasm, and they taunted Him for His claim to "demolish the sanctuary and build it in three days." Before He takes on that assignment, He might first consider His immediate problem: "Save Yourself by coming down from the cross!"

This temptation to come down from the cross is the same one Satan threw at Him in the wilderness (Matt 4:1-11; Luke 4:1-13). It is the same temptation He faced just a few hours earlier in the garden of Gethsemane to forego the cup of suffering (Mark 14:36). Up to the last moment, the evil one is trying to persuade Jesus to reject the cross. He did not want Him there! He knew it would be his ruin and our redemption.

The Great King Was Crucified to Save Others (Mark 15:31-32)

The religious leaders could not resist getting in one last dig at the great King: "He saved others; He cannot save Himself!" They too challenged Him to come down from the cross; then they would believe. How ironic. If our Lord was to save others, Himself He could not save. And save Himself He would not do. These men claim they would have believed if He had come down from the cross, but we believe precisely because He stayed on it!

The two robbers who were crucified with Jesus "were taunting Him" repeatedly (v. 32). However, one of them will have a change of heart before the day ends (Luke 23:39-43). He saw something in Jesus that moved him from insulting Him to trusting Him. He would not be disappointed. He would meet the Lord after death in paradise. We must never forget: no sinner will be disappointed who flees to the crucified King. It is never too late!

Jesus Died Forsaken Even Though He Was God's Son
MARK 15:33-41

Mark highlights six events as Jesus died: (1) the darkness (v. 33); (2) His cry of anguish (vv. 34-36); (3) a final cry and His death (v. 37); (4) the tearing of the temple curtain (v. 38); (5) the confession of the Roman centurion (v. 39); and (6) the witness of women (vv. 40-41).

When you consider all four Gospels, Jesus uttered "Seven Sayings from the Cross."

1. "Father, forgive them, because they don't know what they are doing." Luke 23:34 (Forgiveness)
2. "I assure you: Today you will be with Me in paradise." Luke 23:43 (Salvation)
3. "Woman, here is your son." John 19:26 (Relationship)
4. "My God, My God, why have You forsaken Me?" Matthew 27:46; Mark 15:34 (Abandonment)
5. "I'm thirsty!" John 19:28 (Distress)
6. "It is finished!" John 19:30; cf. Mark 15:37 (Triumph)
7. "Father, into Your hands I entrust My Spirit." Luke 23:46 (Reunion)

Mark will only record the words of one (15:34) and the "cry" of another (15:37). His focus is the forsakenness of the great King.

The Great King Died in Darkness (Mark 15:33)

Jesus has been on the cross for three hours. Suddenly at about "noon," darkness engulfed the whole land "until three." This was not a solar eclipse, since the Passover was held at the time of a full moon. This is a miracle of God, a cosmic sign of God's judgment on sin poured out on His Son (Isa 5:25-30; Amos 8:9-10; Mic 3:5-7; Zeph 1:14-15). The ninth plague in Egypt was a three-day period of darkness followed by the final plague, the death of the firstborn (Exod 10:22-11:9). Wiersbe notes, "The darkness of Calvary was an announcement that God's firstborn and Beloved Son, the Lamb of God, was giving His life for the sins of the world!" (*Be Diligent*, 148–49).

The Great King Died Alone (Mark 15:34-36)

The cry of verse 34 may be the most heart-wrenching one in the whole Bible. It is a quote from Psalm 22:1, and it identifies Jesus as the righteous sufferer of that psalm. Our Savior cried out in Aramaic, His mother tongue, "*Eloi, Eloi, lema sabachthani?*" which means, "My God, My God, why have You forsaken Me?" The cry was not one of physical pain, psychological confusion, or dread of death. No, it was the cry of the Son of God, who was now experiencing something He had never known in all of eternity: separation from and forsakenness by God. Tim Keller captures beautifully the transaction of the moment:

> This forsakenness, this loss, was between the Father and the Son, who had loved each other from all eternity. This love was infinitely long, absolutely perfect, and Jesus was losing it. Jesus was being cut out of the dance.
>
> Jesus, the Maker of the world, was being unmade. Why? Jesus was experiencing our judgment day. "My God, my God, why have you forsaken me?" It wasn't a rhetorical question. And the answer is: For you, for me, for us. *Jesus was forsaken by God so that we would never have to be.* The judgment that should have fallen on us fell instead on Jesus. (Keller, *King's Cross*, 202; emphasis in original)

Jesus' cry and the darkness that covered the land declared the same truth: there was real abandonment from the Father as Jesus took on every sin of every man, woman, and child. As Isaiah 53:6 teaches, "The Lord has punished Him for the iniquity of us all." This was the price He paid as "a ransom for many" (Mark 10:45).

And why "My God" and not "My Father"? Because in this one moment in all of time and eternity, He views Himself and knows Himself not as the Father's Son but as the sinner's sacrifice.

Some standing by mistakenly thought He was calling out to Elijah. They waited, probably with additional ridicule, to see whether Elijah would come to take Him down. However, if the Father would not intervene to spare His Son, it is certain Elijah would not come. The great King would die alone as the sinner's substitute.

God separated from God—who can understand? I may never understand it, but I will forever praise Him for it.

The Great King Died and Opened the Way to God (Mark 15:37-39)

"Jesus let out a loud cry" and died (v. 37). Almost certainly it was the cry recorded in John 19:30, "It is finished!" Atonement has been made, and the work of salvation is done. As tangible evidence, "the curtain of the sanctuary was split in two"—and do not miss this—"from top to bottom" (Mark 15:38). This was God's doing. The significance of the tearing of the curtain that separates the holy place from the holy of holies is rich in symbolic allusions. Pastor Sam Storms notes at least three:

> (1) It points to the complete, perfect, and altogether sufficient sacrifice for sins that Jesus has offered in himself on the cross. The sin that had created a barrier both spiritually and naturally between God and man has been atoned for. (2) It also points to the end of the Mosaic Covenant and its laws, which have been fulfilled in Christ. The "old order" has passed away! (3) It points to the fact that God in all his glory is now freely and fully accessible to all men and women who come to him by faith in Jesus Christ. For centuries before the coming of Christ, God had confined the revelation of his glory and majesty to the Holy of Holies. Now he bursts forth to dwell no longer behind a veil in a house built with wood and stone and precious jewels, but to dwell in the hearts of his people. See Hebrews 10:19-22. (Storms, "The Cross and the Cry")

Now we arrive at the destination Mark has intended since 1:1. On the lips of a Gentile Roman Centurion, we hear the confession, "This man really was God's Son" (15:39). It was not one of His marvelous miracles or tremendous teachings that evoked this confession; it was His passion. Like the centurion, Mark wants his readers to confess Jesus as the Christ. The question is, have you? Will you? It is a question only you can answer.

The Great King Died with Women Looking On in Love (Mark 15:40-41)

While no men are mentioned by Mark, he does note three women who were there: Mary of Magdala whom Jesus had delivered from demonic possession (Luke 8:2), a second Mary who had two sons named James and Joses, and Salome who is only mentioned by name in Mark (15:40; 16:1). This last was the mother of the disciples James and John, and probably the sister of Jesus' mother (Matt 27:56).

Their presence establishes eyewitnesses to His death and burial (Mark 15:47). Further, they were true disciples who had followed Him and ministered to Him (v. 41). They, along with "many other women," were faithful to Him to the bitter end. They may have watched the brutal events of the cross "from a distance," but unlike His male disciples their devotion was not marked by absence. Their love and devotion to Jesus would not go unrewarded (16:4-8)!

Jesus Was Buried Because He Was Dead
MARK 15:42-47

Jesus is dead. John 19:34 tells us "one of the soldiers pierced His side with a spear" just to be certain. Normally, a man who died by crucifixion would be left on the cross to rot or be eaten by dogs or birds of prey. What was left of the corpse would then be thrown into the Valley of Hinnom (see comments on Mark 9:43-48). Jesus, however, would be spared this humiliation because (1) Jewish law demanded that even executed criminals receive a proper burial and that those hanged on a tree be taken down and buried before sunset (Deut 21:23), and (2) Joseph of Arimathea "boldly went in to Pilate and asked for Jesus' body" (Mark 15:43).

The Great King Was Buried in a Rich Man's Tomb (Mark 15:42-46)

It is late Friday afternoon. Preparation for the Sabbath would already be underway so any decision as to what to do with the body of Jesus must be made quickly (v. 42).

Joseph of Arimathea, who (1) was "a prominent member of the Sanhedrin" and (2) "was himself looking forward to the kingdom of God . . . asked for Jesus' body" (v. 43). Luke 23:51 informs us he did not support the Council's decision to seek Jesus' execution. He may have even thought Jesus was the Messiah (John 19:38). As far as he and the others could tell, such hopes had now been lost. Still, his love for Jesus moved him to go public and make clear his affection for Jesus.

Pilate was surprised to hear that Jesus "was already dead." Often, a man would suffer several days on the cross. Receiving confirmation from the centurion that Jesus was in fact dead, "he gave the corpse to Joseph."

Joseph purchased "some fine linen," wrapped the Savior in it, and put Him in his own tomb. Then "he rolled a stone against the entrance." Once again the Scripture was fulfilled, "They made His grave . . . with a rich man" (Isa 53:9).

The Great King Was Buried, and Women Saw Where He Was Laid (Mark 15:47)

In addition to Joseph of Arimathea and Nicodemus (see John 19:38-42), Mary Magdalene and Mary the mother of Joses "were watching where He was placed." Thus the only people at His grave were two Pharisees and two women. The apostles, who had professed proudly that they would die for Him (Mark 14:31), are in hiding. By contrast those who once remained in the shadows or were hardly noticed by the "really important" people are there by His grave. They do not care who knows of their loyalty and love for Jesus.

Conclusion

And so it is over. He is finished. Or . . . is He? I know it's Friday. But Sunday is coming! S. M. Lockridge (1913–2000) was a powerful and passionate African-American preacher. He captured so well what just happened . . . and what's coming in just a few days.

> *It's Friday.* Jesus is praying. Peter's a-sleeping. Judas is betraying. But Sunday's comin'.
>
> *It's Friday.* Pilate's struggling. The Council is conspiring. The crowd is vilifying. They don't even know that Sunday's comin'.
>
> *It's Friday.* The Disciples are running like sheep without a shepherd. Mary's crying. Peter is denying. But they don't know that Sunday's a-comin'.
>
> *It's Friday.* The Romans beat my Jesus. They robe Him in scarlet. They crown Him with thorns. But they don't know that Sunday's comin'.
>
> *It's Friday.* See Jesus walking to Calvary. His blood dripping. His body stumbling. And His spirit's burdened. But you see, it's only Friday. Sunday's comin'.
>
> *It's Friday.* The world's winning. People are sinning. And evil's grinning.

It's Friday. The soldiers nail my Savior's hands to the cross. They nail my Savior's feet to the cross. And then they raise Him up next to criminals.

It's Friday. But let me tell you something: Sunday's comin'.

It's Friday. The disciples are questioning, what has happened to their King. And the Pharisees are celebrating that their scheming has been achieved. But they don't know it's only Friday. Sunday's comin'.

It's Friday. He's hanging on the cross. Feeling forsaken by His Father. Left alone and dying. Can nobody save Him? Ooooh, it's Friday. But Sunday's comin'.

It's Friday. The earth trembles. The sky grows dark. My King yields His spirit.

It's Friday. Hope is lost. Death has won. Sin has conquered. And Satan's just a-laughin'.

It's Friday. Jesus is buried. A soldier stands guard. And a rock is rolled into place. But *It's Friday.* It is only *Friday.* Sunday is a-comin'! (Lockridge, "It's Friday")

Reflect and Discuss

1. How would you respond to someone who says that any man could have fulfilled these prophecies simply by manipulating events and doing certain things?

2. Theologians use the terms "substitutionary atonement," "propitiation," and "reconciliation" to describe what Jesus accomplished. Should the church continue to use these terms? How would you explain these terms to a person not familiar with theological/biblical concepts?

3. When you see a cross, do you think of it as "glorious" or "horrible"? Explain.

4. What took place that showed the inhumanity and cruelty of crucifixion as a method of execution? Why did God ordain that this would be done to His Son?

5. Could Jesus have avoided going to the cross? Was He capable of coming down from the cross? What kept Him there?

6. How would you respond to someone who said the darkness that descended during the crucifixion was a natural phenomenon?

7. Explain in your own words why Jesus exclaimed, "My God, My God, why have You forsaken Me?"

8. How might the Jews have responded to the tearing of the curtain in the sanctuary? What does it mean for Gentiles?

9. How would you respond to those who theorize that Jesus didn't really die on the cross? Why is this fact important?

10. What is the significance in Mark reporting that, of all Jesus' followers, only a few of the women were there during the crucifixion, and only they and two converted Jewish leaders were there at His burial?

The Resurrection of the Great King

MARK 16:1-8

Main Idea: Jesus' resurrection is historically certain and eternally significant. In it He defeated the power of death and guaranteed the future resurrection of His people.

I. The Witness of Mark's Gospel (16:1-8)
II. Resurrection Options
III. Naturalistic or Alternative Theories That Reject the Resurrection
IV. Evidences for the Bodily Resurrection of Jesus
V. Why the Resurrection Is Important

I have a friend who is an atheist or, at least, an agnostic. When he and I were visiting, I asked him, "What is the bottom line when it comes to Christianity?" He responded, "That's easy. It is the resurrection of Jesus Christ." He then quickly added, "If the resurrection is true, then so are a number of other things: (1) There is a God; (2) Jesus is that God; (3) the Bible is true; (4) heaven and hell are real; and (5) Jesus makes the difference whether you go to one or the other."

My friend is right on all counts. I have often wished my seminary students and fellow theologians saw the issue as clearly. Christianity stands or falls on the historical, bodily resurrection of Jesus from the dead. No resurrection, no Christianity. In 1 Corinthians 15:17, Paul plainly writes, "And if Christ has not been raised, your faith is worthless; you are still in your sins."

In 16:1-8, Mark will note several evidences for the resurrection. We will quickly examine them and then provide a bird's-eye view of this most critical issue of the Christian faith. We will examine the different theories that have been set forth and conclude with the massive evidence that leads us to proclaim, "He is risen! He is risen indeed!" The witnesses to the resurrection are rock solid!

The Witness of Mark's Gospel
MARK 16:1-8

Two of the women at the cross (15:40) saw where Jesus was buried (15:47).
When the Sabbath was over, these women—Mary Magdalene and Mary the
mother of James—along with Salome "bought spices, so they could go and
anoint" the body of Jesus. They knew exactly where He was buried, and they
wanted to perfume His body in a final act of devotion.

"Very early . . . at sunrise" on Sunday morning "they went to the tomb."
They were concerned about how they would get to His body—the stone in
front of the tomb "was very large." When they arrived at the tomb, they were
met with a surprise: "The stone . . . had been rolled away." They entered the
tomb to find an even bigger surprise: "They saw a young man dressed in a
long white robe" (16:5). There is no doubt he was an angel, and of course
"they were amazed and alarmed." Fear, wonder, amazement, astonishment,
and distress gripped their souls. This word "alarmed" is the same word used
in Mark 14:33 to describe the agony Jesus experienced in the garden of
Gethsemane.

Luke (24:3-4) and John (20:12) inform us that there were actually two
angels present, the number required to establish a valid witness (Deut 17:6;
19:15). Matthew (28:5) and Mark focus on the spokesman, the one who
conversed with the women.

Aware of their distress, the angel seeks to calm and assure them by
revealing the greatest surprise of all (16:6): "Don't be alarmed. . . . You are
looking for Jesus the Nazarene, who was crucified. He has been resurrected!
He is not here! See the place where they put Him." I deeply appreciate the
insights of James Edwards at this point:

> The Crucified One, says the angel, has been raised! The angel invites
> the women to see the place where they last saw the body of Jesus
> (15:47). The references to the place of his burial and to Jesus as the
> crucified one are of crucial importance. The women are not directed
> to a mystical or spiritual experience or to a numinous encounter.
> They are directed specifically to Jesus, who died by a crucifixion they
> witnessed, was buried in a place they witnessed, and now has been res-
> urrected. The verbs in verse 6 refer to both sides of the Easter event.
> The announcement of the divine emissary establishes an inseparable
> continuity between the historical Jesus and the resurrected Jesus.
> The one whom the angel invites them to know is the one whom they
> have known. The announcement of the gospel is literally, the *gospel*,
> good news, and the place from which the gospel is first preached is
> the empty tomb that both received and gave up the Crucified One.

A new order of existence is inaugurated. . . . At this moment and in this place the women are witnessing "the kingdom of God come with power" (9:1). (Edwards, *Mark*, 494)

The evidence is undeniable. The tomb is empty! Now the women have a new assignment. There is no need to anoint a dead body that is no longer there. It is time to start proclaiming the good news of a risen Lord and Savior who has left the tomb! The angel instructs them to begin with those who had abandoned and denied Him: "But go, tell His disciples and Peter, 'He is going ahead of you to Galilee; you will see Him there just as He told you'" (v. 7). What a word of grace, forgiveness, hope, and promise. What a pledge for a new beginning. Peter would especially be grateful for this word!

Stunned, the women "started running from the tomb" (v. 8). They were overcome with "trembling and astonishment," and "they said nothing to anyone, since they were afraid." Sinclair Ferguson helps us put things in perspective:

> Should they not have returned home rejoicing in the news they had heard? Is there not something unexpected about this response? That in itself is a mark of its authenticity (if we were to invent the story we would not end it in this way). But it is more. In Mark's Gospel, this fear is always man's response to the breaking in of the power of God. It is the fear the disciples experienced when Jesus stilled the storm; the fear of the Gerasenes when Jesus delivered Legion; the fear of the disciples as they saw Jesus setting his face to Jerusalem to die on the cross. This fear is the response of men and women to Jesus as he shows his power and majesty as the Son of God. (Ferguson, *Mark*, 271)

And thus Mark's Gospel comes to an end, and an abrupt one at that. Verses 9-20 are not found in the oldest and most reliable manuscripts. Mark's sudden ending was what he wanted. It makes clear that the disciples of Jesus were stunned by all of this. They did not expect the resurrection. They did not know how to respond. How would they respond to all of this? How will you?

Resurrection Options

On the issue of Jesus' bodily resurrection, there are three basic options. The first is that *Jesus' resurrection is false*. It was a great hoax. Jesus did not rise from the dead and certain persons, probably the disciples, fabricated the story and pulled off perhaps the greatest hoax of all time. The second option is that *Jesus' resurrection is fiction*. It is ancient mythology. The early church made Jesus into someone He really was not by telling stories they embellished over time. Eventually, believers turned Him into God incarnate who died on a cross for our sins and later rose from the dead. Although none of these events really happened, the stories about Jesus continue to evoke wonder and inspire us to live more noble lives, even today. The third option is that *Jesus' resurrection is fact* and is, therefore, the supreme event of history. The New Testament accurately records the historical and supernatural resurrection of Jesus of Nazareth from the dead. His resurrection was bodily and permanent. These are the viable options. There really are no others.

Naturalistic or Alternative Theories That Reject the Resurrection

Naturalistic theories attempt to explain away the idea that Jesus was bodily resurrected by the supernatural power of God. These theories prefer *any* naturalistic (or mystical) explanation over a supernatural one. Ten theories are worth noting, and an additional one (10) that I will throw in for comic relief!

1. *The swoon theory: Jesus did not really die but fainted because of the enormous physical punishment He suffered.* Later regaining consciousness in the cool, damp tomb, He unwrapped Himself from His grave clothes. He then managed to move aside the large stone that sealed the tomb. Jesus emerged bruised and bleeding; then He convinced His followers that He had risen from the dead.

An example of this theory is the best-seller *The Passover Plot*, in which Hugh Schonfield says Jesus planned the whole thing with help from Joseph of Arimathea. Jesus was drugged while on the cross, making it appear that He had died. Unfortunately, He was seriously injured and actually died a short time later. Barbara Thiering says Jesus was given snake poison to fake His death and later recovered. He would go on to marry Mary Magdalene and later Lydia, and He would father several children!

2. *The spirit theory: Jesus was not raised bodily, but He returned in a spirit form.* This view is held by the Jehovah's Witnesses cult, which teaches that Jesus was created by God as the archangel Michael and that while on earth He was only a man. Following His death on the cross, God restored Jesus in a spiritual form only. The Watchtower Society asserts, "King Christ Jesus was put to death in the flesh and was resurrected an invisible spirit creature."

3. *The hallucination theory: Jesus preconditioned His disciples to hallucinate by means of hypnosis.* Ian Wilson says Jesus may have "prepared his disciples

for his resurrection using the technique that modern hypnotists call post-hypnotic suggestion. By this means he could have effectively conditioned them to hallucinate his appearances in response to certain prearranged cues" (Wilson, *Jesus*, 141).

4. The vision theory: the disciples had experiences they interpreted or understood to be literal appearances of the risen Jesus. The disciples saw visionary appearances of the risen Christ, and He communicated to them a call and a mission. This view is similar to the spirit theory.

5. The legend or myth theory basically agrees with the infamous Jesus Seminar. Over time the Jesus stories were embellished and exaggerated. The resurrection is a "wonder story" indicating the significance the mythical Jesus held for His followers.

6. The stolen-body theory: the soldiers who guarded Jesus' tomb were bribed by the Jewish leaders to lie and say, "His disciples came during the night and stole Him while we were sleeping." It is the earliest naturalistic theory, going back to Matthew 28:11-15. Occasionally, it is alleged that the body could also have been stolen by the Jewish leaders, the Romans, or even Joseph of Arimathea.

7. The wrong-tomb theory: belief in Jesus' bodily resurrection rests on a simple mistake. First the women and later the men went to the wrong tomb by accident. Finding that tomb empty, they erroneously concluded that Jesus had risen from the dead.

8. The lie-for-profit theory: Jesus' death by crucifixion was a huge disappointment, but His followers saw a way to turn it for financial profit. They proclaimed that Jesus had risen, they built a substantial following, and they fleeced the people who believed their lie. This theory assigns contemptible motives to the disciples, charging them with perhaps the greatest religious hoax ever perpetrated.

9. The mistaken-identity theory: the women mistook someone else for Jesus. They perhaps ran into a gardener or a caretaker. Because it was early in the morning and still dark, they could not clearly see this man. They wrongly thought he was Jesus.

10. The twin theory: Jesus had an identical twin brother. In a 1995 debate with Christian apologist William Lane Craig, philosopher Robert Greg Cavin argued this theory. Separated at birth, the brothers did not see each other again until the crucifixion. Following Jesus' death, His twin conjured up a messianic identity and mission for Jesus, stole His body, and pretended to be the risen Jesus. All we can say in response is, "Incredible! What an imagination!"

11. *The Muslim theory: the biblical witness of Jesus' crucifixion is false; God provided a substitute for Jesus*, perhaps even making the person look like Jesus. Surah 4:157 in the Qur'an says, "They declared: 'We have put to death the Messiah Jesus the son of Mary, the apostle of Allah.' They did not kill him, nor did they crucify him, but they thought they did." Muslims do not agree on who took Jesus' place. Candidates include Judas, Pilate, Simon of Cyrene, or even one of the disciples. Muslims do not believe in Jesus' bodily resurrection because they do not believe He died on the cross. Instead, Surah 4:158 declares, "Allah took him up unto Himself."

Evidences for the Bodily Resurrection of Jesus

Virtually all scholars acknowledge a number of historical facts surrounding Jesus' death, burial, and resurrection: (1) Jesus died on a Roman cross by crucifixion. (2) Jesus was buried in a tomb not far from the crucifixion site. (3) Jesus' death threw the disciples into a state of despondency, believing their Lord was now dead. (4) Jesus' tomb was discovered to be empty shortly after His burial. (5) The disciples had real experiences that convinced them that Jesus had risen from the dead and was alive. (6) These experiences with the risen Jesus radically transformed the disciples into bold witnesses of His resurrection, which led to martyrdom for many of them. (7) The message of Jesus' death, burial, and resurrection was the heart of the gospel from the beginning. (8) This gospel was preached in Jerusalem, the city where Jesus had been crucified and buried. (9) The good news of Christ's death and resurrection was foundational in the birth of the Christian church. (10) Sunday became the day of worship for the church in celebration of the Lord's resurrection on that day. (11) James, Jesus' half brother and an unbeliever, was converted following an appearance of his resurrected brother. (12) Saul, a persecutor of Christians, was converted to Christianity following an appearance of the risen Christ. Because these facts are well-attested and accepted, any theory or explanation of the empty tomb must properly account for them.

No one witnessed the actual resurrection of Jesus. The proclamation of Jesus' resurrection is based on the fact that He died, He was buried, the tomb in which He was buried was discovered to be empty, and the disciples had experiences that convinced them that Jesus had supernaturally and bodily risen from the dead. Having established these historical facts, we can build a strong case for Jesus' bodily resurrection based on 14 evidences.

1. *The failure of naturalistic or alternative theories to explain the event.* Naturalistic arguments did not stand up to careful analysis. Virtually all of them have

been abandoned or substantially revised. Proponents were selective in the biblical data they affirmed.

2. *The birth of the disciples' faith and the radical change in their lives.* Something happened that caused Jesus' followers to believe they had genuine encounters with the risen Lord. These encounters with Jesus changed them from fearful cowards in hiding to bold witnesses of the resurrected Christ. In addition, according to church tradition, the 11 apostles, with the possible exception of John, died as martyrs, still proclaiming Jesus as the risen Lord. Although people will die for a lie if they think it is the truth, they will not die for what they know to be a lie.

3. *The empty tomb and the discarded grave clothes.* Paul's early testimony in 1 Corinthians 15 supports the truth of the empty tomb, and the account itself is simple and lacks legendary development. The details are not fantastic, including only some discarded clothes.

4. *The fact that women saw the empty tomb first.* In the Jewish culture of the first century, women were not qualified to be witnesses in a legal proceeding. It is astonishing that the Bible records that women saw the risen Jesus first. If the early church were making up a story to persuade people to believe that Jesus rose from the dead, it is inconceivable that they would say women were the first witnesses to the event. The only reason to do so is that women did, in fact, see Him first.

5. *The change in the day of worship from the Sabbath to Sunday.* For centuries Jewish identity had been connected to the observance of the Sabbath, a day that is honored and kept sacred to the Lord. Yet something extraordinary happened around AD 30 that caused a large group of Jews in Jerusalem to change their day of worship from the Sabbath to Sunday. That event is the bodily resurrection of Jesus from the dead.

6. *The unlikely nature of mass hallucination.* Mass hallucination is actually impossible! Hallucinations are inner, subjective experiences of the mind. They occur personally and individually, not as a group experience.

7. *Postresurrection appearances.* The New Testament records many occasions when Jesus appeared to His followers after His resurrection (e.g., Matt 28; Luke 24; John 20–21; Acts 1; 1 Cor 15; Rev 1). The disciples claimed that Jesus appeared at different times and to different people. Some appearances were to groups while others were to individuals. The differing though complementary nature of the resurrection appearances support their authenticity. The appearances lasted for 40 days and then came to an abrupt

stop after Jesus' ascension back to heaven. No other compelling alternative explanation exists.

8. *The 50-day interval between the resurrection and the bold and public proclamation of the gospel at Pentecost in Jerusalem.* Jesus' disciples did not proclaim the gospel of the risen Lord for 50 days after the event took place. Why? They waited until Jesus had ascended (see Luke 24; Acts 1) and until the Holy Spirit had come to empower them for witness (see Acts 2). Christ had to leave before they would act on their own, and the Spirit had to come to give them boldness for witness.

9. *The inability of the Jewish leaders and the Romans to disprove the message of the empty tomb.* It is an undeniable fact of history that those who opposed Jesus could not disprove His resurrection. The disciples could not have preached the resurrection in Jerusalem had the tomb not been empty. The Christian movement could have been quickly crushed by producing Jesus' dead corpse. No one was able to do so because there was no body to produce.

10. *The unexpected nature of Jesus' bodily resurrection.* The disciples did not anticipate that Jesus would rise from the dead though He had predicted this miracle on several occasions (see Mark 8:31-33; 9:31-32; 10:32-34). In fact, Mark 9:32 *tells* us they did not understand. When Jesus was crucified, their hopes were dashed. The disciples being fearful and despondent is especially fatal to any type of hallucination or hypnosis theory.

11. *The conversion of two skeptics: James and Paul.* James, the half brother of Jesus, was an unbeliever in Jesus as Messiah prior to His crucifixion (John 7:5). Yet something transformed James from a doubter to a believer, from a skeptic to a leader in the church at Jerusalem, from one who thought his brother was mad (see Mark 3:21) to one who willingly suffered martyrdom for the gospel. Saul of Tarsus violently persecuted the church (see Acts 7:58; 8:1-3; 9:1-2). Something changed him from a persecutor of Christ to a missionary and evangelist for Christ. His own testimony affirms that he had not been open to the gospel, but he saw the resurrected Christ (see Acts 9:3-6; 22:6-10; 26:12-19; 1 Cor 15:8; Gal 1:15-16).

12. *The moral character of the eyewitnesses.* The New Testament provides the greatest teachings found in any literature on love, truth, honesty, hope, faithfulness, kindness, and other virtues. These teachings came from the pens of men like Matthew, John, Paul, James, and Peter, all of whom claimed to be eyewitnesses of the risen Jesus. To affirm their teachings yet

reject their witness of Jesus as a lie or mistake is nonsensical. If we accept
their teachings, we must trust their testimony about Jesus.

13. The accepted character and claims of Jesus. On numerous occasions Jesus
spoke of His crucifixion and resurrection. He claimed He was God (see
John 8:58; 10:30; 14:9), and He said He would come back from the dead
(see Matt 16:21). To claim Jesus as a great religious figure and moral teacher
while believing that His prediction of His resurrection was wrong would
make Him either a liar or a lunatic. The resurrection is essential to the confession that Jesus is Lord. Everything hinges on it.

14. Reliable eyewitness documents recording the events. The New Testament is the
most well-authenticated document of antiquity, a fact no textual critic of any
theological persuasion would deny. More than 5,600 Greek manuscripts of
the New Testament exist. These are of an earlier date and of a more reliable
nature than those of any other work of antiquity. Eyewitness followers of Christ
wrote many of them, and the books themselves have the ring of history. No
religion has in its sacred writings what Christians have in the New Testament.

These 14 arguments form objective, historically verifiable evidence of
Jesus' resurrection. Combined with a believer's personal experience of Jesus
as living Lord, they provide ample reason to believe that Jesus was physically
raised from the dead by the mighty hand of God.

Why the Resurrection Is Important

The resurrection verifies the truthfulness of the deity of Jesus Christ (see
Acts 2:22-24; Rom 1:3-4) and provides hope for the believer's resurrection
(see Rom 6:8-9; 1 Cor 6:14; 15:20-28; 2 Cor 4:14; 5:10; Phil 3:21; 1 Thess
4:14; 1 John 3:2). The resurrection indicates God's approval of Jesus—who
He is and what He said. God's approval includes Jesus' message about the
way people can receive eternal life (see John 14:6).

The resurrection tells us that the God who raised Jesus from the dead
exists. It establishes Jesus' lordship. The resurrection promises victory over
death (see John 14:1-9; 1 Cor 15:55-57), and it is a pledge of God's final
judgment (see Acts 17:31; Heb 9:26-27).

Jesus said in John 10:18, "No one takes [My life] from Me, but I lay it
down on My own. I have the right to lay it down, and I have the right to take
it up again." Christ is the firstfruits of the resurrection, which all who are
in Him will enjoy (1 Cor 15:22). Christ has been raised for our justification
(Rom 4:25). The penal substitutionary death of Christ on the cross and His
resurrection are both essential for the miracle of salvation.

The definitive text on the resurrection is 1 Corinthians 15. It is both apologetic and theological in its treatment of this great doctrine. Both the death of Christ and His resurrection are part of the definition of the gospel. That gospel is that Christ died for our sins, He was buried, and He was raised again—all according to the Scriptures.[7] The resurrection itself is the crowning moment of the work of atonement provided by our Lord. It is a trinitarian accomplishment with each person of the Godhead participating (Rom 1:1-4).

Jesus is indeed the risen Lord. You can reject Him, but you cannot ignore Him. What Jesus did in rising from the dead demands a response. How will you respond to the risen Lord and King of the universe? It is a question that cannot be avoided. (Most of the content of this message was taken from Akin, *Discovering*.)

Reflect and Discuss

1. When you ponder your faith, or when you face doubts, what is the bottom line for you—what is your anchor? How do you give a brief answer to, Why are you a Christian?
2. If you wanted to make up a story about a man being resurrected from the dead, how would it differ from Mark's account of Jesus' resurrection? Why is the difference actually evidence that Mark's account is true?
3. Why do people create alternative explanations for Jesus' resurrection? Give two or three reasons.
4. Which of the 14 historical facts do you consider to be the strongest support for the reality of the bodily resurrection of Jesus?
5. How does the martyrdom of ten of the apostles provide evidence for the resurrection?
6. How does the founding of the church in the city of Jerusalem provide evidence for the resurrection?
7. Hypothetically, what could the Romans or Jews have done that would have disproved the testimonies to the resurrection and stopped the Christian religion before it started? Why did they not do those things?
8. Toward the end of Jesus' ministry, what were the disciples expecting of Him? When Jesus was crucified, what were they probably thinking? (See Luke 24:19-24.)
9. How do the conversions of James and Paul testify to the resurrection of Christ?
10. How does your own heart and personal experience give testimony to the resurrection of Christ?

---

[7] By "according to the Scriptures," Paul has in view the Old Testament Scriptures and texts like Gen 22:1-19; Pss 16:8-11; 22; Isa 52:13–53:12; Jonah 1:17; 2:10; Zech 12:10.

WORKS CITED

Adams, Edward. "The Coming of the Son of Man." *Tyndale Bulletin* 56 (2005): 39–61.

Akin, Daniel L. *10 Who Changed the World*. Nashville: B&H, 2012.

———. *Discovering the Biblical Jesus*. Nashville: LifeWay, 2003.

———, and Al Mohler. "Why We Believe Children Who Die Go to Heaven." http://www.danielakin.com/wp-content/uploads/2004/08/why-we-believe -children-who-die-go-to-heaven.pdf.

Anderson, Gregg. "Healing in Gennesaret." Sermon at Capitol Ministries Idaho, Boise, ID, August 23, 2007.

Arnold, Clinton E. "Exorcism 101." *Christianity Today*. September 3, 2001. http://www.christianitytoday.com/ct/2001/september3/5.58.html.

———. *Mark*. Zondervan Illustrated Bible Backgrounds Commentary. Grand Rapids, MI: Zondervan, 2007.

Associated Press. "The End of the World as We Know It? Prediction of Saturday 'Rapture' Is Fuel for Faithful, Doubters." *Fox News*. May 19, 2011. http:// www.foxnews.com/us/2011/05/19/rapture-movement-predicts-end-world -saturday.

Barton, Bruce B., Mark Fackler, et al. *Mark*. Life Application Bible Commentary. Wheaton, IL: Tyndale, 1998.

Bavinck, Herman. *Reformed Dogmatics, Volume 3: Sin and Salvation in Christ*. Grand Rapids, MI: Baker Academic, 2006.

Beilby, James K., and Paul Rhodes Eddy, editors. *The Historical Jesus: Five Views*. Downers Grove, IL: IVP Academic, 2009.

Belben, H. A. G. "Fasting." Page 364 in *New Bible Dictionary*. 3rd ed. Edited by I. Howard Marshall et al. Downers Grove, IL: InterVarsity, 1996.

Belz, Mindy. "Ready to Die for a Cause." *World*. March 26, 2011. www.worldmag .com/2011/03/ready_to_die_for_a_cause.

Bliss, Philip P. "Hallelujah, What a Savior!" Public domain.

Blue, Ron, with Jeremy White. *The New Master Your Money: A Step-by-Step Plan for Gaining and Enjoying Financial Freedom*. 4th ed. Chicago: Moody, 2004.

Bonhoeffer, Dietrich. *The Cost of Discipleship*. New York: Macmillan, 1963.

———. *Life Together: A Discussion of Christian Fellowship*. New York: Harper & Row, 1954.

Bonk, Jon. *Between Past and Future: Evangelical Mission Entering the Twenty-First Century*. Pasadena, CA: William Carey Library, 2003.

Brewer, Geoffrey. "Snakes Top List of American's Fears." *Gallup*. March 19, 2001. http://www.gallup.com/poll/1891/Snakes-Top-List-Americans-Fears.aspx.

Calvin, John. *Calvin's Commentaries*. Vol. XVII. Grand Rapids: Baker, 1999.

————. *Commentary on a Harmony of the Evangelists, Matthew, Mark, and Luke.* 3 vols. Translated by William Pringle. Grand Rapids: Baker, 1999.

Carson, D. A. "Matthew." Page 468 in *Matthew, Mark, Luke.* Expositor's Bible Commentary 8. Edited by Frank E. Gaebelein and J. D. Douglas. Grand Rapids, MI: Zondervan, 1984.

Chapman, Wilbur. "Jesus! What a Friend for Sinners." Public domain.

Christian Biblical Errancy Debate. "Welcome to CBED." Christian Biblical Errancy Debate. http://wheresjesus.multiply.com/journal/item/952?&item_id=952 &view:replies=threaded.

Cicero, Marcus Tullius. *Defense of Rabirius.*

Congreve, William. "The Morning Bride." 1697.

Cowman, Charles. *Streams in the Desert.* 14th ed. Los Angeles: Oriental Missionary Society, 1933.

Dawkins, Richard. *The God Delusion.* Boston: Houghton Mifflin Harcourt, 2006.

DeRose, Keith. "Universalism and the Bible: The Really Good News." Yale University, http://pantheon.yale.edu/~kd47/univ.htm.

Dever, Mark. "Ignoring or Hearing?" Sermon at Capitol Hill Baptist Church, Washington, D. C., June 16, 1996. http://www.capitolhillbaptist.org/1996 /06/ignoring-or-hearing-mark-41-25.

————. *It Is Well: Expositions on Substitutionary Atonement.* Wheaton: Crossway, 2010.

————. "Jesus and Filth: The Heart of the Problem." Sermon at Capitol Hill Baptist Church, Washington, D.C., March 22, 1998. http://www.capitolhill baptist.org/audio/1998/03/jesus-filth-the-heart-of-the-problem.

————. "Jesus' Debut." Sermon at Capitol Hill Baptist Church, Washington, D.C., September 10, 1995. http://www.capitolhillbaptist.org/audio/1995/09/jesus -debut-mark-19-13.

————. "Jesus Paid Taxes." Sermon at Capitol Hill Baptist Church, Washington, D.C., September 19, 2010. www.capitolhillbaptist.org/audio/2010/09 /jesus-paid-taxes-mark-1213-17.

Djansezian, Kevork. "Kelly Clarkson: I've Never Been in Love." *USA Today.* June 12, 2007. http://usatoday30.usatoday.com/life/people/2007-06-12-kelly -clarkson_N.htm.

Dodd, C. H. *The Parables of the Kingdom.* New York: Scribner's, 1961.

Duin, Julia. "San Antonio Fundamentalist Battles Anti-Semitism." *The Houston Chronicle.* April 30, 1988.

Edwards, James. *The Gospel of Mark.* Pillar New Testament Commentary. Grand Rapids, MI: Eerdmans, 2001.

Edwards, Jonathan. *The Works of Jonathan Edwards.* Edited by Wallace E. Anderson et al. 26 vols. New Haven, CT: Yale University Press, 1957–2008.

Ferguson, Sinclair B. *Let's Study Mark.* Edinburgh: Banner of Truth, 1999.

Fosdick, Harry Emerson. "Shall the Fundamentalists Win?" Sermon at First Presbyterian Church, New York, NY, May 21, 1922. http://baptiststudies online.com/wp-content/uploads/2007/01/shall-the-fundamentalists -win.pdf.

Gabriel, Charles H. "I Stand Amazed in the Presence." Public domain.

Gaither, William J. "He Touched Me." No. 628 in *The Baptist Hymnal*. Nashville, TN: LifeWay Worship, 2008.

Garland, David E. *Mark*. NIV Application Commentary. Grand Rapids, MI: Zondervan, 1996.

Giles, Jeff. "Lady McCartney: After an Astonishingly Loyal 29 Years of Marriage, Paul Loses His Lovely Linda." *Newsweek*. May 4, 1998, 64.

Grassmick, John D. "Mark." Page 144 in *The Bible Knowledge Commentary: An Exposition of the Scriptures by Dallas Seminary Faculty (New Testament)*. Edited by John F. Walvoord and Roy B. Zuck. Wheaton, IL: Victor, 1983.

Havner, Vance. *Jesus Only*. Old Tappan, NJ: Fleming H. Revell, 1946.

Hewitt, Eliza. "When We All Get to Heaven." Public domain.

Hiebert, D. Edmond. *Mark: A Portrait of the Servant*. Chicago: Moody, 1974.

Hughes, Kent R. *Mark: Jesus, Servant and Savior*. Preaching the Word 1. Westchester, IL: Crossway, 1989.

Hurtado, Larry W. *Mark*. Understanding the Bible Commentary 2. Grand Rapids, MI: Baker, 1989.

Huxley, Aldous. *Ends and Means*. London: Chatto & Windus, 1938.

Josephus. *Josephus*. Translated by H. St. J. Thackeray et al. 10 vols. LCL. Cambridge: Harvard University Press, 1926–1965.

Keller, Timothy J. *The Gospel of Mark*. New York: Redeemer Presbyterian Church, 2005.

———. *King's Cross: The Story of the World in the Life of Jesus*. New York: Dutton Adult, 2011.

Klausner, Joseph. *Jesus of Nazareth: His Life, Times, and Teaching*. Cincinnati: Bloch, 1997.

Lane, William. *The Gospel According to Mark: The English Text with Introduction, Exposition, and Notes*. New International Commentary on the New Testament. Grand Rapids, MI: Eerdmans, 1974.

Lewis, C. S. *The Last Battle*. New York: Harper Collins, 2000.

———. *Mere Christianity*. New York: MacMillan, 1960.

———. *The Screwtape Letters*. New York: MacMillian, 1961.

Ling, Chai. "Can Video of Yue Yue, a Toddler Left for Dead, Change China?" *Fox News*. October 22, 2011. http://www.foxnews.com/opinion/2011/10/22 /can-video-yue-yue-toddler-left-for-dead-change-china.

Lloyd-Jones, D. Martyn. *God the Father, God the Son*. Great Doctrines of the Bible 1. Wheaton, IL: Good News, 1996.

Lloyd-Jones, Sally. *The Jesus Storybook Bible*. Grand Rapids, MI: Zondervan, 2007.

Lockridge, S. M. "It's Friday, but Sunday's Comin'."

Lombardi, Family of Vince. "Vince Lombardi—Quotes." http://www.vince lombardi.com/quotes.html.

Luther, Martin. *Three Treatises Paper.* Translated by Charles M. Jacobs. 2nd ed. Philadelphia: Fortress Press, 1990.

MacArthur, John. "Jesus Is Lord of the Sabbath, Part 1." Sermon at Grace Community Church, Sun Valley, CA, June 7, 2009. http://www.gty.org/resources/sermons/41-11/jesus-is-lord-of-the-sabbath-part-1.

———. "The Scandal of Grace." Sermon at Grace Community Church, Sun Valley, CA, May 24, 2009. http://www.gty.org/resources/sermons/41-9.

Mahaney, C. J. *Humility: True Greatness.* Colorado Springs, CO: Multnomah, 2005.

Massey, Gerald. *Ancient Egypt—the Light of the World: A Work of Reclamation and Restitution in Twelve Books.* Sioux Falls, SD: NuVision, 2008.

Merida, Tony. Twitter Post. February 27, 2013, 5:56 a.m. https://twitter.com/tonymerida/status/306764787612807168.

Morris, Lelia N. "What If It Were Today?" Public domain.

Murray, Andrew. *The Ministry of Intercession: A Plea for More Prayer.* New York: Fleming H. Revell, 1898.

Myers, Kenneth A. "Do Jews Really Need Jesus?" *Christianity Today.* August 1, 2002. http://www.christianitytoday.com/ct/2002/augustweb-only/8-12-52.0.html?start=1.

Newton, John. "Amazing Grace! How Sweet the Sound." Public domain.

———. "Come My Soul, Thy Suit Prepare." *Olney Hymns.* London: W. Oliver, 1779.

———. *The Works of John Newton.* New Haven: Nathan Whiting, 1826.

Packer, J. I. *Evangelism and the Sovereignty of God.* Downers Grove, IL: InterVarsity, 1961.

———. *Knowing God.* Westmont, IL: InterVarsity Press, 1993.

Paris, Twila. "How Beautiful." *Cry for the Desert.* Star Song Music, 1990.

Pierson, T. R. Speech at the New York Ecumenical Missionary Conference, 1900. Cited by Jon Bonk in *Between Past and Future: Evangelical Mission Entering the Twenty-First Century.* Pasadena, CA: William Carey Library Publishing, 2003.

Piper, John. "Beyond Forgiveness: Blasphemy Against the Spirit." Sermon at Bethlehem Baptist Church, Minneapolis, MN, April 1, 1984. http://www.desiringgod.org/resource-library/sermons/beyond-forgiveness-blasphemy-against-the-spirit.

———. *Bloodlines: Race, Cross, and the Christian.* Wheaton, IL: Crossway, 2011.

———. "Christ in Combat: Defense by the Spirit." Sermon at Bethlehem Baptist Church, Minneapolis, MN, March 18, 1984. http://www.desiringgod.org/resource-library/sermons/christ-in-combat-defense-by-the-spirit.

———. *Fifty Reasons Why Jesus Came to Die.* Wheaton, IL: Crossway, 2006.

————. "Missions: The Battle Cry of Christian Hedonism." Sermon at Bethlehem Baptist Church, Minneapolis, MN, November 13, 1983. http://www.desiringgod.org/resource-library/sermons/missions-the-battle-cry-of-christian-hedonism.

————. "Prayer: The Work of Missions." Sermon at ACMC Annual Meeting, Denver, CO, July 29, 1998. http://www.desiringgod.org/resource-library/conference-messages/prayer-the-work-of-missions.

————. "Receiving Children in Jesus' Name." Sermon at Bethlehem Baptist Church, Minneapolis, MN, February 23, 1992. http://www.desiringgod.org/resource-library/sermons/receiving-children-in-jesus-name.

————. "The Son of Man Came to Serve." Sermon at Bethlehem Baptist Church, Minneapolis MN, December 17, 1995. http://www.desiringgod.org/resource-library/sermons/the-son-of-man-came-to-serve.

————. "The Son of Man Must Suffer Many Things." Sermon at Bethlehem Baptist Church, Minneapolis, MN, March 28, 2010. http://www.desiringgod.org/resource-library/sermons/the-son-of-man-must-suffer-many-things.

————. "What God Has Joined Together, Let Not Man Separate, Part 1." Sermon at Bethlehem Baptist Church, Minneapolis, MN, June 24, 2007. Accessed February 8, 2013 at http://www.desiringgod.org/resource-library/sermons/what-god-has-joined-together-let-not-man-separate-part-1.

Platt, David. "The Centerpiece of All History and the Determinant of Our Eternity." Sermon at The Church at Brook Hills, Birmingham, AL, April 1, 2012. http://www.radical.net/media/series/view/1032/the-centerpiece-of-all-history-and-the-determinant-of-our-eternity?month=4&year=2012&filter=date.

————. "My Take: Why My Church Rebelled Against the American Dream." CNN BeliefBlog. 23 December 23 2010. http://religion.blogs.cnn.com/2010/12/23/my-take-why-my-church-rebelled-against-the-american-dream.

————. Radical: Taking Back Your Faith from the American Dream. Colorado Springs, CO: Multnomah, 2010.

Robertson, A. T. A Harmony of the Gospels. New York: Harper & Row, 1950.

————. Word Pictures in the New Testament. Grand Rapids, MI: Kregel, 2003.

Russell, Bertrand. Why I Am Not a Christian. New York: Simon & Schuster, 1967.

Ryle, J. C. Mark. Crossway Classic Commentaries. Wheaton, IL: Crossway, 1993.

Schaeffer, Francis. Compass, Summer 1997.

Sproul, R. C., Jr. "Comfort Ye My People—Justification by Youth Alone: When Does Comfort Become Confusion?" World. May 6, 1995.

Spurgeon, Charles H. "A Defense of Calvinism." The Spurgeon Archive. http://www.spurgeon.org/calvinis.htm.

————. "Infant Salvation." The Spurgeon Archive. http://www.spurgeon.org/sermons/0411.htm.

————. Metropolitan Tabernacle Pulpit. 63 vols. London: Passmore and Alabaster, 1863–1917.

———. "Nothing but Leaves." Sermon at Metropolitan Tabernacle, London, February 21, 1864. http://www.spurgeon.org/sermons/0555.htm.

———. "The Pleading of the Last Messenger." Sermon at Metropolitan Tabernacle, London, March 6, 1887. http://spurgeongems.org/vols31-33 /chs1951.pdf.

———. *Spurgeon's Sermons.* Peabody, MA: Hendrickson Publishers, 2009.

Stein, Robert H. *Mark.* Baker Exegetical Commentary on the New Testament. Grand Rapids, MI: Baker Academic, 2008.

Storms, Sam. "Be Killing Sin or Sin Will Be Killing You." Sermon at Bridgeway Church, Oklahoma City, OK, January, 2, 2011. http://resources.bridgeway church.com/bw.celebrations/main.celebration/audio/podcast.audio /2011/01_02_11%20-%20be%20killing%20sin,%20or%20sin%20will%20 be%20killing%20you%20(26).mp3.

———. "Christ, Our Passover Lamb, Has Been Sacrificed!" Sermon at Bridgeway Church, Oklahoma City, OK, July 3, 2011. http://resources.bridgeway church.com/BW.Celebrations/main.Celebration/audio/podcast.Audio /Mark%20Series%20(2010-2011)/Notes/SermonSummary43.pdf.

———. "The Cross and the Cry of Abandonment." Sermon at Bridgeway Church, Oklahoma City, OK, September 4, 2011. http://resources.bridgeway church.com/BW.Celebrations/main.Celebration/audio/podcast.Audio /Mark%20Series%20(2010-2011)/Notes/SermonSummary51.pdf.

———. "Divorce and Remarriage: Part 1." *Enjoying God Ministries.* November 6, 2006. http://www.enjoyinggodministries.com/article/divorce-and-remarriage -part-i.

———. "Figs, Fakery, and Faith." Sermon at Bridgeway Church, Oklahoma City, OK, March 6, 2011. http://resources.bridgewaychurch.com/BW .Celebrations/main.Celebration/audio/podcast.Audio/Mark%20 Series%20(2010-2011)/Notes/SermonSummary33.pdf.

———. "I Love You, Lord!" Sermon at Bridgeway Church, Oklahoma City, OK, May 1, 2011. http://resources.bridgewaychurch.com/BW.Celebrations /main.Celebration/audio/podcast.Audio/Mark%20Series%20(2010 -2011)/Notes/SermonSummary37.pdf.

———. "Truth on Trial." Sermon at Bridgeway Church, Oklahoma City, OK, July 24, 2011. http://resources.bridgewaychurch.com/BW.Celebrations /main.Celebration/audio/podcast.Audio/Mark%20Series%20(2010 -2011)/Notes/SermonSummary46.pdf.

Stott, John R. W. *Between Two Worlds: The Challenge of Preaching Today.* Grand Rapids, MI: Eerdmans, 1982.

Strauss, Mark L. *Four Portraits, One Jesus: An Introduction to Jesus and the Gospels.* Grand Rapids, MI: Zondervan, 2007.

Thomas, Scott, and Tom Wood. *Gospel Coach: Shepherding Leaders to Glorify God.* Grand Rapids, MI: Zondervan, 2012.

Thring, Godfrey, and Matthew Bridges. "Crown Him with Many Crowns." No. 304 in *The Baptist Hymnal*. Nashville, TN: LifeWay Worship, 2008.

Townend, Stuart, and Keith Getty. "To See the King of Heaven Fall." *Have You Heard: Live from CCK, Brighton*. Colorado Springs, CO: Integrity, 2009.

Trent, John, and Gary Smalley. *The Blessing*. Nashville, TN: Thomas Nelson, 1986.

Watson, Thomas. *The Doctrine of Repentance*. Carlisle, PA: Banner of Truth, 1999.

Watts, Isaac. "Jesus Shall Reign." Public domain.

———. "When I Survey the Wondrous Cross." Public domain.

Weigel, George. "Christian Number-Crunching." *First Things: On the Square*. February 9, 2011. http://www.firstthings.com/onthesquare/2011/02/christian-number-crunching.

Wesley, Charles. "O for a Thousand Tongues." Public domain.

Wessel "Mark." Page 648 in *Matthew, Mark, Luke*. Expositor's Bible Commentary 8. Edited by Frank E. Gaebelein and J. D. Douglas. Grand Rapids, MI: Zondervan, 1984.

Wiersbe, Warren W. *Be Diligent (Mark): Serving Others as You Walk with the Master Servant*. The BE Series Commentary. Wheaton, IL: Victor, 1987.

Wilkins, Michael J. "Study Notes on the Gospel of Matthew." In *The ESV Study Bible*. Wheaton, IL: Crossway, 2008.

Wilson, Ian. *Jesus: The Evidence*. San Francisco: Harper & Row, 1984.

ZENIT.org News Agency. "20th Century Saw 65% of Christian Martyrs." *EWTN News (Rome)*. May 10, 2002, http://www.ewtn.com/vnews/getstory.asp?number=26402.

Zhang, Lijia. "How Can I Be Proud of My China If We Are a Nation of 1.4bn Cold Hearts?" *The Guardian*. October 22, 2011. http://www.guardian.co.uk/commentisfree/2011/oct/22/china-nation-cold-hearts?INTCMP=SRCH.

SCRIPTURE INDEX